*F*UTURES AND *O*PTIONS *M*ARKETS

An Introduction

Colin A. Carter

University of California, Davis

WAVELAND

PRESS, INC.

Long Grove, Illinois

For information about this book, contact:
Waveland Press, Inc.
4180 IL Route 83, Suite 101
Long Grove, IL 60047-9580
(847) 634-0081
info@waveland.com
www.waveland.com

Cover photo: © Image Source/Corbis

10-digit ISBN 1-57766-553-8
13-digit ISBN 978-1-57766-553-3

Printed in the United States of America

7   6   5   4   3   2   1

To Noreen, Dakota, and Olesya

CONTENTS

CHAPTER 4 FINANCIALS   121

CHAPTER 5 FUNDAMENTAL ANALYSIS   151

PREFACE

Futures and options markets are globally linked through round-the-clock computerized trading, and this booming derivatives industry has led the world economy in the recent globalization trend. This book highlights the economic role of futures and options markets in the new global economy and explains how these markets evolved to better serve a more integrated world economy. Starting from the fundamentals of commodity futures, this book advances the reader through the exciting development of financial futures and options, including currencies and equity indexes. The commodity contracts have historical significance and provide a foundation for understanding price formation in the most modern financial futures and options markets—the future of the industry. Using economics logic rather than complex mathematics, this book brings the futures and options markets to life by explaining how and why these markets function and how they are used to manage market risk and as speculative investments.

Futures and options markets are the epitome of the global competitive marketplace. I have been interested in futures and options markets for many years and I have studied and traded these markets with enthusiasm and respect for the splendor of the marketplace. Futures and options markets provide a wonderful laboratory to allow students to see economic theory in action. The markets swifty react to world news events that serve as either a supply or demand shock. The importance of futures and options markets in the global economy has grown remarkably and the industry remains highly dynamic and exciting. Despite the economic importance of futures and options markets, there is a surprisingly high level of ignorance among the public and the media regarding the functioning and economic benefits of these markets. Myths abound regarding the riskiness and undesirability of trading futures and options contracts, yet the volume of trade on these markets continues to expand year after year. As a result of the growth in this industry, more and more universities are beginning to introduce courses on futures and options markets. With the writing of this book, I hope to make a contribution to furthering the understanding of these vital markets.

This book is written as a textbook for an upper level undergraduate course in futures and options markets taught in schools of business, economics, or agricultural and applied economics. Students in an MBA program are also a target audience, as are professional financial planners, and money managers. The objective of this book is to provide an economic understanding of the development and operation of futures and options markets. This book presents an integrated explanation of the market institutions, theory, and empirical evidence. It provides the reader with an intuitive explanation of the complicated nature of futures and options markets. The material in this book is presented in a way that is accessible to students with training in economics, mathematics, and statistics at the principles level. Mathematics and formulas are kept to a minimum in this book because it is meant to be introductory material.

I have attempted to make the material interesting and easy to understand. Numerous real-world examples are provided explaining how practitioners use futures and options markets. A section on market efficiency is included to explain the efficiency debate. An extensive listing of Internet sites is provided to allow students to keep current with the market and access real data. Discussion questions and problems are offered to stimulate students to think about the topics at hand and allow them to test their understanding of the material presented. In addition, each chapter has key references to academic literature that provides the more sophisticated reader with suggestions for more advanced reading.

This book has a distinctive blend of material relating to options, futures, commodities, and financials. It is more general than most futures and options textbooks–for instance, it gives equal treatment to commodities and financials. The chapters on fundamental and technical analysis are somewhat unique, as most textbooks on this topic do not have such chapters. The illustrative examples and text boxes are aimed to make the material user friendly to students who are new to this topic.

This book is designed for a one-semester course and students should easily be able to get through the entire book in one semester. Although the material is difficult in places and intellectually challenging, I hope you find it worth the effort.

ACKNOWLEDGMENTS

I am grateful to the following reviewers for topical suggestions and for the correction of errors in an early draft:

A. Barry Carr–Texas A&M University, Commerce
Leigh Maynard–University of Kentucky
James Pritchett–Colorado State University
David J. Schaffner–California Polytechnic State University, San Luis Obispo
Michael Haigh–University of Maryland
Steve Turner–University of Georgia

Kim Ma and Jesse Tack at UC Davis provided research assistance and I am very grateful to both Kim and Jesse for their excellent help on the manuscript. Special thanks goes to my editor Kimberly Yehle, who assisted in many ways and remained cheerful and polite throughout the long process. In addition, Amy Hackett at Carlisle Communications provided superb technical editing.

CHAPTER 1

The Market

Ken Roberts says the commodities markets are a blast! There is too much fun and too much profit for anyone with a dream not to grab a share.

—*Worth* magazine, October 1997

I have never, ever been in the futures market myself; I don't have the skill for it.

—Philip Johnson, quoted in the *Wall Street Journal*, April 29, 1983

Who are these two guys? Ken Roberts is a former Amway salesman who wrote a popular book on how to trade commodities. Roberts's book promotes trading strategies and systems to people new to futures trading, and he reportedly made over $50 million selling his book through the mail. Philip Johnson is a former chairman of the **Commodity Futures Trading Commission** (CFTC), the U.S. government agency that regulates and oversees the futures industry. Johnson is a lawyer and an expert on commodity law who wrote a treatise on commodities regulation.

It is diverse attitudes like those of Roberts and Johnson that give the futures industry an exciting flavor. Someone as knowledgeable as Johnson believes that **speculating,** or participating in the futures market with the sole intention of making a profit, is too risky (we discuss speculating in a later chapter). In all likelihood, he knows that the futures market is close to being efficient and that there is no reason to believe there is easy money to be made in trading futures. On the other hand, Roberts throws caution to the wind and tells his clients there is effortless money to be made. In fact, this works for Roberts. He sells a lot of books because the industry attracts a small percentage of investors who believe in get-rich-quick schemes, like the Ken Roberts formula. Most of these naive investors ultimately lose money speculating in the futures markets. People like Roberts get rich from selling moneymaking ideas to novice traders, not necessarily from trading according to their own systems.

The get-rich-quick gurus are a fringe group in the industry and the only group that claims to hold the secrets as to how to beat the market gods. The majority of

---

BOX 1.1

In plain English, what are futures and options?

Both futures and options are types of financial derivatives. Derivatives have recently become very important in the financial world, and the derivative business has flourished, but what exactly does the term encompass? Strictly speaking, a derivative is a financial contract the value of which is derived from or linked to the value of an underlying equity (e.g., common stock), bond, index (e.g., Standard and Poor's 500 stock index), or commodity. A derivative is usually a contract, which is nothing more than an agreement between two parties.

Sometimes, the general public mistakenly views derivative trading as legalized gambling. This is unfortunate because derivatives provide the commodity and financial world with a relatively inexpensive way of controlling risk. Derivatives are not a new idea. In fact, one of the earliest derivatives was money, which for many centuries was tied to the value of gold.

A futures contract is an obligation to buy or sell a specific quantity and quality of a commodity or financial instrument at a certain price on a specified future date. Futures contracts are standardized and traded on organized exchanges. Options, on the other hand, give the buyer (seller) the right to buy (sell) futures contracts; but unlike futures, there is no obligation.

---

traders in the industry make no such claims. This majority includes producers and processors of primary products, such as mining companies, oil companies, farmers, food processors, and multinational food dealers. This group also includes banks, airlines, insurance companies, mutual fund managers, and multinational firms trying to cope with price risk, exchange rate risk, or other forms of financial risk. Many of these firms participate in the futures market in order to shift some of the risk of price fluctuations onto other traders. In other words, their motives for trading are dissimilar to those of Roberts's disciples, who seek to profit from price fluctuations.

This book devotes very little attention to the colorful fringe of small speculators who believe in get-rich-quick schemes. Instead, it presents institutional background on futures and options markets and focuses on the economics of the markets and the economics of **hedging,** which entails participating in the futures or options market to neutralize the effects of commodity or financial price risk. Hedging is another important topic we discuss in later chapters. The topics presented in this book were chosen with the objective of providing the reader with an understanding of and appreciation for the economic principles that underlie futures and options markets and the market participants. This book does not survey in detail the academic literature on futures and options markets, but extensive academic literature on the topic is surveyed by Carter (1999), Malliaris (1997), and Williams (2001).

Despite its size and growing economic importance, the futures and options industry remains poorly understood because many view it as a set of derivative markets that are far too complicated and too risky. However, futures and options

BOX 1.2

What is the probability of turning $1,000 into $100,000 in just 10 months of futures trading?

The correct answer is that this feat is virtually impossible, unless you are Hillary Clinton. Clinton made international headlines with her amazing speculative profits in cattle futures contracts. Her ability to trade futures contracts became an issue when her husband was running for president of the United States. According to press reports, Mrs. Clinton started trading commodities in 1978 on the Chicago Mercantile Exchange (CME). Somehow, she was able to turn her initial investment of $1,000 into $100,000 after just 10 months of trading.

A study by Anderson and Jackson investigated the odds of generating a 100-fold return in the cattle futures market. They found the probability is one in approximately 31 trillion. Clinton's cattle futures trades were also studied by Leo Melamed (1996), a former chairman of the CME. He found that in all likelihood most of her profits came from larger trades ordered by someone else and then shifted to her account. It is possible that her broker had two "mirrored" accounts, with one account buying cattle futures and the other selling cattle futures. After the trades were completed, the profitable trades could be credited to one account and the losses to the other.

For further reading, see Anderson and Jackson (1994).

markets have many characteristics in common with other markets. Using a very broad definition, a **market** is a place or situation that puts sellers and buyers in communication with one another, discovers prices, and facilitates ownership transfer. This applies to local street markets in Beijing or San Francisco as well as to futures markets in Chicago, New York, London, and Tokyo. In general, one important economic function of markets is to add time "utility" to a commodity or financial asset. The important role provided by futures and options markets is the provision of the time dimension, which permits buyers and sellers to conduct transactions calling for fulfillment at some future date. This is accomplished using very specific rules and regulations governing trading, that are laid down by the exchange bylaws. These rules, the exchange's highly centralized nature, and the standardized characteristics of futures and options contracts make futures and options markets unique compared to other markets.

Forward (or deferred delivery) contracts are familiar to most people. A **forward contract** is a contract calling for the future delivery of an item or a service at a specified price and at a set time period. If you buy an airline ticket for travel to see your family over Thanksgiving, this is a forward contract between you and the airline. You agree on a price today, but the transportation service and peanuts will not be provided until some future date. An apartment lease is a forward contract. In most college towns, the tenant signs a one-year lease with the landlord, and this constitutes a type of forward contract. In the financial and commodity world, forward contracts are very common. But forward contracts are nonstandardized and are not traded on organized exchanges. A **futures contract** is nothing more than a forward contract that happens to be traded on an organized exchange, which means that it is standardized.

Day-to-day changes in futures prices affect day-to-day changes in **cash** (or **spot**) prices and vice versa. This means that firms or individuals affected by price activity in the underlying cash commodity or financial instrument are indirectly affected by price activity in the futures (and options) market. This is true whether or not these firms or individuals use the futures and options market directly. For instance, as a result of the recent changes in U.S. farm policy, farmers in the United States have become more dependent on supply and demand in both the cash and the commodity futures markets because the government no longer supports the **farmgate prices**. Even if a farmer does not trade directly on the futures market, the local cash price fluctuates daily along with the price changes in the futures market. There is a high degree of correlation between local cash prices and futures prices.

Following deregulation in the electricity market in many parts of the United States, utility companies have become more dependent and knowledgeable regarding electricity cash, forward, and futures markets. The growing importance of contingent markets (i.e., futures and options markets) is also spreading internationally. This means that prices determined by futures markets affect production and consumption decisions of individuals and firms in every corner of the world.

A primary function of futures (and options) markets is the discovery of prices, and these prices ration available supplies. If the weather is expected to turn bad in northern China, the price of wheat on the Chicago futures market will most likely rise on the basis of this news. This price rise signals to the world a possible reduced supply of wheat. Futures and options markets permit this type of supply shock to be transmitted across prices for both near-term and future settlement.

Prices of products ranging from soybeans to gasoline to foreign currencies are determined in futures and options markets. Contracts traded on the futures and options markets fall into four categories of products: (a) agricultural commodities[1] (e.g., corn), (b) metals (e.g., silver), (c) natural resources (e.g., crude oil), and (d) financial instruments (e.g., the European Euro). More than 200 different futures contracts (representing about 75 different commodities/financial instruments) are actively traded on North American markets alone. In addition, there are more than 100 different options contracts traded in North America (see Appendix Table 1.A1). In the United States, there are presently 10 different organized futures and options markets (**exchanges**) in operation (these are listed in Appendix Table 1.A1 along with trading volume). The largest U.S. exchanges are located in Chicago and New York. Outside the United States, there are over 40 exchanges, with several operating in Japan and Europe. Futures traders can buy and sell silk futures in Japan, stock index futures in London or Chicago, white maize futures in South Africa, copper futures in London, coffee futures in New York, treasury bond futures in Chicago, canola futures in Canada, and cotton yarn on the Osaka Textile Exchange.

---

[1] The group of commodities known as the "soft" commodities is composed of food and fiber items that include cocoa, sugar, coffee, orange juice, cotton, and lumber.

BOX 1.3

World's top futures and options markets.

The United States once dominated the futures industry, but this is no longer true because of a tremendous boom in trading on foreign futures and options markets. The commodity and financial volatility of the 1970s brought international attention to futures markets as a mechanism to manage risks. The growth in overseas futures markets was due largely to the initial success of similar markets in the United States. It is also the case that traders based in the United States are active buyers and sellers in overseas futures markets. In the mid-1980s, overseas futures trading volume was approximately 25% of that in the United States. By the early 1990s, this gap closed quickly, with overseas volume equaling about 75% of U.S. volume. Trading volume on non-U.S. exchanges exceeded that on U.S. exchanges by the mid-1990s. Of the 10 busiest futures and options exchanges in the world, only four are in the United States.

2001 FUTURES AND OPTIONS EXCHANGE VOLUME

	Exchange	*(in million contracts)*
1.	Korea Stock Exchange	854.8
2.	Eurex	541.6
3.	Chicago Mercantile Exchange	411.7
4.	Chicago Board of Trade	260.3
5.	LIFFE, UK	205.0
6.	Paris Bourse (Euronext)	149.3
7.	New York Mercantile Exchange	103.0
8.	Brazilian Mercantile and Futures Exchange	97.9
9.	Chicago Board Options Exchange	74.0
10.	London Metal Exchange	59.4

Source: Futures Industry Association.

Note: Volume data excludes options on individual equities.

In addition, "barge freight" futures are traded on the Merchants' Exchange of St. Louis, an electronic exchange. This is one of the few active futures contracts based on a service. It has been traded since 2000 and is used as a hedging device by international commodity merchants.

MARKET PARTICIPANTS: HEDGERS, SPECULATORS, AND ARBITRAGEURS

The major participants in futures and options markets are classified as hedgers, speculators, and arbitrageurs. In many cases, the individual traders are not members of the exchange. Therefore, they must execute their buy and/or sell orders through a member broker. A **broker** is a person or firm that handles futures and options trades on the floor of the exchange for a nominal commission fee. A **hedger** is a person or corporation that transacts business in the underlying commodity or financial instrument specified in the futures contract. For commodities, this classification includes oil and mining companies, energy companies, farmers, grain companies, cattle feeders, and so on. Banks, trust companies, mutual funds, insurance companies, and construction companies are typical hedgers in the financial futures market. Hedgers trade futures and options in order to reduce exposure to price fluctuations. By taking a position in the futures (options) market that is opposite their underlying cash position, they can reduce the risk of price variability. In other words, they take a position in the futures or options market in order to offset risk in their underlying business. Hedging is not necessarily conducted for profit but rather to reduce price risk in the underlying asset market.

Hedging is not much different from buying other forms of insurance. For example, a wheat farmer can purchase insurance against the loss of a crop due to a freak hailstorm. In fact, almost every risky aspect of this business is insurable except product price risk. The reason for the "missing" insurance market is very simple. An insurance company could not afford to offer a price insurance policy to wheat farmers for a reasonable price because during a year of low prices, every client would make a claim. The probability of a single wheat farmer being adversely affected by low prices is not independent from the same event affecting other wheat farmers. For the same reason, earthquake insurance is prohibitively expensive for residents of San Francisco. If there is one claim due to an earthquake loss, there will be hundreds of thousands of claims. The pooling of independent risks is not very effective (and is therefore costly) for earthquake insurance, but it is not even feasible for commodity and financial asset prices. However, futures and options markets serve this important function: they facilitate the transfer of price risk from hedgers to speculators.

On the other hand, futures and options market **speculators** do not normally buy or sell the underlying physical commodity or financial instrument during the normal course of their business activities. They assume the price risk from hedgers and seek to profit from price variability. A futures or options market would be very difficult (or even impossible) to operate without the risk-absorbing service that speculators provide. If a hedger wishes to buy or sell a futures contract, speculators are usually willing to take the other side of the transaction. The risk of price fluctuation is thereby transferred from the hedger to the speculator. The same is true with options on futures.

In addition to outright speculators and hedgers, there is a subclassification of speculators called **arbitrageurs**. These individuals or firms often take very short-term positions in the market, seeking to take advantage of market anomalies. They simultaneously buy and sell futures (or options) contracts in order to profit from a discrepancy in price relationships. Arbitrageurs are invaluable in terms of "making" a market because they often provide needed liquidity and their buying and selling (i.e., arbitrage) activities enhance the pricing efficiency of the futures market. An arbitrage opportunity is a risk-free profit opportunity. It is often said that there is no "free lunch" in the markets. But arbitrageurs are constantly on the lookout for a "free lunch" (e.g., when relative prices for two different futures contracts display an abnormal relationship), and if they find a "free lunch," they quickly exploit it. Three-way arbitrage opportunities also exist among the cash, futures, and options markets.

Given that futures and options trading is a zero-sum game (i.e., aggregate profits equal aggregate losses), there is much debate as to whether speculators consistently earn profits from hedgers. Whether hedgers pay a significant insurance premium to speculators is very difficult to determine empirically. However, in the 1960s, Rockwell found that, as a group, speculators do not earn a large insurance payment from hedgers. In the 1980s, Hartzmark found that in aggregate speculators in some markets lose while hedgers have positive average returns. This is not to say that in certain markets and at certain times an insurance premium does not exist, whereby speculators earn the premium in return for assuming the price risk.

WHAT EXACTLY ARE FUTURES AND OPTIONS MARKETS?

A futures market is an organized marketplace where buyers and sellers come together to establish prices for deferred delivery of a specific commodity (e.g., gold or coffee) or financial asset (e.g., a U.S. Treasury bond or the Japanese yen). It is called a futures market because the price established today is for future delivery. Supply, demand, and expectations interact to determine futures contract prices. Futures traders buy and sell through a public open outcry bid-and-offer system or electronically through a computerized trading system.[2] The futures exchange sets all the specific rules and regulations governing trading except for the price. Prices are established in the trading pit (or through the electronic pits), where futures contracts are bought and sold. Futures markets have been a tremendous growth industry, and they determine intertemporal prices for about 200 different commodities or financial assets. For instance, these markets help establish the world price of a barrel of crude oil, the price of frozen concentrated orange juice exported from Brazil, and the price of European Euros.

To introduce the basics of futures markets, it is useful to discuss in more detail the process of hedging. **Hedging** on a futures market entails taking either a buy or a sell futures position that is opposite to the position in the market for the physical commodity (i.e., the cash or spot market).[3] The hedger participates in the futures and cash markets simultaneously, as a buyer (seller) in one market, and at the

---

[2] The public outcry system conducted in trading pits on the exchange "floor" is the conventional method of trading futures and options contracts and remains the most common in the United States. However, computerized trading is growing in importance in Europe, Asia, and through U.S.-globally linked e-markets. "Floorless" trading may have cost advantages over the old-fashioned trading pit because computers can automatically execute orders once bid and ask prices match. The Chicago Board of Trade uses the Eurex electronic trading system, and the Chicago Mercantile Exchange uses the Globex electronic platform.
[3] The terms *cash market* and *spot market* are sometimes used interchangeably in this book. Technically, there is a subtle difference, with *cash* meaning *now* and *spot* meaning *here*. Spot usually refers to a cash market price for immediate delivery.

same time a potential seller (buyer) in the other. To the extent that futures contract prices tend to be positively correlated with spot market prices over time, having opposite positions in these two markets tends to neutralize the effects of a price change in either direction, hence the term *hedging*. Gains (losses) in the futures market tend to offset losses (gains) in the cash market regardless of the direction of the price movement.

Consider the following hedging example. When Iraq invaded Kuwait in the summer of 1990, the price of crude oil more than doubled—rising on both cash and futures markets from about $17 per barrel to around $40. With the run-up in oil prices, suppose an oilman in Alberta, Canada, determines that it would be profitable to uncap one of his abandoned oil wells. The cost of pumping his oil is estimated to be about $30 per barrel, so $40 yields a handsome profit. However, the decision to uncap the well is somewhat irreversible in the short run, and it will take the oilman about three months to bring the capped well back into production. In the meantime, he runs the risk of the price of oil falling back to the preinvasion level of below $20. The oilman desires some protection against such a potential price drop, so he e-mails his futures broker and instructs him to sell a crude oil futures contract at $40 per barrel.[4] Such a futures contract sale would obligate the oilman to deliver oil to the futures delivery point and receive $40 per barrel in return. The sale of the futures contract is a temporary substitute for the oilman's future sale of crude oil in the cash market.

The New York Mercantile Exchange futures contract calls for delivery of 1,000 barrels of crude oil: the contract size. Suppose the oilman chooses a contract specifying delivery in about five months time, say, the December futures contract. Intuition tells us that once the oilman decides to uncap the well and start pumping oil, he is exposed to the risk of a price decline. To reduce this risk, he sells a futures contract. He therefore would stand to gain from his futures position if prices were to fall because to liquidate (i.e., to close) his futures market position, he would buy back the contract at a lower price than he originally sold it for. Alternatively, if prices rise, he will gain in the spot market for oil but lose in the futures market. The futures contract would have to be "bought back" at a higher price than what it was sold for; hence, a futures loss would be incurred.

As in any other marketplace, for every seller of a futures contract there has to be a buyer. Continuing with our example, consider a trader on the opposite side of the market from the oilman. Suppose a major international airline company from Britain watches the price of oil rise to $40 and is worried that prices could go even higher if the United States steps into the war and invades Iraq. The airline wants to attempt to lock in the current price of oil in order to protect itself against higher jet fuel prices in the future. Higher fuel prices could lead to large financial losses for the airline. The airline company initiates an order with its futures broker to buy a December crude oil futures contract at $40 per barrel. The purchase of the futures contract is a temporary substitute for the future purchase of jet fuel in the cash market. Assume the price of crude oil and jet fuel are highly correlated.

---

[4] Trade in a single futures contract is used for illustrative purposes in this example. Multiple contracts could be used instead, but this would not change the essence of this example.

BOX 1.4

Weather futures and options.

In the business world, it is not uncommon to experience loss due to uncertain and adverse weather patterns. Losses can arise from a number of weather-induced developments, such as physical damage to assets, higher input costs, lower selling prices, or disrupted market conditions. Various futures and options exchanges around the world have offered weather derivative contracts in an attempt to help businesses cope with the weather risk and its financial consequences. However, weather derivatives are relatively new concepts in the futures and options industry, and some of these contracts have not survived. For instance, in the early 1990s, the Chicago Board of Trade (CBOT) introduced catastrophe options based on property claims due to hurricanes, tornadoes, and other climatic events. In the late 1990s, the Bermuda Commodities Exchange introduced similar options based on losses from hurricanes, tornadoes, thunderstorms, windstorms, hail, and winter storms. Both the CBOT and Bermuda catastrophe option contracts failed because of insufficient trading volume. This is not unusual, as Carlton found that about one-third of futures contracts introduced in the United States died within the first two years of trading.

See Carlton (1984).

More recently, the London International Financial Futures and Options Exchange (LIFFE) introduced a weather futures contract. This contract is based on daily average temperature in three European locations in the United Kingdom, France, and Germany. LIFFE offers both monthly and seasonal contracts that are based on an index of daily average temperatures. The contract value is equal to 3,000 Euros per 1-degree-Centigrade change in temperature. Weather contracts are also offered in the United States on the Chicago Mercantile Exchange (CME). The CME trades heating degree days and cooling degree days contracts on futures in 10 different cities. These contracts offered by the CME were the first exchange-traded, temperature-related weather derivatives offered. Currently, weather derivatives are a fast-growing derivatives market.

Technically, the use of crude oil to hedge jet fuel prices is called **cross-hedging**. Jet fuel is the cash commodity being hedged, but there is no futures contract for jet fuel. Instead, the airline uses a different but related futures contract (i.e., crude oil futures). With cross-hedging, prices for the cash commodity being hedged and the related futures market follow similar price patterns over time.

The British airline and the Canadian oilman are both hedgers. Their profits are affected by the price of crude oil in the daily course of their business because they either produce or consume oil, the underlying commodity. In this example, they both trade futures contracts in order to try to reduce price risk.

Suppose both futures contract orders—from the Canadian oilman and the British airline—reach the trading floor of the New York Mercantile Exchange at about the same time. The oilman's broker offers to sell December oil at $40, and the airline's broker bids (i.e., offers to buy) December oil at $40. Since the bid and offer prices match, the trade is immediately completed on the floor of the New York exchange. The price of December oil futures on the exchange is public information, and news of any price change on the exchange is quickly sent out to brokerage firms and other interested parties around the world.

Rather than the British airline buying the contract from the oilman, suppose a university professor from California anticipates that the price of oil will rise to $60. This professor is a speculator—one who buys and sells futures contracts with the sole intention of making money. This is a much different objective for trading futures than was the case for the oilman or the airline, both of which are hedgers. The professor anticipates that an invasion by the United States would push the price of oil up from $40 to $60. The speculator calls his futures broker and puts in an order to buy December crude oil futures at $40. Assume the oilman takes the other side of the position. The intention of the speculator is to wait for the price of oil to rise, and then he will liquidate his futures position by entering into a reverse trade (i.e., he would later sell a December futures contract). If the price rises to $60 before December, the speculator sells a December futures contract and earns a profit of $20,000: $20 per barrel times 1,000 barrels. Of course, if oil futures prices fall instead of rise, the speculator is forced to sell at a lower price than the original purchase price, and thus he loses money. In relative terms, the speculator's position in the futures market is much riskier than is the case for the hedger because the speculator does not hold an underlying position in the cash (spot) market. However, maintaining a well-diversified portfolio would reduce the speculator's risk associated with any position in the futures market.

To illustrate some key features of a typical futures contract, refer to Figure 1.1, which displays daily closing futures prices for (light, sweet) crude oil traded on the New York Mercantile Exchange. The unit of trade is 1,000 U.S. barrels (42,000 gal-

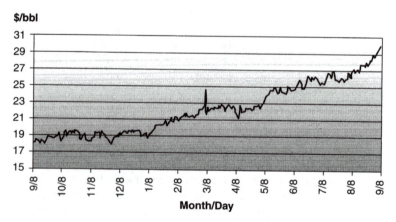

FIGURE 1.1
Daily closing futures prices, crude oil.

lons), and the price on the vertical axis in Figure 1.1 is quoted in $U.S. per barrel. The futures price in Figure 1.1 trended upwards from $18/bbl to $30/bbl, over the 12 months of price history shown. The $12/bbl price change represents a change in contract value of $12,000.

Crude oil is actually the world's most actively traded commodity futures contract and the futures market is used as a principal international pricing benchmark. In 2001, more than 37.5 million crude oil futures contracts were traded on the New York Mercantile Exchange. For the price graph shown in Figure 1.1, the contract specifies that the delivery month is March and the delivery point is Cushing, Oklahoma. The **delivery month** indicates the month during which the futures contract expires (in this case March). Prior to expiry, the contract must be offset (sold if one was previously bought, bought if one was previously sold), settled by the exchange of the physical commodity, or settled in cash. Crude oil futures are somewhat unique in that trading is conducted for 12 consecutive calendar months. Most futures contracts have less than 12 standardized delivery months. For instance, live cattle futures on the Chicago Mercantile Exchange have six standardized trading months: February, April, June, August, October, and December.

Like crude oil, many futures contracts have an underlying cash market in which trading of the physical commodity takes place. For instance, Cushing, Oklahoma, is the U.S. center of cash market trading in oil and is also accessible to participants in the international spot market for crude oil. Trading in the cash market is much less standardized and less regulated than trading in the corresponding futures market. In the futures market, settlement of the contract is managed by the exchange's **clearinghouse** (unlike in the spot market). The clearinghouse is discussed later in this chapter.

ORIGINS OF FUTURES AND OPTIONS TRADING

The characteristics of commodity futures contracts that are traded on modern-day exchanges were developed during the 19th century.[5] However, it is believed that futures markets did have historical counterparts in Japan and Europe in the 18th century, as some form of a rice futures contract was traded in Osaka, Japan, during that time. Around the same period, futures trading was apparently conducted in grains, brandy, whale oil, and coffee in Amsterdam.

In 1848, the Chicago Board of Trade organized futures trading as it exists today. Primarily because of its geographic location between the Great Lakes and the grain belt, Chicago had become the grain marketing center of the United States. Futures trading arose out of the cash grain market in Chicago. Futures trading evolved for two major reasons: to provide economic incentives to encourage grain storage and to correct large seasonal cash price changes. Large volumes of both

[5] For a discussion on the historical evolution of futures trading, see Irwin (1954). Further historical information on commodity markets is contained in Bakken (1952) and Williams (1982). For a discussion of the evolutionary development of futures markets, see Peck (1985).

FIGURE 1.
Seasonal pri...

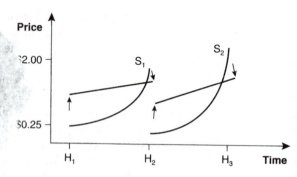

wheat and corn were marketed through Chicago.[6] Wheat generally arrived at this terminal market immediately after harvest because most farmers were eager to receive payment for their crops. This temporary oversupply of wheat at harvest had a tendency to severely depress prices for a period of time.

This issue regarding seasonal price swings is illustrated with the help of Figure 1.2. The figure displays representative cash price behavior over two full crop years (i.e., two seasons). In the figure, three hypothetical harvests are denoted as H_1, H_2, and H_3. Each harvest is depicted as a discrete point in time. The two curved lines, labeled S_1 and S_2, represent typical seasonal cash price patterns for wheat prior to the introduction of a forward market. Immediately following each harvest, cash prices were low (because supply exceeded demand), and then prices rose throughout the crop year as the fixed supply was continuously utilized. During the first season, starting from time H_1, the cash price followed along the S_1 curve upward, and then eventually the price came crashing down from S_1 to S_2 as soon as the next harvest was under way, at point H_2. As shown in Figure 1.2, in the mid-1800s, it was not unusual for grain prices to rise from as low as $0.25 per bushel following harvest to as high as $2.00 per bushel just prior to the next harvest.

This marketing problem of wide seasonal price swings led to the development of "forward," or "to arrive," contracts, which were essentially deferred delivery contracts. The seller was required to deliver a specific amount of grain at a future period and for a preestablished price. These contracts provided economic incentives to store wheat (because the forward price was guaranteed), and this resulted in a more rational flow of the product to market over time.

After the introduction of forward contracts, postharvest prices rose because some grain was placed in storage rather than sold. Much later in the crop year, pre-

---

[6] The development of futures trading in corn arose for a slightly different reason than in wheat. The interested reader is referred to Irwin (1954). Storage facilities in Chicago were inadequate to carry inventory throughout the crop year; thus, ironically, an undersupply of wheat often became a problem in the spring of each year. As a consequence of these severe marketing inefficiencies, large seasonal cash price changes in the wheat market were not uncommon.

harvest prices were reduced because grain was removed from storage and sold on the market. Seasonal price spreads were therefore reduced by arbitrage. Grain was taken off the cash market after harvest and sold forward, only to be placed back on the cash market later during the season. Removing grain from the cash market after harvest served to raise postharvest cash prices. Subsequently, placing that same grain back on the market later served to lower the next season's preharvest prices. This phenomenon is shown by the arrows in Figure 1.2, which shows that seasonal price swings were flattened out. The two straight lines represent the typical seasonal price swings after the introduction of forward trading. The differences between the low and high prices along the two straight lines are much smaller than low–high price differences along S_1 and S_2.

However, a major economic problem remained even after forward contracts were in place. Some traders were reluctant to trade these "forward" contracts because of their heterogeneity. The Chicago Board of Trade played a major role at this point by introducing standardized futures contracts guaranteeing a certain quantity, quality, and delivery at a specific location and time. These contracts soon led to futures contracts, which were very similar to forward contracts except the futures contracts were homogeneous and more easily traded.

Using the Chicago market as a model, standardized futures contracts soon developed in other cities in the United States and around the world. London and Winnipeg set up wheat futures trading, while cotton futures markets were established in New York and Bombay. As a result, there are numerous futures exchanges around the world today. The Chicago and New York markets remain important, but the world's largest exchange is the Eurex, a fully electronic market in Frankfurt, Germany.

To summarize, U.S. futures markets evolved more than 160 years ago to remove agricultural marketing inefficiencies and to facilitate trading in agricultural commodities such as wheat and corn that had short harvest periods and required storage. More than a century later, in the 1960s, commodity exchanges started trading in nonstorable agricultural commodities, and by the 1970s they were offering contracts for many nonagricultural commodities, such as lumber and gold. Of course, the big innovation was financial futures in the 1980s (Hull 2000).

ONGOING EVOLUTION OF FUTURES AND OPTIONS TRADING

The futures industry has grown by such large proportions in the past three decades that it is difficult to overstate the growth. As recently as the early 1970s, only about 30 million futures contracts were traded annually in the United States. By 2001, over 580 million contracts were traded (an 18-fold increase). Trade in nonagriculturals (primarily financials) has outstripped trade in the traditional agricultural commodities. In a span of only 26 years (1975–2001), nonagricultural futures trading volume in the United States went from zero to over 513 million contracts. Over this same time period, agricultural futures displayed slower and erratic growth, with trading volume increasing from 50 million to about 68 million contracts annually. Not only has the overall volume of trade increased steadily, but many innovative contracts, such as Eurodollar futures and Treasury-bond futures, have

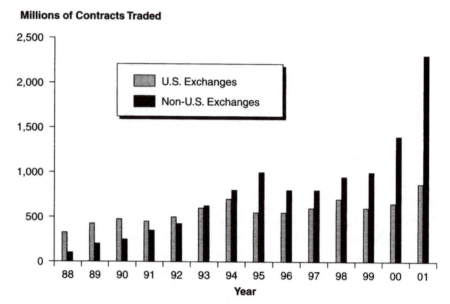

Millions of Contracts Traded

FIGURE 1.3
World futures and options on futures trading volume.
Source. Futures Industry Association.
Note: Individual equity contracts are excluded.

been developed as well. Today, the Eurodollar (on the Chicago Mercantile Exchange) has the largest share of trading volume on U.S. exchanges, at 47%. The volume of Treasury-bond contracts traded on the Chicago Board of Trade rose dramatically from 1986 until the late 1990s and then stagnated. Treasury-bond futures accounted for about 22% of the total volume of all U.S. futures contracts traded in 1998 and ranked number one. The Eurodollar became the largest volume futures contract by 1999 and in 2001 Eurodollar futures accounted for close to 30% of U.S. trading volume. Options on Eurodollar futures are the largest volume options on futures. The number of different futures and options contracts traded in North America and worldwide continues to expand each year.

Trade volume on U.S. futures markets is now 40% of total world trade volume compared to about 80% 15 years ago. This means the U.S. futures exchanges have slowly lost market share to foreign exchanges (Fig. 1.3). The U.S. exchanges are concerned about this issue, and some of their executives argue that this loss of market share is due largely to overregulation of U.S. exchanges.[7] However, market share also depends on competition to introduce new contracts and the willingness of exchanges to be innovative and introduce new technology, such as electronic trading. The European competition for financial futures volume between the

---

[7] For a discussion of the international competitiveness issue, see Commodity Futures Trading Commission (1999).

BOX 1.5

Single-stock futures.
Futures contracts on individual stocks were proposed for trading in the United States in the early 1980s but the government regulatory agencies (the Commodity Futures Trading Commission and the Securities and Exchange Commission) would not approve them at that time. However, the U.S. government reversed policy in 2001 and approved single-stock futures.

In a single-stock futures transaction, the buyer and seller agree to purchase/sell a stock at a set price during a specified future month. For example, an investor might enter into a contract to buy 1,000 shares of Microsoft at $70 per share, one year from now, under the expectation that the share price will increase during that time. The Chicago Mercantile Exchange, the Chicago Board Options Exchange, and the Chicago Board of Trade have formed a joint venture to offer single-stock futures. A competing partnership was formed between the U.S. Nasdaq stock market and the LIFFE futures market in London, with plans to begin listing futures on stocks.

Individual stock futures were introduced on the Sydney futures exchange (in Australia) in 1994. Users include portfolio managers and other hedgers, speculators, and arbitrageurs.

London International Financial Futures and Options Exchange (LIFFE) and the Eurex illustrates this point. LIFFE was the largest exchange in Europe, but in the late 1990s a large share of LIFFEs trading shifted over to the Eurex. LIFFE had a trading floor that lost out to the highly efficient electronic trading system introduced by the Eurex.

Both inside and outside the United States, the increase in the trading of financial futures contracts has been particularly striking. For instance, the Sydney futures exchange was originally established in 1960 as a greasy wool futures exchange and later introduced wheat futures. However, agricultural futures (wool and wheat) were dropped by the Sydney exchange in 2001.

Standard & Poor's (S&P) 500 Index was the seventh most active U.S. futures contract in 2001. One reason for the increased popularity of stock index futures is believed to be greater stock market volatility. However, this contract suffered a setback as a result of the October 1987 stock market crash, when the Dow Jones Industrial Average (DJIA) fell by 22.6% in one day. Some argued that the futures index led the stock market to fall and was therefore responsible for the crash. How could an efficient stock market fall by 22.6% in one day? It seems unbelievable that economic fundamentals could change that much in a single day. After exhaustive study, the futures market was exonerated, but nevertheless daily stock index futures contract volume declined by about 30% after the crash and remained well below precrash levels for a number of years. In 1997, the Chicago Board of Trade started trading the DJIA Futures Index in competition with the

S&P index. However, the DJIA trading volume remains well below that of the Chicago Mercantile Exchange's S&P 500 index.

Given the long history of trading, there have been few recent innovations in agricultural futures (and options) contracts that have been successful. For example, the Chicago Mercantile Exchange initiated a cheddar cheese futures contract in 1997. The contracts were cash settled, so actual delivery or taking of delivery was not possible. Although no longer controversial, the issue of cash settlement was contentious at one time when the Chicago feeder cattle futures contract was converted to cash settlement.[8] The Chicago Board of Trade introduced corn yield futures in 1995. The contracts were cash settled, and the value of the contract was $100 times the average corn yield (in bushels) in a specific region. Both the Board of Trade's corn yield contract and the Mercantile Exchange's cheddar cheese futures contract eventually failed due to lack of speculative and hedging interest.

Literally hundreds of new contracts have been approved by the Commodity Futures Trading Commission in the past decade. Like the cheddar cheese contract, not all of these new contracts are success stories and in fact many new futures instruments fail to attract sufficient trading volume.[9] For instance, in 1985 the Coffee Sugar and Cocoa Exchange launched inflation futures, based on the consumer price index, but it failed miserably, and trading was discontinued in 1991.

Some new contracts, such as the crude oil futures contract, take several years before they blossom. When crude oil futures were introduced on the New York Mercantile Exchange in 1983, several industry analysts predicted that the contract would fail. It did take about four or five years before the contract attracted considerable trading interest, but it turns out that today crude oil ranks as the fourth largest U.S. contract measured by annual trading volume. It ranks behind Eurodollars, Treasury Bonds, and Treasury Note futures.

Potatoes and rice are two examples of commodities that have never been successfully traded on futures exchanges. A potato contract at the New York Mercantile Exchange failed in the 1970s. Subsequently, a new revised potato contract introduced on the New York Cotton Exchange in 1996 failed. The reasons for these failures are not totally clear, and the explanations run from alleged manipulation by both buyers and sellers to quality problems with potatoes to concentration in the potato processing industry. Private contracts between growers and many processors also preclude the need for a traditional hedging instrument, such as a futures contract.

A rice futures contract was introduced on the New York Commodity Exchange in 1981, but it subsequently failed. In the case of rice, the combination of government programs and the preponderance of buying and processing cooperatives also removed the need for a traditional hedging instrument, such as a futures contract. At the present time, rough rice futures are traded on the Chicago Board of Trade, but trading volume is very light.

---

[8] Live cattle futures are physically delivered, whereas feeder cattle futures are cash settled. See Kahl, Hudson, and Ward (1989).

[9] For a discussion of successes and failures of new futures contracts, see Chambers and Carter (1990).

The discovery and introduction of a new futures contract with high volume happens only once or twice in a decade. In 1980, agricultural futures accounted for 64% of the total volume of U.S. futures contracts traded. By 2001, these contracts accounted for only about 12% of total volume. However, futures trading volume does fluctuate from year to year with changing market conditions and changing government commodity programs. For example, in 1988, agricultural futures trading was up by about 30% over the previous year because of the higher prices associated with the severe drought in the midwestern United States.

The volume of trading in some nonagricultural commodities, such as precious and nonprecious metals, was stagnant over the 1980s. Conversely, crude oil contracts increased in trading volume during the late 1980s. The volatility in crude oil prices is believed responsible for this occurrence. Thus, we find that the volume of trading in a particular futures contract is very sensitive to the behavior of the underlying cash price.

Most of the U.S. futures markets, with the exception of the Philadelphia Board of Trade, also trade options on futures contracts. Like futures markets, options have a long history, albeit a more tattered one. Options (or privileges) traded in grains from about the 1840s until the 1930s and were blamed for the excessive volatility of grain prices before the Great Depression and the eventual collapse of prices in the early 1930s. The futures exchanges did not have strict control over options trading, which was often conducted away from the futures trading floor. As a result, the U.S. Congress banned options trading on agricultural commodities in 1936. It was not until 1981 that the Commodity Futures Trading Commission (CFTC) approved options for a very limited number of futures contracts, including gold, sugar, and Treasury bonds. In 1984, several more agricultural options were introduced under a three-year pilot-trading project. This program included options on futures for corn, soybeans, live hogs, live cattle, wheat, and cotton. In January 1987, the CFTC judged the pilot trading successful and approved options trading on all futures contracts. In 2001, options on interest rate futures accounted for 75% of the volume of options on futures. Options on agricultural commodities accounted for 10% of the 2001 trading volume and options on energy futures 9%.

REGULATION

The futures and options markets are regulated by a combination of industry self-regulation and formal government regulation. There is a large set of industry and government rules that govern futures market participants and their trading practices. These rules are designed to promote fair and competitive markets. For instance, market manipulation is prohibited, and rules are in place to prevent a trader from creating an artificial price movement (or "cornering" the market) in order to earn abnormal profits.

Self-regulation is effective in the futures industry because trading is a zero-sum game. This means that if a trader is trying to manipulate the market, then another trader on the other side of the market is getting hurt, financially, and it is in his or her best interest to file a complaint. Unlike the securities industry, insider trading is not a common problem in the futures industry. So there is less of a need for government regulation. For a discussion of some of the issues surrounding self-regulation, see Pirrong (1995).

The CFTC was introduced in 1974 to oversee the operations of the nation's futures and option markets. Regulation of the futures industry was revamped at that time to cover the growing futures trading in nonagricultural contracts, especially financials. Prior to 1974, U.S. futures trading was regulated by the 1936 Commodity Exchange Act, which was administered by the U.S. Department of Agriculture (Peck, 1985). The CFTC is run by five commissioners appointed by the president. In 2000, Congress passed the Commodity Futures Modernization Act (HR 5660), which reauthorized and amended the Commodity Exchange Act. The Commodity Futures Modernization Act created a new structure for regulation of futures and options trading and codified an agreement between the CFTC and Securities and Exchange Commission (SEC) to allow trading of single-stock futures. The SEC regulates stock exchanges.

The CFTC's main responsibilities are to protect the trading public from fraud and trading abuses on and off the exchange, to prevent price distortions and manipulations, and to encourage the overall competitiveness and efficiency of all U.S. exchanges. The CFTC posts pictures on its Web site (*http://www.cftc.gov*) of individuals wanted for financial crimes related to futures and options.

The National Futures Association (*http://www.nfa.futures.org*) is a self-regulatory industry organization that was established in 1981. The National Futures Association (NFA) assumed some regulatory responsibility on behalf of the CFTC. One such responsibility is the registering of every firm or individual who conducts futures or options on futures business with the public. The basic goal of the NFA is to protect all futures and options traders from fraudulent trading activities, and the NFA has an arbitration program that handles complaints against broker or trading firms.

THE EXCHANGE

Futures and options exchanges are associations of members interested in trading as principals (for their own account) or as agents for other firms or the general public. Figure 1.4 schematically presents the major components of a futures and options exchange. Most exchanges are unincorporated, nonprofit organizations. For example, the Chicago Board of Trade is a *not-for-profit*, nonstock corporation that serves individuals and member firms. There is a limited number of memberships on any one exchange. Therefore, the memberships have a capital value that fluctuates over time, and the membership price is closely related to the exchange's volume of trade.

In 2000 the Chicago Mercantile Exchange Inc. became a *for-profit* corporation by converting its membership interests into shares of common stock that trade separately from exchange trading privileges. LIFFE is also a *for-profit* exchange that is owned by shareholders. The exchange establishes all the rules of trading in accordance with government regulations, disseminates market information, and provides physical trading facilities.

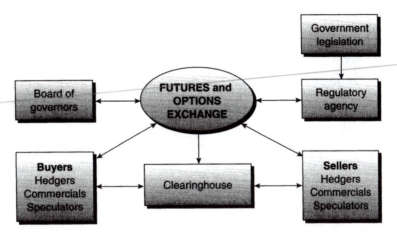

FIGURE 1.4
Organization of futures/options exchange.

A **board of governors**, elected from the membership, (or shareholders) manages the affairs of the exchange. It enforces the bylaws of the exchange and arrives at management decisions when necessary. The financing of an exchange's daily operating costs, such as rent, overhead, employees' salaries, and so on, is covered mainly by annual membership dues and a small transactions fee levied on each trade.

A **clearinghouse** consists of a subgroup of members from the exchange. It financially guarantees all contracts on the exchange and handles the financial settlement of all contracts. There has never been a default on U.S. exchanges because of the financial backing provided by the clearinghouse. The clearinghouse is discussed in more detail later in Chapter 2.

ECONOMIC FUNCTIONS OF FUTURES AND OPTIONS TRADING

As explained previously, the futures market is a very old institution that developed largely in North America and originally served to correct marketing inefficiencies in commodity markets through the provision of intertemporal prices. In more recent years, the futures market has also been adopted by financial markets for many of the same economic reasons that futures have been used by those in agriculture for more than 150 years. The futures market serves several roles: it discovers prices, shifts price risk, disseminates information, and provides returns to hedgers for storage services (if they are hedging a storable commodity). Each of these roles is briefly explained here (for a more in-depth treatment of this topic, see Peck, 1985).

One of the original reasons for the establishment of futures markets was to provide producers and merchants with a liquid market in which to shift the risk of price change onto others. Hedgers enter into both long (buy) and short (sell) positions, and as a consequence some of the risk is shifted to other hedgers. Speculators

---

BOX 1.6

The price of an exchange membership.

Future exchanges were traditionally organized as nonprofit membership associations, but this is changing as the Chicago Mercantile Exchange (CME) and other exchanges have become for-profit organizations with shareholders. There are a finite number of memberships ("seats") on a futures exchange. For instance, the Chicago Board of Trade (CBOT) has about 1,400 full-time members. The Chicago Mercantile Exchange (CME) has about 3,100 members (this number includes all four divisions of the CME). The price of a membership fluctuates according to the supply and demand for these memberships, and memberships are sold through a bid-and-ask system. An individual or company owns every membership. Some members lease their seats to nonmember traders, and there is a lease market.

Demand for a futures exchange seat is dependent largely on the exchange's trading volume, but that is not the only factor. For instance, in 2002 trade volume on the New York Mercantile Exchange (NYMEX) was much less than on either the CBOT or the CME. However, the price of a seat on the NYMEX exceeded that for the CBOT or the CME. At the other end of the spectrum, the Winnipeg Commodity Exchange in Canada has a few hundred members, and memberships sell for a few thousand dollars. Interestingly enough, back in the 1920s, seats on the Winnipeg Commodity Exchange sold for as high as $35,000, while those on the CBOT were less than $2,000. The establishment of a government-marketing agency for wheat, the Canadian Wheat Board, resulted in the termination of wheat futures trading on the Winnipeg Commodity Exchange. As a consequence, the Winnipeg membership fell dramatically in value.

Membership seat prices fluctuate considerably. For instance, the CBOT full-seat prices exceeded $857,000 in 1997 but subsequently fell to $450,000 in 1998 and then traded in the $400,000 range in 2002. The CME full-seat prices traded as high as $925,000 in 1994 and then fell to $310,000 in 1998 but rebounded to $800,000 in 2002.

---

assume that amout of price risk that is not shifted to other hedgers. By reducing their exposure to price risk, producers are more able to make sound production decisions. For merchants, the opportunity to shift price risk through hedging means that their unit costs of marketing are lowered.

The informational role of futures prices is a public good in the sense that many people benefit from the service without paying the cost. Knowledgeable producers view futures prices as market signals that benefit them in the timing of sales. Commercial interests who trade in the futures market reveal their information through trading; thus, their information indirectly becomes public information. For instance, a commodity firm that makes a large sale to an overseas buyer may immediately turn around and hedge this sale on the futures market. Therefore, futures markets serve to transfer information from those who have it to those who do not.

Prior to the introduction of futures markets, many markets were subject to large seasonal or cyclical price swings (see Fig. 1.2). A major reason for the large price changes was that merchants had no guarantee of earning an economic return for storing the commodity. As a result, less-than-optimal amounts of some products were put into storage. The futures market corrected this marketing anomaly and now ensures, through a set of intertemporal prices, that products such as oil or grain are placed in storage to be supplied to the market in a continuous fashion.

SUMMARY

This introductory chapter has covered the basics of where and how futures and options contracts are traded. Futures exchanges are in the price discovery and risk transfer business, and trading started with agricultural commodities in the 19th century. Price discovery and risk transfer are both vital economic functions in any economy. The futures market creates hedging opportunities and enhances price discovery. A futures contract is an obligation to buy or sell a specific quantity and quality of a commodity or financial instrument at a certain price on a specified future date. The following six characteristics of futures and options trading have been discussed:

- Trading is conducted on organized exchanges.
- There are specific rules governing trading.
- Futures and options contracts are highly standardized.
- Futures contracts have symmetrical risks for the buyer and seller, and those risks are legally canceled by making offsetting trades.
- The exchange clearinghouse guarantees all contracts.

The unique aspects of futures exchanges, as compared with other marketplaces, have been the focus of discussion in this chapter. These exchanges have not only an interesting history but also an exciting future. Their role of providing contingent markets in the economy is of utmost importance.

For the past 150 years, the futures industry has been the central point of price discovery for the food industry. Futures have simultaneously enabled producers, merchandisers, and processors of food to reduce their exposure to adverse price movements. In the past three or four decades, the futures industry has expanded to include many contracts for nonfood commodities, such as metals and energy products. In addition, contracts have been developed to enable financial institutions to protect against currency fluctuations, equity index variations, and interest rate changes. The proven usefulness of these derivatives has resulted in phenomenal growth in trading volumes. The U.S. volume of futures and options trading has increased by more than 100 percent in the last decade. What does the next decade hold in store for this industry?

DISCUSSION QUESTIONS

1. Discuss the economic importance of futures and options markets.
2. What role do market prices play in the economy, and how do they ration supply and demand?
3. Can a market be "efficient" if prices fall by over 20% in one day?
4. "Speculating in futures is no more risky than speculating in the stock market." Explain with the use of an example.
5. Do you have to go "long" before you can go "short" in the futures market?
6. Why are the U.S. futures and options markets losing world market share to overseas markets?
7. What type of firms would use single-stock futures as hedging devices? Explain with an example.
8. Explain the role of the Commodity Futures Trading Commission.
9. How do the objectives of hedgers differ from those of speculators?
10. Why do some futures contracts require delivery and others are closed by cash settlement?

SELECTED REFERENCES

Anderson, S. C., & Jackson, J. D. (1994). A note on odds in the cattle futures market. *Journal of Economics and Finance, 18*(3), 357–365.

Bakken, H. (1952). *Theories of markets and marketing.* Madison, WI: Mimir.

Bodie, Z., & Rosansky, V. (1980). Risk and return in commodity futures. *Financial Analysts Journal,* May/June, 27–39.

Carlton, D. W. (1984). Futures markets: Their purpose, their history, their growth, their successes, and failures. *Journal of Futures Markets, 4,* 237–271.

Carter, C. A. (1999). Commodity futures markets: A survey. *Australian Journal of Agricultural and Resource Economics, 43*(2), 209–247.

Chambers, S., & Carter, C. (1990). U.S. futures exchanges as nonprofit entities. *Journal of Futures Markets, 10* (February), 79–88.

Commodity Futures Trading Commission. (1999). The global competitiveness of U.S. futures markets revisited. Division of Economic Analysis, Washington, DC, November. [Available *http://www.cftc.gov/dea*]

Hartzmark, M. L. (1987). Returns to individual traders of futures: Aggregate results. *Journal of Political Economy, 95,* 1292–1306.

Hull, J. (2000). *Introduction to futures and options markets* (4th ed.). Upper Saddle River, NJ: Prentice Hall.

Irwin, H. S. (1954). *Evolution of futures trading.* Madison, WI: Mimir.

Kahl, K. H., Hudson, M. A., & Ward, C. E. (1989). Cash settlement issues for live cattle futures contracts. *Journal of Futures Markets, 9*(3), 237–248.

Malamed, L. (1996). *Escape to the Futures.* New York: John Wiley & Sons.

Malliaris, A. G. (Ed.). (1997). *Futures markets.* Vols. 1–3. Cheltenham: Elgar.

Peck, A. E. (1985). The economic role of traditional futures markets. In Anne E. Peck (Ed.), *Futures markets: Their economic role* (Chapter 1). Washington, D.C.: American Enterprise Institute.

Pirrong, S. C. (1995). The self-regulation of commodity exchanges: The case of market manipulation. *Journal of Law and Economics, 38*(1), 141–206.

Rockwell, C. S. (1967). Normal backwardation, forecasting and the return to speculators. *Food Research Institute Studies, 7* (Suppl.), 107–130.

Williams, J. C. (1982). The origins of futures markets. *Agricultural History, 56:* 306–316.

Williams, J. C. (2001). Commodity Futures and Options. In B. Gardner & G. Rausser (Eds.), *Handbook of agricultural economics: Vol. 1* (Chapter 13). New York, NY: Elsevier Science.

APPENDIX

TABLE 1.A1   Futures and Options Trading Volume (Number of Contracts:) 2001

AMEX	UNIT	VOLUME
Airline Index (XAL)	$100 x Index	9,130
Biotechnology Index (BTK)	$100 x Index	136,860
Computer Hardware Index (HWI)	$100 x Index	
Computer Tech Index (XCI)	$100 x Index	5,111
Credit Suisse First Boston Technology Index (CTN)	$100 x Index	732
Defense Index (DFI)	$100 x Index	112
deJager Year 2000 Index (YTK)	$100 x Index	
Disk Drive Index (DDX)	$100 x Index	184
Eurotop 100 Index (EUR)	$100 x 1/10 Index	15,953
Hong Kong (floating rate) Index (HKO)	$100 x Index	9,268
Institutional Index (XII)	$100 x Index	505
Interactive Week Internet Index (IIX)	$100 x Index	10,988
Japan Index (JPN)	$100 x Index	88,448
Major Market Index (XMI)	$100 x Index	155,573
Mexico Index (MXY)	$100 x Index	
Morgan Stanley Commodity Index (CRX)	$100 x Index	729
Morgan Stanley Consumer Index (CMR)	$100 x Index	7,686
Morgan Stanley Cyclical Index (CYC)	$100 x Index	59,516
Morgan Stanley Internet Index (MOX)	$100 x Index	23,387
Morgan Stanley High Tech 35 Index (MSH)	$100 x Index	196,582
NASDAQ Non-Financial 100 Index (NDX)	$100 x Index	42,988
Mini NASDAQ Non-Financial 100 Index (MNX)		89,494
Natural Gas Index (XNG)	$100 x Index	163,210
Deutsche Bank Energy (DXE)	$100 x Index	1,134
Networking Index (NWX)	$100 x Index	
Oil Index (XOI)	$100 x Index	31,806
Pharmaceutical Index (DRG)	$100 x Index	66,644
Securities Broker/Dealer Index (XBD)	$100 x Index	17,876
S&P MidCap Index (MID)	$100 x Index	25,931
TheStreet.com e-commerce Index (ICX)	$100 x Index	1,568
TheStreet.com e-finance Index (XEF)	$100 x Index	70
All Options on Individual Equities		203,942,399
AMEX Index Total		**205,103,884**

(continued)

TABLE 1.A1 *Cont.*		
CHICAGO BOARD OPTIONS EXCHANGE	**UNIT**	**VOLUME**
S&P 100 Index Options (OEX)	$100 x Index Level	10,028,266
OEX Leaps	$100 x Asset	18,596
S&P 100 European Exercise (XEO)		470,978
S&P 500 Index Options (SPX)	$100 x Index Level	22,829,042
S&P Barra Growth Index (SGX)	$100 x Index Level	
S&P Barra Value Index (SVX)	$100 x Index Level	
Dow Jones Industrial Index (DJX)	$100 x Index	8,987,456
Exchange Traded Funds		
NFT 50 (N-FT)	$100 x Index	
SPX Leaps	$100 x Asset	1,156,347
Sectors Total*	$100 x Index Value	119,337
Mexico Index (MEX)	$100 x Index	634
Latin 15 (LTX)	$100 x Index	
Nikkei 300 Index (NIK)	$100 x Index	
NYSE Composite (NYA)	$100 x Index	2,125
NASDAQ 100 (NDX)	$100 x Index	1,617,443
NASDAQ 100 Mini (MNX)	$100 x Index	6,353,484
Russell 2000 Options (RUT)	$100 x Index	245,346
S&P Small Cap 600 (SML)	$100 x Index	5,736
Stock Index FLEX Options		471,853
Interest Rate Composite	$100 x compLevel	39,303

*Comprised of Biotech, CBOE Comp.,
Software Envir. Indus., S&P, Banking, Healthcare,
Insurance, Retail, Chemical, Transport.

All Options on Individual Equities		232,693,569
CBOE Total		**306,667,851**

CANTOR EXCHANGE		
5 Year U.S. Agency Note	$100,000	
10 Year U.S. Agency Note	$100,000	
WHEN Issued 5 Year Note		26
WHEN Issued 10 Year Note		130
6% U.S. T-Bonds	$100,000	62,550
6% U.S. Five Year T-Notes	$100,000	42
6% U.S. Ten Year T-Notes	$100,000	57,970
Cantor Exchange Total		**162,700**

CHICAGO BOARD OF TRADE		
Wheat	5,000 bu	6,801,541
Corn	5,000 bu	16,728,748
Oats	5,000 bu	440,854
Soybeans	5,000 bu	12,150,369
Soybean Oil	60,000 lb	6,034
Soybean Meal	100 tons	6,743,772
Rice	200,000 lb	121,661
Corn Yield	Yield est x 100	
Silver	1,000 oz	8,634
Mini New York Silver	1,000 oz	1,087
Silver	5,000 oz	161

TABLE A.1 *Cont.*

CHICAGO BOARD OF TRADE	UNIT	VOLUME
Gold	Kilo	4,867
Mini New York Gold	33.2 troy oz	717
Gold	100 oz	
U.S. T-Bonds	$100,000	58,579,290
Mini U.S. T-Bonds	$50,000	4,383
Ten Year T-Notes	$100,000	57,585,828
Mini Ten Year T-Notes	$50,000	213
Five Year T-Notes	$100,000	31,122,401
Two Year T-Notes	$200,000	2,389,165
Ten Year Agency Debt	$100,000	1,189,389
Five Year Agency Debt	$100,000	1,919
Mini Eurodollars	$500,000	483
Mortgage	$1,000 x Index	57,324
Ten Year Interest Rate Swap	$100,000	58,884
Municipal Bond Index	$1,000 x Index	348,319
30 Day Fed Funds	$5,000,000	4,686,695
Dow Jones Industrial Index	$10 x Index	4,901,949
Mini Dow Jones Industrial Index	$2 x Index	20,728
Dow Jones Transportation Index	$20 x Index	2
Dow Jones Utility Index	$200 x Index	2
Dow Jones Composition Index	$20 x Index	
Dow Jones–AIGCI Index	100 x Index	4,292
CBOT Futures Total		*209,988,002*
Wheat	5,000 bu	1,714,041
Corn	5,000 bu	4,864,294
Oats	5,000 bu	70,218
Soybeans	5,000 bu	3,829,236
Soybean Oil	60,000 lb	672,284
Soybean Meal	100 tons	606,187
Rice	200,000 lb	23,233
Corn Yield	Yield est x 100	
PCS Catastrophe Insurance		
Silver	1,000 oz	4
U.S. T-Bonds	$100,000	13,478,771
Ten Year T-Notes	$100,000	19,983,876
Five Year T-Notes	$100,000	4,681,604
Two Year T-Notes	$200,000	44,185
Municipal Bond Index	$1,000 x Index	
Ten Year Agency Debt	$100,000	2,711
Flexible U.S. T-Bonds		38,160
Flexible T-Notes (10 Year)		45,700
Flexible T-Notes (5 Year)		2,200
Dow Jones Industrial Index	$10 x Index	288,364
CBOT Options on Futures Total		*50,345,068*
CBOT Total		**260,333,070**
CHICAGO MERCANTILE EXCHANGE		
Lean Hogs	40,000 lb	2,018,339
E-Mini Lean Hogs	10,000 lb	3,978
Pork Bellies, Frozen	40,000 lb	196,359

(continued)

TABLE 1.A1 *Cont.*

CHICAGO MERCANTILE EXCHANGE	UNIT	VOLUME
Butter	40,0001b	1,374
Dry Whey	44,000 lb	
Fluid Milk	50,000 lb	88,016
Nonfat Dry Milk	44,000 lb	48
Class IV Milk	200,000 lb	6,513
Pork Cutout	40,000 lb	
Live Cattle	40,000 lb	4,279,273
Stocker Cattle	25,000 lb	
Feeder Cattle	50,000 lb	616,988
E-Mini Feeder Cattle	10,000 lb	69
Orient Strand Board Lumber	100,000 sq ft	10,264
Random Lumber	80,000 bd ft	206,840
90 Day T-Bills	$1,000,000	31,113
3 Month Eurodollar	$1,000,000	184,015,496
Euroyen	$100,000,000 yen	494,519
One Month LIBOR	$3,000,000	1,315,593
5 Year Agency Note	$100,000	
10 Year Agency Note	$100,000	
British Pound	62,500	2,078,834
Brazilian Real	100,000	3,937
Canadian Dollar	100,000	2,961,680
Deutsche Mark	125,000	3,232
Euro FX	125,000 x Euro	5,898,429
E-Mini Euro FX	62,500 x Euro	13,244
Japanese Yen	12,500,000	4,552,599
E-Mini Japanese Yen	6,250,000	2,023
Mexican Peso	500,000	1,069,327
New Zealand Dollar	100,000	21,766
Russian Ruble	500,000	
South African Rand	500,000	65,327
Swiss Franc	125,000	2,901,939
Australian Dollar	100,000	832,707
French Franc	500,000	17
Euro/Pound	125,000 x Euro	127
Euro/Yen	125,000 x Euro	98,970
EuroYen/Libor	100,000,000 yen	17,474
Euro/Swiss Franc	125,000 x Euro	182
Nikkei 225	$5 x Index	476,274
S&P 500 Index	$250 x Index	22,478,152
E Mini S&P 500	$50 x S&P Index	39,434,843
S&P 500 Barra Growth Index	$500 x Index	12,408
S&P 500 Barra Value Index	$500 x Index	24,319
S&P 400 Index	$500 x Index	378,526
Fortune E-50	$20 x Index	3,694
NASDAQ 100 Index	$500 x Index	5,586,750
E-Mini NASDAQ 100	$20 x Index	32,550,233
Russell 2000	$500 x Index	714,259
E-Mini Russell	$100 x Index	26,012
Benzene	42,000 gal x Index	36
Mixed Xylenes	42,000 gal x Index	6
HDD Weather	100 x HDD	131

TABLE 1.A1 *Cont.*

CHICAGO MERCANTILE EXCHANGE	UNIT	VOLUME
CDD Weather	100 x CDD	
Goldman Sachs Commodity Index	$250 x Index	479,646
CME Futures Total		*315,971,885*
Lean Hogs	40,000 lb	171,472
Lean Hog Index	40,000 lb	
Pork Bellies, Frozen	40,000 lb	6,901
Butter	40,000 lb	38
Fluid Milk	50,000 lb	23,792
Mini BFP Milk		29
Midi BFP Milk	100,000 lbs	2,836
Class IV Milk	200,000 lbs	1,448
Live Cattle	40,000 lb	688,149
Feeder Cattle	50,000 lb	186,247
Random Lumber	80,000 bd ft	25,752
Euroyen	100,000,00 yen	2,225
3 Month Eurodollar	$1,000,000	88,174,799
One Month LIBOR	$3,000,000	2,105
British Pound	62,500	147,205
Canadian Dollar	100,000	109,908
Deutsche Mark	125,000	727
Japanese Yen	12,500,000	839,069
Mexican Peso	500,000	5,331
Swiss Franc	125,000	119,051
Australian Dollar	100,000	30,050
EuroFX	125,000 x Euro	655,991
Nikkei 225	$5 x Ind	3,339
S&P 500 Index	$250 x Ind	4,381,924
E-Mini S&P 500	$50 x S&P Index	21,777
S&P 400 Index	$500 x Index	4,007
NASDAQ 100 Index	$500 x Index	121,895
Russell 2000	$500 x Index	10,941
Goldman Sachs Commodity Index	$250 x Index	3,343
CME Options on Futures Total		*95,740,352*
CME Total		**411,712,237**

KANSAS CITY BOARD OF TRADE		
Wheat	5,000 bu	2,357,004
Western Natural Gas	10,000 MMBtu	
Value Line Index	$100 x Index	17,773
Mini Value Line	$100 x Index	
ISDEX	$100 x Index	356
KCBOT Futures Total		*2,375,133*
Wheat	5,000 bu	243,311
Value Line Index	$100 x Index	45
ISDEX	$100 x Index	
KCBOT Options on Futures Total		*243,356*
KCBOT Total		**2,618,489**

(continued)

TABLE 1.A1 *Cont.*

MID-AMERICA COMMODITY EXCHANGE	UNIT	VOLUME
Wheat	1,000 bu	52,285
Corn	1,000 bu	118,574
Oats	1,000 bu	1,892
Soybeans	1,000 bu	281,451
Soybean Meal New	20 tons	6,430
Soybean Oil	30,000 lbs	3,246
Live Cattle	20,000 lb	6,529
Lean Hogs	20,000 lb	8,968
New York Silver	1,000 oz	3,066
New York Gold	33.2 oz	3,023
Platinum	25 oz	96
U.S. T-Bonds	50,000	50,936
T-Bills	500,000	90
Ten Year T-Notes	50,000	1,909
Five Year T-Notes	50,000	1
Eurodollars	500,000	7,224
Australian Dollar	50,000	380
British Pound	12,500	6,200
Euro Currency	62,500	1,880
Swiss Franc	62,500	10,999
Deutsche Mark	62,500	42
Japanese Yen	6,250,000	10,466
Canadian Dollar	50,000	7,185
MIDAM Futures Total		*582,872*
Wheat	1,000 bu	832
Corn	1,000 bu	3,590
Soybeans	1,000 bu	5,116
Soybean Oil	30,000 lb	4
New York Gold	33.2 oz	2
U.S. T-Bonds	$50,000	343
MIDAM Options on Futures Total		*9,887*
MIDAM Total		**592,759**

MINNEAPOLIS GRAIN EXCHANGE		
Spring Wheat	5,000 bu	967,666
White Wheat	5,000 bu	227
Durum Wheat	5,000 bu	74
Cottonseed	120 tons	732
White Shrimp	5,000 lb	
Black Tiger Shrimp	5,000 lb	
Twin Cities Electricity—On Peak	736HHW	
Twin Cities Electricity—Off Peak	736HHW	
MGE Futures Total		*968,699*
Spring Wheat	5,000 bu	2,912
European Spring Wheat	5,000 bu	
White Wheat	5,000 bu	
Durum Wheat	5,000 bu	
Cottonseed	120 tons	718

TABLE 1.A1 *Cont.*

MINNEAPOLIS GRAIN EXCHANGE	UNIT	VOLUME
White Shrimp	5,000 lb	
Black Tiger Shrimp	5,000 lb	
MGE Options on Futures Total		*29,830*
MGE Total		**998,529**

NEW YORK BOARD OF TRADE	UNIT	VOLUME
Coffee "C"	37,500 lb	2,199,371
Sugar #11	112,000	5,150,329
Sugar #14	112,000 lb	116,733
Cocoa	10 M tons	2,005,817
BFP Milk		
BFP Large		
Cotton #2	50,000 lb	2,259,665
Orange Juice, Frozen Concentrate	15,000 lb	577,496
Orange Juice, Frozen Concentrate—2	15,000 lb	
Orange Juice, Frozen Concentrate—Diff		15
5 Year T-Note	$100,000	1,904
U.S. Dollar/Canadian	$200,000 US	1,854
U.S. Dollar/Swedish Krona	$200,000 US	2,564
U.S. Dollar/Norwegian Krone	$200,000 US	
U.S. Dollar/Swiss Franc	$200,000 US	10,737
U.S. Dollar/Japanese Yen	$200,000 US	16,338
U.S. Dollar/British Pound	$125,000 BP	17,379
U.S. Dollar/Rand	$100,000 US	4,793
Canadian Dollar/Japanese Yen	$200,000 CAN	18,865
Australian Dollar/U.S. Dollar	$200,000 AUS	2,640
Australian Dollar/Canadian Dollar	$200,000 AUS	17,986
Australian Dollar/New Zealand	$200,000 AUS	12,673
New Zealand Dollar/U.S. Dollar	$200,000 NZ	
Australian Dollar/Japanese Yen	$200,000 AUS	31,250
Pound/Swiss	$125,000 EP	
Pound/Yen	$125,000 BP	
Swiss/Yen	200,000 S. Francs	15,196
Large Euro/U.S. Dollar		64,431
Small Euro/U.S. Dollar		2,299
Euro/Australian Dollar	100,000 Euros	17,006
Euro/Canadian	100,000 Euros	11,712
Euro/Yen	100,000 Euros	
Euro/Krona	100,000 Euros	30,354
Euro/Pound	100,000 Euros	
Euro/Norwegian	100,000 Euros	4,498
Euro/Swiss	100,000 Euros	44,162
U.S. Dollar Index	$1000 x Index	342,948
NYSE Composite Index	$500 x Index	217,772
Russell 1000	$500 x Index	313,318
PSE Tech 100	$500 x Index	128
S&P Commodity Index		8,505
CRB Index	$500 x Index	16,878
NYBOT Futures Total		*14,034,168*

(continued)

TABLE 1.A1 *Cont.*

NEW YORK BOARD OF TRADE	UNIT	VOLUME
Coffee "C"	37,500 lb	799,506
Sugar #11	112,000	1,305,470
Flexible Sugar		12,200
Cocoa	10 M tons	436,295
BFP Milk		
BFP Large		
Cotton #2	50,000 lb	1,025,578
Orange Juice, Frozen Concentrate	15,000 lb	170,756
U.S. Dollar Index	$ 1000 x Index	15,365
Large Euro/U.S. Dollar		932
Euro/Pound	100,000 Euros	936
Euro/Swiss	100,000 Euros	
Euro/Yen		685
Pound/Yen	$125,000 BP	16
Pound/Swiss Franc	$125,000 SP	
Swiss/Yen	200,000 S. Francs	
New Zealand I U.S. Dollar	$200,000 NZ	
U.S. Dollar/British Pound	$125,000 BP	136
U.S. Dollar/Swiss		
U.S. Dollar/Rand	$100,000 US	
U.S. Dollar/Japanese Yen	$12,500,00 ¥	867
NYSE Composite Index	$500 x Index	78,053
Russell 1000	$500 x Index	9,905
PSE Tech 100	$500 x Index	130
CRB Index	$500 x Index	891
NYBOT Options on Futures Total		*3,857,721*
NYBOT Total		**17,891,889**

NEW YORK MERCANTILE EXCHANGE		
COMEX Division		
Gold	100 oz	6,785,340
Silver	5,000 oz	2,569,198
High Grade Copper	25,000 lb	2,856,641
Aluminum	44,000 lb	43,089
Eurotop 100 Index	$100 x Index	976
Eurotop 300 Index	$200 x Index	3,415
COMEX Futures Total		*12,258,659*
Gold	100 oz	1,975,019
Silver	5,000 oz	483,386
High Grade Copper	25,000 lb	50,826
Aluminum	44,000 lb	
COMEX Options on Futures Total		*2,509,231*
COMEX Division Total		**14,767,890**
NYMEX Division		
Palladium	100 oz	25,925
Platinum	50 oz	205,969
No. 2 Heating Oil, NY	1,000 bbl	9,264,472
Unleaded Regular Gas, NY	1,000 bbl	9,223,510

TABLE 1.A1   *Cont.*

NEW YORK MERCANTILE EXCHANGE	UNIT	VOLUME
Crude Oil	1,000 bbl	37,530,568
Brent Crude Oil	1,000 bbl	49,565
Middle East Sour Crude, Oil	1,000 bbl	
Propane	42,000 gal	10,566
Natural Gas	10,000 MMBTU	16,468,355
Central Appalachian Coal (CAPP)	1,500 tons	2,209
Mid-Columbia Electricity	736 Mwh	75
Cinergy Electricity	736 Mwh	
Entergy Electricity	736 Mwh	
Palo Verde Electricity	736 Mwh	109
PfM Electricity	736 Mwh	
California Oregon Border Electricity	736 Mwh	2
NYMEX Futures Total		72,781,325
Platinum	50 oz	1,813
No. 2 Heating Oil, NY	1,000 bbl	704,972
Unleaded Regular Gas, NY	1,000 bbl	1,040,030
Crude Oil	1,000 bbl	7,726,076
Brent Crude Oil	1,000 bbl	741
Natural Gas	10,000 MMBTU	16,468,355
Gas–Crude Oil Spread	1,000 bbl	5,974,240
Heating Oil–Crude Oil Spread	1,000 bbl	14,992
Cinergy Electricity	736 Mwh	13,014
Entergy Electricity	736 Mwh	
Palo Verde Electricity	736 Mwh	
California Oregon Border Electricity	736 Mwh	
NYMEX Options on Futures Total		15,475,878
NYMEX Division Total		**88,257,203**
New York Mercantile Exchange		**103,025,093**

PACIFIC STOCK EXCHANGE		
Wilshire Small Cap Index (WSX)	$100 x Index	
Morgan Stanley Emerging Growth Index (EGI)	$100 x Index	
All Options on Individual Equities		102,701,752
PSE Total		**102,701,752**

PHILADELPHIA STOCK EXCHANGE		
Utility Index (UTY)	$100 x Index	50,877
Value Line Index (VLE)	$100 x Index	
Oil Service Sector (OSX)	$100 x Index	2,896,796
Phone Index (PNX)	$100 x Index	
Forest & Paper Products Index (FPP)	$100 x Index	4,495
Semiconductor Index (SOX)	$100 x Index	731,376
OTC Prime Sector Index (OTX)	$100 x Index	15,390
Computer Box Maker (BMX)	$100 x Index	5,030
Gold/Silver Index (XAU)	$100 x Index	443,028
Bank Index (BKX)	$100 x Index	263,734
Defense Index (DFX)	$100 x Index	999
Drug Index (RXS)	$100 x Index	492

(continued)

TABLE 1.A1   *Cont.*

PHILADELPHIA STOCK EXCHANGE	UNIT	VOLUME
Fiber Optics Index (FOP)	$100 x Index	2,383
Super Cap Index (HFX)	$100 x Index	
TheStreet.com Internet Index (DOT)	$100 x Index	28,687
U.S. Top 100 Index (TPX)	$100 x Index	
Wireless Telecom Sector (YLS)	$100 x Index	12,055
OTC index (XOC)	$100 x Index	608
All Currency Options		557,259
All Options on Individual Equities		96,360,224
PHLX Total		**101,373,433**
U.S. Total Futures		*629,123,443*
U.S. Total Options on Futures		*168,211,323*
U.S. Total Options on Securities		*715,846,920*
Grand Total for the United States		*1,513,181,686*

U.S. COMMODITY GROUPS FUTURES

Interest Rate	342,105,778
Ag Commodities	72,346,731
Energy Products	72,549,431
Foreign Currency/Index	21,725,203
Equity Indexes	107,166,181
Precious Metals	9,608,093
Nonprecious Metals	2,899,730
Chemicals	42
Other	722,264
Total	*629,123,443*
%	
Interest Rate	54.38%
Ag Commodities	11.5%
Energy Products	11.53%
Foreign Currency/Index	3.45%
Equity Indexes	17.03%
Precious Metals	1.53%
Nonprecious Metals	0.46%
Other	0.11%
Total	*100%*

U.S. OPTIONS ON FUTURES

Interest Rate	126,456,680
Ag Commodities	16,892,893
Energy Products	15,474,065
Foreign Currency/Index	1,926,269
Equity Indexes	4,920,380
Precious Metals	2,460,224
Nonprecious Metals	50,826
Other	29,996
Total	*168,211,323*

TABLE 1.A1   *Cont.*

U.S. OPTIONS ON FUTURES	UNIT	VOLUME
%		
Interest Rate		75.18%
Ag Commodities		10.04%
Energy Products		9.20%
Foreign Currency/Index		1.15%
Equity Indexes		2.93%
Precious Metals		1.46%
Nonprecious Metals		0.03%
Other		0.02%
Total		*100%*
Options on Securities		
Interest Rate		39,303
Foreign Currency/Index		557,259
Equity Indexes		79,552,414
Individual Equities		635,697,944
Total		*715,846,920*
%		
Interest Rate		0.01%
Foreign Currency/Index		0.08%
Equity Indexes		11.11%
Individual Equities		88.80%
Total		*100%*
U.S. Grand Total		**1,513,181,686**

INTERNATIONAL VOLUME		
Live Hogs (AVC)		32,437
Piglets (AMB)		243
Eggs (EFA)		3
Potatoes (AAC,APC)		61,184
Agricultural Futures Markets Amsterdam Futures Total		*93,867*
Potato Options (OFAA, OFAJ, OFAP)		8,498
Hog Options (OPF)		1,879
Agricultural Futures Markets Amsterdam Options Total		*10,377*
Agricultural Futures Markets Amsterdam Total		**104,244**
AEX Stock Index (FTI)		3,317,913
Light AEX Stock Index (FTIL)		8,211
Amsterdam Information Technology Index (FIA)		
Amsterdam Financial Sector Index (FFA)		
Amsterdam MidCap Index (FTM)		4,290
FTSE sStars (FTES)		

(continued)

TABLE 1.A1 *Cont.*

INTERNATIONAL VOLUME	VOLUME
FTSE Eurotop 100 Index (FETI)	253
Euro/US Dollar (FED)	2,346
U.S. Dollar/Euro FDE)	2,234
All Futures on Individual Equities	8,387
Amsterdam Futures Total	*3,343,634*
Gold Options	
Silver Options	
Euro/U.S. Dollar (EDX)	29,760
U.S. Dollar/Euro Options (DEX)	39,700
Dutch Gov't Bond Options	10,937
AEX Stock Index Options (AEX)	6,569,129
Light AEX Stock Index Options (AEXL)	50,241
Eurotop 100 Options	2,358
FTSE sStar Options (STAR)	24
FTSE Eurotop 100 Options (ETI)	5,210
Amsterdam Information Technology Index Options (AIS)	53
Amsterdam Financial Sector Index Options (AFS)	28
Amsterdam MidCap, Index (MID)	1,165
Eurotop Bank Sector Index Options (EIS)	2
Eurotop Information Technology Sector Index Options (EIS)	
Dutch Top 5 Index Options	
All Options on Individual Equities	56,348,323
Amsterdam Options Total	*63,057,020*
Amsterdam Exchanges Total	**66,400,654**
ATX Index	271,741
CeCe (5 Eastern European Indexes)	164,278
Wiener Borse Futures Total	*436,019*
ATX Index	123,757
ATX LEOs (Long Term Equity Options)	274
CeCe (5 Eastern European Indexes)	1,633
All Options on Individual Equities	1,239,969
Wiener Borse Options Total	*1,365,633*
Wiener Borse Total	**1,801,652**
Mini Bet 20 Index (MBEL)	2,166,420
Mini Dow Jones Euro Stoxx50 (MEUR)	728,700
Bel 20 Index (BXF)	543,501
Euronext Futures Total	*3,438,621*
Bel 20 Index Options (BXO)	727,853
U.S. Dollar/Euro (USO)	
Gold Index Options (GXO)	
All Options on Individual Equities	404,559
EURONEXT Options Total	*1,132,412*
EURONEXT Brussles Derivatives Market (Formerly BELFOX) Total	**4,571,033**
Arabica Coffee	475,034
Live Cattle	92,365
Sugar Crystal	93,904
Cotton	15

TABLE 1.A1 *Cont.*	
INTERNATIONAL VOLUME	**VOLUME**
Corn	4,588
Soybean Futures	83
Gold Futures	
Gold Forward	484
Gold Spot	42,971
Anhydrous Fuel Alcohol Futures	67,527
Bovespa Stock Index Futures	5,151,572
Bovespa Mini Index	110,943
Bovespa Volatility Index	450
Interest Rate	46,241,111
Interest Rate Swap	964,419
Interest Rate x Stock Basket Swap	
Interest Rate x Exchange Rate Swap	3,645,963
Interest Rate x Reference Rate Swap	28
Interest Rate x Price Index Swap	99,900
Interest Rate x Basic Financial Rate Swap	
Interest Rate x Gold Swap	
Interest Rate x Ibovespa Swap	592
Interest Rate x Ibovespa Index	900
ID x U.S. Dollar Spread Futures	1,375,846
FRA on ID x U.S. Dollar spread	16,524,996
ID Long-Term Futures	
ID Forward with Reset	602,431
C-Bond	3
EI-Bond	407
U.S. Dollar	18,636,578
Mini U.S. Dollar	10,945
Euro	170
Exchange Rate Swap	
Price Index's Exchange Rate	
BM & F Futures Total	*94,174,452*
Gold Options on Actuals	156,447
Gold Options Exercise	58,316
U.S.$ d. Arabica Coffee Options	12,818
U.S.$ d. Arabica Coffee options Exercise	1,130
Corn Options	
Corn Options	
Soybean Options	
Soybean Options Exercise	
Live Cattle Options	1,204
Bovespa Stock Options	41,210
Bovespa Stock Options Exercise	11,750
Interest Rate Options (IDI)	1,129,060
Interest Rate Options (IDI) Exercise	89,013
Flexible Bovespa Stock Index Options	273,889
U.S. Dollar Options on Actuals	1,212
U.S. Dollar Options Exercise	139,057
Flexible Currency Options	570,739
BM & F Options Total	*3,696,233*
BM & F, Brazil Total	**97,870,685**

(continued)

TABLE 1.A1 *Cont.*

INTERNATIONAL VOLUME	VOLUME
Corn	
Euro Wheat	15,733
Feed Wheat	
Feed Barley	2,403
Wheat	433
Extra Wheat	15
Black Seed	98
Rapeseed	1,101
Soybean	21
TAX	39
Ammonium Nitrate	44
Europ I Live Hog	17
Europ 11 Live Hog	
U.S. Dollar	
Japanese Yen	425,125
EUR	226,639
British Pound	1,840,127
Swiss Franc	15,426
Czech Crown	63,010
Three Month LIBOR	
Budapest Commodity Exchange Futures Total	7,585
	2,612,788
Corn	
Milling Wheat	511
Black Seed	
Wheat	
Euro Wheat	164
EUR	
Budapest Commodity Exchange Options Total	11,000
	11,675
Budapest Commodity Exchange Total	
	2,624,463
3 Year Hungarian Government Bond	1,800
Budapest Stock Index (BUX) Futures	1,236,405
DEM/HUF	
EUR0/HUF	
JPY/HUF	41,722
CHF/HUF	3,084
GBP/HUF	7,064
USD/HUF	1,000
All Futures on Individual Equities	116,176
	879,049
Budapest Stock Exchange Futures Total	
	2,286,300
Budapest Stock Index (BUX) Options	
All Options on Individual Equities	9,076
Budapest Stock Exchange Options Total	
	9,076
Budapest Stock Exchange Total	
	2,295,376
DAX	
FOX	14,686,359
NEMAX 50	74,819
Dow Jones Global Titans 50	5,409,482
	871

TABLE 1.A1 *Cont.*	
INTERNATIONAL VOLUME	**VOLUME**
DI Euro STOXX 50	37,828,500
DJ Euro, STOXX Banks	113,478
DJ Euro STOXX Healthcare	2,399
DJ Euro STOXX Technology	82,321
DJ Euro STOXX Telecom	47,967
DJ STOXX 50	452,830
DJ STOXX 600 Banks	11,259
DJ STOXX 600 Healthcare	11,968
DJ STOXX 600 Technology	5,152
DJ STOXX 600 Telecom	6,900
Euro-BUND	178,011,304
Euro-BOBL	99,578,068
1 Month Euribor	0
3 Month Euribor	663,980
3 Month Euromark	0
Euro-BUXL	0
Euro-SCHATZ	92,637,630
EUREX, Frankfurt Futures Total	*429,625,287*
DAX Options	44,102,502
FOX Options	6,053
NEMAX 50	1,726,251
Dow Jones Global Titans 50	104
DJ Euro STOXX 50	19,046,893
DJ Euro STOXX Banks	20,434
DJ Euro STOXX Healthcare	96
DJ Euro STOXX Technology	19,031
DJ Euro STOXX Telecom	9,677
DJ STOXX 50	44
Options on Euro-BUND	22,054,064
Options on Euro-SCHATZ	10,075
Options on 3 Month Euribor	0
Options on Euro-BOBL	6,188,962
All Options on Individual NEMAX Component Equities	16,165,675
All Options on DJ Euro STOXX 50 Component Equities	984,468
All Options on German Equities	240,918
All Options on U.S. Equities	38,196
All Options on Individual DAX Equities	799,751,215
EUREX, Frankfurt Options Total	*200,597,880*
EUREX, Frankfurt Total (Formerly DTB) Total	**630,223,167**
Swiss Market Index (SMI)	5,099,537
Swiss Government Bond (CONF)	416,883
EUREX, Zurich Futures Total	*5,516,420*
Swiss Market Index (SMI) Option	3,179,143
All Options on Individual SMI Component Equities	35,239,133

(continued)

TABLE 1.A1 *Cont.*	
INTERNATIONAL VOLUME	**VOLUME**
EUREX, Zurich Options Total	*38,418,276*
EUREX, Zurich Total (Formerly SOFFEX)	**43,934,696**
EUREX Total	**674,157,863**
STOX Stock Future	988,503
HEX Tech Index	41
FOX Index	
Helsinki Futures Total	*988,544*
FOX Index Options	
HEX Tech Index	3,040
All Options on Individual Equities (STOX)	152,052
Helsinki Options Total	*155,092*
Helsinki Exchanges (Formerly Finnish Options Market Exchange) Total	**1,143,636**
Danish Government Bonds 7% 2004	
Danish Government Bonds 6% 2009 (G09)	
Danish Government Bonds 5% 2005 (G05)	
6% 2026 Mortgage Bonds (A26)	
6% 2029 Mortgage Bonds (A29)	
KFX Stock Index	459,007
All Futures on Individual Equities	
FUTOP Futures Total	*459,007*
Danish Government Bonds 6% 2009 Option (G09)	
KFX Stock Index Options	5,529
All Options on Individual E	26,041
FUTOP Options Total	*31,370*
FUTOP Clearing Centre, Denmark, Total	**490,577**
Brent Crude Oil	18,396,069
Gasoil	7,230,408
Fuel Oil	
Electricity Baseload—Monthly	50
Natural Gas—Seasons	1,005
Natural Gas—Quarters	3,900
Natural Gas BOM	2,570
Natural Gas Daily (NBP)	1,540
Natural Gas Monthly (NBP)	462,665
International Petroleum Exchange Futures Total	*26,098,207*
Brent Crude Oil Options	252,217
Gasoil Options	60,240
International Petroleum Exchange Options Total	*312,457*
International Petroleum Exchange, UK, Total	**26,410,664**
FIB 30 Index	4,634,329
Mini FIB 30 Index	1,400,135
MIDEX	743
Italian Derivatives Futures Total	*6,035,207*

TABLE 1.A1 *Cont.*	
INTERNATIONAL VOLUME	**VOLUME**
MIB 30 Index options	2,716,271
All Options on Individual Equities	8,329,533
Italian Derivatives Options Total	*11,045,804*
Italian Derivatives Market of the Italian Stock Exchange Total	**17,081,011**
Korea Treasury Bonds	9,323,430
CD Interest Rate	1,410
KOSDAQ50 Index	466,479
U.S. Dollar	1,676,979
Gold	608
Korea Stock Exchange Futures Total	*11,468,906*
U.S. Dollar Options	
KOSDAQ50 Index	85
Options	85
Korea Futures Exchange	11,468,991
KOSPI 200	31,502,184
Futures	31,502,184
KOSPI 200 Options	823,289,608
Korea Stock Exchange Options Total	*823,289,608*
Korea Stock Exchange Total	**854,791,792**
High Grade Primary Aluminum	23,767,595
Aluminum Alloy	819,206
Copper—Grade A	17,797,929
Standard Lead	3,096,929
Primary Nickel	3,194,758
Special High Grade Zinc	6,113,484
Silver	
Tin	1,432,814
LMEX	1,780
London Metal Exchange Futures Total	*56,224,495*
High Grade Primary Aluminum Options	1,547,829
Aluminum Alloy Options	5,787
Copper—Grade A Options	1,053,373
Standard Lead Options	86,098
Primary Nickel Options	133,039
Special High Grade Zinc Options	188,147
Tin Options	27,150
Primary Aluminum TAPOS	80,244
Aluminum Alloy TAPOS	
Copper Grade A TAPOS	39,472
Lead TAPOS	1,512
Nickel TAPOS	10,937
Tin TAPOS	360
Special High Grade Zinc TAPOS	14,807
London Metal Exchange Options Total	*3,188,755*
London Metal Exchange Total	**59,413,250**

(continued)

TABLE 1.A1 *Cont.*

INTERNATIONAL VOLUME	VOLUME
3 Month Sterling	34,945,053
3 Month Euroswiss	4,694,391
3 Month Euro Libor (formerly the Ecu)	1,852
3 Month Euribor	91,083,198
3 Month Euroyen Tibor	
10 Year Euro EFB (formerly Deutsche Mark Libor Fin. Bond)	
5 Year Euro EFB (formerly Deutsche Mark Libor Fin. Bond)	
Long Gilt	6,710,557
5 Year Gilt	
2 Year Swapnote	686,450
5 Year Swapnote	1,502,104
10 Year Swapnote	1,967,221
EuroBTP	
Japanese Government Bond	72,182
FTSE 100 Index	12,698,908
Mini FTSE 100 Index	129,283
FTSE 100 techMARK	
FTSE Eurotop 100 Index	130,824
FTSE Eurotop 300 Index	33
FTSE EStars Index	
FTSE Eurobloc 100 Index	1,752
MSCI Euro Index	124,202
MSCI Pan-Euro Index	373,259
FTSE Mid 250 Index	559
Barley	5,614
BIFFEX (Baltic Freight Index)	922
No. 7 Cocoa	1,514,384
Robusta Coffee	1,547,838
Potatoes	12,503
Wheat	95,676
White Sugar	898,261
London Monthly	5
All Futures on Individual Equities	2,325,744
LIFFE Futures Total	*161,522,755*
3 Month Sterling Option	7,692,455
3 Month Sterling Mid Curve Option	427,975
3 Month Euroswiss Option	82
3 Month Euribor Option	21,643,698
3 Month Euribor Mid Curve Option	963,417
3 Month Euro Libor	
Long Gilt Option	1,230
2 Year Swapnote	450
5 Year Swapnote	1,730
10 Year Swapnote	2,429
FTSE 100 Option (ESX)	11,848,155
FTSE 100 Option (SEI)	320,461
FTSE Eurotop 100 Index	28,100
FTSE 100 FLEX Options	229,152
Barley Options	751
No. 7 Cocoa Options	94,505
Robusta Coffee Options	80,197

TABLE 1.A1   *Cont.*

INTERNATIONAL VOLUME	VOLUME
Potatoes Options	
Wheat Options	12,693
White Sugar Options	70,526
All Options on Individual Equities	10,725,183
LIFFE Options Total	*54,225,252*
LIFFE, UK, Total	**215,748,027**
Crude Palm Oil (FCPO)	479,799
3 Month KLIBOR (FKB3)	54,914
KLSE Composite Index (FKL1)	287,528
Malaysia Derivatives Futures Total	*822,241*
KLSE Composite Index Options (OKLI)	564
Malaysia Derivatives Options Total	*564*
Malaysia Derivatives Exchange Berhad (Formerly Kuala Lumpur Options and Financial Futures Exchange and Commodity and Monetary Exchange of Malaysia), Total	**822,805**
EURO National Bond	17,349,421
EURO 5 Year	621,814
EURIBOR	2,965
Wheat #2	57,159
Com	57,664
Wine	68
European Rapeseed Meal	
Rapeseed Oil	
Rapeseed	135,655
MATIF Futures Total	*18,224,746*
Options on EURO Notional Bond	
Options on Rapeseed	7,554
MATIF Options Total	*7,554*
MATIF, Paris, Total	**18,232,300**
CAC 40 10 Euro	22,923,597
DJ EURO STOXXSM 50	887,447
DJ EURO STOXX	2,323
DJ STOXX 50	2,330
DJ STOXX (L&M)	1,606
DJ STOXX (SM) Sector Indexes	624
MONEP Futures Total	*23,817,927*
CAC 40 Index Options	107,251,388
DJ STOXX 50 Options	705
DJ STOXX Sector	
DJ EURO STOXX 50 Options	2,265
All Options on Individual Equities	178,330,328
MONEP Options Total	*285,584,686*
MONEP, France, Total	**309,402,613**
Paris Bourse SA, Total	**627,634,913**

(continued)

TABLE 1.A1 *Cont.*	
INTERNATIONAL VOLUME	**VOLUME**
10 Year Notional Bond	290,608
Meff Renta Fija Futures Total	*290,608*
Meff Renta Fija, Spain, Total	**290,608**
IBEX 35 Plus	4,305,035
Mini IBEX 35	22,423
S&P Europe 350	3,219
S&P Financial	2,223
S&P Technology	5,191
S&P Telecommunications	4,037
All Futures on Individual Equities	8,766,165
Meff Renta Variable Futures Total	*13,108,293*
IBEX 35 Plus Option	998,645
S&P Europe 350	242
S&P Financial	751
S&P Technology	285
S&P Telecommunications	391
All Options on Individual Equities	22,628,132
Meff Renta Variable Options Total	*23,628,446*
Meff Renta Variable, Spain, Total	**36,736,739**
Wheat	44,607
Corn	36,421
Sunflowerseed	8,440
Soybean	59,436
Argentine Wheat Index (ITA)	83
Mercado a Termino de Buenos Aires Futures Total	*148,987*
Wheat Options	20,492
Corn Options	8,140
Sunflowerseed Options	1,764
Soybean Options	16,804
Argentine Wheat Index (ITA)	26
Mercade a Termino de Buenos Aires Options Total	*47,286*
Mercado a Termino de Buenos Aires, Total	**196,273**
Bankers Acceptance Futures 3 Months (BAX)	4,234,236
10 Year Canadian Government Bond (CGB)	1,835,229
5 Year Canadian Government Bond (CGF)	
S&P Canada 60 Index (SXF)	1,174,328
All Futures on Individual Equities	17,206
Bourse de Montreal Futures Total	*7,260,999*
Options on Canadian Government Bond (OGB)	12
Options on Bankers Acceptance Futures 3 Months (OBX)	89,339
Canadian Gov't Bond Options (OBK, OBV, OBZ)	20,369
S&P Canada 60 Index (SXO) (incl. LEAPS)	35,585
i60 Index (XIU) (incl. LEAPS)	127,731

TABLE 1.A1 *Cont.*

INTERNATIONAL VOLUME	VOLUME
All Options on Individual Equities	5,099,894
Bourse de Montreal Options Total	5,372,930
Bourse de Montreal, Total	**12,633,929**
3 Year Government Stock	62,521
10 Year Government Stock	32,319
90 Day Bank Bill	915,225
NZSE—10 Capital Share Price Index	637
New Zealand Electricity	150
New Zealand Futures Exchange Futures Total	1,010,852
90 Day Bank Bill Options	18,320
3 Year Government Stock	1,100
10 Year Government Stock	200
NZSE—10 Capital Share Price Index Options	
All Options on Individual Equities	15,312
New Zealand Futures Exchange Options Total	34,932
New Zealand Futures Exchange, Total	**1,045,784**
Interest Rate	7,033,675
OMX (Index)	14,906,505
NOX (Index)	
All Futures on Individual Equities	1,468,018
OM Stockholm Futures Total	23,408,198
Interest Rate Options	11,000
OMX (Index) Options	4,587,544
NOX (Index) Options	
All Options on Individual Equities	34,729,075
OM Stockholm Options Total	39,327,619
OM Stockholm, Total	**62,735,817**
OBr10	5,220
OBr5	8,310
Forwards	302,497
OBX	521,314
Oslo Stock Exchange Futures Total	837,341
OBX Options	662,394
All Options on Individual Equities	2,346,339
Oslo Stock Exchange Options Total	3,008,733
Oslo Stock Exchange, Total	**3,846,074**
Copper	4,088,943
Aluminum	1,448,192
Rubber	73,200
Shanghai Futures Exchange	5,610,335

(continued)

TABLE 1.A1 *Cont.*	
INTERNATIONAL VOLUME	**VOLUME**
Eurodollar	17,684,054
Singapore Dollar Interest Rate	111,210
Nikkei 225	4,573,348
Nikkei 300	29,439
Straits Times Index	20,023
S&P CNX Nifty Index	1,800
Dow Jones Thailand Index	
MSCI Hong Kong Index	
MSCI Singapore Index	488,489
MSCI Taiwan Index	3,902,738
Brent Crude	50
Euroyen Tibor	2,711,826
Euroyen Libor	452,559
5 Year Singapore Government Bond	79,246
Japanese Government Bond	545,189
All Futures on Individual Equities	6,575
SIMEX Futures Total	*30,606,546*
Eurodollar Options	10
Euroyen Tibor options	47,127
Euroyen Libor Options	2,000
Japanese Government Bond Options	228
MSCI Taiwan Index Options	42,899
Nikkei Option	291,052
SIMEX Options Total	*383,316*
SIMEX, Singapore, Total	**30,989,862**
White Maize (WMAZ)	563,510
Yellow Maize (YMAZ)	77,933
WEAT	23,992
SUNS	25,249
WSEC	240
YSEC	64
All Share Index	8,044,557
Industrial Index	2,304,176
Financial Index (FIND)	10,585
RESI	2,933
Johannesburg Interbank Rate (JBAR)	4
R150	2,055
R153	1,788
All Futures on Individual Equities	811,156
SAFEX Futures Total	*11,868,242*
White Maize (WMAZ)	269,887
Yellow Maize (YMAZ)	27,785
WEAT	8,694
SUNS	5,775
All Share Index	17,926,295

TABLE 1.A1 *Cont.*

INTERNATIONAL VOLUME	VOLUME
Industrial Index	337,289
Financial Index (FINI)	15,804
R150	780
R153	9,449
All Options on Individual Equities	5,705,719
SAFEX Options Total	24,307,477
South African Futures Exchange (SAFEX),Total	**36,175,719**
TAIEX Futures	2,844,707
Mini TAIEX Futures	413,343
Taiwan Stock Exchange Electronic Sector Index Futures	635,661
Taiwan Stock Exchange Bank and Insurance Sector Index Futures	452,541
Taiwan Futures Exchange Futures Total	4,346,252
TAIEX Options	5,137
Taiwan Futures Exchange Options Total	5,137
Taiwan Futures Exchange,Total	**4,351,389**
All Ordinaries Share Price Index	58,016
SPI 200	3,823,729
Australian Dollar Futures	40,654
Bank Bills 90 Day	9,108,108
3 Year Treasury Bonds	15,718,248
10 Year Treasury Bonds	5,296,233
NSW Base Load Electricity	125
NSW Peak Period Electricity	40
VIC Base Load Electricity	30
VIC Peak Period Electricity	151
Wheat	4,044
Fine Wool	2,385
Broad Wool	944
Barley	120
Canola	556
Sorghum	959
Greasy Wool	8,621
All Futures on Individual Equities	12,545
Sydney Futures Exchange Futures Total	34,075,508
All Ordinaries Share Price Options	11,478
SP1 200	504,954
90 Day Bank Bill Options	267,808
Overnight 90 Day Bank Bills Options	300
3 Year Treasury Bond Options	301,782
Overnight 3 Year Treasury Bond Options	618,011
10 Year Treasury Bond Options	36,341
Overnight 10 Year Treasury Bond Options	29,671
Wheat	6
Greasy Wool	20
Sydney Futures Exchange Options Total	1,770,371
Sydney Futures ExchangeTotal	**35,845,879**

(continued)

TABLE 1.A1   *Cont.*

INTERNATIONAL VOLUME	VOLUME
Wheat	166,932
Oats	0
Flax Seed	72,476
Canola	2,424,973
Canola Meal	676
Feed Peas	0
Field Peas	1,195
Western Barley	237,574
Futures	2,903,826
Wheat Options	243
Flax Options	2,300
Western Barley Options	5,728
Canola Options	125,236
Winnipeg Commodity Exchange Options Total	*133,507*
Winnipeg Commodity Exchange Total	**3,037,333**
Hang Seng Index	4,400,071
Mini Hang Seng Index	769,886
MSCI China Free Index	3,141
Hang Seng 100	78
Hang Seng Properties Sub-Index	
Red-Chip Index	533
Rolling Forex	4,226
One Month HIBOR	14,315
Three Month HIBOR	629,491
Three Year Exchange Fund Note	1,175
All Futures on Individual Equities	7,756
HKFE and HKSE Futures Total	*5,830,672*
Hang Seng Index	716,114
Hang Seng 100	111
Hang Seng Properties Sub-Index	
Red Chip Index	
All Options on Individual Equities	4,002,655
HKFE and HKSE Options Total	*4,718,880*
Hong Kong Exchanges and Clearing-Derivatives Unit (HKFE and HKSE), Total	**10,549,552**
Red Beans	54,845
Imported Soybeans	122,429
Non-GMO Soybeans	1,478,070
Refined Sugar	1,437
Corn	2,016,968
Broiler	2,693,858
Fukuoka Futures Exchange (formerly the Kanmon Commodity Exchange) Total	**6,367,607**
Red Beans	30,069
U.S. Soybeans	465,057
Non-GMO Soybeans	971,980
Refined Sugar	2,874
Raw Sugar	94,961

TABLE 1.A1   *Cont.*

INTERNATIONAL VOLUME	VOLUME
Raw Silk	269,199
Corn 75 Index	263,520
Coffee Index	371,272
Kansai International Grain Index	432,619
KANSAI Futures Total	*2,901,551*
Raw Sugar Options	6,097
KANSAI Options Total	*6,097*
Kansai Commodities Exchange Total	**2,907,648**
Red Beans	29,614
Imported Soybeans	60,759
Non-GMO Soybeans	22,471
Refined Sugar	345
Dried Cocoon	90,267
Cotton Yarn (40S)	307,768
Wool Yarn	
Shell Egg	596,415
Gasoline	14,392,478
Kerosene	12,346,595
Central Japan Commodity Exchange Total	**27,846,712**
Nikkei 225 Futures	9,516,875
Nikkei 300 Futures	961,566
High-Tech Index	
Financial Index	
Consumer Index	
Osaka Securities Exchange Futures Total	*10,478,441*
Nikkei 225 Options	6,953,222
Nikkei 300 Options	609
All Options on Individual Equities	38,077
Osaka Securities Exchange Options Total	*6,991,908*
Osaka Securities Exchange Total	**17,470,349**
Wool Yarn	
Cotton Yarn (20S)	113,074
Cotton Yam (40S)	90,591
Rubber (RSS3)	710,872
Rubber (TSR20)	66,268
Rubber Index	967,915
Aluminum	1,438,450
Osaka Mercantile Exchange Total	**3,387,170**
Gold	9,791,711
Silver	660,864
Platinum	16,244,583
Palladium	117,098
Aluminum	735,366
Gasoline	16,441,056
Kerosene	8,301,559
Crude Oil	911,597

(continued)

TABLE 1.A1 *Cont.*	
INTERNATIONAL VOLUME	**VOLUME**
Rubber	3,334,411
Cotton Yam	
The Tokyo Commodity Exchange Total	**56,538,245**
American Soybeans	1,740,613
Non-GMO Soybeans	3,342,542
Soybean Meal	268,513
Arabica Coffee	4,465,044
Red Beans	1,093,922
Corn	10,341,897
Refined Sugar	2,874
Robusta Coffee	420,873
Raw Sugar	1,031,530
Tokyo Grain Exchange Futures Total	*22,707,808*
American Soybeans Option	19,040
Corn Options	52,012
Raw Sugar Options	37,544
Tokyo Grain Exchange Options Total	*108,596*
Tokyo Grain Exchange Total	**22,816,404**
3 Month Euroyen	7,624,711
3 Month Euroyen LIBOR	2,904
U.S. Dollar–Japanese Yen	1,294
Tokyo International Financial Exchange Futures Total	*7,628,909*
3 Month Euroyen Options	13,553
Tokyo International Financial Exchange Options Total	*13,553*
Tokyo International Financial Futures Exchange Total	**7,642,462**
5 Year Yen Government Bond	2,198
10 Year Yen Government Bond	7,377,641
TOPIX Stock Index	5,071,946
Electric Applicance Index	350
Transportation Equipment Index	
Bank Index	13,298
Tokyo Stock Exchange Futures Total	*12,465,433*
TOPIX Options	7,623
Yen Government Bond (10 Yr) Options	1,062,235
Tokyo Stock Exchange Options Total	*1,069,858*
Tokyo Stock Exchange Total	**13,535,291**

TABLE 1.A1 *Cont.*	
INTERNATIONAL VOLUME	**VOLUME**
Japan Raw Silk	602,727
International Raw Silk	241,004
Dried Cocoon	69,789
Potato	399,351
Yokohama Commodity Exchange Total	**1,312,871**

INTERNATIONAL COMMODITY GROUPS

Futures	
Interest Rate	674,551,544
Equity Indices	223,845,921
Ag Commodities	66,390,811
Energy Products	78,539,565
Foreign Currency/Index	23,114,699
Precious Metals	26,858,319
Nonprecious Metals	64,008,646
Other	927
Futures on Individual Equities	14,302,601
Total Futures International	*1,171,633,033*
Options	
Interest Rate	72,945,191
Equity Indices	1,054,840,753
Ag Commodities	900,083
Energy Products	312,457
Foreign Currency/Index	2,001,947
Precious Metals	214,763
Nonprecious Metals	3,188,755
Other	0
Options on Individual Equities	462,664,706
Total Options International	*1,597,068,655*
Grand Total International	**2,768,701,688**

Source: Futures Industry Association, *Monthly Volume Report*, December 2001.

CHAPTER 2

Futures and Options Market Mechanics

This chapter explains the market mechanics and the jargon of futures and options markets. The options contracts discussed in this chapter are options written on underlying futures contracts. Hedgers and speculators trade options as either substitutes for or in conjunction with futures contracts. This chapter emphasizes futures more than options because options are covered in greater depth in later chapters. In any case, options described in this chapter are based on futures contracts, so an understanding of futures markets goes a long way toward an understanding of options on futures. The basic workings of the markets explained in this chapter cover both commodity (e.g., minerals and agricultural) and financial (e.g., interest rate and exchange rate) futures and options markets.

THE FUTURES CONTRACT

As explained in Chapter 1, a futures contract is very similar to either a deferred delivery contract or a forward contract. Traders entering into a futures contract establish a price for subsequent delivery (or cash settlement) of a certain type of a designated commodity or financial instrument. The contract itself specifies a geographic area (if there is delivery) and a given time period for settlement or delivery. To serve as an example, Table 2.1 illustrates the specifications for the New York Mercantile Exchange crude oil futures contract. These specifications cover the major terms and conditions of the contract. Units of 1,000 barrels of oil are traded, and the contract specifies delivery of light "sweet" crude oil. Open outcry trading is conducted from 10:00 A.M. to 2:30 P.M., and in addition, there is after-hours electronic trading (Box 2.1). Each crude oil contract can be traded for up to a 30-month consecutive time period before its expiration date. Trading in crude oil futures is conducted for 12 delivery months (i.e., for all 12 months of the calendar year). As explained in Chapter 1, 12 delivery months is unusual, as most futures contracts have less than nine delivery months. For example, lumber futures have only six

---

TABLE 2.1   New York Mercantile Exchange Specifications

New York Mercantile Exchange
NYMEX/COMEX. Two divisions, one marketplace

NYMEX: LIGHT, SWEET CRUDE OIL FUTURES AND OPTIONS CONTRACT SPECIFICATIONS

Trading Unit Futures: 1,000 U.S. barrels (42,000 gallons). Options: One NYMEX Division light, sweet crude oil futures contract.	**Delivery** F.O.B. seller's facility, Cushing, Oklahoma, at any pipeline or storage facility with pipeline access to TEPPCO, Cushing storage, or Equilon Pipeline Co., by in-tank transfer, in-line transfer, book-out, or interfacility transfer (pumpover).
Trading Hours Futures and Options: 10:00 A.M.–2:30 P.M. for the open outcry session. After-hours trading is conducted via the NYMEX ACCESS® electronic trading system starting at 3:15 P.M. on Monday through Thursday and concluding at 9 A.M. On Sunday, the electronic session begins at 7 P.M. All times are New York time.	**Delivery Period** All deliveries are rateable over the course of the month and must be initiated on or after the first calendar day and completed by the last calendar day of the delivery month.
Trading Months Futures: 30 consecutive months plus long-dated futures, which are initially listed 36, 48, 60, 72, and 84 months prior to delivery. Additionally, trading can be executed at an average differential to the previous day's settlement prices for periods of 2 to 30 consecutive months in a single transaction. These calendar strips are executed during open outcry trading hours. Options: Twelve consecutive months, plus three long-dated options at 18, 24, and 36 months out on a June–December cycle.	**Alternate Delivery Procedure (ADP)** An Alternate Delivery Procedure is available to buyers and sellers who have been matched by the Exchange subsequent to the termination of trading in the spot month contract. If buyer and seller agree to consummate delivery under terms different from those prescribed in the contract specifications, they may proceed on that basis after submitting a notice of their intention to the Exchange.
Price Quotation Futures and Options: Dollars and cents per barrel.	**Exchange of Futures for, or in Connection with, Physicals (EFP)** The commercial buyer or seller may exchange a futures position for a physical position of equal quantity by submitting a notice to the Exchange. EFPs may be used to either initiate or liquidate a futures position.

(continued)

TABLE 2.1   *Cont.*

NYMEX: LIGHT, SWEET CRUDE OIL FUTURES AND OPTIONS CONTRACT SPECIFICATIONS

Minimum Price
Futures and Options: $0.01 (1¢) per barrel ($10 per contract).

Deliverable Grades
Specific domestic crudes with 0.42% sulfur by weight or less, not less than 37° API gravity nor more than 42° API gravity. The following domestic crude streams are deliverable: West Texas Intermediate, Low Sweet Mix, New Mexican Sweet, North Texas Sweet, Oklahoma Sweet, South TexaSweet.

Specific foreign crudes of not less than 34° API nor more than 42° API. The following foreign streams are deliverable: U.K. Brent and Forties, and Norwegian Oseberg Blend, for which the seller shall receive a 30¢-per-barrel discount below the final settlement price; Nigerian Bonny Light and Colombian Cusiana are delivered at 15-cent premiums; and Nigerian Qua Iboe is delivered at a 5-cent premium.

Maximum Daily Price Fluctuation
Futures: Initial limits of $3.00 per barrel are in place in all but the first two months and rise to $6.00 per barrel if the previous day's settlement price in any back month is at the $3.00 limit. There is no limit for the two contracts nearest expiry. In the event of a $7.50 per barrel move in either of the first two contract months, limits on all months become $7.50 per barrel from the limit in place in the direction of the move following a one-hour trading halt.
Options: No price limits.

Inspection
Inspection shall be conducted in accordance with pipeline practices. A buyer or seller may appoint an inspector to inspect the quality of oil delivered. However, the buyer or seller who requests the inspection will bear its costs and will notify the other party of the transaction that the inspection will occur.

Last Trading Day
Futures: Trading terminates at the close of business on the third business day prior to the 25th calendar day of the month preceding the delivery month. Options: Beginning with the August 1997 contract, trading will end three business days before the underlying futures contract. All prior contracts, as well as the December 1997, June 1998, and December 1998 contracts already listed as long-dated options, expire on the Friday before the termination of futures trading, unless there are less than three trading days left to futures termination, in which case options expire two Fridays before the futures contract.

Position Limits
20,000 contracts for all months combined, but not to exceed 1,000 in the last three days of trading in the spot or 10,000 in any one month.

Exercise of Options
By a clearing member to the Exchange clearing–house not later than 5:30 P.M., or 45 minutes after the underlying futures settlement price is posted, whichever is later, on any day up to and including the option's expiration.

Margin Requirements
Margins are required for open futures or short options positions. The margin requirement for an options purchaser will never exceed the premium.

Source: NYMEX.

BOX 2.1

Open outcry versus electronic trading.

Shouting buy and sell orders in the futures exchange trading pit and waving hand signals is the traditional futures price discovery mechanism. It is a somewhat crude system, but it is one that has worked well in the U.S. markets for the past 150 years. However, the traditional open outcry trading is slowly giving way to computerized electronic trading. The Chicago Board of Trade and the New York Mercantile Exchange both have introduced electronic trading systems for overnight trades. The Chicago Mercantile Exchange also has an electronic system (Globex) for financial products. Many foreign exchanges in London, Tokyo, Paris, and Frankfurt have moved fully to electronic futures screen trading. The exchanges in Europe and Asia are newer, and compared to the U.S. exchanges, they have met less member resistance to change toward computerized trading.

There are pros and cons associated with open outcry versus electronic trading. The debate over which system is better has focused on cost, market liquidity, pricing transparency, speed, and regulatory issues related to minimizing trading abuse. The traditional open outcry system is more expensive than computerized trading, but some participants in the industry argue that human interaction among floor traders provides greater market liquidity. Electronic trading is faster, more efficient, and easier to regulate. It is difficult to determine which system is superior, but we do know one thing—the free market will ultimately decide whether electronic trading will replace open outcry as the dominant system.

For further reading on this topic, see Tse and Zabotina (2001) and Pirrong (1999).

---

delivery months. The crude oil options contracts are typically traded for a shorter time period compared to futures. The options contracts are normally traded for up to 12 consecutive months prior to expiry.

On entering a futures contract, the buyer and seller make equal and offsetting commitments. In the trade's terminology, a buyer of a futures contract enters into a "long" position, whereas the seller enters into a "short" position. The seller of one December crude oil contract, for example, is going **short** in the market by agreeing to deliver 1,000 barrels of light "sweet" crude oil to Oklahoma during the month of December. On the other side of the transaction, the buyer of the crude oil futures contract is going **long** in the market by agreeing to accept delivery in December and on delivery to pay for the 1,000 barrels in full. Table 2.1 reports that the central delivery point for crude oil is Cushing, Oklahoma, with several alternative delivery opportunities.

On entering the futures market, a trader can either sell or buy a futures contract. The initial trade must be subsequently offset either by taking an opposite position (e.g., the seller later buys) or through delivery. Many students may ask the

---

BOX 2.2

Is sound just noise?

How futures and options markets process information in reaching a price and volume equilibrium is an important issue in financial economics. Some market observers claim that market participants do not rely solely on easily observable data, such as past prices, trading volumes, or news announcements, to determine how much they are willing to buy or sell and at what price. Indeed, a computer is not a perfect substitute for humans in the trading pits. Current electronic trading mechanisms are not equipped to convey the same kinds of signals as a sound level. For instance, the noise level of a trading pit can be very insightful to a trader. It has been found through research that following a rise in the sound level of a trading pit, prices become more volatile. Considering that traders often make decisions on the basis of price volatility, the sound level of the trading pit can be a very useful price indicator. At a time when many futures and options exchanges around the world are investigating the pros and cons of fully electronic trading systems, replacing the trading floor with a network of computers, the importance of face-to-face human interaction is an extremely relevant question that cannot be overlooked.

For further reading on this topic, see Coval and Shumway (2001).

---

obvious question: How can a trader first sell a futures contract before they actually buy one? The answer is that by selling a futures contract, the trader enters into an agreement to deliver (and thus sell) the commodity or asset during the delivery month. Selling a futures contract is a *promise* to sell at a future date, and for that reason futures traders can "sell" an asset they may not even own. Of course, they either have to buy the physical asset before the delivery month or simply cancel their initial promise to sell by later buying a futures contract for the same delivery month.

Most futures contracts do not result in actual delivery and some do not even permit delivery, but this does not detract from their usefulness in the economy. Unlike trading in most other markets (including the stock market) where equity ownership or ownership of physical assets changes hands with every trade, the execution of a futures market trade involves future commitments on the part of the buyer and seller. These commitments are legally binding but can easily be offset, as described next.

A unique characteristic of a futures contract, and that which distinguishes it from a forward contract, is that it affords both the buyer and the seller a continuing opportunity to avoid making or taking delivery. To avoid delivery any time after the initial transaction, traders execute an equal but opposite transaction in the same commodity (or asset) and futures month. For example, to absolve himself of the commitment to accept 1,000 barrels of crude oil in December, the original buyer of the futures contract could subsequently sell one December contract. This offsetting trade can be done at any time before the contract expires. For each trader, if the selling price of a futures contract is higher than the buying price, then a profit is recorded (ignoring transaction costs such as brokerage fees); otherwise, there is a loss.

For most futures contracts, the futures exchange establishes a limit on the extent to which futures prices may change during a single day. Prices are restricted from moving by more than some prescribed amount from the previous day's settlement price. If prices reach the upper or lower limit, then the market is "locked limit," and trading is suspended for a period of time. As shown in Table 2.1, there is no daily maximum price change for crude oil for the two contracts nearest expiry. For the more distant contracts (beyond the two nearest contracts), the limit is $3.00 per barrel per day, which is more binding with respect to how far the price can

---

BOX 2.3

Futures price manipulation.

Given the highly competitive nature of the futures and options markets, there are relatively few instances of attempts by futures traders to manipulate prices through cornering the market. The U.S. Commodity Futures Trading Commission (CFTC) is constantly on the alert for possible market manipulation and is responsive to any complaint about possible market manipulation.

However, there are some famous examples of alleged futures price manipulation. Some of these examples are as follows:

- Bunker, Herbert, and Lamar Hunt, members of a rich and colorful Texas oil and ranching family, were found to have manipulated the silver futures market during 1979 and 1980.
- Ferruzzi Finanziaria SpA, an Italian multinational agribusiness firm, was ordered by the CFTC to liquidate its soybean futures positions when it was found Ferruzzi had built up long positions of more than 50% of deliverable supply of soybeans in Chicago and Toledo. This case led to changes in the delivery points for CBOT soybeans and other grains.
- Merrill Lynch & Co. and Japan's Sumitomo Corp. allegedly worked together to manipulate the New York and London copper futures markets in 1995 and 1996. These two firms were found to have conspired to keep the price of copper high and to artificially force prices higher in late 1995.
- A Spokane energy company paid a $2.1 million fine to settle civil charges that its former employees tried to manipulate the electricity futures market in 1998. Avista Energy agreed to pay the fine and accept a "cease and desist" order from the CFTC. The CFTC found that on four occasions, Avista Energy manipulated the settlement prices of electricity futures contracts in order to increase the company's net gain. Avista had placed large orders for futures contracts that influenced prices on the entire Western market. Avista provides electric power for much of eastern Washington and northern Idaho.

move in one day. This means that at all times during a given day, crude oil contract prices must be within $3.00 of the previous trading day's contract settlement price.

The reason for having daily price limits is to serve as a type of circuit breaker when trading becomes volatile. This reduces the risk of trader default and reduces the effects of emotional reactions to information. The exchanges seek to avoid "panics" by forcing traders to stretch large price moves across days, thus giving everyone time to rationally evaluate new information. In cases where significant price changes are based on economic factors, the daily price limits are often increased by the exchange on a temporary basis. For example, in the case of crude oil, if a "back month" futures contract price closes "at the limit" (either up or down), the limit is doubled from $3.00 to $6.00 per barrel. In this way, futures exchanges seek to maintain order in the pricing process while still allowing the markets to work.

The exchange also establishes minimum price movements. For example, for crude oil, this is $0.01 per barrel, or $10 per contract. Table 2.A1 reports the trading symbol for crude oil futures: CL. This is an industry abbreviation, and there is a separate symbol for each futures and options contract. For instance, a crude oil futures contract traded on the New York Mercantile Exchange and expiring in March 2004 is abbreviated as CLH4, where CL represents the crude oil futures, H represents the month of March, and 4 is the last digit in the expiration year. For a complete listing of these abbreviations, see Appendix Table 2.A1.

Table 2.2 presents a sample of some of the daily futures prices reprinted from the *Wall Street Journal*. Basic information reported for each contract includes the names of the delivery months for which contracts are currently being traded, the first (called the "open") and last ("close") price at which each contract traded during the day, the highest and lowest prices at which transactions occurred during the day, and the change between the previous and current settlement prices. Some newspapers, such as the *Wall Street Journal, Barron's*, or *Investor's Business Daily*, also report trade volume and open interest (explained in a later section) and the highest and lowest prices at which a particular contract has ever traded during its lifetime. Prices are supplied by futures exchanges and are also available on the Internet with a 10- to 20-minute delay. You can also find delayed prices at the interactive *Wall Street Journal* (http://www.wsj.com). To get real-time futures and options prices, you must subscribe to Reuters or Telerate, but these services are quite expensive.

One of the first things we notice in Table 2.2 is that there are various categories of futures contracts. These include grains (wheat, corn, and soybeans), livestock and meat (cattle, hogs, and pork bellies), food and fiber (cocoa, coffee, and sugar), metals and petroleum (gold and platinum), interest rates (Treasury bonds and Treasury notes), indexes (Dow Jones Industrial Average, S&P 500 Index, and Nasdaq 100), currencies (Japanese yen, Euro, and Canadian dollar). At the top of Table 2.2, there is a small box that contains exchange abbreviations. These abbreviations allow us to determine where each contract in Table 2.2 is traded (i.e., on which exchange). All futures price and trading volume quotes are from the previous trading day, so Monday's newspaper reports trading activity for the previous Friday, Tuesday's paper reports Monday's prices and volume, and so on. The open interest figures are reported with a one-day lag, so Monday's newspaper reports

TABLE 2.2 Daily Futures Prices from the *Wall Street Journal*

Exchange Abbreviations

For commodity futures and futures options

CBT-Chicago Board of Trade;
CME-Chicago Mercantile Exchange;
CSCE-Coffee, Sugar & Cocoa Exchange, New York;
CMX-COMEX (Div. of New York Mercantile Exchange);
CTN-New York Cotton Exchange;
DTB-Deutsche Terminboerse;
EUREX-European Exchange;
FINEX-Financial Exchange (Div. of New York Cotton Exchange;
IPE-International Petroleum Exchange;
KC-Kansas City Board of Trade;
LIFFE-London International Financial Futures Exchange;
MATIF-Marche a Terme International de France;
ME-Montreal Exchange;
MCE-MidAmerica Commodity Exchange;
MPLS-Minneapolis Grain Exchange;
NYFE-New York Futures Exchange (Sub. of New York Cotton Exchange);
NYM-New York Mercantile Exchange;
SFE-Sydney Futures Exchange;
SGX-Singapore Exchange Ltd.;

Futures prices reflect day and overnight trading
Open interest reflects previous day's trading

Thursday, May 16, 2002

Grain and Oilseed Futures

	OPEN	HIGH	LOW	SETTLE	CHG	LIFETIME HIGH	LIFETIME LOW	OPEN INT

Corn (CBT)-5,000 bu.; cents per bu.

	OPEN	HIGH	LOW	SETTLE	CHG	HIGH	LOW	OPEN INT
July	216.00	216.00	212.75	213.25	-3.00	279.50	198.00	210,786
Sept	222.25	222.50	219.00	219.50	-3.00	262.00	205.25	48,178
Dec	231.75	231.75	228.00	228.50	-3.25	272.00	215.00	110,404
Mr03	239.00	239.00	235.50	235.75	-3.00	258.50	224.00	18,266
May	241.00	241.25	239.25	239.50	-2.75	252.00	229.25	5,447
July	243.00	243.50	241.75	242.25	-2.50	272.00	233.75	8,660
Dec	241.00	242.75	240.50	241.75	...	269.00	235.00	11,352
Mr04	248.50	248.50	248.00	248.25	.75	255.00	242.75	746
Dec	241.00	243.00	240.50	242.50	1.75	260.00	239.25	914

Est vol 58,000; vol Wed 65,619; open int 414,997, +4,000.

Oats (CBT)-5,000 bu.; cents per bu.

July	151.50	156.00	150.00	153.50	1.75	179.75	129.00	4,293
Sept	130.25	131.00	129.00	129.25	-1.00	151.00	117.50	547
Dec	130.00	131.00	129.50	130.75	-.25	153.00	123.00	4,030

Est vol 2,000; vol Wed 2,373; open int 9,000, +234.

Soybeans (CBT)-5,000 bu.; cents per bu.

July	481.00	487.25	479.00	484.75	2.75	533.00	425.00	86,680
Aug	476.00	482.00	475.25	479.75	2.75	529.00	425.00	11,153
Sept	471.00	475.00	468.00	471.75	1.00	495.00	425.00	7,283
Nov	467.25	469.25	464.00	466.25	-1.00	561.00	428.50	35,457
Ja03	471.00	473.50	468.50	470.25	-1.25	488.00	445.00	3,962
Mar	473.50	475.00	471.00	471.75	-3.50	491.00	449.00	2,853
May	473.00	475.50	472.00	472.50	-2.00	492.00	461.00	2,508
July	474.50	477.00	474.50	475.00	-2.50	525.00	450.00	1,516
Nov	477.00	478.00	475.25	475.25	.25	515.00	453.00	856

Est vol 48,000; vol Wed 49,458; open int 152,269, +3,769.

Soybean Meal (CBT)-100 tons; $ per ton.

July	163.50	165.70	162.30	165.10	1.20	170.50	141.00	60,345
Aug	161.00	162.30	159.70	161.80	.80	168.50	141.10	12,985
Sept	157.80	159.40	156.80	158.60	.70	168.00	141.90	11,719
Oct	155.50	156.20	154.00	155.10	-.10	165.00	141.50	8,461
Dec	154.50	155.10	152.80	154.40	-.30	160.70	142.70	25,657
Ja03	154.50	154.50	153.00	153.80	-.80	160.00	143.50	3,566
Mar	153.30	153.50	152.00	152.00	-1.50	156.50	145.50	2,165
May	151.00	151.80	149.80	149.80	-1.40	163.70	146.00	1,401
July	151.00	151.00	149.50	149.50	-2.20	156.00	147.00	1,069

Est vol 26,000; vol Wed 32,806; open int 127,757, +1,137.

Soybean Oil (CBT)-60,000 lbs.; cents per lb.

July	16.82	17.17	16.75	16.93	.10	20.55	15.48	61,540
Aug	17.00	17.29	16.99	17.04	.10	20.33	15.62	12,410
Sept	17.13	17.40	17.10	17.15	.10	18.00	15.73	10,937
Oct	17.28	17.45	17.21	17.25	.10	18.35	15.15	8,311
Dec	17.36	17.72	17.36	17.52	.12	20.50	16.10	22,813
Ja03	17.78	17.78	17.68	17.68	.09	17.99	16.35	2,610
Mar	17.85	18.05	17.85	17.85	.10	18.45	16.70	1,695
May	18.05	18.25	18.00	18.00	.10	18.25	16.80	1,240
July	18.15	18.15	18.15	18.15	.05	20.05	16.95	1,246

Est vol 19,500; vol Wed 16,860; open int 125,366, +895.

Wheat (CBT)-5,000 bu.; cents per bu.

July	283.50	284.00	275.00	276.50	-7.00	365.00	264.50	65,744
Sept	287.25	287.50	280.50	281.25	-6.50	315.00	271.00	8,855
Dec	298.75	298.75	290.00	291.50	-6.00	365.00	283.50	14,541
Mr03	300.50	301.00	296.00	296.00	-5.50	320.00	291.00	2,174
July	289.00	290.00	286.00	286.25	-3.75	336.00	286.00	1,090

Est vol 22,500; vol Wed 26,446; open int 92,847, -980.

Wheat (KC)-5,000 bu.; cents per bu.

May	280.00	280.00	276.50	276.50	-5.50	357.00	271.25	6
July	290.50	290.50	282.50	283.50	-6.00	384.50	279.50	39,326
Sept	297.50	297.50	289.00	290.00	-5.75	338.00	286.75	8,300
Dec	304.00	304.75	296.75	297.50	-6.25	348.00	293.50	10,667
Mr03	304.50	305.50	301.25	301.75	-6.25	326.00	299.00	2,639

Est vol 7,029; vol Wed 12,700; open int 62,265, -2,570.

Wheat (MPLS)-5,000 bu.; cents per bu.

May	...	...	...	288.25	...	376.00	285.00	0
July	297.50	297.50	293.00	294.50	-3.25	381.00	289.50	12,650
Sept	303.00	303.00	298.50	299.75	-4.00	385.00	295.50	4,775
Dec	312.50	312.50	309.00	310.00	-4.00	390.00	305.50	2,913
Mr03	319.50	319.50	318.50	319.50	-4.00	355.00	315.50	469

Est vol na; vol Wed 2,277; open int 21,508, -115.

Livestock Futures

Cattle-Feeder (CME)-50,000 lbs.; cents per lb.

May	76.05	76.07	75.80	75.85	-.05	90.30	69.85	2,603
Aug	77.10	77.27	76.45	76.50	-.57	89.50	71.82	7,089
Sept	76.60	76.80	76.10	76.12	-.57	87.45	71.87	1,050
Oct	76.85	76.90	76.30	76.35	-.42	86.25	72.27	1,320
Nov	77.30	77.30	76.75	76.82	-.40	86.50	72.75	579

Est vol 1,582; vol Wed 1,048; open int 13,024, +183.

Cattle-Live (CME)-40,000 lbs.; cents per lb.

June	63.10	63.15	62.65	62.72	-.35	74.85	59.32	32,369
Aug	63.80	63.90	63.32	63.57	-.20	75.20	59.75	26,614
Oct	66.57	66.70	66.15	66.30	-.25	75.95	62.52	25,544
Dec	68.00	68.10	67.50	67.80	-.30	73.80	64.25	10,300
Fb03	68.82	68.82	68.30	68.60	-.27	74.55	65.35	2,804
Apr	70.00	70.15	69.75	70.15	-.10	74.97	66.60	1,345

Est vol 10,340; vol Wed 7,027; open int 98,976, +156.

Hogs-Lean (CME)-40,000 lbs.; cents per lb.

June	53.35	53.75	52.70	52.82	-.95	68.20	50.25	14,227
July	54.55	54.70	53.65	53.85	-.87	64.90	50.50	10,106
Aug	53.00	53.10	52.17	52.55	-.72	62.50	49.00	3,857
Oct	43.70	43.77	43.00	43.20	-.62	55.80	41.90	2,834
Dec	40.90	40.90	40.10	40.27	-.65	52.00	39.85	2,650
Fb03	43.00	43.00	42.30	42.30	-.82	53.10	42.25	461

Est vol 5,617; vol Wed 6,028; open int 35,487, +701.

Pork Bellies (CME)-40,000 lbs.; cents per lb.

May	65.70	65.70	64.10	65.02	-.17	87.25	60.90	22
July	65.70	65.85	64.07	64.87	-.25	87.30	61.95	2,582
Aug	65.00	65.10	63.50	64.20	...	86.50	62.00	602

Est vol 401; vol Wed 494; open int 3,228, -51.

Food and Fiber Futures

Milk (CME)-200,000 lbs., cents per lb.

(continued)

TABLE 2.2 Cont.

Month	Open	High	Low	Settle	Change	High	Low	Open Int
May	10.80	10.80	10.80	10.80	...	12.30	10.79	1,890
June	10.85	10.85	10.76	10.76	-.05	12.64	10.70	2,611
July	11.53	11.55	11.30	11.35	-.18	13.40	11.20	2,882
Aug	12.30	12.32	12.28	12.28	-.02	13.45	11.75	2,216
Sept	12.71	12.75	12.68	12.72	.02	13.56	12.30	2,256
Oct	12.52	12.55	12.50	12.50	-.02	13.11	12.25	1,549
Nov	12.05	12.06	12.03	12.06	...	12.69	11.98	983
Dec	11.81	11.82	11.77	11.82	...	12.50	11.77	760

Est vol 561; vol Wed 734; open int 15,536, -126.

Cocoa (CSCE)-10 metric tons; $ per ton.

Month	Open	High	Low	Settle	Change	High	Low	Open Int
July	1,581	1,598	1,561	1,595	57	1,598	875	32,182
Sept	1,543	1,567	1,532	1,562	57	1,567	907	17,024
Dec	1,475	1,493	1,475	1,497	55	1,493	936	12,863
Mr03	1,435	1,454	1,435	1,455	51	1,454	986	12,340
Sept	1,426	1,426	1,426	1,438	58	1,426	1,090	10,772
Dec	1,400	1,410	1,400	1,418	54	1,410	1,092	5,983

Est vol 13,423; vol Wed 7,800; open int 102,447, +399.

Coffee (CSCE)-37,500 lbs.; cents per lb.

Month	Open	High	Low	Settle	Change	High	Low	Open Int
May	...	...	...	48.40	.95	87.00	45.60	30
July	49.25	50.80	49.20	50.75	1.35	84.00	48.10	31,921
Sept	51.85	53.45	51.80	53.35	1.35	85.75	49.40	16,533
Dec	54.65	56.00	54.55	55.95	1.20	72.25	51.25	8,397
Mr03	56.70	58.00	56.70	57.90	1.25	64.75	52.90	5,168
May	57.75	59.75	59.20	59.10	1.35	64.90	54.50	1,904
July	58.75	59.25	58.75	59.80	1.25	65.00	55.90	1,953
Sept	60.00	60.00	60.00	60.30	1.20	63.50	59.25	1,141

Est vol 6,539; vol Wed 7,613; open int 67,047, -10.

Sugar-World (CSCE)-112,000 lbs.; cents per lb.

Month	Open	High	Low	Settle	Change	High	Low	Open Int
July	5.78	5.99	5.78	5.98	.13	9.60	4.83	74,187
Oct	5.67	5.83	5.67	5.83	.11	8.50	4.92	34,504
Mr03	5.92	6.03	5.92	6.03	.08	8.00	5.29	20,441
May	5.95	6.05	5.95	6.05	.07	7.65	5.35	7,424
July	5.89	5.98	5.89	5.98	.07	7.35	5.30	12,107
Oct	6.08	6.12	6.08	6.13	.05	6.60	5.55	7,733

Est vol 21,590; vol Wed 16,356; open int 158,609, +404.

Sugar-Domestic (CSCE)-112,000 lbs.; cents per lb.

Month	Open	High	Low	Settle	Change	High	Low	Open Int
July	19.20	19.36	19.20	19.36	.12	21.82	19.12	3,051
Sept	19.70	19.70	19.70	19.70	.05	21.82	19.45	2,803
Nov	19.63	19.70	19.63	19.69	.09	21.45	19.55	2,988
Ja03	19.70	19.80	19.70	19.80	.10	21.32	19.50	2,251
Mar	19.92	19.92	19.92	20.00	.02	21.22	19.92	1,844
May	20.15	20.15	20.15	20.15	.03	21.10	20.05	341
July	20.28	20.28	20.28	20.28	.02	20.95	20.25	330

Est vol 92; vol Wed 56; open int 13,640, +23.

Cotton (NYCE)-50,000 lbs.; cents per lb.

Month	Open	High	Low	Settle	Change	High	Low	Open Int
July	36.33	36.50	35.30	35.48	-.63	68.50	31.90	36,093
Oct	38.80	39.00	37.50	37.88	-.70	65.50	33.85	1,623
Dec	40.50	40.60	39.45	39.65	-.52	64.45	34.65	23,327
Mr03	42.50	42.55	41.60	41.68	-.47	55.25	36.20	3,569
May	45.00	45.00	45.00	44.15	-.50	54.00	38.70	2,316
Dec	46.80	47.00	46.80	46.25	-.75	51.00	43.80	302

Est vol 8,369; vol Wed 8,160; open int 68,426, -471.

Orange Juice (NYCE)-15,000 lbs.; cents per lb.

Month	Open	High	Low	Settle	Change	High	Low	Open Int
July	89.80	91.40	89.80	91.20	1.35	99.60	86.20	11,751
Sept	89.30	90.50	89.30	90.10	.80	100.00	86.50	2,570
Nov	90.50	90.50	90.50	89.70	.40	101.60	86.50	2,670
Ja03	90.20	90.60	90.20	90.45	.45	102.40	87.80	3,686
Mar	90.80	91.00	90.80	90.90	.50	102.00	88.25	2,186

Est vol 4,350; vol Wed 1,696; open int 23,115, -185.

Metal Futures

Copper-High (CMX)-25,000 lbs.; cents per lb.

Month	Open	High	Low	Settle	Change	High	Low	Open Int
May	73.90	73.90	73.30	73.40	-0.90	89.60	61.90	2,404
June	n.a.	74.00	73.55	73.55	-0.95	89.50	62.35	5,430
July	74.75	74.75	73.70	73.85	-0.90	88.90	62.30	36,298
Aug	74.40	74.45	74.40	74.10	-0.90	82.90	62.90	1,973
Sept	74.90	74.90	74.35	74.30	-0.90	88.00	62.95	8,379
Ja03	75.35	75.35	75.15	75.05	-0.90	79.95	64.90	575
June	76.45	76.45	76.10	75.90	-0.90	76.80	70.80	216
Dec	76.80	76.80	76.80	76.60	-0.90	78.90	71.50	1,479

Est vol 8,000; vol Wed 6,497; open int 74,580, +405.

Gold (CMX)-100 troy oz.; $ per troy oz.

Month	Open	High	Low	Settle	Change	High	Low	Open Int
May	...	...	...	309.80	1.10	311.00	306.80	4
June	309.00	310.80	308.80	310.10	1.10	385.00	264.50	111,066
Aug	310.40	311.80	309.90	311.30	1.20	315.00	272.60	19,014
Dec	312.30	313.70	311.80	312.90	1.00	358.00	268.10	21,383
Fb03	313.20	313.20	313.20	313.80	0.90	316.70	286.50	7,511
Apr	315.70	315.70	315.70	314.80	0.90	317.00	281.50	2,536
Dec	320.00	321.00	319.60	320.40	0.80	359.30	280.00	5,158

Est vol 33,000; vol Wed 31,064; open int 186,230, -5,491.

Platinum (NYM)-50 troy oz.; $ per troy oz.

Month	Open	High	Low	Settle	Change	High	Low	Open Int
July	533.00	542.50	533.00	536.00	3.10	558.00	405.00	5,639

Est vol 362; vol Wed 216; open int 5,733, -13.

Silver (CMX)-5,000 troy oz.; cnts per troy oz.

Month	Open	High	Low	Settle	Change	High	Low	Open Int
May	463.0	464.0	461.5	463.9	1.3	525.0	407.0	77
July	463.5	465.5	462.0	465.0	1.3	559.0	409.5	56,081
Sept	465.0	465.0	465.0	466.6	1.2	480.5	412.5	4,302
Dec	468.5	470.0	465.0	469.1	1.3	613.0	412.0	9,025

Est vol 6,000; vol Wed 7,314; open int 75,490, +603.

Petroleum Futures

Crude Oil, Light Sweet (NYM)-1,000 bbls.; $ per bbl.

Month	Open	High	Low	Settle	Change	High	Low	Open Int
June	27.60	28.55	27.20	27.95	-0.20	29.54	17.35	81,169
July	27.40	27.56	26.40	27.08	-0.13	28.58	18.75	170,285
Aug	27.02	27.28	26.40	26.93	...	28.18	18.70	52,843
Sept	26.74	26.91	26.20	26.66	0.06	27.76	19.10	33,106
Oct	26.39	26.64	25.90	26.45	0.14	27.42	19.50	19,715
Nov	26.15	26.44	25.92	26.25	0.19	27.07	19.55	11,952
Dec	26.00	26.24	25.60	26.05	0.24	26.95	15.50	44,867
Ja03	25.70	25.70	25.45	25.81	0.28	26.50	19.90	19,866
Feb	25.45	25.45	25.45	25.58	0.32	26.10	19.70	8,383
Mar	25.25	25.25	25.25	25.37	0.37	28.85	20.05	9,366
June	24.79	24.79	24.50	24.75	0.42	25.35	19.82	16,848
Sept	24.00	24.00	24.00	24.28	0.48	24.11	21.05	4,295
Dec	23.70	23.76	23.70	23.89	0.57	24.44	15.92	19,361
Dc05	22.00	22.00	22.00	22.18	0.71	23.00	17.00	3,694
Dc08	21.10	21.10	21.10	21.12	0.71	21.55	19.75	4,090

Est vol 261,051; vol Wed 246,639; open int 543,976, +3,811.

Heating Oil No. 2 (NYM)-42,000 gal.; $ per gal.

Month	Open	High	Low	Settle	Change	High	Low	Open Int
June	.6850	.6915	.6670	.6816	.0037	.7280	.5110	30,703
July	.6900	.6975	.6725	.6866	.0034	.7300	.5210	32,035
Aug	.7010	.7010	.6810	.6921	.0039	.7260	.5300	16,757
Sept	.7005	.7075	.6935	.6991	.0044	.7300	.5390	12,541
Oct	.7050	.7050	.7015	.7061	.0049	.7345	.5460	7,754
Nov	.7140	.7140	.7080	.7121	.0054	.7500	.5570	5,820
Dec	.7230	.7230	.7095	.7166	.0059	.7570	.5660	15,150
Ja03	.7240	.7240	.7150	.7191	.0064	.7510	.5680	7,284
Feb	.7140	.7140	.7100	.7151	.0074	.7441	.5710	5,386
Mar	.7025	.7025	.6960	.6996	.0089	.7261	.5640	3,998
Apr	.6800	.6820	.6765	.6796	.0104	.7041	.5500	1,805
May	.6560	.6560	.6560	.6591	.0119	.6800	.5450	902
June	.6500	.6500	.6500	.6536	.0129	.6751	.5600	2,822

Est vol 38,004; vol Wed 33,746; open int 144,579, -1,030.

Gasoline-NY Unleaded (NYM)-42,000 gal.; $ per gal.

Month	Open	High	Low	Settle	Change	High	Low	Open Int
June	.7920	.7975	.7810	.7953	.0071	.8685	.5900	44,241
July	.7960	.8020	.7850	.8000	.0117	.8510	.5925	34,264
Aug	.7869	.7940	.7820	.7925	.0112	.8290	.5800	15,786
Sept	.7640	.7670	.7640	.7693	.0100	.8000	.5788	18,236
Oct	.7260	.7260	.7260	.7318	.0095	.7550	.5815	4,584
Ja03	.7000	.7000	.7000	.7053	.0095	.7260	.5775	802

Est vol 38,711; vol Wed 45,913; open int 121,881, +422.

Natural Gas (NYM)-10,000 MMBtu.; $ per MMBtu

TABLE 2.2 Cont.

	Open	High	Low	Settle	Chg	High	Low	Open Int
Aug	3.750	3.780	3.685	3.735	-.026	4.790	2.380	39,705
Sept	3.765	3.800	3.710	3.756	-.016	4.770	2.380	31,105
Oct	3.788	3.820	3.730	3.786	-.011	4.785	2.410	48,312
Nov	3.750	4.070	3.750	4.046	-.011	4.900	2.630	28,416
Dec	4.192	4.290	4.192	4.271	-.006	5.010	2.720	27,439
Ja03	4.330	4.380	4.310	4.366	-.006	5.049	2.730	31,487
Feb	4.264	4.300	4.250	4.296	-.001	4.874	2.700	20,014
Mar	4.135	4.150	4.100	4.146	.009	4.710	2.710	19,240
Apr	3.910	3.920	3.900	3.928	.009	4.520	2.610	15,466
May	3.880	3.900	3.860	3.898	.012	4.490	2.630	11,144
June	3.905	3.915	3.890	3.920	.012	4.400	2.610	15,435
July	3.875	3.935	3.875	3.955	.017	4.530	2.550	8,206
Aug	3.945	3.955	3.940	3.990	.029	4.535	2.890	11,823
Sept	3.945	3.945	3.945	3.980	.029	4.445	2.880	9,742
Oct	3.975	3.975	3.975	4.010	.029	4.455	2.910	12,175
Ja04	4.342	4.430	4.342	4.440	.034	4.880	3.300	9,850
Mar	4.170	4.170	4.170	4.170	.037	4.510	3.150	6,246
Apr	3.890	3.890	3.890	3.897	.044	4.190	2.970	7,077

Est vol 115,566; vol Wed 108,894; open int 554,445, -8,129.

Brent Crude (IPE) 1,000 net bbls.; $ per bbl.

	Open	High	Low	Settle	Chg	High	Low	Open Int
Jun	26.30	26.61	26.09	26.22	0.05	28.76	17.70	19,500
Jul	26.52	26.90	25.90	26.38	-0.18	27.50	17.35	82,975
Aug	26.22	26.54	25.70	26.11	-0.15	27.15	17.95	47,526
Sep	26.14	26.23	25.53	25.89	-0.10	26.80	18.19	19,396
Oct	25.87	25.96	25.40	25.66	-0.03	26.48	18.30	10,948
Nov	25.66	25.66	25.15	25.41	0.01	26.08	19.10	8,557
Dec	25.40	25.40	24.81	25.18	0.04	25.95	17.35	36,887
Ja03	25.12	25.12	24.75	24.92	0.08	25.40	19.15	12,280
Feb	24.88	24.88	24.85	24.70	0.12	25.08	19.20	3,763
Mar	24.60	24.60	24.60	24.50	0.17	24.88	19.22	3,420
Sep	23.40	23.60	23.40	23.56	0.39	23.85	20.21	3,140
Dec	22.75	22.85	22.75	23.20	0.48	23.43	19.15	11,060

Est vol 110,000; vol Wed 109,146; open int 269,507, -7,884.

Interest Rate Futures

Treasury Bonds (CBT)-$100,000; pts 32nds of 100%

	Open	High	Low	Settle	Chg	High	Low	Open Int
June	100-15	101-00	100-10	100-28	16	110-00	96-30	413,568
Sept	99-26	99-26	99-06	99-22	15	109-00	96-07	49,208
Dec	98-05	98-24	98-05	98-21	15	101-04	96-06	7,365

Est vol 165,000; vol Wed 247,530; open int 470,143, -4,580.

Treasury Notes (CBT)-$100,000; pts 32nds of 100%

	Open	High	Low	Settle	Chg	High	Low	Open Int
June	104-25	05-115	04-215	105-08	17.0	107-10	101-10	686,776
Sept	103-31	103-11	103-11	103-28	17.0	08-165	100-25	103,154

Est vol 370,000; vol Wed 350,459; open int 789,946, +3,994.

10 Yr Agency Notes (CBT)-$100,000; pts 32nds of 100%

	Open	High	Low	Settle	Chg	High	Low	Open Int
June	00-315	101-12	00-255	101-09	17.0	102-05	97-04	25,793

Est vol 500; vol Wed 2,657; open int 25,844, -344.

5 Yr Treasury Notes (CBT)-$100,000; pts 32nds of 100%

	Open	High	Low	Settle	Chg	High	Low	Open Int
June	105-28	06-075	05-255	06-055	10.5	106-21	03-115	569,155
Sept	04-285	04-285	04-205	04-275	10.5	105-07	102-17	65,972

Est vol 140,000; vol Wed 156,362; open int 635,127, +2,753.

2 Yr Treasury Notes (CBT)-$200,000; pts 32nds of 100%

	Open	High	Low	Settle	Chg	High	Low	Open Int
June	104-14	104-20	04-137	104-19	4.5	104-26	03-005	93,472

Est vol 7,000; vol Wed 8,219; open int 93,594, +247.

30 Day Federal Funds (CBT)-$5,000,000; pts of 100%

	Open	High	Low	Settle	Chg	High	Low	Open Int
May	98.245	98.250	98.245	98.245	...	98.400	97.640	44,786
June	98.23	98.23	98.23	98.23	...	98.37	96.62	46,750
July	98.20	98.21	98.20	98.21	.01	98.23	97.68	59,939
Aug	98.12	98.15	98.12	98.14	.03	98.17	97.47	37,954
Sept	98.02	98.05	98.02	98.04	.04	98.09	97.27	9,569
Dec	97.45	97.48	97.45	97.48	.06	97.48	96.60	297

Est vol 14,500; vol Wed 39,249; open int 210,789, +16,439.

10 Yr Interest Rate Swaps (CBT)-$100,000; pts 32nds of 100%

	Open	High	Low	Settle	Chg	High	Low	Open Int
June	101-13	101-27	101-07	101-24	19	102-26	97-14	23,149

Est vol 3,500; vol Wed 500; open int 25,899, +273.

Treasury Bills (CME)-$1,000,000; pts of 100%

	OPEN	HIGH	LOW	SETTLE	CHG	YIELD	CHG	OPEN INT
June	...	...	...	98.24	.01	1.76	-.01	333

Est vol 2; vol Wed 2; open int 387, -2.

Libor-1 Mo. (CME)-$3,000,000; pts of 100%

	OPEN	HIGH	LOW	SETTLE	CHG	YIELD	CHG	OPEN INT
June	98.12	98.13	98.11	98.13	.01	1.87	-.01	16,843
July	98.09	98.09	98.08	98.09	.02	1.91	-.02	13,453
Aug	97.94	97.96	97.94	97.96	.03	2.04	-.03	4,065
Sept	97.79	97.81	97.79	97.81	.07	2.19	-.07	1,898
Dec	97.04	97.04	97.03	97.05	.08	2.95	-.08	300

Est vol 1,894; vol Wed 4,163; open int 38,256, +464.

Eurodollar (CME)-$1,000,000; pts of 100%

	OPEN	HIGH	LOW	SETTLE	CHG	YIELD	CHG	OPEN INT
June	97.99	98.02	97.99	98.02	.02	1.98	-.02	683,345
July	97.89	97.91	97.89	97.90	.03	2.10	-.03	19,001
Aug	97.75	97.76	97.73	97.75	.04	2.25	-.04	7,112
Sept	97.51	97.62	97.51	97.59	.07	2.41	-.07	632,008
Dec	96.86	96.98	96.86	96.94	.07	3.06	-.07	784,169
Mr03	96.24	96.35	96.24	96.32	.08	3.68	-.08	445,438
June	95.67	95.79	95.67	95.74	.07	4.26	-.07	292,185
Sept	95.25	95.35	95.25	95.32	.07	4.68	-.07	241,282
Dec	94.96	95.05	94.96	95.02	.07	4.98	-.07	190,860
Mr04	94.79	94.88	94.79	94.85	.07	5.15	-.07	147,377
June	94.60	94.70	94.60	94.67	.07	5.33	-.07	133,387
Sept	94.46	94.54	94.46	94.51	.07	5.49	-.07	126,931
Dec	94.32	94.36	94.31	94.34	.07	5.66	-.07	91,578
Mr05	94.22	94.30	94.22	94.27	.07	5.73	-.07	91,231
June	94.16	94.19	94.13	94.16	.07	5.84	-.07	62,509
Sept	94.04	94.08	94.03	94.06	.07	5.94	-.07	68,390
Dec	93.88	93.94	93.88	93.92	.07	6.08	-.07	51,608
Mr06	93.88	93.91	93.85	93.89	.07	6.11	-.07	48,381
June	93.79	93.82	93.76	93.80	.07	6.20	-.07	48,884
Sept	93.71	93.74	93.68	93.72	.07	6.28	-.07	45,735
Dec	93.59	93.62	93.56	93.60	.07	6.40	-.07	30,884
Mr07	93.56	93.60	93.54	93.58	.07	6.42	-.07	25,192
June	93.47	93.52	93.46	93.51	.07	6.49	-.07	13,463
Sept	93.39	93.46	93.39	93.44	.06	6.56	-.06	11,375
Dec	93.31	93.34	93.29	93.33	.06	6.67	-.06	10,685
Mr08	93.30	93.33	93.28	93.32	.06	6.68	-.06	7,413

Est vol 867,316; vol Wed 926,027; open int 4,364,064, -23,712.

Currency Futures

	OPEN	HIGH	LOW	SETTLE	CHG	LIFETIME HIGH	LIFETIME LOW	OPEN INT

Japanese Yen (CME)-12.5 million yen; $ per yen (.00)

	OPEN	HIGH	LOW	SETTLE	CHG	HIGH	LOW	OPEN INT
June	.7847	.7866	.7797	.7816	-.0028	.8776	.7449	81,533
Sept	.7882	.7902	.7837	.7854	-.0028	.8620	.7495	1,653

Est vol 5,801; vol Wed 19,697; open int 84,072, +750.

Canadian Dollar (CME)-100,000 dlrs.; $ per Can $

	OPEN	HIGH	LOW	SETTLE	CHG	HIGH	LOW	OPEN INT
June	.6418	.6443	.6413	.6431	.0008	.6700	.6180	71,991
Sept	.6414	.6430	.6400	.6418	.0008	.6590	.6175	6,523
Dec	.6408	.6415	.6400	.6407	.0008	.6555	.6190	2,112
Mr03	.6388	.6400	.6388	.6396	.0008	.6400	.6198	391

Est vol 3,784; vol Wed 8,215; open int 81,260, +634.

British Pound (CME)-62,500 pds.; $ per pound

	OPEN	HIGH	LOW	SETTLE	CHG	HIGH	LOW	OPEN INT
June	1.4574	1.4594	1.4516	1.4542	-.0030	1.4670	1.3910	44,733
Sept	1.4488	1.4520	1.4440	1.4458	-.0030	1.4600	1.3990	1,157

Est vol 2,865; vol Wed 12,440; open int 45,910, +983.

Swiss Franc (CME)-125,000 francs; $ per franc

	OPEN	HIGH	LOW	SETTLE	CHG	HIGH	LOW	OPEN INT
June	.6268	.6282	.6244	.6265	-.0001	.6320	.5813	53,017
Sept	.6277	.6290	.6257	.6275	-.0001	.6330	.5860	513

Est vol 3,594; vol Wed 12,946; open int 53,576, +17.

Australian Dollar (CME)-100,000 dlrs.; $ per A$

	OPEN	HIGH	LOW	SETTLE	CHG	HIGH	LOW	OPEN INT
June	.5471	.5491	.5466	.5473	.0001	.5491	.4885	45,011
Sept	.5428	.5449	.5426	.5433	.0001	.5449	.4790	409

(continued)

TABLE 2.2   Cont.

Est vol 739; vol Wed 4,277; open int 45,905, +335.

Mexican Peso (CME)-500,000 new Mex. peso, $ per MP

June	.10530	.10530	.10465	.10495	–00032	.11010	.09730	24,269
Sept	.10340	.10363	.10335	.10345	–00032	.10830	.09930	3,272

Est vol 2,592; vol Wed 4,017; open int 29,040, –406.

Euro FX (CME)-Euro 125,000; $ per Euro

June	.9100	.9130	.9074	.9106	.0005	.9275	.8365	130,175
Sept	.9065	.9090	.9038	.9069	.0005	.9235	.8375	4,898
Dec	.9034	.9055	.9010	.9038	.0004	.9175	.8390	840

Est vol 8,648; vol Wed 33,418; open int 136,033, +3,421.

Index Futures

DJ Industrial Average (CBOT)-$10 times average

June	10274	10318	10226	10293	28	10951	9080	33,292
Sept	10260	10315	10235	10297	28	10705	9670	992

Est vol 15,000; vol Wed 23,663; open int 34,492, +451.
Idx prl: Hi 10318.83; Lo 10230.68; Close 10289.21, +45.53.

S&P 500 Index (CME)-$250 times index

June	109300	110080	108950	109910	460	170550	95030	473,671
Sept	109200	110180	109150	110060	450	165670	95530	58,333

Est vol 59,692; vol Wed 80,080; open int 538,072, –176.
Idx prl: Hi 1099.29; Lo 1089.17; Close 1098.23, +7.16.

Mini S&P 500 (CME)-$50 times index

June	109350	110075	108925	109900	450	118000	104575	231,886

Vol Wed 433,421; open int 232,090, +9,732.

S&P Midcap 400 (CME)-$500 times index

June	545.50	546.50	541.00	542.50	–2.50	555.90	417.85	16,643

Est vol 984; vol Wed 1,355; open int 16,645, +6.
Idx prl: Hi 545.72; Lo 540.91; Close 542.17, –2.36.

Nikkei 225 Stock Average (CME)-$5 times index

June	11700.	11780.	11680.	11775.	175	13400.	9245.	16,692

Est vol 1,455; vol Wed 1,426; open int 16,764, –172.
Idx prl: Hi 11747.35; Lo 11579.12; Close 11738.69, +95.72.

Nasdaq 100 (CME)-$100 times index

June	131600	133000	129700	132350	300	173650.	112600	64,485

Est vol 19,680; vol Wed 28,576; open int 64,569, +3,578.
Idx prl: Hi 1319.52; Lo 1296.11; Close 1315.85, +4.80.

Mini Nasdaq 100 (CME)-$20 times index

June	1316.5	1331.0	1297.0	1323.5	3.0	1714.0	1144.5	161,165

Vol Wed 313,639; open int 161,186, +27,739.

GSCI (CME)-$250 times nearby index

June	205.50	205.70	201.30	204.00	–1.60	210.60	187.00	19,769

Est vol 165; vol Wed 529; open int 20,515, –193.
Idx prl: Hi 205.88; Lo 201.46; Close 203.92, –2.20.

Russell 2000 (CME)-$500 times index

June	513.50	514.00	505.75	506.65	–7.60	528.95	394.95	29,481

Est vol 2,306; vol Wed 2,763; open int 29,481, –40.
Idx prl: Hi 513.54; Lo 506.02; Close 507.40, –6.14.

	OPEN	HIGH	LOW	SETTLE	CHG	LIFETIME HIGH	LIFETIME LOW	OPEN INT
Russell 1000 (NYFE)-$500 times index								
June	579.75	584.00	578.50	584.00	3.00	622.00	555.00	49,383

Est vol 250; vol Wed 207; open int 49,393, –42.
Idx prl: Hi 582.68; Lo 577.97; Close 582.17, +2.81.

NYSE Composite Index (NYFE)-500 times index

June	579.25	582.50	579.00	581.40	1.15	611.50	550.00	2,768
Sept	...	...	...	582.40	1.15	607.00	561.40	410

Est vol 1,500; vol Wed 1,201; open int 3,378, –90.
Idx prl: Hi 582.44; Lo 578.98; Close 581.68, +2.14.

U.S. Dollar Index (FINEX)-$1,000 times index

June	114.29	114.65	114.01	114.34	.04	121.23	113.65	9,188
Sept	114.81	115.07	114.60	114.86	.04	121.00	114.18	2,925

Est vol 1,100; vol Wed 773; open int 12,126, –30.
Idx prl: Hi 114.47; Lo 113.84; Close 114.13, +.01.

Share Price Index (SFE)-A$25 times index

June	3381.0	3402.0	3369.0	3388.0	8.0	3516.0	2945.0	154,128
Sept	3388.0	3391.0	3388.0	3402.0	8.0	3511.0	3305.0	1,620
Dec	3407.0	3407.0	3407.0	3414.0	8.0	3497.0	3319.0	1,066
Mr03	3430.0	3430.0	3430.0	3431.0	8.0	3440.0	3335.0	658

Est vol 12,309; vol Wed 17,885; open int 157,666, +2,650.
Index: Hi 3403.5; Lo 3376.1; Close 3395.2, +19.1.

CAC-40 Stock Index (MATIF)-Euro 10.00 x index

May	4454.0	4473.0	4417.0	4444.0	–11.0	4627.0	4211.5	436,973
June	4423.0	4452.0	4410.0	4433.0	–10.5	4980.0	4200.0	102,506
Sept	4468.5	4496.0	4452.5	4467.5	–11.0	4645.5	4269.0	29,439

Est vol 43,580; vol Wed 46,293; open int 584,785, +3,536.

Xetra DAX (EUREX)-Euro 25 per DAX index point

June	5072.0	5120.0	5050.0	5068.5	–21.5	5520.0	4036.5	238,637
Sept	5117.0	5160.0	5100.0	5114.0	–21.5	5565.0	4806.5	5,862
Dec	5162.0	5162.0	5158.5	5165.0	–22.0	5552.5	4898.0	2,338

Vol Thu 54,961; open int 246,837, –7,945.
Index: Hi 5101.12; Lo 5032.08; Close 5047.45, –24.94.

FT-SE 100 Index (LIFFE)-£10 per index point

June	5274.5	5295.0	5250.5	5260.0	–19.0	5312.5	5089.5	316,357
Sept	5290.5	5307.5	5270.5	5276.0	–19.0	5321.0	5110.0	17,238
Dec	5329.0	5329.5	5329.0	5320.5	–18.5	5369.5	5151.0	9,498
Mr03	5349.5	5349.5	5341.0	5337.0	–17.5	5387.5	5192.0	3,089

Est vol 29,414; vol Wed 40,937; open int 346,182, –1,182.

DJ Euro STOXX 50 Index (EUREX)-Euro 10.00 x index

June	3563.0	3592.0	3520.0	3549.0	–47.0	3880.0	3010.0	899,527
Sept	3585.0	3604.0	3539.0	3561.0	–48.0	3871.0	3379.0	36,879
Dec	3626.0	3638.0	3572.0	3595.0	–47.0	3832.0	3412.0	14,196

Vol Thu 178,982; open int 950,602, +4,003.
Index: Hi 3606.48; Lo 3566.97; Close 3579.03, –16.70.

DJ STOXX 50 Index (EUREX)-Euro 10.00 x index

June	3530.0	3560.0	3525.0	3535.0	–14.0	3728.0	3289.0	25,505
Sept	...	...	...	3545.0	–14.0	3665.0	3385.0	756

Vol Thu 753; open int 26,261, +199.
Index: Hi 3559.57; Lo 3521.05; Close 3531.89, –15.55.

Source: Reprinted by permission from the *Wall Street Journal*, May 17, 2002.

open interest for the previous Thursday, and Tuesday's paper reports Friday's open interest.

Corn futures prices are reported under the "Grain and Oilseed" heading in Table 2.2. Corn production in the United States is used primarily as a feed grain for livestock, and U.S. corn production averages about 200 million metric tons per year, about 40% of the world's production. The United States accounts for three-fourths of the world's corn exports. Corn futures contracts are traded on the Chicago Board of Trade in units of 5,000 bushels, and prices are reported in cents per bushel.[1] This information is shown in bold letters under the Grain and Oilseed section in Table 2.2. Each row under the corn futures category reports information for a separate contract delivery month. Each column reports monetary units, except for the column titled Open Interest. **Open interest is the number of open futures contracts for which a trader remains obligated to the Exchange's clearinghouse because no offsetting sale or purchase has yet been made.** The December corn contract occupies the third row under Corn in Table 2.2, and it has an "opening" price of 231.75¢ per bushel. The opening price is the average price generated through trading during the opening minutes of the trading day. If you look down to the seventh row, you will see another December contract listed under Corn, and this contract is for the subsequent year.

Referring back to the nearby July corn contract occupying the top row (Table 2.2), the three columns to the right of the opening price report the "high," "low," and "settle" prices. For July corn, these prices are 216.00¢, 212.75¢, and 213.25¢, respectively. The high and low prices are simply the highest and lowest prices at which a trade was conducted that day for July corn. The "settlement" (or closing) price is the average of prices at which the contract traded just before the close of trading at the end of the day. The settlement price is extremely important because it is the price used by the clearinghouse to **mark to market** all outstanding positions at the end of the day. Sometimes an exchange pit committee determines the settlement price if the last trade prices of the day are not representative of what happened during the market close. The pit committee has the discretion to determine the settlement price. The fifth column shows the "change," or the change in the closing price from the previous day. On the right-hand side of the corn table, we see the season high and low prices, which are the highest (279.50¢) and lowest (198.00¢) prices recorded for the July contract over the duration of its trading life. Most corn contracts are traded for a year or more before their expiry. The Open Interest column is reported in numbers of contracts. For the July corn contract, the open interest shown in Table 2.2 is 210,786 contracts.

Now consider the foreign currency futures prices shown in Table 2.2 under the heading Currency Futures. These currency prices indicate the number of U.S. dollars it takes to buy one unit of foreign currency for future delivery. In Table 2.2, the December Canadian dollar contract closed at U.S. $0.6407 per Canadian dollar. Canada's national currency also happens to be called the dollar, just like the U.S. national currency. A trader who purchased (i.e., went long) a December Canadian dollar contract would have agreed to purchase $100,000 Canadian dollars at a price of 64.07¢ U.S. per Canadian dollar.

Table 2.3 provides further information on this futures trade. Assume the Canadian dollar rose in value to 70.50¢ U.S. after the initial trade. Suppose that on August 1, the trader went long in December Canadian dollars and held that position open until October 1. On October 1, the trader in question liquidates his

---

[1]Corn futures are also traded on the Beijing Commodity Exchange, the Budapest Commodity Exchange, the Tokyo Grain Exchange, and the Mid-American Commodity Exchange.

TABLE 2.3   Futures Trade Example: Canadian Dollar (CME) 100,000 Dollars; $U.S. per Canadian $

DATE OF FUTURES TRADE	FUTURES TRADE	DELIVERY MONTH	FUTURES PRICE
August 1	Go long	December	U.S. $0.6407
October 1	Go short	December	U.S. $0.7050
Profit (loss)			$0.0643 x 100,000 = $6,430 profit

TABLE 2.4   Futures Trade Example: Canadian Dollar (CME) 100,000 Dollars; $U.S. per Canadian $

DATE OF FUTURES TRADE	FUTURES TRADE	DELIVERY MONTH	FUTURES PRICE
August 1	Go long	December	U.S. $0.6407
October 1	Go short	December	U.S. $0.6100
Profit (loss)			$0.0307 x 100,000 = ($3,070) loss

position by selling (i.e., going short) one December Canadian dollar contract at $0.7050. The profit from this transaction is $6,430 (= $0.0643 x $100,000) before transactions and brokerage fees.

Alternatively, suppose the Canadian dollar fell in value after August 1. This outcome is shown in Table 2.4. In this case, the Canadian dollar declined from U.S. $0.6407 to U.S. $0.61. A *futures trader* who is long Canadian dollars would experience a loss of $3,070 = $0.0307 x $100,000.

Now consider the Japanese yen futures contract in Table 2.2 under the Currency Futures heading. Japanese yen are traded on the Chicago Mercantile Exchange in units of 12.5 million yen, and like all other currency futures, yen futures are quoted as U.S. dollars against the yen. One yen futures contract corresponds to 12.5 million yen. June yen futures in Table 2.2 had a closing price of $.007816, which means that it cost less than one cent (0.7816¢) to buy one yen for March delivery. If we take the inverse of this price (i.e., 1/.007816), this gives 127.94 yen per U.S. dollar. This way of reporting the Japanese currency (as yen per dollar) might be more familiar to the reader, but the standard for Chicago Mercantile Exchange currency quotation is in dollars per yen. Note the heading for Japanese yen in Table 2.2 shows that prices are quotes in dollars per 100 yen, which means that the decimal place for the yen prices in Table 2.2 must be moved two places to the left to calculate profit or loss. The June futures settlement price is printed as $.7816, and after we move the decimal place, this converts to $.007816. Moving the decimal place saves the newspaper both space and ink.

Suppose a currency trader goes short (i.e., sells) one June yen futures contract calling for delivery of 12.5 million yen, at a price of $.007816. This transac-

TABLE 2.5 Futures Trade Example: Japanese Yen (CME) 12.5 Million Yen; $U.S. per Yen

DATE OF FUTURES TRADE	FUTURES TRADE	DELIVERY MONTH	FUTURES PRICE
January 19	Go short	March	U.S. $0.007816
February 1	Go long	March	U.S. $0.007416
Profit (loss)			$0.0004 x 12,500,000 = $5,000 profit

tion is recorded in Table 2.5. The initial trade is entered into on January 19, and by February 1 the yen subsequently falls in value. When the yen falls in value, the dollars-per-yen price decreases because it costs fewer dollars to purchase one yen. If the June futures price falls from $0.007816 to $0.007416 and the currency trader liquidates his position on February 1, a profit of $5,000 is earned before brokerage fees (= $0.0004 x 12,500,000 ¥ = $5,000 profit). Note that a futures price quote in dollars per yen times a contract size in yen gives a profit or loss in dollars.

THE OPTIONS CONTRACT

Options on futures are contractual obligations that are traded on organized futures exchanges through an open outcry or electronic auction system. These characteristics they share in common with futures contracts, but there are some important differences between options on futures and futures contracts themselves. An option, as the name implies, gives its buyer the right but not the obligation to exercise the option and take possession of a futures contract at a predetermined price. For this right, the option buyer pays a premium to the option seller. Options on futures contracts specify delivery of either a long or a short futures contract. A **call** option specifies that the seller must deliver a long futures position to the option buyer, and a **put** option specifies delivery of a short futures position. The seller of the option (i.e., the option's **writer**) has to provide the futures position to the option buyer only if the option is exercised. This means that the buyer of an option has the right to either purchase (in the case of a call option) or sell (in the case of a put option) a futures contract at a preestablished price within a given period of time. The predetermined futures price is referred to as either the **strike price** or the **exercise price**; they are identical in meaning.

For example, in June a trader who expects crude oil futures prices to increase may decide to purchase a December crude oil call option at a strike price of $34 per barrel. If the current December futures price is trading in the $34 range, then the premium paid for this call option may be approximately $2.00 per barrel (or $2,000 per contract). If the December crude oil futures price rises above $34 before the option expires in December, then the holder of the option may exercise the option and take possession of a long December futures position at a price of $34. Alternatively, the holder of the option could reverse his position by selling an identical option contract and profit from the rise in the premium.

The financial obligations involved in options trading are different from those in futures trading. Futures traders have obligations to deliver (in the case of the seller) or accept delivery of (in the case of the buyer) a specified product or asset at a specified price and time in the future. For nondeliverable futures contracts the obligation is to settle at the spot price during the delivery month. With options, in contrast, only the option buyer has the right to exercise the option, and the option seller is obligated to comply. When a call option is exercised, the holder of the option will acquire a long futures position at the option strike price. If a call option is exercised, the exchange (through the clearinghouse) assigns a short futures position to a trader who previously sold an identical call option. Alternatively, when a put option is exercised, the option holder acquires a short futures position at the option strike price, and a long futures position is assigned to a trader who previously sold an identical put. An option can be exercised by its holder at any time before it expires.

The prices of options are reported publicly in the same manner as futures prices. One difference is that there is a much larger number of options, each of which is traded in relatively smaller volumes, so only the settlement price is reported in newspaper summaries. Table 2.6 is a summary from the *Wall Street Journal* for futures options prices. The option price (i.e., the **premium**) is the price paid for the right to buy or sell a futures contract. For each commodity or asset, call and put options with different strike prices and (futures contract) expiration dates are listed. The strike price is the price at which the futures contract will be bought or sold.

Table 2.6 contains the futures options prices for some of the futures contracts selected from Table 2.2. The left panel of Table 2.6 reports corn options prices. The far left-hand column shows the strike prices reported for corn options. The other columns show either the **call** option settlement prices or the **put** option settlement prices for the July, September, and December contracts. For instance, consider the fourth row under Corn in Table 2.6. The **strike price** is 220, which means the buyer of the option will have the right to obtain a futures position at a price of 220¢ per bushel. The premium for a July call is shown to be 5.25¢ per bushel, which means the buyer of that call would have the right to go long in July corn at a price of 220¢ sometime before July. The total premium would be $262.50 (= $0.0525 x 5,000 bu). In addition, there would be brokerage fees. Alternatively, the buyer of a 220 July put option would pay a total premium of $600 (= $0.12 x 5,000 bu). The options buyer pays the premium to the **writer** (i.e., seller) of the option.

Consider the U.S. Treasury bond (T-bond) option prices in Table 2.6. T-bond futures are priced as a percentage of par plus 32nds of a point (e.g., $97\frac{8}{32}$ = 97-08). With each 32nd the futures price advances, the contract will increase in value by $31.25. So, if a trader buys a futures contract at 97-08 and then subsequently sells it at 98-08, this is a price move of $\frac{32}{32}$, or "one full point," which equals $1,000, or 32 x $31.25. Alternatively, if the price moved from 97-08 to 97-30, then this would represent a change in value of $\frac{22}{32}$, or $687.50.

The prices of U.S. T-bond options on futures are quoted in 64ths instead of 32nds, which is the standard for the underlying bond prices. Referring back to Table 2.6, consider the U.S. T-bond option with a strike price of 102-00. This strike price indicates that the options buyer would obtain the right to a T-bond futures

---

TABLE 2.6   Daily Futures Options Prices from the *Wall Street Journal*

Futures Options Prices

Thursday, May 16, 2002

Final or settlement prices of selected contracts. Volume and open interest are totals in all contract months.

Grain and Oilseed

Corn (CBT)
5,000 bu.; cents per bu.

STRIKE	CALLS-SETTLE			PUTS-SETTLE		
Price	Jly	Sep	Dec	Jly	Sep	Dec
190	23.750	...	...	.750	2.375	2.250
200	15.500	24.250	32.500	2.375	5.000	4.500
210	9.500	18.500	25.750	6.250	9.250	7.750
220	5.250	14.125	20.250	12.000	14.500	11.750
230	3.000	10.750	15.875	19.750	21.125	17.250
240	1.750	8.250	12.500	28.375	28.625	24.000

Est vol 20,000 Wd 17,164 calls 6,567 puts
Op int Wed 303,191 calls 171,177 puts

Soybeans (CBT)
5,000 bu.; cents per bu.

Price	Jly	Sep	Nov	Jly	Sep	Nov
440	46.000	40.500	39.875	1.250	9.000	14.000
460	29.250	29.000	29.500	4.500	17.250	23.500
480	16.750	20.500	22.500	12.000	28.750	36.000
500	8.750	15.500	16.750	24.000	...	50.000
520	4.250	11.500	12.500	39.500	...	...
540	2.250	8.500	10.000	57.500	...	...

Est vol 12,000 Wd 8,139 calls 4,490 puts
Op int Wed 120,485 calls 58,063 puts

Soybean Meal (CBT)
100 tons; $ per ton

Price	Jly	Sep	Dec	Jly	Sep	Dec
155	11.20	...	7.75	1.25	...	8.50
160	7.75	6.75	6.00	2.70	8.25	...
165	4.75	...	5.00	4.75	...	...
170	3.00	4.00	4.00	...	...	...
175	2.00	...	...	...	...	...
180	1.25	2.60	...	...	...	...

Est vol 1,100 Wd 1,921 calls 747 puts
Op int Wed 14,720 calls 13,637 puts

Soybean Oil (CBT)
60,000 lbs.; cents per lb.

Price	Jly	Sep	Dec	Jly	Sep	Dec
160	1.010	...	...	.080	.270	.250
165	.600	1.130	1.400	.150	.480	.420
170	.350	.850	1.150	.400	.720	.640
175	.200	.670	.950	.770	1.020	...
180	.110	.520	.750	...	...	...
185	.070	...	.600	...	...	1.550

Est vol 2,700 Wd 1,868 calls 565 puts
Op int Wed 31,162 calls 19,509 puts

Wheat (CBT)
5,000 bu.; cents per bu.

Price	Jly	Sep	Dec	Jly	Sep	Dec
260	18.500	25.250	...	2.000	4.250	4.000
270	11.625	18.750	28.125	5.125	7.750	7.000
280	6.750	13.750	22.375	10.250	12.375	11.125
290	4.000	10.000	17.625	17.500	18.750	16.125
300	2.125	7.250	14.000	25.625	25.500	22.375
310	1.125	5.250	11.250	34.625	33.500	29.375

Est vol 5,500 Wd 3,774 calls 2,648 puts
Op int Wed 58,088 calls 32,279 puts

Wheat (KC)
5,000 bu.; cents per bu.

Price	Jly	Sep	Dec	Jly	Sep	Dec
260	...	...	...	...	...	...
270	15.500	...	...	2.125	3.750	...
280	8.750	17.125	...	5.375	7.125	8.125
290	4.750	12.000	...	11.250	12.000	12.750
300	2.625	8.500	15.875	19.125	18.500	18.250
310	1.500	6.125	12.375	27.875	26.000	...

Est vol 597 Wd 1,112 calls 201 puts

STRIKE	CALLS-SETTLE			PUTS-SETTLE		

Food and Fiber

Cotton (NYCE)
50,000 lbs.; cents per lb.

Price	Jly	Oct	Dec	Jly	Oct	Dec
33	2.89	5.58	7.18	.42	.77	.71
34	2.17	4.86	6.44	.70	1.04	.94
35	1.58	4.20	5.73	1.10	1.36	1.10
36	1.10	3.58	5.07	1.62	1.73	1.52
37	.74	3.05	4.47	2.25	2.18	1.89
38	.49	2.57	3.92	3.00	2.69	2.31

Est vol 4,136 Wd 3,852 calls 2,450 puts
Op int Wed 75,758 calls 47,578 puts

Orange Juice (NYCE)
15,000 lbs.; cents per lb.

Price	Jly	Sep	Nov	Jly	Sep	Nov
80	11.20	10.15	9.95	.05	.20	.65
85	6.30	5.55	6.10	.20	.80	1.50
90	1.90	2.70	3.60	1.00	2.60	3.80
95	.45	1.15	2.30	4.50	6.10	7.50
100	.25	.65	1.55	9.00	10.45	11.55
105	.05	.45	.95	13.80	15.00	15.70

Est vol 396 Wd 266 calls 568 puts
Op int Wed 7,750 calls 8,678 puts

Coffee (CSCE)
37,500 lbs.; cents per lb.

Price	Jly	Aug	Sep	Jly	Aug	Sep
45	6.08	8.91	9.42	.35	.61	1.15
47.5	4.19	7.02	7.93	.95	1.20	2.01
50	2.50	5.40	6.47	2.00	2.07	3.15
52.5	1.55	4.25	5.35	3.29	3.41	4.65
55	1.00	3.38	4.51	5.24	5.02	6.15
57.5	.68	2.74	3.85	7.41	6.87	7.96

Est vol 2,493 Wd 1,370 calls 443 puts
Op int Wed 41,341 calls 20,686 puts

Sugar-World (CSCE)
112,000 lbs.; cents per lb.

Price	Jly	Aug	Sep	Jly	Aug	Sep
500	1.01	.90	.93	.03	.07	.11
550	.59	.54	.60	.11	.21	.28
600	.27	.26	.35	.29	.43	.51
650	.12	.13	.19	.64	.80	.85
700	.04	.06	.10	1.06	1.22	1.26
750	.01	.03	.06	1.53	1.69	1.71

Est vol 6,620 Wd 3,404 calls 3,058 puts
Op int Wed 98,996 calls 55,419 puts

Cocoa (CSCE)
10 metric tons; $ per ton

Price	Jly	Aug	Sep	Jly	Aug	Sep
1500	111	110	129	16	49	68
1550	79	82	105	34	71	93
1600	52	60	80	57	98	118
1650	30	44	60	90	131	147
1700	16	31	46	123	169	183
1750	8	22	35	163	209	221

Est vol 5,217 Wd 705 calls 452 puts
Op int Wed 29,881 calls 37,221 puts

Petroleum

Crude Oil (NYM)
1,000 bbls.; $ per bbl.

Price	Jun	Jly	Aug	Jun	Jly	Aug
2700	0.95	1.23	1.59	0.01	1.15	1.66
2750	0.45	1.03	1.37	0.01	1.45	1.94
2800	0.01	0.83	1.16	1.05	1.75	2.22
2850	0.01	0.66	0.99	0.55	2.07	...
2900	0.01	0.52	0.84	1.05	2.43	...
2950	0.01	0.40	0.70	1.55	2.81	3.25

Est vol 60,678 Wd 20,413 calls 21,805 puts
Op int Wed 551,334 calls 604,168 puts

Heating Oil No.2 (NYM)
42,000 gal.; $ per gal.

Price	Jun	Jly	Aug	Jun	Jly	Aug
66	.0305	.0464	.0589	.0089	.0199	.0270
67	.0242	.0405	.0533	.0126	.0240	.0313

STRIKE	CALLS-SETTLE			PUTS-SETTLE		
69	.0142	.0304	.0430	.0226	.0338	.0409
70	.0106	.0262	.0386	.0290	.0396	.0465
71	.0077	.0225	.0346	.0361	.0458	.0524

Est vol 1,625 Wd 883 calls 654 puts
Op int Wed 34,678 calls 36,788 puts

Gasoline-Unlead (NYM)
42,000 gal.; $ per gal.

Price	Jun	Jly	Aug	Jun	Jly	Aug
78	.0316	.0502	.0570	.0163	.0303	.0445
79	.0260	.0449	.0521	.0207	.0349	.0496
80	.0211	.0399	.0477	.0258	.0399	.0552
81	.0170	.0356	.0436	.0317	.0456	.0610
82	.0135	.0316	.0398	.0382	.0515	.0671
83	.0106	.0279	.0364	.0452	.0578	...

Est vol 3,577 Wd 1,640 calls 489 puts
Op int Wed 45,469 calls 30,410 puts

Natural Gas (NYM)
10,000 MMBtu.; $ per MMBtu.

Price	Jun	Jly	Aug	Jun	Jly	Aug
350	.213	.366	.471	.104	.178	.238
355	.184	.338	.445	.125	.200	.261
360	.159	.313	.419	.150	.224	.285
365	.137	.288	.395	.178	.249	.310
370	.117	.265	.372	.208	.276	.337
375	.100	.244	.350	.241	.305	.365

Est vol 72,595 Wd 27,718 calls 31,219 puts
Op int Wed 870,569 calls 812,197 puts

Brent Crude (IPE)
1,000 net bbls.; $ per bbl.

Price	Jly	Aug	Sep	Jly	Aug	Sep
2550	1.52	1.80	1.99	0.64	1.19	1.60
2600	1.24	1.54	1.75	0.86	1.43	1.86
2650	1.00	1.31	1.53	1.12	1.70	2.14
2700	0.81	1.11	1.34	1.43	2.00	2.45
2750	0.66	0.93	1.16	1.78	2.32	2.77
2800	0.52	0.78	1.00	2.14	2.67	3.11

Est vol 400 Wd 200 calls 200 puts
Op int Wed 8,425 calls 9,304 puts

Livestock

Cattle-Feeder (CME)
50,000 lbs.; cents per lb.

Price	May	Aug	Sep	May	Aug	Sep
7400	1.92	3.72	...	0.07	1.25	1.95
7500	1.00	...	...	0.15	1.40	...
7600	0.40	2.47	...	0.55	1.95	2.50
7700	0.07	...	...	1.22	...	...
7800	0.02	1.45	1.40	2.17	2.95	3.25
7900	0.00	...	...	...	...	...

Est vol 398 Wd 287 calls 266 puts
Op int Wed 5,847 calls 9,666 puts

Cattle-Live (CME)
40,000 lbs.; cents per lb.

Price	Jun	Aug	Oct	Jun	Aug	Oct
61	2.20	...	...	0.47	1.25	...
62	1.50	3.20	...	0.77	1.62	1.25
63	0.90	2.57	...	1.17	2.00	...
64	0.57	1.95	4.20	1.85	2.37	1.92
65	0.35	1.50	...	2.62	2.92	...
66	0.25	1.05	3.05	3.52	3.45	2.75

Est vol 2,135 Wd 526 calls 870 puts
Op int Wed 27,274 calls 27,033 puts

Hogs-Lean (CME)
40,000 lbs.; cents per lb.

Price	Jun	Jly	Aug	Jun	Jly	Aug
51	2.97	...	...	1.15	1.60	...
52	2.35	3.85	3.50	1.52	2.00	2.95
53	1.82	...	...	2.00	2.40	...
54	1.37	2.75	2.45	2.55	2.90	3.90
55	1.05	...	...	3.22	...	...
56	0.77	1.87	1.72	3.95	4.02	5.15

Est vol 316 Wd 243 calls 118 puts

(continued)

TABLE 2.6 Cont.

Metals

Copper (CMX)
25,000 lbs.; cents per lb.

Price	Jun	Jly	Aug	Jun	Jly	Aug
70	3.65	4.45	4.90	0.10	0.60	1.85
72	1.95	3.00	3.50	0.40	1.15	1.40
74	0.80	1.85	2.30	1.25	2.00	2.20
76	0.25	1.05	1.45	2.65	3.20	3.35
78	0.05	0.65	0.90	4.50	4.75	4.75
80	0.05	0.35	0.50	6.45	6.50	6.35

Est vol 550 Wd 147 calls 153 puts
Op int Wed 2,824 calls 1,211 puts

Gold (CMX)
100 troy ounces; $ per troy ounce

Price	Jly	Aug	Oct	Jly	Aug	Oct
300	12.40	13.50	17.30	1.10	2.30	5.30
305	8.70	10.30	13.80	2.40	4.00	6.80
310	5.10	7.40	10.40	3.80	6.10	8.30
315	3.40	5.60	8.70	7.10	9.30	11.60
320	2.50	4.20	7.30	11.20	12.90	15.10
325	1.70	3.20	6.00	15.40	16.90	18.70

Est vol 3,800 Wd 2,303 calls 1,320 puts
Op int Wed 112,810 calls 54,036 puts

Silver (CMX)
5,000 troy ounces; cts per troy ounce

Price	Jly	Aug	Sep	Jly	Aug	Sep
425	40.9	43.4	44.8	1.0	1.8	3.5
450	19.3	23.7	26.5	4.3	7.1	10.0
475	7.0	11.9	14.9	17.0	20.2	23.3
500	2.5	6.0	8.8	37.5	39.4	42.0
525	1.5	3.5	5.7	61.4	61.8	63.7
550	0.8	2.2	3.9	85.7	85.5	86.8

Est vol 1,200 Wd 677 calls 248 puts
Op int Wed 50,097 calls 9,836 puts

Interest Rate

T-Bonds (CBT)
$100,000; points and 64ths of 100%

Price	Jun	Jul	Aug	Jun	Jul	Aug
99	1-61	1-38	2-07	0-05	0-58	1-27
100	1-07	1-04	1-37	0-15	1-24	...
101	0-32	0-43	...	0-40	1-63	2-29
102	0-11	0-25	0-52	1-19	2-45	3-07
103	0-03	0-14	0-36	2-11	...	...
104	0-01	0-07	...	3-08	...	...

Est vol 25,000;
Wd vol 12,238 calls 30,343 puts
Op int Wed 295,021 calls 252,103 puts

T-Notes (CBT)
$100,000; points and 64ths of 100%

Price	Jun	Jul	Aug	Jun	Jul	Aug
103	2-17	1-27	1-51	0-01	0-35	0-59
104	1-21	0-54	1-15	0-05	0-62	1-23
105	0-36	0-28	0-52	0-20	1-36	1-59
106	0-10	0-13	0-32	0-58	...	...
107	0-02	0-06	0-19	1-50	...	...
108	0-01	0-11	2-48	...	...	...

Est vol 90,000 Wd 47,272 calls 51,105 puts
Op int Wed 867,337 calls 702,886 puts

5 Yr Treas Notes (CBT)
$100,000; points and 64ths of 100%

Price	Jun	Jul	Aug	Jun	Jul	Aug
10500	1-13	0-35	...	0-02	0-44	...
10550	0-48	0-22	...	0-05	...	...
10600	0-25	0-13	0-26	0-14	...	...
10650	0-10	0-08	...	0-31	...	...
10700	0-03	0-05	...	0-56	...	...
10750	0-01	...	...	...	...	...

Est vol 24,000 Wd 9,955 calls 17,937 puts
Op int Wed 291,222 calls 266,854 puts

Eurodollar (CME)
$ million; pts. of 100%

Price	Jun	Jul	Aug	Jun	Jul	Aug
9750	5.22	2.00	2.22	0.00	1.05	1.27

9800	0.55	0.20	0.32	0.32	...	...
9825	0.02	0.05	0.10	2.30	...	...
9850	0.00	0.00	...	4.77	...	...
9875	0.00	...	...	7.27	...	...

Est vol 315,534;
Wd vol 145,639 calls 68,839 puts
Op int Wed 4,932,752 calls 3,975,113 puts

1 Yr. Mid-Curve Eurodlr (CME)
$1,000,000 contract units; pts. of 100%

Price	Jun	Jul	Aug	Jun	Jul	Aug
9525	5.17	2.62	3.15	0.22	1.87	2.40
9550	3.10	1.42	...	0.65	...	...
9575	1.55	0.65	...	1.60	...	...
9600	0.55	0.27	...	3.10	...	...
9625	0.22	...	...	5.27	...	...
9650	0.07	...	...	...	...	...

Est vol 92,500 Wd 27,605 calls 32,121 puts
Op int Wed 734,800 calls 576,348 puts

2 Yr. Mid-Curve Eurodlr (CME)
$1,000,000 contract units; pts. of 100%

Price	Jun	Sep	Dec	Jun	Sep	Dec
9425	4.40	4.27	4.15	0.20	1.65	3.25
9450	2.40	2.85	...	0.70	2.70	...
9475	1.05	1.70	...	1.85	...	...
9500	0.40	...	...	...	...	...
9525	...	...	...	...	...	...
9550	0.05	...	...	...	...	...

Est vol 250 Wd 500 calls 500 puts
Op int Wed 50,425 calls 38,155 puts

Euribor (LIFFE)
Euro 1,000,000

Price	Jun	Jul	Aug	Jun	Jul	Aug
96125	0.28	0.08	0.11	0.00	0.11	0.14
96250	0.17	0.04	0.06	0.02	0.20	0.21
96375	0.08	0.01	0.03	0.05	0.29	0.31
96500	0.02	0.00	0.01	0.12	0.41	0.41
96625	0.00	...	0.00	0.23	0.53	0.53
96750	...	...	...	0.35	0.65	0.65

Vol Th 49,356 calls 12,425 puts
Op int Wed 2,196,374 calls 906,469 puts

Euro-BUND (EUREX)
100,000;pts. in 100%

Price	Jun	Jul	Aug	Jun	Jul	Aug
10450	0.83	0.86	1.09	0.06	0.42	0.65
10500	0.45	0.57	0.81	0.18	0.63	0.87
10550	0.19	0.37	0.59	0.42	0.93	1.15
10600	0.06	0.22	0.42	0.79	1.28	1.48
10650	0.02	0.13	0.29	1.25	1.69	1.85
10700	0.01	0.07	0.20	1.73	2.13	2.26

Vol Th 13,881 calls 355,789 puts
Op int Wed 13,212 calls 331,080 puts

Currency

Japanese Yen (CME)
12,500,000 yen; cents per 100 yen

Price	Jun	Jly	Aug	Jun	Jly	Aug
7700	1.38	1.93	...	0.22	0.40	...
7750	1.02	1.59	...	0.36	0.55	0.83
7800	0.73	1.27	1.57	0.57	0.73	1.03
7850	...	...	...	...	...	...
7900	0.35	0.78	...	1.19	1.24	...
7950	0.24	0.61	0.90	...	...	...

Est vol 1,105 Wd 104 calls 496 puts
Op int Wed 37,895 calls 64,361 puts

Canadian Dollar (CME)
100,000 Can.$, cents per Can.$

Price	Jun	Jly	Aug	Jun	Jly	Aug
6350	0.91	...	...	0.10	0.28	...
6400	0.53	0.63	0.80	0.22	0.45	...
6450	0.26	...	...	0.45	...	...
6500	0.12	0.24	0.40	0.81	...	...
6550	0.05	0.13	...	...	...	...
6600	0.03	0.08	...	...	...	...

Est vol 655 Wd 371 calls 233 puts

British Pound (CME)
62,500 pounds; cents per pound

Price	Jun	Jly	Aug	Jun	Jly	Aug
1430	2.56	...	...	0.14	0.70	...
1440	1.70	1.62	...	0.28	1.04	1.50
1450	1.04	1.12	...	0.62	...	...
1460	0.54	0.74	1.14	1.12	...	...
1470	0.26	...	0.82	1.84	...	...
1480	0.12	0.28	...	...	...	...

Est vol 80 Wd 131 calls 120 puts
Op int Wed 6,923 calls 6,270 puts

Swiss Franc (CME)
125,000 francs; cents per franc

Price	Jun	Jly	Aug	Jun	Jly	Aug
6150	1.32	...	...	0.17	...	...
6200	0.94	...	...	0.29	0.55	...
6250	0.65	...	...	0.50	...	...
6300	0.42	0.78	...	0.77	...	...
6350	0.27	...	...	1.12	...	...
6400	0.18	0.44	0.70	1.53	...	...

Est vol 90 Wd 52 calls 49 puts
Op int Wed 6,518 calls 3,810 puts

Euro Fx (CME)
125,000 euros; cents per euro

Price	Jun	Jly	Aug	Jun	Jly	Aug
9000	1.39	1.55	1.97	0.33	0.86	1.28
9050	1.06	1.26	...	0.50	1.07	...
9100	0.78	1.04	...	0.72	1.35	...
9150	0.56	...	...	1.00	...	...
9200	0.41	0.69	1.08	1.35	1.99	...
9250	0.28	0.55	...	...	...	...

Est vol 2,936 Wd 1,345 calls 433 puts
Op int Wed 35,167 calls 27,448 puts

Index

DJ Industrial Avg (CBOT)
$100 times premium

Price	May	Jun	Jly	May	Jun	Jly
101	20.00	33.60	41.00	0.25	14.70	...
102	10.50	27.25	...	1.25	18.25	...
103	4.00	21.50	...	4.50	22.50	...
104	1.00	16.65	25.00	11.50	27.65	...
105	0.50	12.70	20.00	21.00	33.65	...
106	0.35	8.95	...	...	40.30	...

Est vol 700 Wd 514 calls 2,118 puts
Op int Wed 7,239 calls 21,807 puts

S&P 500 Stock Index (CME)
$250 times premium

Price	May	Jun	Jly	May	Jun	Jly
1090	10.70	28.50	37.60	1.60	19.40	27.10
1095	6.90	25.50	...	2.80	21.40	...
1100	4.10	22.70	32.10	5.00	23.60	31.50
1105	2.30	20.20	...	8.20	26.10	...
1110	1.00	17.80	26.70	11.90	28.70	...
1115	0.45	15.60	...	16.30	31.50	...

Est vol 9,590 Wd 12,881 calls 95,197 puts
Op int Wed 12,145 calls 157,883 puts

Other Options

Nasdaq 100 (CME)
$100 times NASDAQ 100 Index

Price	May	Jun	Jly	May	Jun	Jly
1320	16.00	63.60	...	...	...	...

Est vol 48 Wd 93 calls 688 puts
Op int Wed 2,696 calls 3,247 puts

NYSE Composite (NYFE)
$500 times premium

Price	May	Jun	Jly	May	Jun	Jly
582	1.55	10.10	15.00	2.15	10.65	14.60

Est vol 575 Wd 395 calls 584 puts

Source: Reprinted by permission from the *Wall Street Journal*, May 17, 2002.

contract that is priced at 102% of its face (i.e., par) value. For a T-bond with a $100,000 face value, 102% of its face value converts to $102,000.

If each 32nd of a T-bond futures contract is worth $31.25, then each 64th of an option on that futures contract is worth one-half that amount, or $15.62. Referring back to Table 2.6, a June put option with a strike price of 102-00 traded for a premium of 1-19, or $1^{19}\!/_{64}$. The full amount of the premium is then $1,296.78 (= 1 x $1,000 + 19 x $15.62 = $1,296.78).

In Table 2.6, some of the strike prices have no corresponding premiums reported. Instead, the newspaper reports either "...," "no tr," or "no op," which means there was no trading for that particular option.

THE CLEARINGHOUSE

The **clearinghouse** is a corporation that is separate from but associated with the futures exchange. The clearinghouse is responsible for recording each futures transaction, reconciling all trades, and ensuring the financial integrity of each transaction. All futures trades must be "cleared" through the clearinghouse at the end of each trading day. Any member of the exchange who does not also hold a membership in the clearinghouse must have trades "cleared" through a member of the clearinghouse and pay a commission fee for this service. There is a separate clearing corporation for each futures exchange.

In addition to "clearing" trades, the clearinghouse is responsible for balancing the books of all outstanding futures accounts at the end of each trading day. The clearinghouse adjusts the monetary value of open positions (i.e., futures positions entered into and not yet liquidated) to reflect daily settlement prices. Daily margin calls (requests for additional capital) are made to clearing members whose balances show a loss as a result of daily price activity. Those members showing a gain due to the day's activity can withdraw their funds on a daily basis.

Another important function performed by the clearinghouse is facilitation of delivery on futures contracts. If a seller of a futures contract chooses to settle contractual obligations by making delivery, the clearing corporation selects the clearing member with an open long position who will receive delivery. The final invoicing and payment procedures are conducted between the buyer and the seller under rules of the clearing corporation. In this way, individual traders need not be concerned about identifying or negotiating with other traders who are interested in taking the opposite side of delivery.

In essence, the clearinghouse becomes each buyer's seller and each seller's buyer. That is, the clearinghouse breaks each futures transaction apart after the initial trade. For example, if an individual enters into a long futures position, then the clearinghouse sold it to him or her for all further reference after the initial trade. Denoting this individual trader as person A, the initial position is shown in the first row of Table 2.7 as the buyer of one New York Mercantile Exchange gold futures contract valued at $36,000. Person A has committed himself to buy 100 ounces of gold for $360 per ounce at some point in the future. On the other side of the market, person B has simultaneously agreed to sell to A one gold contract for $360 per

TABLE 2.7   The Operation of the Clearinghouse: An Illustration from the New York Mercantile Exchange Gold Futures Market

TIME PERIOD	FUTURES BUYER	FUTURES SELLER	CONTRACT VALUE	CLEARINGHOUSE POSITION	OPEN LONGS	OPEN SHORTS
1	A	B	$36,000	A's seller and B's buyer	A	B
2	C	A	$37,000	C's seller and A's buyer	C	B
3	B	C	$36,500	B's seller and C's buyer	—	—

ounce. After the initial futures trade is completed between person A and B, the clearinghouse immediately becomes A's seller and B's buyer. Thus, the clearinghouse has a commitment to accept delivery from B and to deliver to A.

Suppose that on the following day, person A decides to liquidate his position by selling a gold futures contract for the same delivery month previously bought. Assume this contract is purchased by a third person, C. If the price of gold increases from $360 to $370 per ounce before A sells, then after A sells, the clearinghouse will pay person A (through the broker) the difference between the selling and the buying price times the number of ounces in question, or $1,000 in this case (ignoring commissions). However, because the clearinghouse brings to market all contracts at the end of each trading day, it will call on person B to deposit an additional $1,000 on day 2. Person B went short at $360 per ounce, and then the market moved "against" him to $370. When his commitment is "marked to market" at the end of day 2, he is therefore required to put up $1,000 as a margin call, which in turn is paid to person A.

To complete this scenario in Table 2.7, assume that on day 3 the price of gold falls back to $365 from $370. If both persons C and B liquidate their positions at $365, then the clearinghouse collects $500 net from person C. In addition, it returns $500 to person B.

If no further trading takes place, the result is that person A gained $1,000, and $500 was lost by both B and C. The clearinghouse never encounters a deficit or surplus because it "brings" each contract to the market price from its original trading price at the end of each day. This process is called "marking to market." The operating costs of the clearinghouse are covered by transaction fees levied on its members.

MARGIN DEPOSITS

Futures trading does not involve the exchange of any physical assets or financial instruments unless delivery takes place during the delivery month. This means that buyers and sellers of a futures contract do not have to provide the full monetary value of their commitment at the time a trade is executed. Instead, they are required only to deposit a good-faith, or **margin**, deposit. The leverage resulting from margin deposits is one reason speculators are attracted to futures trading. The clearinghouse (for each exchange) establishes minimum margin requirements for each particular contract. For example, for New York Mercantile Exchange gold

TABLE 2.8   Sample Minimum Margin Requirements

CONTRACT	INITIAL MARGIN	MAINTENANCE MARGIN
Cotton (NYCE)	$1,000	$750
Frozen orange juice (NYCE)	$1,000	$750
Corn (CBT)	$800	$600
Soybeans (CBT)	$1,350	$1,000
Wheat (CBT)	$675	$500
T-bonds (CBT)	$2,430	$1,800
Dow Jones Index (CBT)	$3,840	$3,200
Japanese yen (CME)	$2,900	$2,200
Lean hogs (CME)	$1,000	$800
Frozen pork bellies (CME)	$1,600	$1,200

(symbol is GC), this is $2,500 per 100-ounce contract, or roughly 7% of the total value. Margin requirements set by individual brokerage firms are often above this minimum and vary from firm to firm. With a 7% margin deposit, a 7% change in the futures price will result in a 100% change in the equity of a trader's account. Thus, futures trading is viewed as a risky venture for speculators. Yet both price volatility and the leverage afforded a commodity futures trader make trading risky.

On execution of a trade, a margin deposit is required by the brokerage firm (for nonmember traders) and in turn by the clearinghouse. In the case of cotton futures, for example, the required "initial" margin deposit for one contract is approximately $1,000, and the "maintenance" margin is about $750. Table 2.8 reports a sample of minimum margin requirements established by various exchanges. Margin requirements change quite often, with changing market conditions. The Web sites for both the Chicago Board of Trade and the Chicago Mercantile Exchange report current margin requirements at *(http://www.cbot.com/mplex/contract/margins.htm orhttp://www.cme.com/clearing/pbrates)*. Margin requirements differ among speculators and hedgers, and there are special margin considerations for spread trading. Hartzmark (1986) wrote an interesting article that looked at changing margin requirements and the impact on the composition of traders in the futures pit.

For public traders, the margin requirements are set by brokerage firms and normally will be above the minimum levels shown in Table 2.8. The initial margin is required on the day the futures trade in initiated, while the maintenance margin is the amount required to keep the trader's account in the black every day thereafter, as long as the futures position remains outstanding. As long as the market moves in favor of the trader, no additional margin money is required, and in fact profits can be claimed by the trader at the end of each trading day. This is because the clearinghouse forwards any profit, realized or unrealized, to the broker, and thus the client has the right to this money.[2]

---

[2] Interest on temporarily unclaimed and unrealized profit has provided a large source of revenue to brokerage firms over the years.

TABLE 2.9   Margin Calls: An Illustration of a Long Position in a Lean Hog Futures Contract

TIME PERIOD	MARGIN DEPOSIT	CONTRACT PRICE	CONTRACT SIZE	TOTAL VALUE	MARGIN CALL
1	$1,000	$.50	40,000 lb	$20,000	—
2	$1,000	$.48	40,000 lb	$19,200	$ 600
3	$1,000	$.42	40,000 lb	$16,800	$1,800

Margin requirements for options on futures are different. Unlike in the case with futures, the buyer of an option is not required to deposit margin money with the clearinghouse because the maximum risk exposure is the premium, which is paid in full at the time a position is taken. However, the seller of an option is exposed to significant risk and thus is required to deposit margin money in the same fashion as one who either bought or sold a futures contract outright. The seller (writer) of an option is normally required to deposit margin money equal to the margin on the underlying futures contract plus the current value of the option's premium.

Once the market moves against a trader, the brokerage firm, on behalf of the clearinghouse, will demand additional margin money from the trader. Table 2.9 provides an illustration of margin calls using the lean hog futures market as an example. If the individual in question goes long, then he is subject to margin calls if the price begins to fall. Suppose he goes long in lean hog futures at 50¢ per pound and the price subsequently falls to 48¢. Over this period, he will be required to deposit a total of $600 in addition to the initial $1,000 margin. The 2¢ decline in price resulted in a loss of contract value equal to $800, so the initial margin of $1,000 was drawn down to only $200. In order to restore the margin money in the account to the maintenance margin level (of $800), the individual would receive a $600 margin call from his broker. The margin calls must be paid immediately. If the price continued to fall to 42¢, additional margin equal to $2,400 (6¢ x 40,000) would be required. Thus, it is often the case that margin calls equal to the full value of unrealized losses must be made by the futures trader. Margin money must be in the form of cash or near-cash instruments, such as Treasury bills.

VOLUME AND OPEN INTEREST

Volume is the number of contracts traded over a given time interval, and normally it is measured on a daily basis. Since for every buyer of a futures contract there must be a seller, volume is the total number of purchases or sales but not the sum of the two. Volume is a useful indicator of market activity and market liquidity.

Open interest is the number of unliquidated contracts at any point in time; thus, it is a cumulative figure. It is measured by either the number of open long positions or the number of open short positions but not the sum of the two. Table 2.10 illustrates how open interest and volume are calculated. Suppose that on day 2, a

TABLE 2.10 Illustration of Open-Interest and Volume Calculations for Futures Contracts

	TRANSACTION					
DAY NO.	BUYER	SELLER	OPEN "LONGS"	OPEN "SHORTS"	DAILY VOLUME	OPEN INTEREST
1					0	0
2	A(2)	B(2)	A(2)	B(2)	2	2
3	C(1)	D(1)	A(2), C(1)	B(2), D(1)	1	3
4	B(1)	E(1)	A(2), C(1)	B(1), D(1), E(1)	1	3
5	D(1)	C(1)	A(2)	B(1), E(1)	1	2
6	E(1)	A(1)	A(1)		1	1
7	B(1)	A(1)			1	0

Note: Number of contracts either bought or sold are in parentheses. Letters A to E denote individual traders.

new futures contract begins trading and that person A buys two contracts from person B. At the end of the day, the clearinghouse records would indicate that person A has two open long positions and that person B has two open short positions. Both the daily volume and open interest at the end of the day would be reported as two contracts.

On day 3, suppose that there is a sale of one contract by person D (a "new" seller) to person C (a "new" buyer). At the end of day 3, the cumulative open interest will have increased from two to three, and the daily volume will be recorded as one contract. Open interest rises to three contracts because trader A still has two open long contracts, and now trader C also has one open long contract, for a total of three open interest. On the other side of the market, both traders B and D have open short positions, and these positions also sum to three.

Further illustration of how volume and open interest change over time is provided in Table 2.10 for days 4 through 7. As can be seen from the table, if there is a purchase by an "old" seller from an "old" buyer, open interest declines. On the other hand, if there is a purchase by a "new" buyer from an "old" buyer, open interest is unchanged.

OPTIONS VERSUS FUTURES

There are some important fundamental differences between futures and options. First, the obligation involved in buying an options contract is much different from that involved in buying a futures contract. The holder of a futures contract has the obligation to either deliver or accept delivery of the underlying asset or financial instrument. This obligation must either be "met" or "offset" by the holder of a futures contract. It is most often offset by the trader entering into an equal and opposite futures position. Alternatively, the holder of an option has the "right" but not an "obligation" to either buy or sell the underlying futures contract. For example, a buyer of a T-bond futures contract must either accept delivery or sell an offsetting

TABLE 2.11   Basic Differences Between Futures Contracts and Options on Futures

ALTERNATIVE POSITION	TRADER'S RIGHTS	TRADER'S OBLIGATIONS	MARGINS REQUIRED
Futures contract buyer		Accept commodity or asset at contract price	Yes
Futures contract seller		Deliver commodity or asset at contract price	Yes
Put option buyer	Sell futures contract at strike price		No
Put option seller		Buy futures contract at strike price	Yes
Call option buyer	Buy futures contract at strike price		No
Call option seller		Sell futures contract at strike price	Yes

futures contract before contract expiration. On the other hand, a buyer of a T-bond "call" option can either exercise his right and obtain a long position in T-bond futures or, alternatively, choose not to exercise the option and simply let it expire. The basic differences between futures and options contracts are outlined in Table 2.11.

To reiterate, an option is a contractual agreement to either purchase or sell a futures contract at a preestablished price and within a specified time period. As briefly explained earlier in this chapter, there are two types of options: "puts" and "calls." A call option gives a buyer the right (but not the obligation) to purchase a futures contract at a specified strike price and during a specified period of time (before the expiry date). A put option gives a buyer of the option the right (but not the obligation) to sell a futures contract at a specified price and during a specified period of time. The seller (writer) of an option receives a premium, which is the amount paid by the buyer of the option in return for the right to control a futures contract. The premium is the price of the option, and thus it fluctuates with the supply and demand for the option itself. The holder can exercise an option at any time during the life of the option.

A few examples will help illustrate these basic concepts. Consider Table 2.12, where representative futures options prices are reported for options written on wheat and gold futures contracts. The top panel of Table 2.12 reports wheat option prices. On the day in question, the purchaser of a call option in wheat would have numerous different strike prices to choose from, ranging from $2.60 to $3.10 per bushel. If the option buyer chooses $2.80 as the appropriate strike price, then he would pay 6.75¢ per bushel for the right to go long one July wheat futures contract at a strike price of $2.80 per bushel. He may exercise this right any time before the month of July.[3] The total premium he pays to the seller of the

---

[3] For most futures options, the expiration date is in the early portion of the contract month or late in the previous month. In contrast, most futures contracts expire near the end of the contract month.

TABLE 2.12   Wheat and Gold Futures Options

Wheat (CBT)

5,000 bu.; cents per bu.

Price	Jly	Sep	Dec	Jly	Sep	Dec
260	18.500	25.250	...	2.000	4.250	4.000
270	11.625	18.750	28.125	5.125	7.750	7.000
280	6.750	13.750	22.375	10.250	12.375	11.125
290	4.000	10.000	17.625	17.500	18.750	16.125
300	2.125	7.250	14.000	25.625	25.500	22.375
310	1.125	5.250	11.250	34.625	33.500	29.375

Est vol 5,500 Wd 3,774 calls 2,648 puts
Op int Wed 58,088 calls 32,279 puts

Gold (CMX)

100 troy ounces; $ per troy ounce

Price	Jly	Aug	Oct	Jly	Aug	Oct
300	12.40	13.50	17.30	1.10	2.30	5.30
305	8.70	10.30	13.80	2.40	4.00	6.80
310	5.10	7.40	10.40	3.80	6.10	8.30
315	3.40	5.60	8.70	7.10	9.30	11.60
320	2.50	4.20	7.30	11.20	12.90	15.10
325	1.70	3.20	6.00	15.40	16.90	18.70

Est vol 3,800 Wd 2,303 calls 1,320 puts
Op int Wed 112,810 calls 54,036 puts

Source: Reprinted by permission from the *Wall Street Journal*, May 17, 2002.

option is $337.50 (6.75¢ per bushel × 5,000 bushels), and this is paid immediately at the time the option is purchased. If the price of wheat falls and he chooses not to exercise the option, then his total loss is limited to $337.50. However, if the price of wheat rises and he exercises his option, he will acquire a "long" futures position at the option strike price of $2.80. At the same time, the exchange clearing-house will assign a "short" futures position to a trader who has previously sold an identical "call" option, with the same underlying futures contract and the same strike price.

Turning to the gold example in Table 2.12, consider the buyer of a put option. If the purchaser chooses a strike price of $300 per ounce and an August expiry date, the premium paid to the option seller is $2.30 per ounce, or $230 for one put option. The holder of this option has the right to acquire a short position in August gold futures at a price of $300. If the price of gold falls before the month of August and the option is exercised, the holder obtains a short futures position from the exchange clearinghouse. He must then liquidate his futures position in order to capture the full profit available to him at the time. Alternatively, if the price falls, he may choose to sell his option for a profit before the expiry month. He will profit from selling the option because its premium will rise when the price of gold falls.

> ### BOX 2.4
>
> ### Harry Potter and the Sorcerer's Stone *futures contracts?*
> Based at the University of Iowa Business School, the Iowa Electronic Market is a futures market in which contract payoffs depend on economic and political events, such as elections and box office movie revenues. Various contracts are offered, including *Harry Potter and the Sorcerer's Stone*, Monsters Inc., mayoral elections, presidential elections, and the Federal Reserve monetary policy. Specifically, the Harry Potter contracts pay off depending on the movie's box office receipts. For example, one contract will pay $1.00 if, in the period November 16–December 13, Harry Potter grosses less than $160 million at the box office. The Iowa Electronic Market is a fun and interesting way for students to introduce themselves to the intricacies of a futures market contract and how cash-settled contracts work compared to those contracts that specify delivery. The Iowa market can be found on the Web at *http://www.biz.uiowa.edu/iem/index.html.*

WHY SPECULATE IN FUTURES AND OPTIONS CONTRACTS?

It was established in Chapter 1 that hedgers trade futures for commercial reasons to manage the impact of price risk on the profitability of their business. Futures markets exist primarily to facilitate hedger interests, but the speculator is also very critical to the functioning of the market. The volume of futures and options trading has grown rapidly in recent years because of growing hedger and speculative interest. It is a fast-moving industry and offers a speculator certain advantages that are not available in more conventional investments.

One of the most attractive aspects of futures trading for speculators is the high leverage ratio they are afforded because futures contracts are bought and sold on margin money. Leverage means that you need commit only a small amount of money in order to control a futures contract that is highly valuable. Most contracts may be purchased or sold with only 10% of the total value of contract initially invested (initial margin money). For instance, the initial margin on a short or long Canadian dollar futures position may be $7,500. The market value of the position may be $75,000, so the initial margin represents only 10% of the value of the futures position.

Whereas a $10,000 investment in the stock market would control $10,000 worth of securities, the same $10,000 investment in the futures market could control $100,000 worth of commodities or financial instruments. A 10% change in the value of a stock would affect an investor's account by 10%. Alternatively, a 10% change in the value of a futures contract would result in a 100% change in an investor's account. Contrary to popular belief, futures prices are no more volatile than stock market prices, but trading in futures is riskier because accounts are highly leveraged.

Futures and options are very liquid forms of investments compared to many alternatives. At the other end of the spectrum is real estate, for example, a highly illiquid investment. Futures and options contracts can be easily bought and sold on a daily basis, and the highly standardized nature of futures contracts contributes to market liquidity. An exchange's clearinghouse guarantees each contract, and there is essentially no risk of default for an investor.

For the most part, brokerage fees for the purchase and sale of a futures contract are very low compared to many other forms of investment. The typical brokerage fee to initiate and then liquidate a one-contract position is approximately $50. This amount is insignificant compared to the transaction fees on other investments, such as real estate.

There is a diverse set of contracts traded on futures and options markets that provide not only many different trading opportunities but also diversification possibilities for the investor. Another attractive aspect of futures and options trading is that an investor can profit from price declines as well as price increases. Speculators can take a short (sell) position in the futures market as easily as they can take a long (buy) position. Spreads or straddles—going long in one contract and short in another—also provide a unique investment strategy for speculators.

Options on futures are attractive to investors for many of the same reasons. The buyer of an option is required to pay a premium to the seller, and in return the buyer gets a predetermined level of risk. The potential return is high, but the risk exposure is relatively small as long as the premium is not excessive. Limited risk is the major advantage associated with speculating in options rather than futures.

Given the generally high level of risk associated with a leveraged futures investment, it is important to appreciate the risk-return trade-off in futures and the merits of diversification. A high expected return from holding a futures contract as a speculator is normally associated with a high level of risk. Speculators often run the risk of losing more than their initial investment. However, risk exposure can be reduced if a speculator spreads investments among different commodities and financial instruments. Generally, the larger the number of different commodities and instruments held in a portfolio, the lower the risk exposure. This is a major reason the commodity futures funds have become so popular for investors.

While reducing the exposure to risk by investing in more than one commodity or financial instrument, a speculator will not necessarily forgo potential returns. This is particularly true if the futures contracts chosen for the portfolio do not follow similar price patterns. The fundamental basis for diversification rests on choosing investments that are not closely correlated. For example, a portfolio comprised of one silver contract and one soybean contract is less vulnerable to risk than a portfolio comprised of two silver contracts, although the two portfolios may yield a similar expected rate of return.

Combining stock market investments with futures and options investments can also attain the merits of diversification. For example, stock and commodity futures prices are often negatively correlated. Futures tend to be good inflationary hedges, while common stocks tend to be poor inflationary hedges. Research has shown that diversification in the stock and futures market can lower portfolio risk without affecting the expected return (see Box 2.5).

BOX 2.5

Portfolio diversification benefits of futures and options.
Commodity futures and options contracts are becoming more and more acceptable as a legitimate class of financial assets for purposes of portfolio diversification. Specifically, an investment in a commodity futures index may offer the diversifying properties that investors seek to balance their exposure to stocks and bonds. Despite the popular perception that commodity futures are highly risky, research supports the claim that the utility of investing in commodity futures is higher the more risk averse the investor. Commodity futures indexes have demonstrated significant positive correlation with the rate of inflation as well as changes in the rate of inflation. However, the utility of investing in commodity futures for diversification purposes will be different for different investors. The actual level of investment for a risk-averse investor will depend on the investor's individual utility function, level of risk tolerance, and current portfolio composition.

For more on this topic, see Anson (1999).

SUMMARY

This chapter has provided an overview of the main characteristics of futures and options contracts. Differences between futures and options contracts were emphasized, and the mechanics of trading in these contracts were explained with several examples. A futures contract is very similar to either a deferred delivery contract or a forward contract, except that each futures contract is standardized and is traded on an organized exchange. Both the buyer and the seller of a futures contract enter into a binding commitment to exchange commodities or financial instruments at an agreed price at some future date. The risks and rewards for the buyer and seller of futures contracts are symmetrical. Alternatively, options on futures give the buyer the right (but not the obligation) to either buy or sell a futures contract at a specified strike price at some future date. Alternatively, the seller of the option is obligated to deliver the underlying futures contract at the strike price if the option is exercised by its holder. For options on futures, the risks and rewards for the buyer and seller are asymmetrical.

Futures and options contracts can be easily bought and sold on a daily basis, and the highly standardized nature of futures contracts contributes to market liquidity. A call option specifies that the seller must deliver a long futures position to the option buyer, and a put option specifies delivery of a short futures position. The financial obligations involved in options trading are different from those in futures trading.

The important role of the exchange clearinghouse was also covered in this chapter, with examples of how the clearinghouse "marks to market" each trade at the end of each trading day. Trading on margin is an important characteristic of futures markets, a concept that was also explained in this chapter.

DISCUSSION QUESTIONS

1. Why will electronic trading gradually fully replace the open outcry system of trading? What are the pros and cons of the two alternative systems?
2. How does the clearinghouse ensure the financial integrity of futures and options trading?
3. Explain why the risks for buyers and sellers of futures contracts are symmetrical.
4. Explain why the risks for buyers and sellers of options on futures are asymmetrical.
5. Explain how margin trading provides leverage to speculators in the futures market.
6. "Daily trading volume was higher than normal but open interest remained unchanged." Explain this statement and the conditions under which open interest rises, remains unchanged, or falls.

SELECTED REFERENCES

Anson, M. J. P. (1999). Maximizing utility with commodity futures diversification. *Journal of Portfolio Management, 25*(4), 86–94.

Coval, J. D., & Shumway, T. (2001). Is sound just noise? *Journal of Finance, 56*(5), 1887–1910.

Hartzmark, M. L. (1986). The effects of changing margin levels on futures market activity, the composition of traders in the market, and price performance. *Journal of Business, 59*, (pt. 2), S147–S180.

Pirrong, Stephen Craig. (1999). Electronic exchanges are inevitable and beneficial. *Regulation, 22*(4), 20–26.

Tse, Y., & Zabotina, T. V. (2001). Transaction costs and market quality: Open outcry versus electronic trading. *Journal of Futures Markets, 21*(8), 713–735.

APPENDIX

TABLE 2.A1 Futures Contract Symbols

The futures industry code for a particular futures contract employs abbreviations for both the contract and its expiration. Typically, two letters represent the contract, one letter represents the contract expiration month, and a final number represents the last digit of the expiration year. For example, the March 2003 Crude Oil futures contract is represented as CLH3. CL represent crude oil, H represents March, and 3 represents 2003. Contract and month codes are listed here.

Delivery Month Symbol Codes

Jan = F	Feb = G	Mar = H	Apr = J	May = K	Jun = M
Jul = N	Aug = Q	Sep = U	Oct = V	Nov = X	Dec = Z

(continued)

TABLE 2.A1 *Cont.*

CONTRACT SYMBOLS

CHICAGO MERCANTILE EXCHANGE (CME)

CURRENCIES	SYMBOL
Australian Dollar	AD
Brazil Real	BR
British Pound	NB
Canadian Dollar	CD
Deutsche Mark	DM
EuroFx	EC
E-Mini EuroFx	E7
French Franc	FR
Japanese Yen	JY
E-Mini Japanese Yen	J7
Mexican Peso	MP
New Zealand Dollar	NE
Russian Ruble	RU
South African Rand	RA
Swiss Franc	SF
Euro/British Pound	RP
Euro/Japanese Yen	RY
Euro/Swiss Franc	RF

Weather

HDD Weather	H1-HO
CDD Weather	K1-KO

Food and Fiber

Class 3 Milk	DA
Class 4 Milk	DK
Butter	DB
Non-Fat Dry Milk	NF
Lumber, Random Length	LB

Indexes

E-Mini Midcap	ME
E-Mini NASDAQ	NQ
E-Mini Russell	ER
E-Mini S&P 500	ES
Fortune E-50	FE
Goldman-Sachs Commodity Index	GI
NASDAQ 100 Index	ND
Nikkei 225 Stock Index	NK
Russell 2000 Index	RL
S&P 500	SP
S&P Midcap 400	MD
S&P 500/BARRA Growth Index	SG
S&P 500/BARRA Value Index	SU

Chemicals

Benzene	BZ
Mixed Xylene	MX

TABLE 2.A1 *Cont.*

CURRENCIES	SYMBOL
Interest Rates	
Eurodollar	ED
Euroyen (LIBOR)	EL
Euroyen (TIBOR)	EY
Libor 1 Month	EM
Overnight Fed Funds-Turn Rate	TZ
90 Day T-Bill	TB
2 Year Midcurve	E2
10 Year Agency Note	FO
5 Year Bundle	Y5
QBI	QB
Japanese Yen Government Bond	JB
1 Year Midcurve	EO
5 Year Agency Note	F5
Livestock and Meat	
Pork Cutouts	PC
E-Mini Lean Hogs	HM
Feeder Cattle	FC
Lean Hogs	LH
Live Cattle	LC
Fresh Pork Bellies	FR
Frozen Pork Bellies	PB

CHICAGO BOARD OF TRADE (CBOT)

	SYMBOL (outcry, electronic)
Grains and Oilseeds	
Corn	C,ZC
Wheat	W, ZW
Oats	O, ZO
Rough Rice	RR, ZR
Soybeans	S, ZS
Soybean Oil	BO, ZL
Soybean Meal	SM, ZM
Mini-Sized Corn	N/A, YC
Mini-Sized Soybeans	N/A, YK
Mini-Sized Wheat	N/A, YW
Indexes	
CBOT X-Fund Index	To Be Announced
Dow Jones Industrial Average	DJ, ZD
Mini-Sized Dow Jones Industrial Average	N/A, YJ
Dow Jones Composite Average	DE, DC
Dow Jones Transportation Average Index	DQ, DV
Dow Jones Utility Average Index	DR, DU
Dow Jones AIG Commodity Index	AI, AI
Interest Rates	
Long-Term Municipal Bond	MB, ZU
30 Year U.S. Treasury Bonds	US, ZB

(continued)

TABLE 2.A1 *Cont.*

CHICAGO BOARD OF TRADE (CBOT)

SYMBOL (outcry, electronic)

Interest Rates

10-Year Treasury Notes	TY, ZN
10-Year Agency Notes	DN, AN
10-Year Interest Rate Swap	NI, SR
5-Year Treasury Notes	FV, ZF
5-Year Agency Notes	DF, AF
2- Year Treasury Notes	TU, ZT
30 Day Federal Funds	FF, ZQ
Mini-Sized 10-Year Treasury Notes	N/A, YN
Mini-Sized 30 Year U.S. Treasury Bonds	N/A, YH
Mini-Sized Deferred Eurodollar	N/A, YE2
Mini-Sized Eurodollar Futures	N/A, YE

Metals

Mini-Sized New York Gold	N/A, YG
Mini-Sized New York Silver	N/A, YI
Kilo Gold	KI, N/A
1,000-Ounce Silver	AG, AG

NEW YORK BOARD OF TRADE (NYBOT)

SYMBOL

Currencies

Australian Dollar/Canadian Dollar	AS
Australian Dollar/Japanese Yen	YA
Australian Dollar/New Zealand Dollar	AR
Australian Dollar/U.S. Dollar	AU
British Pound/Japanese Yen	SY
British Pound/Swiss Franc	SS
Canadian Dollar/Japanese Yen	HY
Euro/Australian Dollar	RA
Euro/Canadian Dollar	EP
Euro/Japanese Yen	EJ
Euro/Norwegian Krone	OL
Euro/Sterling	GB
Euro/Swedish Krone	RK
Euro/Swiss Franc	RZ
Euro/U.S. Dollar Large	EU
Euro/U.S. Dollar Regular	EO
New Zealand Dollar/U.S. Dollar	ZX
Swiss Franc/Japanese Yen	YZ
U.S. Dollar/British Pound	YP
U.S. Dollar/Canadian Dollar	YD
U.S. Dollar/Japanese Yen	YY
U.S. Dollar/New Zealand Dollar	ZX
U.S. Dollar/Norwegian Krone	NS
U.S. Dollar/South African Rand	ZR
U.S. Dollar/Swedish Krone	KU
U.S. Dollar/Swiss Franc	YF

TABLE 2.A1 *Cont.*	
	SYMBOL

Food and Fiber

Cocoa	CC
Coffee	KC
Cotton	CT
FCOJ	OJ
FCOJ Differential	OD
FCOJ Differential Par = 0	OD2
FCOJ #2	OK
Sugar #11 World	SB
Sugar #14 Domestic	SE

Indexes

Commercial Markets Index	CI
CRB/Bridge Index	CR
Dollar Index	DX
NYSE Large Composite Index	YL
NYSE Composite Index	YX
NYSE Small Composite Index	YS
S&P Commodity Index	I
Russell 1000 Large Index	RQ
Russell 1000 Index	R
Russell 1000 Mini Index	RM

Interest Rates

Treasury Auction 5 Year Note	FY
Treasury Auction 10 Year Note	TW
8% 2 Year Treasury Note	A
8% 5 Year Treasury Note	F
8% 10 Year Treasury Note	T
8% 30 Year U.S. T-Bond	B
6% 2 Year Treasury Note	V
6% 5 Year Treasury Note	X
6% 10 Year Treasury Note	Y
6% 30 Year U.S. T-Bond	Z
5 Year U.S. Agency Note	XZ
10 Year U.S. Agency Note	YZ

NEW YORK MERCANTILE EXCHANGE (NYMEX)

Energy

Brent Crude Oil	SC
Light Sweet Crude Oil	CL
California/Oregon Border Electricity	MW
Central Appalachian Coal	QL
Cinergy Electricity	CN
Entergy Electricity	NT
Heating Oil	HO
Henry Hub Natural Gas	NG
Henry Hub Natural Gas Swaps	NN
Mid-Columbia River Electricity	KM

(continued)

TABLE 2.A1   *Cont.*

NEW YORK MERCANTILE EXCHANGE (NYMEX)

	SYMBOL
Unleaded Gasoline	HU
PJM Electricity	QJ
Palo Verde Electricity	KV
Propane	PN
Metals	
Aluminum	AL
Copper	HG
Gold	GC
Palladium	PA
Platinum	PL
Silver	SI

KANSAS CITY BOARD OF TRADE (KCBT)

Indexes	
ISDEX Internet Stock Index	IS
Value Line Stock Index	MV
Energy	
Western Natural Gas	KG
Grains and Oilseeds	
Wheat	KW

MINNEAPOLIS GRAIN EXCHANGE (MGE)

Grains and Oilseeds	
Durum Wheat	DW
Wheat, Hard Red	MW

MIDAMERICA EXCHANGE (MIDAM)

Currencies	
British Pound	XP
Canadian Dollar	XD
Grains and Oilseeds	
Corn	XC
Oats	XO
Soybean Meal	XE
Soybean Oil	XR
Soybeans	XS
Wheat	XW
Livestock and Meats	
Lean Hogs	XH
Live Cattle	XL

Note: This table reports only those contracts with active trading volume.

CHAPTER 3

Commodities

The essence of futures and options markets is their role as a vehicle to establish prices across time (i.e., intertemporal prices). For example, on any given day, the Chicago Board of Trade corn futures market establishes prices for five different months: March, May, July, September, and December. The basic economics of commodity intertemporal price relationships are examined in this chapter. We focus on understanding fundamental intertemporal price relationships, such as the price differential between May and September soybean futures on a given date or between May and September coffee futures. Is the September futures price normally higher than the May price, and if so, by how much? What economic factors influence this price spread over time? This chapter also examines the price relationship between cash and futures prices. How does the cash price for crude oil in the Middle East relate to the New York futures price? How does the cash price for wheat in New Orleans relate to the Chicago wheat futures price? Does a supply or demand shock have an equal impact on the New Orleans cash price and the Chicago futures price? The difference between the Chicago futures price and the New Orleans cash price is called a **basis**, a price spread between the futures and cash markets.

An understanding of **intertemporal** commodity market price relationships is essential for a full comprehension of cash, futures, and options markets. There are three dimensions to commodity price relationships: time, space, and product form. This chapter focuses on the time dimension of commodity markets because futures and options markets provide a time dimension to commodity prices. The basis relates to the spatial dimension of commodity markets, and in this chapter some attention is also devoted to this topic.

The **law of one price** captures much of the economic theory of intertemporal commodity prices for storable commodities. In general, the *law of one price* says that there is one price for a commodity—the cash price of the underlying product—and that all other prices are related to that price through storage and transport costs. Storage costs reflect the time dimension, and transport costs reflect the spatial dimension. If intertemporal and spatial price relationships do not reflect storage and transport costs, this may provide an **arbitrage** opportunity for traders. In reality, it is the threat of arbitrage that keeps cash and futures prices in line with each other.

Although the law of one price is not always empirically supported for international markets because of international trade barriers (e.g., tariffs and quotas) and unanticipated exchange rate fluctuations, it accurately describes the workings of domestic commodity markets where arbitrage is more effective.

The **price-of-storage** theory is consistent with the law of one price. In the discussion that follows, the *price of storage* theory is used to explain the pattern of intertemporal price relationships among futures contracts for **storable** commodities. The price-of-storage theory predicts that intertemporal price relationships are determined by the net cost of carrying inventory. For example, the theory suggests that in the presence of normal inventory levels, the price of a futures contract for December delivery tends to be the price for October delivery plus the net (positive or negative) cost of storing the commodity from October to December. This means that the futures price for any delivery month is equal to the current spot price plus the cost of storage.

The concept of the **basis** is also touched on in this chapter. The basis is the linkage between cash and futures prices. Since there are numerous cash markets for any one futures market, there are numerous bases in any market. For every cash market, there is a unique basis associated with that market. For example, in the U.S. corn market there are a few key terminal cash markets such as the Gulf, the Pacific Northwest, Kansas City, Toledo, and Minneapolis. Most of the local rural corn prices are based off these terminal markets, and the terminal markets are closely tied to the Chicago corn futures price.

From the hedger's perspective, the *basis* is one of the most important factors associated with cash, futures, and options markets. Intertemporal price relationships are integrated into a simple spatial equilibrium model in this chapter to help illustrate the important role of supply and demand for commodity storage in determining intertemporal price spreads.

FUTURES CONTRACT PRICE PATTERNS OVER TIME

For any commodity futures contract, trading is conducted simultaneously for different delivery months. For example, Table 3.1 reports alternative soybean futures contracts traded on the Chicago Board of Trade. The price for the nearby delivery month (November) is $4.69 per bushel, and prices for subsequent delivery months

TABLE 3.1   Delivery Months and Futures Prices for Chicago Board of Trade Soybean Futures Contracts

CROP YEAR	DELIVERY MONTH	FUTURES PRICE ($/BU)
Old	November (nearby month)	4.69
Old	January	4.77
Old	March	4.83
Old	May	4.84
Old	July	4.87
New	November (distant month)	4.81

are progressively higher, except for the most distant delivery month, November, in the following year. The distant November contract price is $4.81, and this contract specifies delivery in a "new" crop year, whereas the nearby November contract is the "old" (i.e., current) crop year. The old crop year is separated from the new crop year by a harvest.

In Table 3.1, the intertemporal price relationship for the "old" crop (nearby November through July) is in **contango,** a situation where futures prices are progressively higher for the more distant delivery months. Alternatively, the intertemporal price relationships between some of the old crop contracts and the distant (new crop) November contract represent **inverted markets, as the nearer months are trading at price premiums** to the more distant month. Specifically, July soybeans are trading at $4.87, a 6¢-per-bushel premium over the more distant November price of $4.81 per bushel. Thus, we can say that the July-distant November price spread is inverted. In addition, the March-distant November spread and May-distant November spread are also inverted. A contango is a more normal intertemporal price relationship, although inverted markets are not uncommon.

Futures price patterns can be analyzed as relationships among contracts at a specific point in time (e.g., the November–January–March soybean price spreads as reported in Table 3.1) or as price changes of a specific futures contract over time (e.g., the behavior of January soybean futures prices over time).

The price pattern expected for a specific commodity is at least partially dependent on whether the commodity is classified as **storable** or **nonstorable**. Gold, silver, sugar, soybeans, wheat, corn, cotton, crude oil, heating oil, and coffee are examples of storable commodites with futures contracts. Alternatively, electricity, live cattle, feeder cattle, and lean hogs are examples of nonstorable commodities that trade on futures markets.

PRICES BETWEEN TIME PERIODS
FOR A STORABLE COMMODITY

Consider a simple economic model for allocating a storable commodity between two time periods: the present time period and a future time period. Suppose the present time period is the *summer* season and the future time period the *winter* season. In this example, the commodity is assumed to be heating oil, but the model can be applied to a broad range of storable commodities. Heating oil is refined from crude oil, and the demand for heating oil is highly seasonal because there is a large demand for use in furnaces to heat homes in the northeastern United States during the winter months. Heating oil is also used in water heaters, and there is considerable industrial use of heating oil.

Assume that each of the two time periods (i.e., summer and winter) has a unique demand and supply curve (presented in Fig. 3.1). The summer demand (D_s) and supply (S_s) schedules are known with certainty, and the winter demand (D_w) and supply (S_w) schedules are based on market expectations of what lies ahead for the upcoming winter months. The demand curve is a schedule indicating the quantity demanded of the commodity at each price level. Along the

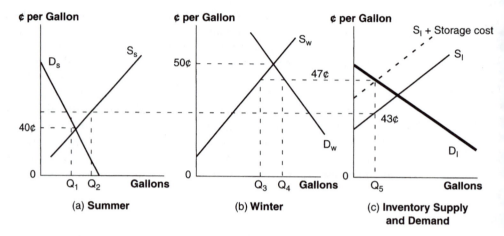

FIGURE 3.1
Heating oil price relationship between two time periods: (a) summer, (b) winter, and (c) inventory supply and demand.

demand curve, only the commodity's price and the quantity demanded are allowed to change; all other factors, such as income, expected winter weather patterns, and prices of other goods, are assumed to remain constant. The supply curves in Figure 3.1 are assumed to be short-run supply curves, which imply that all factors of production are assumed variable except for industry capacity. The summer and winter supply curves are a summation of the supply curves for all firms producing in the market. Each firm's supply curve is equal to the portion of its marginal cost curve at or above the minimum of the average variable cost curve.

A commodity such as heating oil will be stored from the summer to the winter as long as there is an economic incentive to store. One strong incentive is a price differential between the two time periods. With the model presented in Figure 3.1, in order for storage to take place, a price differential must exist between the two periods that is sufficient to pay for full storage costs. Suppose at prevailing prices there is excess supply in the summer and excess demand in the winter. These conditions will generate a price differential between the winter and summer seasons that will provide an incentive to store heating oil.

Figure 3.1 can be used to show that as long as storage costs are positive, the price in the *winter* season must be higher than the price in the *summer* season if storage is to occur. The equilibrium price without storage for cash heating oil is assumed to be 40¢ per gallon in the summer and 50¢ in the winter (Fig. 3.1a, b). The equilibrium price for each season (i.e., 40¢ in the summer and 50¢ in the winter) is determined by the intersection of its respective supply and demand curve. Given the specified 10¢ per gallon price differential between the winter and summer price, conditions indicate a "potential" case in which storage will occur. The term "potential" is used because the size of storage costs in relation to the price differential will determine whether storage actually occurs. If full storage costs are less than the 10¢ price differential, storage is undertaken; otherwise, no economic incentive for storage exists.

Inventory Supply

In this simple model, how many gallons of heating oil will be stored from summer to winter, and what is the equilibrium price spread between summer and winter? Even if storage costs were zero, all summer production would be sold during that season if the price of heating oil were expected to be equal to or below 40¢ per gallon in the winter. Demand during the summer is large enough to ensure that all summer production would be consumed in the summer if the summer price is 40¢ or less.

The potential inventory supply (S_I in Fig. 3.1c), before storage costs, is implicit in Figure 3.1a because the summer period is the most likely period to have excess supply that could be placed into storage. Demand for heating oil is relatively low in the summer, as shown by the positioning of D_s relative to D_w. The inventory supply schedule (S_I) is equal to the summer quantity supplied (S_s) minus the summer quantity demanded (D_s) at any price above 40¢, as shown in Figure 3.1c. As the price increases during the summer, the quantity demanded by consumers decreases, and the quantity supplied by producers increases, so S_I is upward sloping.

Inventory Demand

Winter's heating oil inventory demand schedule (D_I) is determined relative to the equilibrium market price in the winter. For prices at or above 50¢ per gallon, the quantity supplied by producers in the winter is sufficient to meet demand during that season (Fig. 3.1b). Inventory demand (D_I in Fig. 3.1c) equals winter quantity demanded (D_w) minus winter quantity supplied (S_w) at prices below 50¢ per gallon.

Inventory carried into the winter will result in lower prices in the winter compared to a situation where no stocks are carried into the winter season. If prices decrease in the winter, consumers increase their quantity demanded, and producers decrease their quantity supplied, ceteris paribus. As a result, inventory demand (D_I) is drawn as downward sloping in Figure 3.1c because the lower the market price in winter, the greater the demand for inventory carried from the summer to the winter. Inventory demand is not simply the portion of the demand curve below the equilibrium price without storage; rather, it is the horizontal difference between winter demand and supply in Figure 3.1b.

Storage Costs

Positive storage costs exist because of the cost of operating physical storage facilities plus interest, insurance, and other expenses. Assume storage costs between the two time periods are equal to 4¢ per gallon of heating oil, independent of the quantity stored. In Figure 3.1, this is represented by a parallel upward shift in the inventory supply curve, S_I, to the dashed line denoted as S_I + storage cost (Figure 3.1c). These storage costs must be paid (through the market price) to reward those merchants who are willing to hold inventory from the summer until the winter.

The quantity of heating oil stored from summer to winter is indicated by the intersection of the inventory demand curve (D_I) and the inventory supply plus storage cost curve (S_I + storage cost in Figure 3.1c). The equilibrium quantity stored from summer to winter is shown as $0Q_5$ in Figure 3.1c. The price paid by consumers in the winter is 47¢, while summer producers receive 43¢ (47¢ minus the 4¢ storage cost, which is captured by the merchants providing the storage services).

The storage activity links market-clearing prices in the two seasons, and therefore the summer and winter heating oil prices will be highly correlated from day to day. This linkage becomes clear if there is an exogenous shock that shifts the demand or supply function in either season. Prices in both seasons will move in the same direction in reaction to such a shock. For instance, if OPEC countries agree to cut production, this would be a supply-side shock that would drive prices higher in both seasons. Of course, this intertemporal price relationship breaks down if the two seasons are not linked through storage.

No storage occurs between the two time periods in Figure 3.1 if storage costs exceed 10¢ per gallon. If storage costs were sufficiently high to preclude storage between two time periods, then lower correlations between prices for the different time periods would be expected. In other words, price changes in one time period would not be readily reflected in another time period.

To illustrate the effects of a potential market shock, refer to Figure 3.2 and suppose that during the summer there is a change in market expectations with a surprise weather forecast of an unusually cold winter ahead. The expectation of a very cold winter will shift demand in the winter (D_w) to a higher level, and of course the higher demand will raise expected prices in the winter. Suppose the demand curve in the winter period shifts upward to the dashed line D_w^c (Fig. 3.2b). If storage takes place, the new weather forecast would shift the inventory demand curve (D_I) rightward in Figure 3.2c to D_I^c, expanding the volume of storage to $0Q_6$ and resulting in

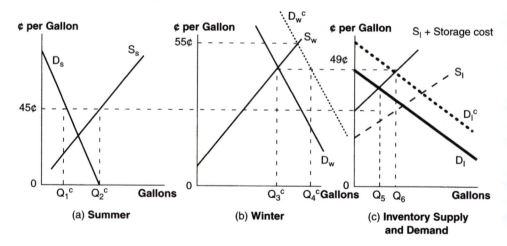

FIGURE 3.2
Change in heating oil price relationship after forecast of cold weather: (a) summer, (b) winter, and (c) inventory supply and demand.

a winter price of 49¢. The winter price increases from the 47¢ level in Figure 3.1, but the expanded volume of storage dampens the extent of this price rise.

Suppose the volume of storage expands from $0Q_5$ to $0Q_6$. This higher level of stocks takes heating oil off the market in the summer and places it into storage for use in the winter. So the heating oil price in the summer will also increase to 45¢ from the 43¢ level shown in Figure 3.1.

TEMPORAL PRICES WITHIN A SINGLE PRODUCTION PERIOD

The previous discussion assumed two distinct production periods while describing the market linkage effects of carrying inventory between the two time periods. There was production in both the summer and the winter seasons. However, an alternative temporal allocation situation exists within a single production period, say, within a given crop-year. The quantity supplied for a single crop-year is fixed, based on current production and inventories carried forward from the previous crop-year. This describes many commodity markets where production takes place only once a year. For example, grain markets (such as corn) have a relatively short harvest period, but inventories are consumed throughout the year.

Figure 3.3 depicts an expected price pattern within a single crop-year for a commodity with a short and single harvest. The solid line in Figure 3.3 shows the expected path of the cash price over the "crop year." The lowest cash price occurs during harvest (August in this example). Steadily increasing cash prices are expected until additional production becomes available during the next harvest period. This is a fairly typical seasonal cash price pattern for commodities. A **seasonal pattern** is any systematic fluctuation in prices within the marketing (or crop) year.

FIGURE 3.3
Futures and cash price patterns for a storable agricultural commodity with seasonal production.

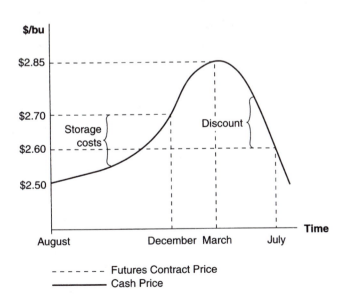

Figure 3.3 is drawn to depict the expected pattern of cash and futures prices as of one point in time (i.e., in August). The cash price in the figure is for the same location as specified in the futures contract. If the harvest was just completed, then Figure 3.3 captures the market's expectation of how the cash price will most likely behave over the full marketing year until the next harvest. Assume that futures contract prices provide an unbiased forecast of forthcoming cash prices. Assume also that no "new" information becomes available that would alter the price forecasts—in other words, Figure 3.3 is a single "snapshot" in time of how the market expects the cash price to unfold over the marketing season. In addition to cash prices, the figure also shows futures prices, which can be viewed as unbiased forecasts of forthcoming cash prices. The futures prices in Figure 3.3 are represented as horizontal dashed lines. If the cash price were expected to rise from $2.50 in August to $2.85 by March, then the current March futures price would equal $2.85 and so on.

Convergence of the cash and futures contract prices in Figure 3.3 results from declining storage costs as the delivery month approaches. Storage costs are largely a function of time, and the time factor becomes less important as the delivery month approaches. This means that futures and cash prices will be identical at the time of futures contract expiry. Situations where the cash and futures do not fully converge are explained later in this chapter.

Given that Figure 3.3 is a snapshot in time, the "expected" March futures contract price is constant, while the "expected" cash price increases from $2.50 in August to $2.85 by the following March. Futures contract prices therefore reflect expected cash price changes. On the other hand, when new information does come into the market (as it surely will), the snapshot of prices changes and the entire spectrum of prices in Figure 3.3 will move up or down simultaneously with changing expectations. All prices in Figure 3.3 move up if the new information is bullish, and they all move down if the news is bearish.

If prices for futures contracts with later maturity dates are higher than prices for those contracts with earlier maturity dates, this typical intertemporal price pattern is referred to as a positive **carrying charge market**, or a **contango**. The difference between the prices of alternative contracts indicates what the market is willing to pay inventory holders for storing the commodity: the **price of storage**. For example, referring to Figure 3.3, an inventory holder would expect to receive 15¢ per bushel ($2.85–$2.70) for carrying stocks from December to March, an amount equal to the carrying charge reflected in the spectrum of futures prices.

If the price for contracts with more distant delivery dates is lower than that for contracts expiring earlier, the market is **inverted**. As shown in Figure 3.3, the inventory holder would expect to suffer a 25¢-per-bushel loss ($2.60–$2.85) between the March and July contract delivery dates. There is an economic incentive to deliver the commodity immediately when a "negative" price for storage exists (Wright and Williams, 1989). Normally, an inverted market arises when there is a relatively low carryover of stocks (and a normal harvest or production year coming up) or, alternatively, when there is a temporary shortage of stocks in a position to be delivered against futures contracts.

TABLE 3.2   Examples of Positive and Negative Intertemporal Carrying Charge Markets, Chicago Board of Trade

DELIVERY MONTH	CORN, POSITIVE CARRY, SEPTEMBER 26, 2001 ($/BU)	OATS, NEGATIVE CARRY, SEPTEMBER 26, 2001 ($/BU)
December 2001	$2.16	$1.60
March 2002	$2.28	$1.51
May 2002	$2.35	$1.45

Inverted Carrying Charge Markets and Normal Backwardation

Actual price patterns between futures contracts and expected cash prices may deviate considerably from the theoretical patterns described in the previous section. Consider the intertemporal price spreads for oats shown in Table 3.2. Oats are used primarily as horse feed and as breakfast cereal. On September 26, 2001, the closing price for the December 2001 Chicago Board of Trade oats futures contract was 15¢ higher than the May 2002 futures contract price (Table 3.2). This intertemporal price relationship is abnormal because oats are not harvested in North America between December and May, and therefore the December and May contracts are in the same crop year. The oats example in Table 3.2 is an example of a negative carrying charge, or an inverted market. The spread between the December and March oats futures was a negative 9¢ per bushel. At the time, the market was not paying a return for storage of oats, and the market signal this sends to inventory holders is to sell in the spot market rather than carry oats forward.

There are alternative explanations for the inversion in the oats market shown in Table 3.2. One possibility is that the volume of trade in the distant months is relatively low—a **thin market** situation (Box 3.1). In a thin market, a relatively large **risk premium** might explain the inversion. There might be an imbalance in the supply and demand for futures contracts and a shortage of speculators willing to hold long futures positions. In this case, long speculators would earn a financial reward (i.e., the risk premium) for holding futures contracts. Another possible explanation of the inversion in oats is a short-term shortage of deliverable stocks, which would push up the nearby futures price relative to the distant contract prices. Traders with short positions would be unable to obtain stocks to deliver and therefore would be forced to bid up the price of the nearby contract in order to offset (or cover) their open short positions. To summarize, if the cash or nearby futures contract price is higher than prices for futures contracts with later delivery dates, then this is an inverted market. The market is not paying for storage, and this is reflected in the negative price difference when the nearer futures price is subtracted from the more distant futures price.

Refer again to the set of intertemporal prices, shown in Table 3.2, for corn and oats futures on the Chicago Board of Trade. A positive carry of 12¢ existed between the December 2001 and March 2002 corn contracts. Is this a "sufficient" price for storing the commodity over that three-month time period? Along with insurance and warehousing charges, interest expense is a major cost in carrying inventory. An estimate of the interest expense can be calculated by multiplying the March futures contract price by the annual prime interest rate. The result is then multiplied by the fraction of a year the corn would be in storage. Using a prime interest rate of 5%, the interest component of the cost of carry would then be about 1¢ per bushel per month (3¢ ≈ .05 × ³⁄₁₂ × $2.28), or 3¢ from December to March. Therefore, the price spread shown in Table 3.2 seems sufficient to compensate the inventory holder, assuming that the noninterest expenses did not exceed 3¢ per bushel per month, and it is doubtful that these other costs would push the total storage costs above 4¢ per month.

Even when a positive carrying charge exists, the price differences between futures contracts may be insufficient to cover all storage costs. Arbitrage opportunities would exist for commercial grain merchants if the carrying charge between futures contracts exceeded the storage costs; hence, storage costs typically represent the maximum price difference between delivery months that will be observed in an efficient market. However, there is no corresponding limit to the size of an inversion in the market.

When positive carry markets have price differences between the contracts that are insufficient to cover full costs of storage, this can be explained by the **theory of normal backwardation**. This theory says that hedgers must compensate speculators for assuming the price risk associated with holding futures contracts. However, the fact that storage occurs when negative carrying charge markets exist (such as the previous oats example) continues to be a controversial economic phenomenon with alternative explanations. One possible explanation (not mentioned here) is that when current inventories are abnormally low, merchants are willing to hold inventories in the presence of an inverted market because the stocks provide a type of **convenience yield**. Convenience yield can be best explained with an analogy. Consider a person who walks around with large sums of cash in his pocket. This may seem irrational to some observers because the individual is not earning interest on that money in his pocket, and if he were rational, he would keep the money in the bank rather than in his pocket. However, the cash on hand may provide a *convenience yield* to the individual because it saves him the inconvenience of running back and forth to the bank. He may also encounter a situation where he needs a large sum of cash, and forgoing the interest paid by the bank may be worthwhile. Cash in the pocketbook yields a flow of services not obtainable from money sitting in a bank account; hence, there is a **liquidity premium** for holding money.

THEORIES OF INTERTEMPORAL PRICES: STORABLE COMMODITIES

Over the years, economists have strived to explain intertemporal price spreads in commodity markets. Some very famous economists have worked on this question. John Maynard Keynes is credited with the **theory of normal backwardation**, which

---

BOX 3.1

Thin markets.

A thin market is synonymous with an inactive or illiquid market—a market where the volume of trading is small. In a thin market, there are relatively few transactions per unit of time, and price fluctuations are high relative to the volume of trade. Since a small number of transactions establishes prices, this often results in large price swings. In financial markets, liquidity may be measured by the bid–ask spread, with a larger spread indicating market *thinness*. Actual market prices in a thin market may be biased indicators of the true supply and demand situation. Thin markets create liquidity risk—the inability to buy or sell an asset quickly with little or no price change from a previous transaction, assuming that no new information has come into the market. For example, the international rice market is often characterized as being a thin market because only a small portion (about 3%) of the total annual global production of rice is traded on the world market. In contrast, about 20% of the world's wheat supply is traded in any given year, and this market is considered to be liquid.

---

emphasizes the financial burden posed by the necessity of carrying inventories, and he suggested that futures markets exist to facilitate hedging. On the other hand, Holbrook Working promoted the idea that the primary function of futures markets is the provision of returns for storage services. The two theories of Working and Keynes are considered the most important contributions to the theoretical understanding of intertemporal price spreads in commodity futures markets.

In the view of Keynes, futures prices are unreliable estimates of the cash price prevailing on the date of expiration of the futures contract. He believed it "normal" for the futures price to be a downward-biased estimate of the forthcoming spot price. This theory, in effect, argues that speculators sell "insurance" to hedgers and that the market is "normally" inefficient because the futures price is a biased estimate of the subsequent spot price.

The three critical assumptions of the theory of normal backwardation are that speculators are net long, that they are risk averse (i.e., they require positive expected profits to hold futures positions), and that they are unable to forecast prices (i.e., all their profits can be viewed as a reward for risk bearing). Given these assumptions, two major implications are associated with the theory. The first is that over time speculators can earn profits merely by holding long positions in futures markets. The second implication is that there is an upward trend in futures prices, relative to spot prices, as the contract approaches maturity.

A graphical presentation of the theory of normal backwardation is presented in Figure 3.4. On the horizontal axis is the number of days until the first day of delivery for a specific futures contract (moving from left to right). Both the futures contract price and the cash price converge to $3.00 on the delivery day in this

FIGURE 3.4
Backwardation and risk
premium in a futures
contract price.

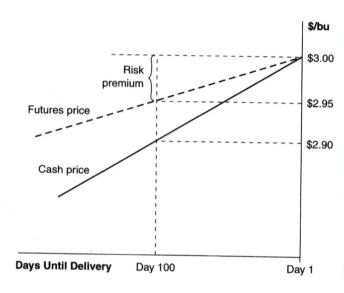

example. Assume that full carrying costs are 10¢ per bushel for storing the commodity 100 days until delivery. This would imply a cash price of $2.90, 100 days
out from delivery. If hedgers initially sell futures contracts to speculators, it is implied that speculators must later sell these contracts to offset their original long position. For speculators to profit from this transaction, the expectation must be that
futures contract prices will increase because they are holding long positions. For
speculators to earn this compensation consistently with rising futures prices, a **risk
premium** must exist. The *risk premium* would result in a reduction in the initial
prices that speculators pay to purchase a futures contract from hedgers. For example, assuming the risk premium is 5¢ on day 100, the actual futures contract price
would be only $2.95 rather than $3.00. The expected cash price on delivery is $3.00,
but the futures price trades for only $2.95 (100 days prior to delivery) because if
speculators paid $3.00, their expected profit would be zero.

Several economists have tested the validity of the theory of normal backwardation. One example is the work of Hartzmark (1987), who analyzed actual profit
and loss data and found little empirical support for the theory of normal backwardation. His study showed that large commercial agricultural firms (hedgers)
earn substantial profits from futures trading in some markets, which suggests that
they do not pay a risk premium to speculators. However, he did find that some individual speculators do earn profits on a regular basis. This is an interesting and
valuable research paper, largely because it used actual trading histories of individual futures traders. In a follow-up study, Hartzmark (1991) attempted to answer the question as to why certain futures traders earn positive profits and others
sustain losses. Hartzmark found that it is inherent luck that largely determines
trader performance. This result seems less plausible than his 1987 finding.

Fama and French (1987) studied monthly returns for 21 commodities and
found weak statistical evidence of an average risk premium. Kolb (1992) used a
similar methodology to study daily returns for 29 commodities, and he found that

most commodities do not exhibit a risk premium. Bessembinder (1992), on the other hand, finds some evidence of risk premia in live cattle, soybeans, and cotton, yet the risk premium in agricultural futures is far less than in financial futures returns, such as Treasury bills. Economic research results are therefore mixed about whether there is a risk premium and whether there is normal backwardation. If a risk premium does exist, it is most likely very small in most futures markets.

Theory of the Price of Storage

An important theoretical extension of the theory of normal backwardation was presented by Working (1949). His theory was critical of the view that futures markets existed solely for the purposes of transferring risk from the hedger to the speculator. Additionally, he criticized the view that the cash and futures markets are autonomous. Working's **theory of the price of storage** hypothesized that intertemporal price relationships are determined by the net cost of carrying stocks.

It should be noted that the theory of price of storage and the theory of normal backwardation are not mutually exclusive, as the former adopted Keynes's notion of a risk premium as one component of the cost of holding stocks. However, the relative importance of the risk premium is greatly reduced by the theory of price of storage.

The theory of storage refers to the demand and supply of commodities as inventories. The term *storage* does not refer to the amount of available storage capacity or the price charged for such storage. Rather, *storage* refers to the level of inventories.

According to the theory of the price of storage, the equilibrium relationship between the futures price and the spot price is as follows:

$$F_{t,T} = S_t (1 + r_{t,T}) + w_{t,T} + c_{t,T}, \qquad (3.1)$$

where $F_{t,T}$ is the futures price at time t for delivery at a future time T, S_t is the spot price at time t, $r_{t,T}$ is the opportunity cost of tying up funds in inventory from time t through time T (i.e., the financing cost), $w_{t,T}$ is the total cost of carrying the inventory (i.e., warehouse costs, insurance, spoilage, and so on), and $c_{t,T}$ is the convenience yield over the time interval t through T. If the equality in Equation 3.1 is not satisfied (i.e., if $F_{t,T} > S_t (1 + r_{t,T}) + w_{t,T} + c_{t,T}$), then an arbitrage opportunity exists for merchants who are in a position to buy and hold inventory.

If a situation arises where $F_{t,T} < S_t (1 + r_{t,T}) + w_{t,T}$, then the theory suggests that the futures price contains an implicit convenience yield ($c_{t,T}$). Rewriting Equation 3.1 provides a definition of convenience yield:

$$c_{t,T} = S_t (1 + r_{t,T}) + w_{t,T} - F_{t,T}. \qquad (3.2)$$

A convenience yield is a negative cost, hence the term *yield*, which implies a return to the owner of inventory derived from the flow of services yielded by a unit of inventory over a given time period. Working's theory predicts that the marginal convenience yield is decreasing in aggregate inventory and approaches zero for high inventory levels.

Fama and French (1987) found that marginal convenience yield varies seasonally for most agricultural commodities but not for metals. Brennan (1991) studied precious metals, oil, lumber, and plywood futures and provided evidence that the convenience yield is inversely related to the level of inventories.

Fama and French (1987) argued that

> there are two popular views of commodity futures prices. The theory of storage ... explains the difference between contemporaneous spot and futures prices in terms of forgone interest in storing a commodity, warehousing costs, and a convenience yield in inventory. The alternative view splits a futures price into an expected risk premium and a forecast of a future spot price. The theory of storage is not controversial (p. 55).

However, Fama and French failed to anticipate the controversy surrounding convenience yield. Without reference to convenience yield, Khoury and Martel (1989) developed a model that offers an explanation as to why inventories would be held with negative expected spot price changes. Wright and Williams (1989) point out that studies that have found evidence of convenience yield have always used aggregate storage data and correlated these data with intertemporal prices measured at a terminal market. They argue that any apparent convenience yield could be illusionary and could be due to spatial aggregation of stocks and attribution of intertemporal incentives at one locality to all locations. In addition, they suggest that variations over time in the marginal cost of transformation from one subaggregate to another could explain why some researchers have claimed to have found support for the notion of convenience yield. Brennan, Williams, and Wright (1997) extended this line of inquiry and examined convenience yield from the perspective of an individual firm. They develop a mathematical programming model of shipments and storage in the wheat marketing system of Western Australia. Brennan et al. found that if intertemporal price spreads are properly measured (at the local level), then stocks are not held at a monetary loss. This result questions previous empirical work that has supported the convenience yield argument. The results from Brennan et al. were later criticized by Frechette and Fackler (1999). However, Frechette and Fackler focused their analysis on explaining factors that generate backwardation rather than on whether storage under backwardation exists (the main issue addressed by Brennan et al.).

Ng and Pirrong (1994) studied the dynamics of industrial metals prices and found that price behavior in those markets is consistent with the theory of storage. Building on the piece by Fama and French (1987), Ng and Pirrong use the theory of storage to derive fundamental relations between the storage adjusted forward–spot price spread and the variances and correlations of spot and forward prices. Ng and Pirrong conclude that spot-and-forward return dynamics are strongly related to fundamental factors in the market rather than to speculative trading.

The Formal Theory of the Price of Storage

We now turn to a complete and formal model of the theory of price of storage. The purpose of this section is to show that intertemporal price spreads (e.g., the difference between the price of May wheat futures and the January cash price during the month of January) are related to the level of stocks (i.e., inventories) that are carried from one period to the next (e.g., from January to May). This section demonstrates that the intertemporal price spread is a market-determined price of storage that can be positive or negative. Frequently, demanders of a commodity require a continuous quantity supplied throughout the year even though production may be seasonal and occur only once during the year. In this case, the (inverse) demand for a commodity in period t can be written as a function of consumption in period t (Brennan, 1958):

$$P_t = f_t(C_t), \tag{3.3}$$

where $\partial f / \partial C_t = f_t'(C_t) < 0$,
P_t = price in period t,
C_t = consumption in period t.

The total stocks available in period t equal beginning stocks (S_{t-1}) plus quantity supplied (X_t). Therefore, consumption can be expressed as total stocks available minus ending stocks (S_t) in period t. Equation 3.3 can be rewritten as

$$P_t = f_t(S_{t-1} + X_t - S_t), \tag{3.4}$$

where
S_{t-1} = stocks at end of period $t - 1$, which is equal to beginning stocks for period t;
X_t = production during period t; and
S_t = stocks at end of period t.

To derive the demand for storage between two periods, consider the effect of an increase in ending stocks during period t (S_t) on the price of storage. The price of storage equals the price in period $t + 1$ minus the price in period t, or $P_{t+1} - P_t$. This price spread, $P_{t+1} - P_t$, can be viewed as a nearby futures price (P_{t+1}) minus the current cash price (P_t). Alternatively, $P_{t+1} - P_t$ could represent the price spread between two different futures contracts with different delivery months. For the discussion that follows, think of $P_{t+1} - P_t$ as the spread between the nearby futures price and the cash price. The nearby futures price is viewed as the expected cash price in the next period, $t + 1$.

Assume that S_{t-1}, production levels (X_t and X_{t+1}), and S_{t+1} are given so that only S_t is allowed to change. In that case, the expression for the price of storage is

$$P_{t+1} - P_t = f_{t+1}(S_t + X_{t+1} - S_{t+1}) \\ - f_t(S_{t-1} + X_t - S_t), \tag{3.5}$$

where $S_t + X_{t+1} - S_{t+1} = C_{t+1}$ and $S_{t-1} + X_t - S_t = C_t$.

Differentiating Equation 3.5 with respect to S_t gives

$$\frac{\partial(P_{t+1} - P_t)}{\partial S_t} = \frac{\partial f_{t+1}}{\partial C_{t+1}} \frac{\partial C_{t+1}}{\partial S_t}$$

$$-\frac{\partial f_t}{\partial C_t} \frac{\partial C_t}{\partial S_t} < 0. \tag{3.6}$$

The entire partial derivative in Equation 3.6 is negative because $\partial f_{t+1}/\partial C_{t+1} < 0$, $\partial C_{t+1}/\partial S_t > 0$, $\partial f_t/\partial C_t < 0$, and $\partial C_t/\partial S_t < 0$. This means that the first expression ($\partial f_{t+1}/\partial C_{t+1} \times \partial C_{t+1}/\partial S_t$) on the right-hand side of Equation 3.6 is negative. The second expression ($\partial f_t/\partial C_t \times \partial C_t/\partial S_t$) is positive but is subtracted from the first expression, so the derivative expressed in Equation 3.6 is negative.

If we examine the first expression on the right-hand side of Equation 3.6, we know that an increase in S_t, by definition, implies an increase in consumption in period C_{t+1}, so $\partial C_{t+1}/\partial S_t$ is positive. This follows because S_t becomes the beginning inventory in period $t + 1$, and S_{t+1} and X_{t+1} are assumed to be constant in Equation 3.6, so consumption (C_{t+1}) must increase in period $t + 1$. There will be an increase in consumption (C_{t+1}) in period $t + 1$ if and only if there is a lower price in period $t + 1$, so $\partial f_{t+1}/\partial C_{t+1} < 0$, based on the **law of demand** (see Equation 3.3).

Turning to the second expression on the right-hand side of Equation 3.6, $\partial f_t/\partial C_t < 0$, based on the law of demand (see Equation 3.3); $\partial C_t/\partial S_t$ is also < 0 because an increase in S_t, by definition, implies declining consumption in period t (C_t), given that incoming stocks (S_{t-1}) and production (X_t) are assumed to be constant in Equation 3.6.

Based on Equation 3.6, the **demand for storage** can be drawn as a downward-sloping curve, as in Figure 3.5. We see from Figure 3.5 that the expected price in the next period (P_{t+1}) minus the price in the current period (P_t) may be expressed as a decreasing function of stocks carried out of the current period.

FIGURE 3.5
The demand for storage.

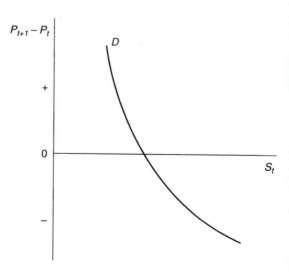

There is an intuitive explanation for the downward-sloping demand curve in Figure 3.5. Suppose that firms decide to carry a smaller level of stocks out of period t and into period $t + 1$. This implies that more of the commodity is offered for sale in period t and less in period $t + 1$. As a result, P_t falls, and P_{t+1} rises. A decrease in stocks carried out of period t decreases the price in t relative to the price in period $t + 1$.

The **supply of storage** arises from firms that carry stocks from period t to $t + 1$. The supply of storage refers to the supply of commodities as inventories, not to the supply of storage space. In a competitive market, firms will hold stocks (i.e., they will "supply" storage) from one period to the next if the net marginal cost of storage equals the expected change in price. Equilibrium requires that the net marginal cost of storage (positive or negative) must equal the price of storage. The total **net cost of storage** was specified by Brennan as a function of three components: physical costs of storage (o_t), risk aversion factor (r_t), and convenience yield (c_t). The term **net cost** refers to the fact that convenience yield is subtracted from the two other components. The total net cost of storage (m_t) can then be written as

$$m_t(S_t) = o_t(S_t) + r_t(S_t) - c_t(S_t),$$ (3.7)

where it is assumed when differentiating with respect to S_t, that
$o_t' > 0$ and $o_t'' \geq 0$ (physical costs)
$r_t' > 0$ and $r_t'' \geq 0$ (risk aversion factor)
$c_t' \geq 0$ and $c_t'' \leq 0$ (convenience yield).

Since supply curves are marginal cost curves above the minimum of average variable costs, differentiating the total net cost of storage gives the supply of storage. This means that net marginal cost (m_t') equals the marginal outlay on physical storage (o_t') plus the marginal risk aversion factor (r_t') minus the marginal convenience yield on stocks (o_t'). Therefore, the net marginal cost of storage in period t is

$$m_t'(S_t) = o_t'(S_t) + r_t'(S_t) - c_t'(S_t).$$ (3.8)

Graphically, Equation 3.8 can be represented by Figure 3.6d. The three components of the equations are illustrated in Figure 3.6a through 3.6c. The effects of each component are explained as follows.

Physical costs of storage include interest expense, insurance, handling, and other direct costs associated with storing a product. These costs are assumed to increase at a constant rate except at high levels of inventory. When inventory is high, physical costs of storage rise at an increasing rate because of capacity limitations. The marginal outlay on physical storage (o_t') is presented in Figure 3.6a.

The marginal risk aversion factor (r_t') is positively related to stocks. The greater the level of stocks, the greater will be the loss to the firm from an unexpected price fall (Fig. 3.6b).

Marginal convenience yield (c_t') is inversely related to the level of stocks. At low levels of inventories, merchandisers and processors potentially could experience **stockouts**. Stockouts may cause orders not to be filled or plants not to run at

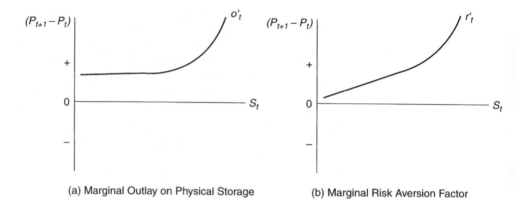

(a) Marginal Outlay on Physical Storage   (b) Marginal Risk Aversion Factor

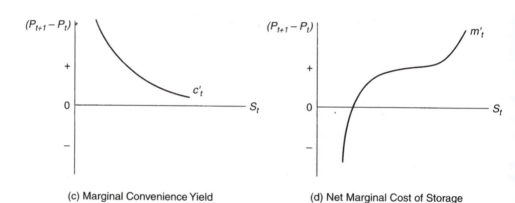

(c) Marginal Convenience Yield   (d) Net Marginal Cost of Storage

FIGURE 3.6
Components of net marginal cost of storage and the supply of storage:
(a) marginal outlay on physical storage,
(b) marginal risk aversion factor,
(c) marginal convenience yield, and
(d) net marginal cost of storage.

full capacity. In addition, costs of obtaining the inventory later may be sufficiently high, which justifies carrying the inventory. Therefore, convenience yield becomes high with low stock levels because pipeline stocks are necessary.

The beer industry provides an excellent example of where pipeline stocks are crucial and where convenience yield comes into play. Breweries in the United States (and around the world) produce a differentiated consumer product: a malt beverage that has a distinct taste. For example, Anheuser Busch spends hundreds of millions of dollars each year advertising its distinct product—Budweiser, the "King of Beers." Budweiser tastes different than Coors, according to the ads. Anheuser Busch has a very large share of the U.S. beer market, and Budweiser's position in the market is highly dependent on the uniform quality of the barley that is used to produce Budweiser. Anheuser Busch is susceptible to any problems with

---

BOX 3.2

Wine futures.
There is a large and growing global market for quality wine, and price volatility is relatively high in this market. As a result, there is both speculator and hedger interest in the wine market. Euronext, a European exchange (*http://www.euronext.com*), introduced trading in wine futures in 2001 to provide retailers and wine merchants a means of hedging wine price risk. The contract is based on new red wines from leading Bordeaux vineyards in France. The futures contract is based on a case of 12 identical bottles delivered 29 months after the contract opens. Euronext plans to offer contracts on wines from other French regions, Australia, South America, California, and southern Europe.

---

the barley harvest because in the United States barley is harvested but once a year, in the fall season.

Beer has a rather short shelf life, and it is produced throughout the year, so the consumer can purchase a freshly brewed product at any time. If Anheuser Busch were to run out of good-quality barley, it could not produce Budweiser with its distinct taste. This would be a disaster for the company. The quality of the barley crop varies from year to year because of weather conditions, and if there was a crop failure, this could jeopardize the supply of Budweiser. As a result, Anheuser Busch carries a very large inventory of barley, and the company places a high convenience yield on its barley inventories.

Firms benefit from convenience yield; therefore, this component is a negative cost and is subtracted in Equations 3.7 and 3.8. At low levels of inventory, further reductions in inventory levels raise convenience yields from holding inventory. Therefore, the marginal convenience yield is a decreasing function of the inventory level (Fig. 3.6c).

SUPPLY OF STORAGE

The supply of storage, which is equal to the net marginal cost of storage, is presented in Figure 3.6d, with the difference between the two price periods on the vertical axis and the horizontal axis representing the inventory level. Unlike a standard supply curve, storage is provided even with a negative price. A negative price for storage would occur when the futures price is less than the current cash price (i.e., an inverted market).

As inventory levels increase, convenience yield declines, and the supply curve for storage flattens and approaches the full cost of storage (see Fig. 3.6d). For large inventories, the cost of carry will increase significantly. These increased costs for a merchandiser can result from inadequate facilities that, in turn, cause higher levels of product deterioration. In addition, expensive additional facilities may have to be built to store the inventory. In such a situation, the price of storage must provide an incentive to merchants to carry the commodity.

IMPLICATIONS OF THE THEORY

According to the theory of the price of storage, the set of intertemporal prices established on the futures market provides a direct indication of the expected return from storage and provides a means of ensuring receipt of storage returns. It is evident that storage is supplied even when the price of storage is zero or negative because of the importance of convenience yield. The convenience yield offsets any loss associated with the sum of physical and risk costs.

In Figure 3.7, the demand and supply of storage are combined in order to demonstrate equilibrium conditions. With the aid of Figure 3.7, comparative static equilibrium points can be traced out. First, it can be assumed that the supply of storage is relatively stable. It is largely the demand for storage that shifts back and forth with changing market conditions. However, such factors as changing interest rates will shift the supply curve. The shifting demand gives rise to variations in the price of storage.

Consider a leftward shift of D in Figure 3.7. This would lower the price of storage. A leftward shift in D could occur due to the following reasons:

- Production decreases in period t.
- Expected production in period $t + 1$ increases.
- Expected carryout of stocks in period $t + 1$ decreases.

FIGURE 3.7
Supply of and demand for storage.

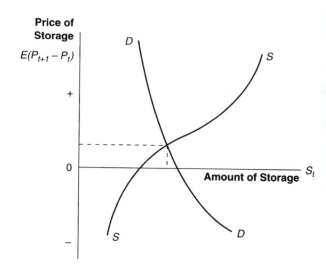

Alternatively, consider what happens when D shifts to the right. In this case, the price of storage increases. A rightward shift could arise for the following reasons:

- Production increases in period t.
- Expected production in period $t + 1$ decreases.
- Expected carryout of stocks in period $t + 1$ increases.

In Figure 3.7, the dashed lines show a storage demand and supply equilibrium above the 0 horizontal line. This equilibrium represents a carrying charge market (or contango), where $P_{t+1} > P_t$. Alternatively, if the demand curve shifted leftward so that the supply and demand equilibrium was below the 0 horizontal line, then intertemporal prices would be inverted (i.e., $P_{t+1} < P_t$).

Suppose that in the month of April the price of September wheat is trading at $0.15 below the price of May wheat futures. We know from the price differential that this is an inverted market, but what accounts for the price differential? According to the theory of storage, the amount by which the price of September wheat is discounted relative to the price of May wheat *does not* depend on the expected size of the wheat crop to be harvested between May and September. Rather, the expected size of the harvest (which occurs between May and September) will affect the price of the May futures contract by approximately the same amount as it will affect the price of the September futures price. The correct explanation of the inverted market is that the price of May wheat (in April) is above the price of September wheat because the previous crop was small. It is important to note that supplies *already in existence* have an impact on the current intertemporal set of prices.

In summary, prices of storable commodities are linked over time through storage costs, and futures markets play an important role in guiding inventory levels and forward pricing. In addition, cash and futures prices are strongly related through time for storable commodities due to arbitrage.

INTERTEMPORAL PRICES OF NONSTORABLE COMMODITIES

The prices of "nonstorable" commodities are not strongly linked over time through storage costs since, by definition, inventories cannot be carried from one period to the next, because the commodity will deteriorate or spoil. Futures prices for these nonstorable commodities basically reflect market participants' current expectations with regard to supply and demand conditions likely to exist at the time of contract maturity. As a result, for *perfectly* nonstorable commodities, no strong relationship is expected to exist between current cash and distant futures prices or between prices of futures contracts with different maturity dates (Naik and Leuthold 1988).

Intertemporal price patterns for nonstorable commodities (such as electricity, live cattle, feeder cattle, and lean hogs) do not adhere to the theory of price of storage. Because of the laws of physics (for electricity) and biology (for livestock), these commodities are "perishable" and therefore cannot be held in inventory from one futures maturity month to another. For example, once cattle or hogs reach their optimum weight, they are ready for market and must be slaughtered. Once electricity is generated, it must be used, or it soon dissipates traveling back and forth over the transmission lines. This means that in the short run, the supply of nonstorable commodities is **price inelastic** and can be represented as a vertical line.

The production period is continuous for most nonstorable commodities (that are traded on futures markets), and supply and demand expectations drive traders' price expectations. The cash price for nonstorables reflects current supply and demand conditions. Alternatively, the various futures prices reflect anticipated supply and demand conditions that will prevail during the maturity month. For instance, the U.S. Department of Agriculture's National Agricultural Statistics Service releases quarterly reports on the hog market. It is not unusual for this government report to signal that the short-term price trend is down while the long-term trend is up and vice versa. This means that the April lean hog contract is almost like a different commodity than the July lean hog contract.

Given that different information sets affect cash versus futures prices, the cash and futures prices are not necessarily highly correlated as for storable commodities. Furthermore, intertemporal prices for nonstorable futures markets are as likely to be inverted as in contango. Price spreads may be in contango for some futures months and, at the same time, inverted for other months. For instance, the April–June spread in lean hogs could be in contango at 10¢ per pound, with June above April. At the same time, the June–August spread could be inverted by 5¢ per pound, while the August–December spread is in contango at 12¢ per pound.

However, cash and futures prices for nonstorables do converge as the maturity date approaches. The possibility of delivery during the maturity month forces price convergence through arbitrage, as does cash settlement for some contracts.

THE BASIS

The principal measure for linking cash and futures prices for storable commodities is the **basis**. For most of this book, the basis is calculated as the futures price minus the cash price, following the lead of Peck (1975). However, it is also common (especially in the industry) to define the basis as the cash price minus the futures price. In domestic and international grain markets, traders have made the cash-minus-futures method the norm. The effect of using one definition over the other is simply to reverse the sign of the difference between the two prices. Both methods appear in the futures literature, and it makes no appreciable difference whether the basis is defined as futures minus cash or vice versa. See Gillis (1986) for a discussion of the definition of basis.

Commodity price quotes in local markets are frequently made in terms of the basis. For example, the cash price for corn in Iowa might be quoted as 30¢ under the nearby CBOT corn futures price. The basis is an indicator of a broad range of factors affecting cash and futures markets. These factors include the following (Kahl and Curtis 1986):

a. Cost of transportation
b. Supply and demand conditions in the cash market relative to delivery points for the futures market
c. Quality differences between the cash commodity and the product specified in the futures contract
d. Quantity of stocks and storage space in the cash market

These factors can create numerous basis patterns over time, as illustrated in Figure 3.8. The left-hand side of the figure shows examples of a narrowing of the basis, where the cash and futures prices come together over time. Five possibilities (N-1 through N-5) of how the basis may narrow are shown on the left-hand side of the figure. N-3 and N-4 are the most common scenarios, where both the cash and the futures prices are moving in the same direction, but they are coming closer together, hence the basis is narrowing.

The right-hand side of Figure 3.8 graphically shows five ways that the basis can widen (W-1 through W-5). W-3 and W-4 are the most likely because the cash and futures prices are moving either down together (W-3) or up together (W-4). In both W-3 and W-4, the cash and futures move in the same direction, but they are diverging from each other, and therefore the basis is widening. The importance of either a widening or a narrowing of the basis becomes clear later in this book when we discuss hedging (Chapter 7).

The basis can be used to estimate spatial price relationships. For example, consider the following case where a Chicago Board of Trade September futures contract for corn is trading at $3.00 per bushel (Table 3.3). Market I is a cattle-producing region that imports corn from other regions, and it has a corn cash price of $3.40 per bushel. Market E is a corn-exporting region, which has a cash price of $2.80 per bushel. Recall that we can define the basis as being equal to the cash price minus the specified futures contract price. Defined as cash minus futures, the basis for market I equals +40¢, while the basis is −20¢ for market E. The positive basis for market I can be stated as "40¢ over" because the cash price is "over" the futures contract price. Similarly, the basis for market E can be described as being "20¢ under" for the opposite reason.

The difference between the two cash market prices (I and E) is equal to 60¢ per bushel, which is equal to the difference between the two bases. It may seem unnecessary to calculate the basis when absolute price levels can be reported instead. But commodity merchants and traders are interested in price relationships *among or between* markets. A common reference point for different cash markets is provided with the basis relative to the futures price. Table 3.3 can be used to make several preliminary conclusions based on simple spatial economics.

First, we know that corn will not be shipped from market I to market E because market I is a relatively high-priced market and market E a relatively low-priced market. Second, market E is a potential supplier of corn to market I if transfer costs of moving corn from E to I are less than 60¢ per bushel.

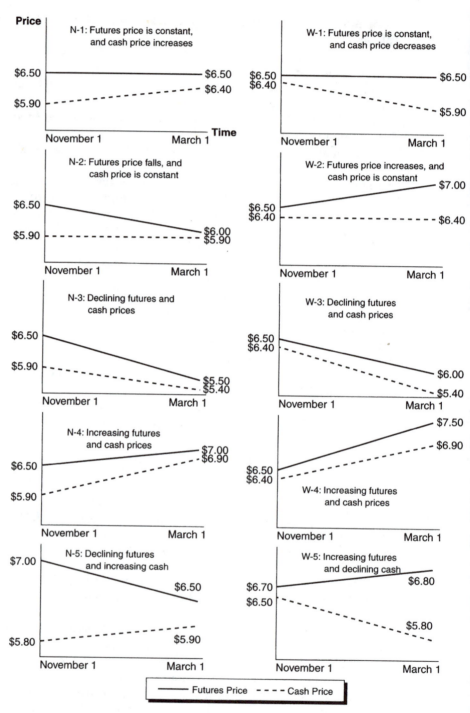

FIGURE 3.8
Scenarios of how the basis may change over time.

TABLE 3.3   Basis and Spatial Price Difference Markets

DESCRIPTION OF MARKET	DOLLARS PER BUSHEL
Market I cash price for corn	3.40
Market E cash price for corn	2.80
Difference in cash market prices	0.60
Chicago Board of Trade September futures contract price for corn	3.00
Basis for market I (cash minus futures)	0.40
Basis for market E (cash minus futures)	− 0.20
Difference in basis between cash markets	0.60

Basis quotes are typically used in commodity trading rather than price quotes because market participants can more readily predict how the basis will change over time, compared to trying to predict absolute price levels. In other words, changes in the basis are somewhat systematic. However, confidence in basis predictions depends on the type of cash market. For instance, the basis in the corn market is more stable than the basis in the natural gas market. It is also the case that the basis for nonstorable commodities (such as lean hogs) is much more difficult to predict than for storable commodities (such as corn).

Cash markets can be categorized by their relationship to futures market delivery points. Some cash markets are viewed as terminal markets if they are high volume liquid markets and/or designated as either primary or alternate delivery points for futures contracts. For instance, Toledo and Omaha are considered terminal markets for corn.

Most commodity futures contracts enable a seller to make actual delivery of the commodity anytime during the delivery month, although delivery still accounts for a relatively small share of open interest in most futures markets. Corn is such a commodity where delivery is possible and is not uncommon. During the delivery month, the actual delivery of corn will occur at one of the locations specified by the Chicago Board of Trade's contract specifications. The seller of the futures contract decides whether delivery will be made, and if there is delivery, then the price received by the seller is that which the seller previously agreed to when the futures contract was sold.

Most traders have definite expectations concerning the behavior of the basis at a futures contract delivery point because the cash price and the futures price will converge during the delivery month (even for nonstorables). The reason for the convergence is the existence of arbitrage between futures and cash markets. Arbitragers will monitor the price relationships between the futures and cash markets to determine whether profitable transactions are possible. Producers, processors, merchandisers, and speculators will assume the arbitrage role.

Consider the case where an arbitrager is evaluating profit opportunities in a cash market, which is also a delivery point for a futures contract. Such an arbitrager has two basic strategies available. One alternative is to buy a futures contract and sell forward the cash commodity at the delivery point. The arbitrager accepts

---

BOX 3.3

Electricity futures.

Electricity futures are traded on the New York Mercantile Exchange (NYMEX) in New York. The NYMEX offers trading in more than one electricity contract because the U.S. spot electricity market is physically broken into regions because of the complicated logistics of transmission over existing power lines. For instance, NYMEX has one contract that is based on delivery at the California/Oregon border.

Electricity is a commodity that flows across power lines, much the same as oil or natural gas flows through pipelines. However, unlike gas and oil, electricity cannot be stored, and therefore electricity flows in a continuous circuit, sometimes flowing backward and forward until consumed.

Within a regional electricity transmission grid (e.g., the western grid), arbitrage is effective in this market. For example, if Los Angeles experiences a surge in demand due to a heat wave, the Department of Power and Water can import electricity from the Pacific Northwest (Washington and Oregon), a region that has less demand for electricity in the summer. By the same token, in the winter, California can sell excess power to the Pacific Northwest. Electricity can be in short supply in some regions, and at the same time there may be a surplus in other regions.

Electricity is an important input cost for many industries, and this gives rise to hedging demand from manufacturing firms. At the same time, suppliers of electricity are exposed to significant price risk, and they also have a reason to hedge. The interest in electricity futures has risen because there have been some huge jumps in electricity prices with deregulation of the markets across the United States. An extreme incident occurred in California in December 2000, when the wholesale price of electricity surged to $1,400 per megawatt hour (a megawatt will supply about 1,000 homes), up from $30 a year earlier (a 4,500% increase).

---

delivery of the commodity specified in the futures contract and then, in turn, uses the delivered commodity to make delivery on the forward cash transaction. The second alternative is to sell a futures contract, simultaneously buy the cash commodity, and then deliver on the futures contract.

The exact strategy that is selected by the arbitrager will be determined by the futures contract price relative to the cash market price. The futures price is either the price received by the arbitrager if she delivers (F_r) or the price paid if she takes delivery (F_p). In addition, the cash market price is either the price paid when buying the commodity (C_p) or the cash market price received when selling (C_r). If the net futures delivery price is higher than the cash price, $F_r > C_p$, then the arbitrager buys the commodity in the cash market and delivers (sells) the commodity to the futures contract buyer. The arbitrager is buying "low" in the cash market and sell-

Potato futures.

Potatoes are one commodity for which futures trading has been unsuccessful, and the reasons for the failure of potato futures are not entirely obvious. Potatoes are a nonstorable and highly perishable commodity, which may be one reason why the contract has been unsuccessful despite numerous attempts over the years to trade a successful contract. In May 1976, there was serious debacle with potato futures due to a "squeeze" on holders of short positions in potato futures. Most "shorts" were unable to satisfy delivery requirements. Holders of short futures positions were unable to either find potatoes or procure transportation services to ship potatoes to New York, where the futures contract called for delivery. Cash market potato prices fluctuated wildly, and futures traders holding short futures positions could not meet their delivery obligations. The resulting default brought an end to potato futures trading.

---

ing "high" in the futures market. If the futures price received on delivery is lower than the cash price received through a forward sale, $F_p < C_r$, then the arbitrager buys a futures contract and accepts delivery. After taking delivery, the arbitrager redelivers on the forward cash sale.

The futures contract price and cash prices are forced to converge through this type of arbitrage process. If the futures contract price is too high relative to the cash price, arbitragers will sell futures contracts and buy cash. As arbitragers sell futures contracts, the futures contract price will fall, while increased buying in the cash market causes cash prices to rise. Decreasing futures contract prices and increasing cash prices cause the profit opportunity to disappear as the two prices converge. As explained in the next section, full convergence is not required to halt arbitrage trading. As soon as the two prices differ by an amount less than total transactions costs (brokerage fees, storage costs, transport costs, and so on), no arbitrage profit opportunity exists.

Basis convergence is affected by two factors: whether a cash market is a "par" delivery point and the delivery costs. A **par** delivery point is a cash market where no deductions (premiums) are taken from (added to) the futures contract price on settlement for either grade or location reasons. A nonpar delivery point would involve an adjustment to the futures price for a location differential. If the grade that is delivered is nonpar, then a grade differential is also made to the price. If the delivery point has a **premium**, the buyer must pay the futures contract price plus the premium. If there is a **discount** for either location or grade, the discount is subtracted from the price received by the seller.

For example, the CBOT soybean futures contract specifies premiums and discounts according to the grade that is actually delivered and the delivery location. No. 2 yellow soybeans is delivered at par value, No. 1 yellow at 6¢ per bushel over

FIGURE 3.9
Basis convergence when grade and location are at par.

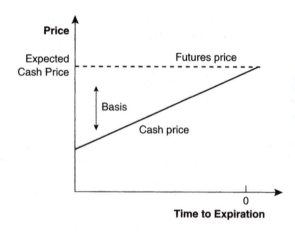

contract price, and No. 3 yellow at 6¢ per bushel under contract price. In addition, delivery in Chicago is at par, whereas delivery in St. Louis, Missouri, is at a premium of 6¢ per bushel over the contract price, subject to the grade differential. Delivery in St. Louis is at a premium because St. Louis is on the Mississippi River and therefore closer to overseas markets than Chicago. Most U.S. soybeans are exported via the Mississippi and the Gulf ports.

The convergence of cash and futures prices is illustrated in Figure 3.9, assuming there is no location or grade discount. Time is measured on the horizontal axis, and the commodity price is represented on the vertical axis. The delivery market is assumed to be a par delivery point. Therefore, the arbitrage process will ensure that the basis will converge to zero.

As previously discussed, additional assumptions are necessary regarding the behavior of the futures and cash prices. In Figure 3.9, the futures contract price is assumed to be an unbiased forecast of the forthcoming cash price. If there is no new supply and demand information entering the market, then price expectations are unchanged, and the futures contract price is constant, as represented by the horizontal dotted line in the figure. The cash corn price is assumed to increase steadily over time to compensate economic agents storing the commodity. However, as new supply and demand information comes into the market, the (horizontal) expected cash price (i.e., the futures price) will move up and down, as will the (upward sloping) trajectory of the cash price. In all cases, the two prices will converge during the delivery month.

For a par futures delivery point, the expected cash price pattern is straightforward. All other cash markets are related through a price grid, which reflects surplus and deficit regions. If a competitive situation exists, local cash market prices are expected to equal the futures delivery point cash price plus or minus transfer costs. Figure 3.10 represents a situation where there is a cash price discount relative to the futures contract price at the time of delivery. This discount could be due to either a grade or a location differential. In this case, the cash and futures prices will still converge over time as storage costs decline. However, the basis will not converge to zero because of the expected discount for grade or location.

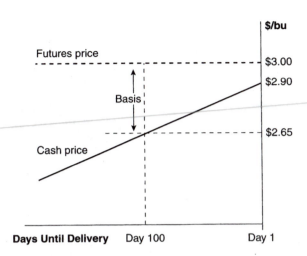

FIGURE 3.10
Basis convergence when grade or location are nonpar.

Of course, there are cash markets that are not directly linked through commodity arbitrage with the market specified as the futures delivery point. In this case, the price transmission from one market to the other is more indirect, and expectations concerning the basis are more unpredictable. This is true of most foreign cash markets in terms of Chicago or New York futures markets. If a wheat grower in Australia is trying to hedge on the Chicago market or a cocoa producer in Africa is trying to hedge on the New York market, then the basis in each case will be volatile. No direct arbitrage occurs to ensure a consistent convergence of cash and futures prices. Marketing the cash commodity and simultaneously using the futures market in such markets is more risky because of the weaker linkage between the cash and futures market, not to mention the exchange rate risk.

Consider two extreme examples of basis behavior. In the first case, consider a corn basis for central Illinois, a market that can deliver corn against the Chicago Board of Trade corn contract with minimal transactions costs. The Illinois corn basis is shown in Figure 3.11 for the September 1999 to January 2001 time period. The futures price in Figure 3.11 is the monthly average of the January 2001 Chicago Board of Trade (No. 2 yellow) corn contract, and the cash price is the monthly average price quote in central Illinois for No. 2 yellow corn. The basis in Figure 3.11 follows a traditional pattern of narrowing as the delivery date approaches.

Over the 17-month period in Figure 3.11, the corn basis fell from about 70¢ per bushel to approximately 14¢ per bushel. The basis in the early part of the time period was large because 17 months of storage is costly, and monthly storage costs are reflected in the basis. The decline in the basis resulted from lower and lower storage costs as the futures maturity approached. At maturity, there was not complete convergence of the cash and futures corn prices, presumably because of transactions costs associated with delivery on the futures contract.

To illustrate the other extreme, where the basis follows a nontraditional pattern and is unpredictable, refer to Figure 3.12. In this example, the monthly average crude oil basis is calculated for the Dubai (United Arab Emirates) cash price

FIGURE 3.11
Example of Central Illinois corn basis.
Source: Commodity Research Bureau

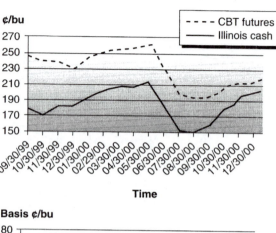

Time

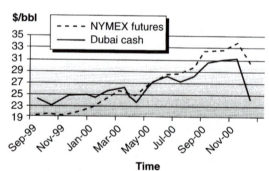

Time

FIGURE 3.12
Example of Dubai crude oil basis.
Source: Commodity Research Bureau

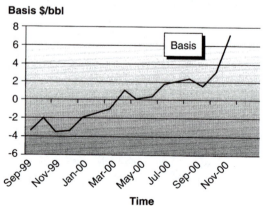

Time

relative to the January 2001 New York Mercantile Exchange crude oil futures contract. As shown in Figure 3.12, the mean basis was approximately zero, but there was a range of over $10.50 per barrel, with the maximum close to $7/bbl and the minimum $3.50/bbl for the September 1999 to January 2001 period.

The contrast between basis levels in Figures 3.11 and 3.12 is striking, and the differences between the corn and crude oil bases highlight the important role of physical market linkages (through transportation) in the convergence process. From day to day, the central Illinois cash corn market is closely linked to the Chicago Board of Trade futures market, whereas the Dubai crude oil cash market is only weakly related to the New York Mercantile Exchange futures market.

BASIS AND INTERNATIONAL TRADE

Basis risks and other complications increase rapidly when transactions cross international borders, especially when foreign currency transactions are involved. Within the United States, commodities can generally move between regions without unnecessary fees or restrictions. For example, corn moves freely from the Midwest to California, and the price differential reflects primarily transfer costs. For most nonperishable commodities, price differences that exist among cash markets in the United States generally reflect supply and demand conditions and transfer costs. The existence of standardized grading systems enhances the spatial pricing efficiency of markets.

Alternatively, price differences among countries may be significantly impacted by border policies that restrict trade. Canada's policy toward wheat is an excellent example of how a government can use policy to isolate domestic producers from changes in international prices. Wheat growers in Canada must market their wheat through a government agency (the Canadian Wheat Board), and all growers receive a common yearly "average" price. As a result, the "basis" is difficult if not impossible to predict for wheat growers in Canada. This means they have little information as to how the value of their crop changes over time. Furthermore, the usefulness of futures or options as means of risk transfer is dramatically reduced for Canadian wheat growers.

International exchange rate fluctuations can also affect price relationships between countries. As a result, international hedging of commodities has been less successful than domestic hedging programs. For example, exchange fluctuations adversely affect the financial returns from hedging Australian cattle sales on U.S. futures exchanges because it reduces the degree of correlation between prices in the two countries. Haigh and Holt (2000) studied both commodity and freight futures contracts for their effectiveness in reducing uncertainty for international traders. They used various economic models to illustrate the importance of hedging volatile price and basis levels in international trade between the United States and Europe. They also illustrate the importance of hedging transportation rates and show the benefits that an international trader realizes through hedging.

> ### BOX 3.5
>
> ### *Domestic versus world sugar market.*
>
> This chapter has emphasized how arbitrage links prices in markets separated by space or time. The sugar market is a counterexample to the *law of one price* because arbitrage is not allowed to work because of U.S. government policy on sugar. The U.S. government restricts imports of sugar from abroad in order to protect a relatively small number of politically powerful and rich U.S. sugar farmers. As a result, the price of domestic sugar in the United States is set at approximately two times world levels. U.S. production has increased in response to the high domestic price, and imports have fallen. Soft drink manufacturers in the United States stopped using sugar a number of years ago and moved toward a sweetener substitute because the U.S. trade restriction makes domestic sugar too expensive. Sugar is a primary example of how government policy can disrupt markets and create economic waste.
>
> The New York Coffee, Sugar and Cocoa Exchange, under the New York Board of Trade, trades both a domestic and a world sugar futures contract. The domestic price is always well above the world price because firms cannot freely import sugar into the United States.

PRICE RELATIONSHIPS ACROSS PRODUCT FORMS

As commodities move through marketing channels, various stages of processing change the commodity's form. Recall that time, space, and product form are the three dimensions associated with marketing. Processing of a raw commodity generally results in a number of products. In a competitive market structure, a processor plays a role that is analogous to that of a market arbitrager. A firm will engage in processing only if its margin from processing equals at least its processing cost. Obviously, a firm will continue processing in the short run as long as its margin is enough to cover variable costs. In the long run, however, the firm will engage in processing only if the margin is enough to cover total costs. The firm's margin is basically the value of processed products obtained from each unit of base commodity minus the base commodity's price.

For any processing technology, the cost of processing and yields of processed products obtained from a unit of base commodity are approximately fixed and predetermined. Given the information on processing yields and product prices, a processor can easily calculate the margin. By comparing this margin with processing costs, a firm can determine whether it is profitable to engage in processing.

Whenever market prices are such that processors' margins exceed processing cost, firms will have a profit opportunity and will try to expand their operation. Their actions, however, will push the price of processed products down and/or the price of the raw commodity up, thereby decreasing processors' margins. This adjustment will continue until a new price relationship is established and the margin is just enough to cover processing costs. On the other hand, if the price relationship is such that processors' margins are less than costs, processing will entail a loss, and firms will not perform the function. This will result in upward pressure on processed product prices and/or downward pressure on the base commodity's price

Processing usually does not stop after the raw commodity has been transformed into one or more products. The products obtained from processing a base commodity are generally intermediate products. These intermediate products are processed further before the final consumer good is produced. The correlation between the price of a raw commodity and the prices of processed products derived from it declines as the degree of processing increases. See the Appendix for a detailed example of the effects that processing has on prices of commodities traded on futures and options markets.

SUMMARY

This chapter has emphasized the economic principle that price patterns among futures contracts for storable commodities (such as corn or natural gas) are affected by inventory supply and demand. The theory of price of storage and the theory of normal backwardation was explained. For storable commodities, intertemporal prices are highly correlated, as they are linked through storage. In contrast, intertemporal prices for nonstorable commodities (such as electricity or lean hogs) are not highly correlated. For nonstorables, each delivery month is somewhat independent from other months.

The concept of the basis was introduced in this chapter, and it was explained that the basis can be defined as the cash price minus the futures price or vice versa. Arbitrage will cause futures and cash prices to converge to essentially zero at futures contract par delivery markets and to converge to transfer costs for other cash markets. The value to which the basis will converge is much more uncertain for some markets than others.

For a commodity to be physically transferred between regional markets, there must be some economic incentive to do so. For instance, the importing region must have a higher price than the exporting market. If the price difference between markets is less than transfer costs, trade is not expected between regions. The lack of physical arbitrage between markets will result in reduced correlation in prices between markets. This is particularly true for international trade, where exchange rates and trade barriers reduce the correlation in prices between countries.

Finally, it was stressed that processing changes the form of a product and therefore affects the price relationship between the raw commodity and products derived from it. In general, the greater the amount of processing, the lower the correlation between prices of related product forms. For instance, the use of natural gas to produce electricity transforms a storable commodity into a nonstorable commodity. Intertemporal futures prices for natural gas are highly correlated, but this is not the case for intertemporal electricity prices.

DISCUSSION QUESTIONS

1. Explain why the inventory supply from one time period to the next is not simply equal to the segment of the supply curve above the equilibrium price in the market in the first time period.

2. Cash markets can be classified into three categories: a cash market designated as a futures contract delivery point, a cash market that can deliver to a futures market delivery point, and a cash market that cannot profitably deliver to the delivery point. Explain and discuss the convergence of basis for each of these cash markets categories.

3. Define and explain how the basis terms *under* and *over* used in grain trading are different from *strengthening* and *weakening*.

4. You have been requested by the secretary of agriculture of a Central American country to determine whether cattle produced in that country could be hedged using the Chicago Mercantile Exchange live cattle contract. What information would you need to collect to determine whether this is feasible? What conditions could exist that would improve the probability of this activity being successful?

5. Assume you are an analyst for an oil company that is hedging using crude oil futures. Your job is to forecast the basis for crude oil at a Midwest refinery. Assume the delivery point for the futures contract is in Texas. Discuss and explain whether the basis would strengthen or weaken in each of the following situations:

   a. The major pipeline supplying your region has an oil spill, and the EPA closes the pipeline for one month.
   b. A major cold front decreases gasoline mileage, and a gasoline shortage develops in your trade area.
   c. OPEC embargoes oil shipments to the United States.
   d. Local storage areas overestimated the demand for crude oil and now have excessive supplies of crude in storage.
   e. A major supplier is able to deliver only a lower-quality crude oil, which greatly increases the costs of processing.

6. You are given the following price information on December 21: Chicago Board of Trade May soybean futures contract price ($8.05), market A cash ($7.58), market B cash ($7.08), and market C cash ($8.75). Calculate the basis for each cash market and discuss the relationships between markets. Assume market A is a delivery market for the soybean contract. In addition, transfer costs are 50¢ between market A and B and 90¢ between Market A and C. Forecast and discuss the basis during the delivery month for each of the cash markets.

7. What is the difference between a "positive" and "negative" carrying charge market? What are the implications of this difference for commercial storage firms at a delivery market?

8. Define *normal backwardation* and explain its expected effects on price relationships and risk premiums.

9. What is the price of storage, and how does convenience yield affect this *price*? How is the inventory level related to the price of storage?

SELECTED REFERENCES

Bessembinder, H. (1992). Systematic risk, hedging pressure, and risk premia in futures markets. *Review of Financial Studies, 5*(4), 637–667.

Brennan, D., Williams, J., & Wright, B. D. (1997). Convenience yield without the convenience: A spatial-temporal interpretation of storage under backwardation. *Economic Journal, 107*(443), 1009–1022.

Brennan, M. J. (1958). The supply of storage. *American Economic Review, 48,* 50–72.

Brennan, M. J. (1991). The price of convenience and the valuation of commodity contingent claims. In D. Lund & B. Oksendal (Eds.), *Stochastic Models and Option Values,* Vol. 200, (pp. 33–71). Elsevier Science, New York.

Fama, E., & French, K. (1987). Commodity futures prices: Some evidence on forecast power, premiums, and the theory of storage. *Journal of Business, 60*(1), 55–73.

Frechette, D., & Fackler, D. L. (1999). What causes commodity price backwardation? *American Journal of Agricultural Economics, 88*(4), 761–771.

Gillis, K. (1986). A note on the definition of basis. *Canadian Journal of Agricultural Economics, 34,* 253–256.

Haigh, M. S., & Holt, M. T. (2000). Hedging multiple price uncertainty in international grain trade. *American Journal of Agricultural Economics, 82*(4), 881–896.

Hartzmark, M. L. (1987). Returns to individual traders of futures: Aggregate results. *Journal of Political Economy, 95,* 1292–1306.

Hartzmark, M. L. (1991). Luck versus forecast ability-determinants of trader performance in futures markets. *Journal of Business, 64*(1), 49–74.

Kahl, K. Hand, & C. E. Curtis, Jr. (1986). A comparative analysis of the corn basis in feed grain deficit and surplus areas. *Review of Research in Futures Markets, 53,* 220–232.

Keynes, J. M. (1923). Some aspects of commodity markets. *Manchester Guardian Commercial.* European Reconstruction Series, Section 13, 784–786.

Khoury, N. T., & Martel, J. M. (1989). A supply of storage theory with asymmetric information. *Journal of Futures Markets, 9*(6), 573–581.

Kolb, R. W. (1992). Is normal backwardation normal? *Journal of Futures Markets, 1*(12), 75–91.

Naik, G., & Leuthold, R. (1988). Cash and futures price relationships for nonstorable commodities: An empirical analysis using a general theory. *Western Journal of Agricultural Economics, 13,* 327–338.

Ng, V. K., & Pirrong, S. C. (1994). Fundamentals and volatility: Storage, spreads, and the dynamics of metals prices. *Journal of Business, 67*(2), 203–230.

Peck, A. E. (1975). Hedging and income stability: Concepts, implications, and an example. *American Journal of Agricultural Economics, 57,* 410–419.

Working, H. (1949). The theory of the price of storage. *American Economic Review, 39* (December), 1254–1262.

Wright, B., & Williams, J. (1989). A theory of negative prices for storage. *Journal of Futures Markets, 9,* 1–13.

APPENDIX

Example of Price Linkages Associated with Commodity Processing

Most commodities are processed into either intermediate products, consumer products, or both. For example, coffee goes through a roasting process and is turned into a consumer product (i.e., coffee beans) with just one process, whereas wheat is first milled into flour, and bakeries further process most flour into baked goods.

The crushing of soybeans is another example, and crushing yields two intermediate products: unrefined soy oil (for human consumption) and soy meal (for animal feed). One bushel of soybeans yields soy oil and soy meal in relatively fixed proportions. One 60 pound bushel of soybeans typically yields 48 pounds of soybean meal and 11 pounds of soybean oil. All three products are traded on the Chicago Board of Trade futures market. Therefore, the soybean *complex* provides a good illustration of the price relationship between a raw commodity (soybeans) and two joint products (soy oil and soy meal). The linkage between these three markets is shown in Figure 3.A1.[1]

The top, middle, and bottom panels in Figure 3.A1 represent soy oil, soy meal, and soybean markets, respectively. Note that the quantity scales for soy oil, soy meal, and soybeans are selected so that they are comparable in terms of soybean equivalence. Crushing 5,000 bushels (i.e., 300,000 lbs) of soybeans produces 55,000 pounds of soy oil. In addition, 147.5 tons of soy meal is produced from 5,000 bushels of soybeans. In their respective panels, the points representing 55,000 pounds of soy oil, 147.5 tons of soy meal, and 5,000 bushels of soybeans are the same distance from their origin.

The demand for soybeans is derived from the demand for soy oil and soy meal, net of crushing costs. Therefore, the "crush value" of soybeans is derived by deducting the crushing cost per bushel from the sum of the value of soy oil and soy meal obtained from a bushel of soybeans. For example, if July soybean meal, soybean oil, and soybean futures prices are trading at $167/ton, 17.96¢ per lb, and $5.00 per bu, respectively, the crush value would be $.98/bu = ($167 × 2,000/48) + ($0.1796 × 11) − $5.00. The soy oil supply curve is derived from the soybean supply curve plus crushing costs. The soy meal supply curve is derived from the soybean supply curve plus crushing costs.

---

[1]This example assumes that

a. A bushel of soybeans (60 pounds) yields an average of 11 pounds of soy oil (18%) and 48 pounds of soy meal (80%).
b. Crushing costs are 98¢ per bushel and are independent of the quantity of soybeans crushed.
c. The demand for soy oil and soy meal is known and fixed.
d. The supply of soybeans is known and fixed.
e. Soybeans are demanded exclusively for crushing to meet the demand for soy oil and soy meal.

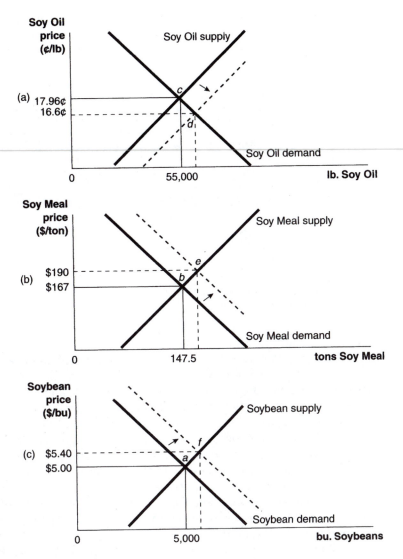

FIGURE 3.A1
Price relationships between soybeans, soy meal, and soy oil.

Because of this interdependence between demand and supply of both joint products, a shift to the right (left) in the demand for one product will be associated with a shift to the right (left) in the supply of the other. Market-clearing prices in all three markets are determined simultaneously. In Figure 3.A1, soybeans, soy meal, and soy oil markets are initially at equilibrium at points *a*, *b*, and *c*, respectively. The soybean price is $5.00 per bushel, and the soy meal and soy oil prices are $167 per ton and 17.96¢ per pound, respectively. In equilibrium in a competitive market (as shown in Figure 3.A1), the crushers' margin will exactly equal their crushing costs: 98¢ per bushel.

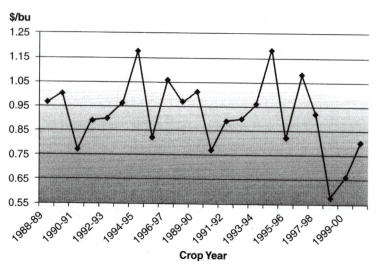

FIGURE 3.A2
Spread between price of soybeans and soybean oil and soy meal.
Source: Commodity Research Bureau

If the demand for soy meal rises, say, because of an expansion of livestock feeding, the soy meal price will increase. Higher soy meal prices will encourage crushers to expand their crushing operation, resulting in larger quantities of soy oil being available, and hence the soy oil supply curve will shift to the right, decreasing soyoil prices. The new soy meal prices may increase the crushers' margin initially. However, competition on the part of crushers to expand their crushing will shift the soybean demand curve to the right and increase soybean prices. As a result, opportunities for excessive profit from crushing will be soon eliminated.

As shown in Figure 3.A1, the new equilibria in soy oil, soy meal, and soybean markets will be at points *d*, *e*, and *f*, respectively, with new prices of 16.6¢ per pound for soy oil, $190 per ton for soy meal, and $5.40 per bushel for soybeans. The crushers' margin will fall until it equals marginal crushing costs (of 98¢ per bushel).

Figure 3.A2 displays the annual average spread between the value of soybeans and the two products, soy oil and soy meal, from 1988 to 2000 (i.e., the crush value). The spread is the gross crush margin, and it averaged about 90¢ per bushel over the time period shown. The maximum crush value was approximately $1.20 per bushel, and the minimum was about 55¢ per bushel. The crush value fluctuates from year to year. Sometimes the soy complex is driven by strength in the soy meal market, and during other periods the soy oil price leads the complex. If the crush value is relatively high, then soybean processors may be willing to bid more for soybeans and this will serve to lower the crush value. Alternatively, if the crush value is relatively low, then processors will be reluctant to bid for soybeans and this will result in a higher crush value as the price of soybeans falls.

CHAPTER 4

Financials

This chapter outlines the basic economics of financial futures and options markets, which are derivatives based on underlying stocks and stock indexes, foreign currencies (**FX**), and interest rates. The fundamentals of financial futures and options markets are slightly different and perhaps more complicated than for commodity futures and options, such as crude oil, coffee, or cattle futures. However, the core economic principles applying to commodity futures and options are similar for financials. For instance, the intertemporal prices of financial futures contracts are linked through a cost-of-carry relationship, much like the economic principles for storable commodities outlined in Chapter 3. Financing costs play a critical role in terms of influencing the contemporaneous determination of intertemporal prices in the financial futures market.

This chapter on financials is important because financial futures (and options) are clearly the booming segment of the futures and options industry, as explained in Chapter 1. There are three broad categories of financial futures and options traded at the present time:

a. Currencies (e.g., Japanese yen and European Euro)
b. Debt instruments (e.g., U.S. Treasury bonds and European bonds)
c. Equity instruments (e.g., Standard & Poor's 500 Stock Index and single-stock futures)

This chapter begins with a description of each of these three general categories, followed by a discussion of price formation within various financial futures and options markets.

CURRENCIES

The rate at which one country's currency can be converted into the currency of another country is called the **exchange rate**. The foreign exchange (**FX**) market is an international market, with active trading in New York, London, Tokyo, and other financial centers (Copeland, 2000). International banks buy and sell currencies 24 hours a day. These banks post their **bid** (the price they are willing to buy at) and **ask** (the price they are willing to sell at) prices for currencies so that they are available to traders around the world. This market is known as the interbank market in foreign exchange. Bid and ask quotes are offered for both the **spot** and the **forward** market. Most foreign exchange interbank payments are handled by the Clearing House Interbank Payment System (CHIPS), an electronic system operated by a New York clearinghouse. CHIPS links more than 130 banks to its central computer. For more information on this market and how this clearing arrangement works, go to *http://www.chips.org*.

A recent innovation in the currency market is nonbank on-line currency trading, such as FXCM, which offers an Internet trading platform for currencies (see *http://www.fxcm.com*). This type of on-line FX trading is designed to give individuals and small institutional investors greater access to the FX market. Most of the over-the-counter trading (i.e., the interbank market) was previously controlled by the large international banks, and it was difficult for the small investor to directly access this market.

BOX 4.1

The black market for foreign currency.

Anyone who has lived or traveled in a developing country has most likely had firsthand experience with the workings of the "black market" in foreign currency. Even though exchanging money on the black or "parallel" market is illegal in many developing countries, the local newspapers in these countries often quote black market rates. If you are a foreigner walking down a street in Egypt or Kenya, chances are that strangers will approach you and ask you whether you want to change money at a better rate than what the banks are offering.

In many developing countries, the government artificially fixes the price of the domestic currency by pegging the currency to a foreign exchange rate, such as the U.S. dollar, or by restricting the range of values that the exchange rate may take on (i.e., a price band). This fictitious exchange rate becomes the official rate at which foreign currency transactions are to be conducted. Often, this policy creates a black market in the domestic currency because the economic fundamentals do not support the "pegged" rate and black market traders try to establish the real rate. Invariably, a price gap develops between the black market rate and the official rate, indicating that there is excess demand for foreign currency. The relative value of foreign currency in the black market typically becomes higher than in the official market. Put differently, this signals that in these countries there is a scarcity of foreign "convertible" currencies, such as the U.S. dollar.

The daily turnover in the CHIPS global foreign exchange (**FX**) market was $1.2 trillion, on average in 2000, making it the world's largest market of any kind. In comparison, the daily value of world trade in goods and services was $30.4 billion in 2000, which means the global currency market is about 30 times larger than the global market for all goods and services.

The currency market is a large network of spot, forward, futures, and options markets, and currency values are established through supply and demand. The long run value of, say, the U.S. dollar versus the Japanese yen depends on economic fundamentals, such as government budgets, the money supply, the balance of trade, economic growth rates, interest rates, and relative expected inflation levels in the two countries. This means that both merchandise trade flows (e.g., imports and exports of manufactured goods and food products) and financial flows (e.g., foreign investment) jointly determine exchange rates. Of course, political uncertainty is also an important factor in the exchange rate market, especially for developing and emerging economies.

Over a period of several years in the latter part of the 1990s and early 2000s, the U.S. dollar strengthened relative to the Japanese yen by 30% to 40% (Fig. 4.1). This long-term currency realignment was based largely on economic fundamentals in the United States versus Japan. Through most of this time period, Japan experienced a slow-moving banking crisis, and dismal economic growth characterized the Japanese economy. On the other hand, the strong economic fundamentals and consistent economic growth in the United States shifted investor faith away from Japan and toward U.S. financial markets.

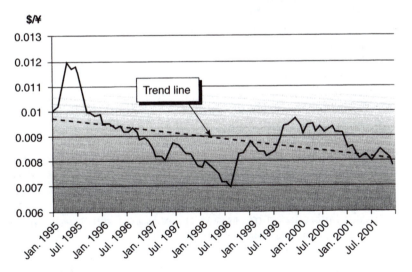

FIGURE 4.1
Japanese yen in dollars per yen.
Source: Commodity Research Bureau

GLOBALIZATION

Globalization is a term that describes a growing trend toward internationally integrated markets and the free movement of goods, services, and factors of production. For instance, the North American Free Trade Agreement (NAFTA) was signed in 1989 between the governments of Canada, Mexico, and the United States. NAFTA helped globalize the three economies because its goal was to facilitate trade in goods and services in North America by reducing trade barriers and promoting fair trade in the area.

One by-product of globalization is that exchange rates now play a greater role in the domestic economy. As more and more goods become **tradable** through globalization and open economies, the prices of many domestic goods have become heavily influenced by exchange rates. The average consumer may be unaware of this development, but nevertheless he or she is affected by exchange rates whenever they purchase food items, gasoline, sporting goods, clothing, and so on. This is true even if the goods are not actually traded but are tradable. Goods are tradable if they can be consumed away from the point of production.

For instance, lumber, beef, and tomatoes are traded within NAFTA, and the prices of these goods are more closely linked to exchange rate fluctuations because of NAFTA. Alternatively, Canadian clothing factories responded to NAFTA's lower trade barriers, and garments made in Canada made inroads into the U.S. market and captured a significant market share. Canadian manufacturers have also benefited from the steady weakening of the Canadian dollar from 85¢ (U.S.) in the early 1990s to only 63¢ (U.S.) in 2002. The weaker Canadian dollar effectively made Canadian labor and other costs cheaper in U.S.-dollar terms.

As a result of globalization, many U.S. and foreign multinational companies now have a large share of their costs and revenues denominated in foreign currencies (Friberg, 1999). For example, Callaway Golf, a U.S. manufacturer of golf clubs and golf equipment, is dependent on Asia as an important market for golf club and equipment sales, and Callaway's sales revenue is impacted by fluctuations in Asian exchange rates. Golf is popular in Japan and South Korea, and the demand for U.S.-made golf clubs in those countries is affected by the international purchasing power of the Japanese yen and South Korean won.

Callaway experienced a significant drop in both the volume and the value of exports to Asia as a result of the 1997–98 Asian financial crisis, when the value of many Asian currencies plunged. Consumers in Asia paid for their Callaway golf equipment in their local Asian currency, and the local price rose when the local currency fell. At the same time, consumer incomes were falling in Asia during the financial crisis. As a result of lower incomes, the Asian demand for imported golf clubs shrunk inward. Concurrently, the supply of Callaway clubs (priced in the Asian currencies) shifted upward and to the left because of the Asian devaluations.

After it sells golf clubs in Asia, Callaway must exchange the Asian currency earned from the sale. The yen or won are exchanged for U.S. dollars in order to cover Callaway's manufacturing costs in the United States. During the period of the Asian crisis, revenue per unit exported fell when measured by Callaway in U.S. dollars. Even though the golf club prices in the local Asian currencies rose, the increase in price did not match the rise in the value of the U.S. dollar.

In addition to the growing importance of FX earnings and receipts for domestic firms, in recent years there has been a massive increase in foreign investment in many host countries, and this has strengthened the linkage of global financial markets. For instance, multinational insurance companies doubled their level of foreign investment between 1995 and 2000 to reach $1.4 trillion. Pension funds in rich countries have also expanded their share of foreign investment to a level where foreign investment now typically accounts for about 20% of a pension fund's portfolio. China is one of the largest recipients of **foreign direct investment**, and during the 1996–2001 time period, the annual average foreign direct investment in China exceeded U.S.$42 billion.

HOW ARE EXCHANGE RATES DETERMINED?

Generally, the stronger a country's economy, the better its currency will perform and the more valuable it will become relative to other currencies (Isard, 1995 and Taylor, 1995). Typically, a certain currency will lose value if there is a high level of inflation in that country or if inflation levels are perceived to be rising. This is because inflation erodes purchasing power and demand for that particular currency. Inflation is an important factor in exchange rate determination because the exchange rate provides the link between a country's price and cost structures. Are hotel rooms expensive in London? Is Mexico a low-cost producer of fruits and

---

BOX 4.2

The European monetary union.
On January 1, 2002, 12 European countries abandoned their national currencies and adopted a single currency—the Euro—as their official currency. This was a big step toward economic integration in Europe. Germans gave up the deutschemark, the French discarded the franc, and the Italians gave up the lira. However, some countries, like Britain, Denmark, and Sweden, did not initially join the single-currency union.

One of the main economic impacts of the single currency is that national governments gave up the ability to determine monetary policy and set interest rates. Instead, the European Central Bank now establishes a single interest rate for the entire Euro region. Another economic impact is the elimination of exchange rate risk for trade within the region. The introduction of the Euro also reduced transactions costs for trade between foreign countries and Europe. With the single Euro, foreign firms trading with Europe no longer have to repeatedly convert receipts and expenses from one currency to the other. Multinationals that sell products throughout Europe now set only one price in the Euro zone. Prior to the adoption of the Euro, multinationals were constantly revising their prices across Europe as exchange rates fluctuated.

vegetables? From the U.S. perspective, these questions can be answered only by converting the foreign currency price into U.S. dollars via the exchange rate.

Domestic firms and individuals demand foreign currency in order to purchase goods or services from a foreign country or to invest in that foreign host country. Foreigners supply foreign currency through their purchases of home goods or services or through investment in the home market. For example, as Japanese banks purchase U.S. financial assets, they provide a supply of Japanese yen in exchange for U.S. dollars. At the same time, U.S. purchases of Japanese automobiles will result in a demand for Japanese yen.

In international trade of goods, services, and financial assets, each participant measures the value of a transaction in terms of his or her home currency. The linkage to all participants is through the exchange rate. For instance, in 1999 and 2000, the European Euro slowly depreciated (Fig. 4.2), largely because of significant financial flows from western Europe to the United States and other destinations. European investors were seeking higher returns on their investments in bonds, stocks, and real estate in the United States and elsewhere.

For the most part, developed countries, such as the United States, the United Kingdom, and Japan, have had floating or **flexible exchange rates** since the early 1970s. Under floating rates, supply and demand are allowed to determine the value of the currency, and the currency's value fluctuates accordingly. In contrast, many developing countries (such as China, Brazil, and India) have had fixed exchange rates for a number of years, although some developing countries have experimented with floating rates. A fixed exchange rate means the exchange rate is rigid relative to the value of outside currencies. For example, following the Asian financial crisis in 1997–98, Malaysia shifted from a flexible to a fixed exchange rate and imposed foreign exchange controls that "pegged" the Malaysian ringgit at

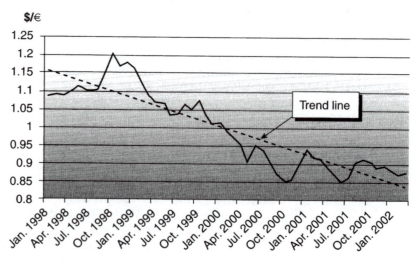

FIGURE 4.2
European Euros in dollars per Euro.
Source: Commodity Research Bureau

RM3.80 to the U.S dollar. The purpose of this move was to control capital flowing out of the country and to halt any further devaluation of the ringgit brought about during the Asian financial crisis.

However, currency pegs cannot last forever, and in most developing countries the currency eventually becomes overvalued (Box 4.1), which affects a country's international competitiveness relative to competing nations. For example, in 1991, Argentina pegged its currency (the peso) to the U.S. dollar in order to control hyperinflation. Unfortunately for Argentina, the U.S. dollar appreciated and (the pegged) Argentinian peso appreciated with it, making Argentine goods uncompetitive in global markets. Under the pegged system, Argentines were allowed to swap pesos for U.S. dollars, resulting in a reduction of the peso's circulation at home and raising the interest rate in Argentina (della Paolera and Taylor, 2001). As a result, Argentina's export markets collapsed, economic growth slowed, and unemployment grew to double-digit levels by 2001. A severe economic crisis resulted, and Argentina suddenly abandoned its currency's peg to the dollar, triggering a devaluation of 70%. Subsequently, Argentina defaulted on U.S.$152 billion in debt, the largest default in the history of global financial markets. Some economists point to the meltdown of the Argentinean economy in 2001 as evidence of the danger of a currency system that does not reflect economic fundamentals—artificial currency pegs are destined to fail. However, as a counterexample, Hong Kong's monetary authority, along with its currency board system, has successfully maintained the ratio of HK$7.80 to U.S.$1 since 1983.

As mentioned previously, the fundamental economic factors that determine exchange rates include the money supply, government budgets, economic growth, relative price levels (i.e., inflation), and interest rate differentials. These economic determinants ought to establish long-term equilibrium exchange rate levels. The traditional model of exchange rate equilibrium is the **purchasing power parity (PPP) theory** (Harvey, 2001). Purchasing power parity is based on the concept that goods and services in different countries should cost the same when measured in a common currency. This implies that exchange rates between currencies are in equilibrium when their purchasing power is identical. In equilibrium, this indicates that the exchange rate between two countries should equal the ratio of the two countries' price levels for a fixed basket of goods and services. So, according to the PPP theory, $1,000 buys as much in the United States as $1,000 worth of Euros buys in western Europe.

According to the PPP, when a country's domestic price level is increasing (i.e., a country experiences inflation), that country's exchange rate must depreciate in order to return to PPP. For example, if the inflation rate in the United States is 4% and in Europe it is 2%, then the U.S. dollar should fall by 2% against the Euro in order to maintain PPP.

As an example of how a country's exchange rate may change over time relative to its long-run PPP equilibrium, consider China, an emerging giant in international financial markets. China's currency is officially known as the renminbi (RMB), but it is often referred to as the yuan in the popular press. The renminbi is not a freely floating currency but rather is managed by China's central government.

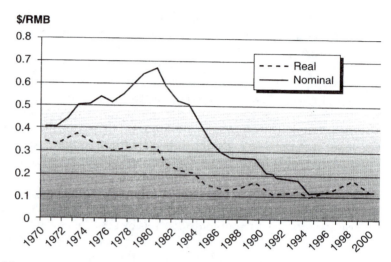

FIGURE 4.3
China's real and nominal exchange rate.
Source: U.S. Department of Agriculture

Figure 4.3 reports the nominal and real (i.e., PPP) exchange rate for China from 1970 to 2000. The nominal exchange rate is the solid line, and the real exchange rate is the dashed line. From 1970 until the mid-1990s, the renminbi was overvalued because the nominal exchange rate (dollars per renminbi) was above the real exchange rate. China experienced a sharp depreciation of its real exchange rate from the early 1980s through 1994; however, the renminbi remained overvalued until about 1994. In the latter part of the 1990s, the renminbi was slightly undervalued, according to these data.

China's rapid economic growth in the 1990s is a well-known story. Part of this economic success was due to China's rapidly expanding exports, and the role of the renminbi was important in fueling the growth of these exports. As shown in Figure 4.3, there was a significant depreciation of the renminbi from 1980 to 1994 (when the currency lost more than 80% of its value).

China's managed exchange rate went from about 1.5 yuan per dollar in the early 1980s to 8.3 yuan per dollar in 2000. A cheaper renminbi certainly accounts for the great success China had in attracting foreign direct investment and expanding exports. However, this changed about the time of the Asian financial crisis, and China's currency appreciated by nearly 30% (in real terms) in the mid-1990s (Figure 4.3). As a result, the nation's exports became expensive compared to those of other Asian countries, and China was threatening to devalue again.

In practice, currencies deviate from their PPP rates for long time periods, and therefore the PPP model does a notoriously poor job of forecasting short-term exchange rate changes. The most likely explanation is that the PPP theory is too simplistic and does not capture the importance of international capital flows. Dornbusch (1987) developed a more complicated model of exchange rates focused on asset markets to explain short-term exchange rates. His model assumes that capital will move freely among countries seeking out the highest expected return based on interest rates and expected currency appreciation or depreciation. The movement of capital will continue until the expected return is equalized across countries.

To illustrate this concept, assume that government bonds in Canada pay 8% interest and U.S. government bonds pay 4%. Investors might begin to invest capital in the Canadian money market (i.e., buy Canadian bonds), and the flow of capital north to Canada will expand the demand for Canadian dollars and drive up the value of the Canadian dollar. The Canadian dollar rate will continue to strengthen against the U.S. dollar until a point is reached where the market participants believe the Canadian dollar has become too strong and is likely to depreciate in the future. If the expectation of a change in the exchange rate gets to the level where the Canadian dollar is expected to depreciate by 4%, then investors would no longer view Canadian 8% bonds as a superior investment opportunity compared to the U.S. market. In other words, the Canadian/ U.S. exchange rate will continue to change up until the point where the U.S. interest rate is equal to the Canadian interest rate plus the expected change in the exchange rate.

A formal representation of the (approximate) relationship between international interest rates and exchange rates is the **interest rate parity** condition:

$$i_{\text{U.S.}} = i_{\text{CDN}} + (e^f - e^s) / e^s, \tag{4.1}$$

where $i_{\text{U.S.}}$ is the interest rate in the United States, i_{CDN} is the interest rate in Canada, e^f is the forward (or futures) exchange rate (U.S. dollars per Canadian dollar), and e^s is the spot exchange rate (U.S. dollars per Canadian dollar). The interest rate parity condition holds exactly when the rate of return on U.S. dollar deposits is equal to the expected rate of return on Canadian dollar deposits. Of course, Equation 4.1 applies to any pair of countries with **convertible currencies**. The United States and Canada are used here for illustrative purposes only.

According to the interest rate parity condition, a country with relatively high interest rates will experience a **depreciation** of its currency. At the same time, a country with relatively low interest rates will experience an **appreciation** of its currency. These expectations will be reflected in the futures (and forward) exchange rates (i.e., e^f in Equation 4.1). If interest rate parity does not hold, arbitrage will kick in, and a trader could profit by borrowing in a low-interest-rate country and simultaneously lending in a high-interest-rate country.

To further illustrate the interest rate parity condition, consider the following example. Suppose that the interest rate on a 90-day government Treasury bill is 1.91% in Canada (i_{CDN}) and 1.75% in the United States ($i_{\text{U.S.}}$). At the same time, assume the spot exchange rate (U.S. dollars per Canadian dollar) is 0.6242 (e^s) and the exchange rate on a futures contract price for delivery in three months time is 0.6237 (e^f). In this example, the Canadian dollar is trading at a forward discount to the U.S. dollar because the futures exchange rate is below the spot rate. Does the interest parity condition hold in this example?

BOX 4.3

It's "deflation" George, not "devaluation."
President George W. Bush caught foreign currency traders by surprise in early 2002. President Bush emerged from private discussions with Japan's prime minister in Tokyo and announced that the two leaders had talked about Japan's "devaluation" issue. Currency markets around the world reacted, and the Japanese yen immediately fell in response to Bush's statement. Currency traders interpreted Bush's statement to mean that Japan was going to let the yen fall in order to bolster its exports. However, after the currency markets reacted, presidential aides sheepishly corrected Bush's statement to indicate that he meant to say "deflation" instead of "devaluation." Deflation means falling domestic prices, something totally different than devaluation, which means allowing the value of one's currency to fall relative to other currencies.

This was a classic example of where a politician was confused over economic terminology. In this case, it cost people money, as Bush's *faux pas* no doubt resulted in losses for some currency traders.

Substituting the previous exchange rate and interest rate figures into Equation 4.1 gives

$$1.75 \cong 1.91 + (0.6237 - 0.6242) / 0.6242 \tag{4.2}$$

and

$$1.75 < 1.909. \tag{4.3}$$

Since the expected rate of return in Canada exceeds that in the United States, the interest parity condition does not hold. The U.S. investor could expect to make money by purchasing the Canadian three-month Treasury bill. As a result, capital would be expected to flow from the United States to Canada.

CURRENCY FUTURES AND OPTIONS

Currency futures began trading on the Chicago Mercantile Exchange (CME) in 1972. Currency futures trading has grown in importance because of globalization, the growth of foreign trade in goods and services, and the growth of foreign investment. The CME quotes exchange rates as the dollar price of one unit of foreign currency. Sometimes, price quotes in the spot market will be the other way around, namely, the foreign currency price of one U.S. dollar. For example, if one U.S. dollar is convertible into Japanese yen at an exchange rate of 120 yen per dollar, this means it costs 120 yen to purchase one U.S. dollar. Conversely, it costs

> ### BOX 4.4
>
> #### The investment biker.
> Jim Rogers is a writer and former currency trader. His Web site says that he got his start in business at the age of five, selling peanuts. As an adult, he states that he made a small fortune trading foreign currency futures. After he made his millions, Rogers started traveling the world, enjoying life and looking for investment opportunities overseas. One of his first trips around the world was on a motorcycle, and he wrote a best-selling book titled the *Investment Biker.* It is a wonderful read. Rogers has continued writing about his travel experiences and has published numerous magazine articles on travel and overseas investment opportunities. At the turn of the millennium, Rogers and his female companion struck out on a three-year round-the-world journey in a custom-designed Mercedes-Benz. His fascinating stories about the people and countries visited are available on his Web site at *http://www.jimrogers.com.*

$0.008333 (= $\frac{1}{120}$) to buy one Japanese yen, which is how the futures market quotes the exchange rate. Whether the home or foreign currency is in the numerator is totally arbitrary, but the CME futures price quote always has the U.S. dollar in the numerator.

Table 4.1 reports currency futures quotations from the *Wall Street Journal.* Consider the Canadian dollar contract, traded in units of $100,000 ($Cdn) on the CME. Suppose that a trader sold one June Canadian dollar contract at $.6431, and then the Canadian dollar subsequently strengthened to $.6500 (i.e., the Canadian dollar became more expensive, denominated in U.S. dollars). In this case, the trader would lose $.0069 × $100,000 = $690 (before commission fees).

In Table 4.1, the Japanese yen contract is quoted in dollars per yen (i.e., the CME standard way of reporting currency values with U.S. dollars in the numerator). For example, the settlement price shown for September yen is $.007854 per yen. Note that the *Wall Street Journal* moves the decimal point on the yen's price two places to the right in order to save ink. This convention of dropping the two zeros from the price is indicated in the *Wall Street Journal* by "(.00)" to the right of "$ per yen" in the "Japan Yen" header in Table 4.1.

The CME also trades options on the underlying currency futures contracts that are shown in Table 4.1. There is active trading in options on futures for the Japanese yen, Canadian dollar, British pound, Swiss franc, and European Euro.

DEBT INSTRUMENTS

Debt instrument (i.e., interest rate) futures have a much shorter history than commodity futures, but debt instrument contracts now dominate the futures industry in terms of trading volume. Interest rate futures are based on the same principle as

---

TABLE 4.1   Currency Futures Quotations

	OPEN	HIGH	LOW	SETTLE	CHG	LIFETIME HIGH	LIFETIME LOW	OPEN INT
Currency Futures								
Japanese Yen (CME)-12.5 million yen; $ per yen (.00)								
June	.7847	.7866	.7797	.7816	-.0028	.8776	.7449	81,533
Sept	.7882	.7902	.7837	.7854	-.0028	.8620	.7495	1,653
Est vol 5,801; vol Wed 19,697; open int 84,072, +750.								
Canadian Dollar (CME)-100,000 dlrs.; $ per Can $								
June	.6418	.6443	.6413	.6431	.0008	.6700	.6180	71,991
Sept	.6414	.6430	.6400	.6418	.0008	.6590	.6175	6,523
Dec	.6408	.6415	.6400	.6407	.0008	.6555	.6190	2,112
Mr03	.6388	.6400	.6388	.6396	.0008	.6400	.6198	391
Est vol 3,784; vol Wed 8,215; open int 81,260, +634.								
British Pound (CME)-62,500 pds.; $ per pound								
June	1.4574	1.4594	1.4516	1.4542	-.0030	1.4670	1.3910	44,733
Sept	1.4488	1.4520	1.4440	1.4458	-.0030	1.4600	1.3990	1,157
Est vol 2,865; vol Wed 12,440; open int 45,910, +983.								
Swiss Franc (CME)-125,000 francs; $ per franc								
June	.6268	.6282	.6244	.6265	-.0001	.6320	.5813	53,017
Sept	.6277	.6290	.6257	.6275	-.0001	.6330	.5860	513
Est vol 3,594; vol Wed 12,946; open int 53,576, +17.								
Australian Dollar (CME)-100,000 dlrs.; $ per A$								
June	.5471	.5491	.5466	.5473	.0001	.5491	.4885	45,011
Sept	.5428	.5449	.5426	.5433	.0001	.5449	.4790	409

Source: Reprinted with permission from the *Wall Street Journal*, May 17, 2002

any other futures market contract, but the asset is money, and its price can be loosely described as the interest rate, which is the cost of borrowing money over a certain time period. Inflation erodes the time value of money, and therefore interest rates have two components. The first component covers expected inflation, called the inflation premium, and the second component reflects the real rate of return. The expected **real rate of interest** is the difference between the nominal rate of interest and the expected rate of inflation. In other words, the real interest rate is the nominal interest rate adjusted for the expected erosion of purchasing power resulting from inflation. For example, with a nominal interest rate of 6% and an expected rate of inflation of 2%, the expected real rate of interest is 4%.

The supply and demand for money determines interest rate levels, and important supply and demand fundamentals include monetary policy, fiscal policy, inflationary expectations, and international capital flows. The term **fiscal policy** refers to government expenditures on goods and services and to the way in which the government finances these expenditures (through borrowing or taxes). The term **monetary policy** refers to actions taken by the central government to influence the amount of money and credit in the economy.

Interest rate futures were first traded in Chicago in 1975. Futures contracts written on fixed-income Government National Mortgage Association (Ginnie Mae) "**mortgage-backed securities**" were the first interest rate futures contracts launched by the Chicago Board of Trade (CBOT). A "**fixed-income security**" generates a fixed income each year. The following year, Treasury-bill (T-bill) futures contracts were introduced on the CME. Treasury-bond futures were then launched in 1977 on the CBOT.

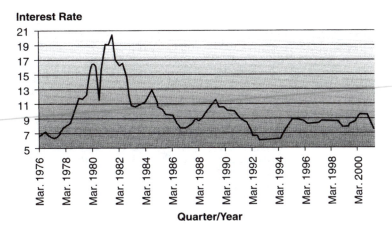

FIGURE 4.4
U.S. prime interest rate.
Source: Commodity Research Bureau

The introduction of these various interest rate contracts revolutionized the futures market by introducing a vehicle to hedge interest rate risk. The futures industry's timing with the introduction of interest rate futures was impeccable. In the late 1970s, annual interest rates in the United States rose to more than 20% and became very volatile. Prior to this, there had been a long period of interest rate stability. Financial firms that used the futures market to hedge during the period of high interest rates in the late 1970s and early 1980s outperformed their competitors because those firms that hedged were successful in reducing the risks associated with large interest rate fluctuations. Such hedgers included banks, investment banks, insurance companies, pension funds, and bond traders. The volume of trade in interest rate futures grew dramatically in the early 1980s and has continued to expand rapidly since then. Figure 4.4 plots the U.S. prime interest rate, which averaged 9.6% over the 1976–2000 time period and exceeded 20% in 1981.

The single most successful futures contract ever introduced and one of the largest volume futures contracts in the world is the U.S. Treasury-bond (T-bond) contract (traded on the CBOT). In less than four years after its introduction, the T-bond futures contract became the world's most actively traded futures contract. Treasury-bond futures and options volume peaked in 1998 at about 150 million contracts and then began to fall as the U.S. government moved away from borrowing money through long-term debt (Box 4.5). In 2001, about 72 million T-bond futures and options contracts, each covering $100,000 in bonds, changed hands on the CBOT.

Prior to the introduction of debt instrument futures and options, government securities (such as T-bills or T-bonds) were traded solely in a decentralized over-the-counter market, and prices were not highly visible to the public. The futures and options market brought increased transparency with regard to market activity. Prices and information became readily available, and soon corporations, banks, and other commercial and financial institutions turned to the financial futures and options markets as a way to manage financial risk through hedging. In addition, debt instrument futures provide speculators with a market opportunity to speculate whether interest rates will rise or fall.

Reasons for increased trade volume in debt instrument futures include interest rate volatility, globalization of financial assets, and the fact that debt instruments are highly sensitive to interest rate changes (due to changes in monetary and fiscal policy, inflation, and capital flows). The debt instrument futures market is a very liquid market, and there is increased awareness of hedging benefits associated with trading on this market.

As with commodity futures, interest rate futures prices (theoretically) adhere to the cost-of-carry model:

$$F_{t,T} = S_t(1 + C_{t,T}), \tag{4.4}$$

where $F_{t,T}$ = futures price for delivery at time T, S_t = spot price at time t, and $(C_{t,T})$ = net cost of carry from time t to T. Storing a financial instrument such as a T-bond is conceptually the same as storing a commodity such as coffee or wheat, except that the relative importance of certain storage cost components (such as warehouse costs) differs. Arbitrage is also at work in the financial market to ensure that the equality in Equation 4.4 roughly holds. The net cost of carry is equal to returns minus carrying charges, with interest rate futures carrying charges essentially equal to the net costs of financing.

Suppose that the equality in Equation 4.4 did not hold and that $F_t > S(1 + C_{0,t})$. In this case, a trader could borrow money to buy the underlying financial instrument at a net cost of $S(1 + C_{0,t})$ and simultaneously sell a futures contract for price F_t. A riskless arbitrage profit would be earned through buying the spot and selling the futures contract, and as a result, futures prices would be driven down and spot prices driven up until the arbitrage profit was driven to zero as in Equation 4.4.

In a similar fashion, Equation 4.4 holds for two different futures months:

$$F_{t+1} = F_t(1 + C_{t,t+1}), \tag{4.5}$$

where F_{t+1} is the futures price for delivery at time $t + 1$ and $C_{t,t+1}$ is the net cost of carry from period t to period $t + 1$.

Suppose that June T-bond futures are trading at 97-30 (which is equivalent to a contract value of $97,937) and September futures are trading at 96-29 (for a contract value of $96,906). If a trader purchases a June contract and simultaneously sells a September contract, is there an arbitrage profit opportunity? The net cost of carrying the bond from June to September ($C_{t,t+1}$) has two components: the financing cost associated with purchasing the bond and the interest paid by the bond (which is a negative cost). Suppose that the 90-day T-bill rate is 2½%, which approximates the financing cost of holding the bond. The T-bond futures contract specifies delivery of a 6% $100,000 bond, which returns $1,500 to the holder for the June–September time period. Therefore, the net cost of financing is .025/4 × ($97,937) − $1,500 = $888. Substituting into Equation 4.5 gives

$$\$96,906 \cong \$97,937 - \$888 \tag{4.6}$$

and

$$\$96,906 < \$97,049. \tag{4.7}$$

So, the left- and right-hand sides of Equation 4.6 are approximately equal, with a difference of only $143. This is a small fraction of the total value of the bond. In all likelihood, transactions costs would exceed $143, so the cost-of-carry arbitrage condition in Equation 4.5 approximately holds in this T-bond example. Keep in mind that this is a simplified example because it ignores the fact that the seller of a bond futures contract has both timing and quality delivery options. Therefore, Equation 4.6 is only an approximation of the true and exact arbitrage condition.

When we solve Equation 4.4 for the cost of carry, the result is the implied **repo rate** ("repo" is short for "repurchase"):

$$C_{0,t} = (F_t \: / \: S) - 1. \tag{4.8}$$

The implied repo rate in Equation 4.8 is the interest rate implied by the difference between the futures and spot price. The term *repo rate* is derived from a repurchase agreement that is very common in financial markets. In a repurchase agreement, a financial asset owned by one party is sold to a second party at one price and then repurchased by the first party after a period of time at a slightly higher price. In other words, the second party is essentially providing the first party with a loan. The difference in the buying and selling price is the interest earned by the second party, which, on an annualized basis, is called the repo rate.

THE TERM STRUCTURE OF INTEREST RATES AND THE YIELD CURVE

The **yield curve** is a simple relationship that reveals an extensive amount of information about the market for debt instruments and overall government macroeconomic policy. The yield curve is the relationship between yield (i.e., the average rate of return, or the interest rate) and term to maturity. In other words, a yield curve is a graph that plots interest rates paid by bonds and short-term debt instruments as a function of time to maturity. The yield curve for Treasury debt, for example, plots yields for (default free) instruments with maturities ranging from 90-day T-bills to 30-year T-bonds. This relationship is often referred to as the "term structure of interest rates." The yield curve is a very popular tool for financial investors because it provides an indication of the expected future level of interest rates.

Figure 4.5 plots a Treasury debt yield curve where the horizontal axis represents the length of time to maturity and the vertical axis reports the yield on each instrument. Figure 4.5 displays the yield curve for September 2000 and another curve that existed in October 2001. The September 2000 yield curve is shown by a downward-sloping dashed line, and the October 2001 yield curve is the upward-sloping solid line. The 2000 curve lies above the 2001 curve as all interest rates were higher in 2000 compared to 2001. The difference in the slopes between the two yield curves is striking.

FIGURE 4.5
Treasury yield curve.

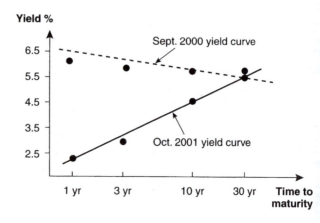

Normally, the yield curve has a positive (i.e., upward) slope, as shown by the October 2001 curve in Figure 4.5, because longer-term investments typically pay higher interest rates than shorter-term investments. This is due, in part, to investors' **liquidity preference** and the fact that longer-term investments are more risky than shorter-term investments because of uncertainty surrounding future inflation rates.

The slope (i.e., steepness) of the yield curve changes when interest rates change. The yield curve often has a relatively steep slope when short-term interest rates are low (e.g., in the fall of 2001). However, it is possible that the yield curve takes on a negative slope when short-term interest rates are high (e.g., in the fall of 2000). The downward-sloping yield curve appears periodically, but its slope was most pronounced in the early 1980s, when short-term interest rates were close to 20% (see Figure 4.4) and at the same time long-term bonds yielded about 14%. The yield curve sometimes flattens out and becomes almost horizontal, which means that investors buying long-term bonds receive no premium over shorter-term investments.

Economists have developed different explanations for the shape of the yield curve: the **expectations** theory, the **liquidity preference** theory, and the **market segmentation** theory. Each of these theories offers a partial explanation for the shape of the yield curve (i.e., the term structure).

The expectations theory states that the shape of the yield curve is a market forecast of forthcoming spot interest rates. If investors are risk neutral, then forward interest rates represent the market's expectations of future spot interest rates. Investors are assumed to be risk neutral because they are indifferent to the security's maturity and are interested only in the yield. This theory assumes that the forward rate is an unbiased estimator of what the future interest rate is expected to be. This means that if the yield curve has a positive slope, then the market believes that spot interest rates will be higher in the future. This could be due to a market belief that the inflation rate is going to increase in the future. Conversely, if inflation were expected to decline in the future, then the yield curve would slope down under the expectations theory.

According to the expectations theory, if investors can obtain a higher return on 30-year bonds, they will then arbitrage the market by selling 10-year bonds and buying 30-year bonds instead. This action will drive up the price of 30-year bonds and drive down the price of 10-year bonds. Soon market equilibrium will be reached, and the return from both bonds will be equal. At this point, investors will be indifferent as to whether they hold the 10-year bond or the 30-year bond.

The liquidity preference theory contends that the shape of the yield curve is affected by a liquidity premium between long- and short-term securities. In financial markets, a liquidity (risk) premium may be required to attract risk-averse investors to buy risky assets. For example, a government bond maturing in one year may be considered low risk by such an investor because the probability of a dramatic change in interest rates is small compared to a longer-term bond. Therefore, investors are willing to pay more for shorter-term bonds compared to longer-term bonds. If this theory were correct, then long-term interest rates would exceed short-term interest rates by the amount of the liquidity premium.

The liquidity preference theory rejects the notion that investors are indifferent to maturity lengths. This theory maintains that investors prefer shorter-term maturities, all other things being equal, and this is why they will pay more for shorter-term bonds than for longer-term bonds. The extra amount paid is the **liquidity premium**. This means that buying a 30-year bond will bring a greater return than a 10-year bond by the amount of the liquidity premium.

The market segmentation theory assumes that each maturity is segmented from the other maturities. Each maturity has a unique group of investors with different investment goals and horizons, and these investors do not view alternative maturities as being substitutable. This theory asserts that there is a market for short-term securities, another market for medium-term securities, and a third market for long-term securities. According to this theory, spot rates are determined by supply and demand conditions in each market.

For example, banks have short-term preferences, and life insurance companies have long-term preferences. These institutions prefer to make bond purchases that match their respective needs. However, they will buy bonds outside their preferred maturity range if the yield is sufficiently attractive. Therefore, according to the market segmentation theory, the yield curve is determined primarily by the interaction of these large institutions in the marketplace.

The expectations, liquidity preference, and market segmentation theories all help explain the shape of the yield curve, and no one theory dominates over time. The following quotation from *Barron's* newspaper on October 19, 1998, helps illustrate factors that influence the yield curve. In late 1998, Federal Reserve Chairman Alan Greenspan ordered a quarter-percentage-point cut in both federal funds and discount rates to keep the economy on a stable growth path. As a result of his decision, the shape of the yield curve changed. *Barron's* reported that as a result of Greenspan's move,

> The yield curve's slope steepened following the Fed's rate move as investors shifted from 30-year bonds to the short end of the market, most in the two-to-five-year-note range. The rationale is that with the Fed likely to ease further and the U.S. dollar softening, the curve will maintain a steepening trend. But given recent volatility in the slope of the curve, market dynamics may not be as predictable as some think. For example, if expectations for a November rate cut wane, yields on the short end could rebound.

T-Bond Futures

As explained previously, a T-bond is an interest-bearing certificate sold by the U.S. federal government. T-bonds are assets that earn money with essentially no default risk because they come with the federal government's guarantee of payment. Selling bonds is one of the federal government's methods of borrowing money in order to help finance its spending. The reason that bonds are essentially free of default risk is that the government can always print more money in order to provide payment. The owner of a T-bond can hold the bond for a long period of time and collect (a fixed amount of semiannual) interest (i.e., coupon payments). Alternatively, the owner can sell the bond in the secondary market, that is, the market in which previously issued securities are traded, and a profit would be earned if the price of the bond moves up. The bond's price is sensitive to interest rate changes (explained shortly). The T-bond's face value (e.g., $100,000) is the amount to be repaid by the government on maturity, and the fixed amount of interest paid on the bond is the coupon value. For example, a bond with a 6% coupon and a face value of $100,000 will pay annual interest of $6,000. Bonds, however, usually pay semiannually, and in this example the bond will pay $3,000 each six months.

T-bonds are long-term financial instruments. Related government medium-term and short-term debt securities include T-bills with maturities of up to one year and T-notes with maturities between 1 and 10 years. The U.S. government is not the only institution that sells bonds. State and local (municipal) governments also issue bonds in order to raise money, as do corporations and foreign governments.

Spot market bonds are traded around the world, and there is no central exchange or market for the majority of bonds that are traded in the spot or cash market. Hence, the bond market is known as an **over-the-counter** market rather than an exchange market. However, bond futures and options are traded on exchanges, even though the overwhelming majority of bonds do not trade on exchanges.

A bond's return comes from the fixed amount of interest the bond pays (i.e., the coupon rate) plus or minus changes in the value (or price) of the bond, which depends on the interest rate. The annual interest paid is a fixed amount, but the price of the bond fluctuates with market interest rates. Suppose that initially the market interest rate is equal to the bond's fixed coupon rate. In this case, the T-bond would trade at its full face value in the secondary market. In other words, it would trade at its **par value**. If the market interest rates rise and exceed the bond's fixed coupon rate, then the market price of the bond falls, and it trades at a **discount** to par value. The reason the price of the bond falls is that a buyer expects to earn at least the going market interest rate, and if the buyer bids the par value, then he or she would earn less than the market rate. A bond's value falls when interest rates rise, and, conversely, a bond's value rises when interest rates fall. Therefore, a speculator who believes that long-term interest rates will rise is going to sell bond futures because he or she is expecting the value of the bond to fall. In contrast, the speculator expecting long-term interest rates to fall will buy bond futures, with the expectation that bond prices will rise.

A bond's current yield is equal to the annual interest or coupon payment divided by the prevailing market price. For example, if a bond that is currently worth $97,000 on the secondary market has a fixed payment of $8,000 per year, then its effective yield is $8,000/$97,000 = .0824 (or 8.24%). If the current yield rises, then the bond price falls and vice versa.

The basic bond pricing formula is

$$\text{Price(\$)} = \frac{\text{Face Value}}{(1 + r)^t},\tag{4.9}$$

where r is yield and t is time. For example, today's price of a bond with a $1,000 face value that matures in one year with a yield of 10% is equal to

$$\text{Price} = \$1,000/1.1 = \$909.09.\tag{4.10}$$

When there is a stream of payments, the bond's price is

$$P_{i0} = \sum_{t=1}^{M} C_{it}/(1 + r)^t,\tag{4.11}$$

where P_{i0} is the current price and C_{it} is the payment in each time period t.

T-bonds are the U.S. government's long-term bonds, and they are issued in only one maturity: 10 years. The 10-year bonds are sold by the government through auction three times a year—in February, August, and November. For many years, the U.S. government sold 30-year bonds, but this practice was discontinued in 2001 (Box 4.5).

BOX 4.5

Death of the 30-year U.S. T-bond.

The 30-year U.S. T-bond was introduced in 1977 to finance large U.S. government deficits during the 1980s and 1990s. At the time, the government had a huge demand for long-term loans. For many years, the government's 30-year bond served as a financial benchmark. Many domestic and foreign investors viewed it as a very safe and liquid asset. Insurance companies and pension funds, with long-term liabilities, were regular purchasers of the 30-year bonds. However, in 2001, the government decided that it no longer needed the 30-year bond to meet its financing needs, and the U.S. Treasury announced that the government would no longer issue the long-term bonds. One reason the 30-year bond was abandoned was that the federal government's budget moved from a deficit to a surplus.

Following the Treasury's announcement in 2001, buyers bid up the price of existing 30-year bonds, and this lowered the long-term interest rates.

Two government agencies, the Federal National Mortgage Association (Fannie Mae) and the Federal Home Loan Mortgage Corporation (Freddie Mac), continue to issue 30-year bonds. These two agencies saw demand for their bonds expand following the cancellation of the long-term T-bonds.

The CBOT's T-bond contract calls for delivery of the equivalent of a 15-year T-bond with a $100,000 face value and a 6% coupon rate. However, the government does not issue 15-year bonds, and therefore any government T-bond is deliverable as long as it has more than 15 years to maturity on the first day of the delivery month and is not callable within 15 years. When a particular bond is delivered, the exchange applies a "conversion factor" to adjust the price to correspond to the hypothetical bond specified by the futures contract. The holder of the short futures position delivering the bond will receive a price that equals the futures settlement price times the conversion factor plus accrued interest. The CBOT publishes the conversion factors covering each possible deliverable bond. The conversion adjusts the different coupon rates and maturity dates to equate with the 6% standard. This conversion ensures that any deliverable bond will receive a fair price if delivered on a futures contract. The conversion factor is the price of the delivered bond ($1 par value) to yield 6%.

Table 4.2 is a table of interest rate futures quotations from the *Wall Street Journal.* The first contract shown is for T-bonds. The T-bond contract is for a $100,000 bond, and bond futures are priced as a percentage of par plus 32nds of a point (e.g., $94\frac{25}{32}$ = 94-25). The price is in points ($1,000) and 32nds of a point, and each 32nd is worth $31.25 since 32 × $31.25 = $1,000. For example, in Table 4.2 the settlement price for the June contract is 100-28, which equals $100\frac{28}{32}$% of par value. For a $100,000 bond, this means the market price is $100,875.

So, if you buy a futures contract at a price of 100-28 and subsequently sell it at 101-28, this equals "one full point ($\frac{32}{32}$)", which is equal to $1,000 (or 32 × $31.25). Each 32nd is worth $31.25 per $1,000 of bonds.

Eurodollar Futures

Internationally, the U.S. dollar is considered to be a reserve asset. As a result, many world residents (firms) wish to hold part of their wealth (capital) in U.S. dollars, but they do not necessarily wish to place their dollars in U.S. banks. In addition, because a large percentage of world merchandise trade is denominated in U.S. dollars, there is a large business and financial community outside the United States that borrows and lends U.S. dollars. For example, if a wheat exporter in Kazakhstan sells a cargo of wheat to Iran, payment will most likely be made in U.S. dollars. The Iranian importer may have to borrow the U.S. dollars in the international money market, and the Kazak exporter may in turn deposit the U.S. dollars in a European bank rather than converting the funds on the currency market into the local currency, the tenge.

Eurodollars are deposits of U.S. dollars in foreign banks or foreign branches of U.S. banks. These deposits are not subject to U.S. banking regulations or **reserve requirements**. In the United States, the Federal Reserve Bank requires that financial institutions hold a certain percentage of the deposits they receive in reserve. Reserve requirements apply to transaction accounts but not to savings accounts or time deposits. The Federal Reserve requirement is 10%, which means that when a bank accepts a $1,000 deposit from a customer, the bank must keep $100 in reserve and can lend out only $900 of that deposit.

TABLE 4.2 Interest Rate Futures Quotations

	OPEN	HIGH	LOW	SETTLE	CHG	LIFETIME HIGH	LOW	OPEN INT

Interest Rate Futures

Treasury Bonds (CBT)-$100,000; pts 32nds of 100%

	OPEN	HIGH	LOW	SETTLE	CHG	HIGH	LOW	OPEN INT
June	100-15	101-00	100-10	100-28	16	110-00	96-30	413,568
Sept	99-26	99-26	99-06	99-22	15	109-00	96-07	49,208
Dec	98-05	98-24	98-05	98-21	15	101-04	96-06	7,365

Est vol 165,000; vol Wed 247,530; open int 470,143, −4,580.

Treasury Notes (CBT)-$100,000; pts 32nds of 100%

	OPEN	HIGH	LOW	SETTLE	CHG	HIGH	LOW	OPEN INT
June	104-25	05-115	04-215	105-08	17.0	107-10	101-10	686,776
Sept	103-11	103-31	103-11	103-28	17.0	08-165	100-25	103,154

Est vol 370,000; vol Wed 350,459; open int 789,946, +3,994.

10 Yr Agency Notes (CBT)-$100,000; pts 32nds of 100%

	OPEN	HIGH	LOW	SETTLE	CHG	HIGH	LOW	OPEN INT
June	00-315	101-12	00-255	101-09	17.0	102-05	97-04	25,793

Est vol 500; vol Wed 2,657; open int 25,844, −344.

5 Yr Treasury Notes (CBT)-$100,000; pts 32nds of 100%

	OPEN	HIGH	LOW	SETTLE	CHG	HIGH	LOW	OPEN INT
June	105-28	06-075	05-255	06-055	10.5	106-21	03-115	569,155.
Sept	04-285	04-285	04-205	04-275	10.5	105-07	102-17	65,972.

Est vol 140,000; vol Wed 156,362; open int 635,127, +2,753.

2 Yr Treasury Notes (CBT)-$200,000; pts 32nds of 100%

	OPEN	HIGH	LOW	SETTLE	CHG	HIGH	LOW	OPEN INT
June	104-14	104-20	04-137	104-19	4.5	104-26	03-005	93,472

Est vol 7,000; vol Wed 8,219; open int 93,594, +247.

	OPEN	HIGH	LOW	SETTLE	CHG	YIELD	CHG	OPEN INT

Treasury Bills (CME)-$1,000,000; pts of 100%

	OPEN	HIGH	LOW	SETTLE	CHG	YIELD	CHG	OPEN INT
June	...	...	...	98.24	.01	1.76	−.01	333

Est vol 2; vol Wed 2; open int 387, −2.

Libor-1 Mo. (CME)-$3,000,000; pts of 100%

	OPEN	HIGH	LOW	SETTLE	CHG	YIELD	CHG	OPEN INT
June	98.12	98.13	98.11	98.13	.01	1.87	−.01	16,843
July	98.09	98.09	98.08	98.09	.02	1.91	−.02	13,453
Aug	97.94	97.96	97.94	97.96	.03	2.04	−.03	4,065
Sept	97.79	97.81	97.79	97.81	.07	2.19	−.07	1,898
Dec	97.04	97.04	97.03	97.05	.08	2.95	−.08	300

Est vol 1,894; vol Wed 4,163; open int 38,256; +464.

Eurodollar (CME)-$1,000,000; pts of 100%

	OPEN	HIGH	LOW	SETTLE	CHG	YIELD	CHG	OPEN INT
June	97.99	98.02	97.99	98.02	.02	1.98	−.02	683,345
July	97.89	97.91	97.89	97.90	.03	2.10	−.03	19,001
Aug	97.75	97.76	97.73	97.75	.04	2.25	−.04	7,112
Sept	97.51	97.62	97.51	97.59	.07	2.41	−.07	632,008
Dec	96.86	96.98	96.86	96.94	.07	3.06	−.07	784,169
Mr03	96.24	96.35	96.24	96.32	.08	3.68	−.08	445,438
June	95.67	95.79	95.67	95.74	.07	4.26	−.07	292,185
Sept	95.25	95.35	95.25	95.32	.07	4.68	−.07	241,282
Dec	94.96	95.05	94.96	95.02	.07	4.98	−.07	190,860
Mr04	94.79	94.88	94.79	94.85	.07	5.15	−.07	147,377
June	94.60	94.70	94.60	94.67	.07	5.33	−.07	133,387
Sept	94.46	94.54	94.46	94.51	.07	5.49	−.07	126,931
Dec	94.32	94.36	94.31	94.34	.07	5.66	−.07	91,578
Mr05	94.22	94.30	94.22	94.27	.07	5.73	−.07	91,231
June	94.16	94.19	94.13	94.16	.07	5.84	−.07	62,509
Sept	94.04	94.08	94.03	94.06	.07	5.94	−.07	68,390
Dec	93.88	93.94	93.88	93.92	.07	6.08	−.07	51,608
Mr06	93.88	93.91	93.85	93.89	.07	6.11	−.07	48,381
June	93.79	93.82	93.76	93.80	.07	6.20	−.07	48,884
Sept	93.71	93.74	93.68	93.72	.07	6.28	−.07	45,735
Dec	93.59	93.62	93.56	93.60	.07	6.40	−.07	30,884
Mr07	93.56	93.60	93.54	93.58	.07	6.42	−.07	25,192
June	93.47	93.52	93.46	93.51	.07	6.49	−.07	13,463
Sept	93.39	93.46	93.39	93.44	.06	6.56	−.06	11,375
Dec	93.31	93.34	93.29	93.33	.06	6.67	−.06	10,685
Mr08	93.30	93.33	93.28	93.32	.06	6.68	−.06	7,413

Est vol 867,316; vol Wed 926,027; open int 4,364,064, −23,712.

Source: Reprinted with permission from the *Wall Street Journal*, May 17, 2002

The interest paid on Eurodollar deposits is usually higher than that on deposits in the United States (see the section "Spread Trading" later in this chapter) because the depositor does not have the protection afforded by U.S. banking regulations. But over time, Eurodollar interest rates move very closely with short-term U.S. interest rates, such as T-bill rates. For more detailed information on the Eurodollar, the Bank for International Settlements Web site, *http://www.bis.org*, is a good source.

The Eurodollar futures contract is a short-term interest rate contract that was introduced in 1981. Eurodollar futures are traded on the CME, the London International Financial Futures Exchange (LIFFE), and the Singapore International Monetary Exchange (SIMEX). After hours and on weekends, this contract is also traded on the CME's GLOBEX, an electronic order-matching system.

The interest rate (i.e., yield) on Eurodollar futures is the 90-day deposit rate on U.S. dollars traded between banks in London. It is known as the **London Inter-Bank Offered Rate (LIBOR)** interest rate. The LIBOR rate quoted in the *Wall Street Journal* is an average of rate quotes from five major banks: the Bank of America, Barclays, the Bank of Tokyo, the Deutsche Bank, and the Swiss Bank.

Eurodollar futures are the highest volume futures contract worldwide. The CME's futures and options volume in Eurodollars in 2001 was more than 272 million contracts. Eurodollar futures are settled in cash during the expiry month because the underlying asset is a nontransferable time deposit that cannot be "delivered." At the time of contract expiry, all Eurodollar open futures positions are debited or credited based on the final settlement cash price, which is calculated as 100 minus the three-month LIBOR interest rate. Table 4.2 reports price quotations for Eurodollar futures. The Eurodollar futures price is an index calculated as 100 minus the 90-day LIBOR deposit rate. Therefore, as short-term interest rates rise, Eurodollar futures fall in price. Alternatively, when interest rates decline, Eurodollar futures rise in price. The futures contract face value is $1 million.

In Table 4.2, the settlement (i.e., closing) price on the nearest July Eurodollar futures contract is 97.90, which means the interest rate is 2.10% (= 100 − 97.90). For Eurodollar futures, a change in one **tick**, or one **basis point** (¹⁄₁₀₀th of a percentage point), is worth $25. So, if the price of the July contract falls to 97.50 (for example), then the value of the futures contract changes by 40 basis points, or $1,000. This futures contract price change associated with an interest rate change of 40 basis points (i.e., 0.4%) is identical to the profit/loss calculation for T-bill futures, as one T-bill futures contract tick is also worth $25. The tick value is determined by the relationship shown in Equation 4.12:

$$\$1,000,000 \times .0001 \times 90/360 = \$25. \tag{4.12}$$

In Equation 4.12, $1,000,000 is the face value of the futures contract, and .0001 represents one tick. The 90/360 ratio in Equation 4.12 accounts for the fact that Eurodollars (and T-bills) are 90-day instruments, and therefore the annualized interest rate must be converted to the quarterly (i.e., 90-day) counterpart. For example, 1% of $1 million equals $10,000 for 360 days, but for a 90-day loan, each 1% of $1 million equals $10,000/4, or $2,500.

Unlike Eurodollars, 90-day T-bills are securities that can be delivered. T-bills are sold at a discount to their face value (e.g., $1 million) and are redeemed at face (or par) value on maturity. For a T-bill, the price of the security on any given day is

$$Price = Face\ Value - Discount. \tag{4.13}$$

So,

$$Discount = Face\ Value - Price = (FV \times y \times t/360), \tag{4.14}$$

where FV is face value,
y is yield, and
t is days to maturity.

So, a T-bill futures quote of 96.51 implies an interest rate of 3.49% (= 100 − 96.51), and (solving Equation 4.14) a discount of $1,000,000 × .0349 × 90/360 = $8,725. This means that the price of the T-bill is equal to $1,000,000 − $8,725 = $991,275.

The interest rate on Eurodollar deposits is added onto the principal amount instead of a discount rate, as in the case of T-bills. This means that for a given discount, the **add-on rate** will slightly exceed the **discount rate**. The Eurodollar add-on rate is determined as follows:

$$Add\text{-}On\ Rate = Discount/Face\ Value \times 360/t. \tag{4.15}$$

So, for this example, where the discount is $8,725, the add-on rate = $8,725/$1,000,000 × 360/90 = .0352, or 3.52%. This is slightly higher than the T-bill yield of 3.49%.

Financial Swaps

In the commodity and financial markets, a **swap** is an agreement between two parties whereby each party agrees to initially exchange (i.e., swap) an asset and then reexchange the assets at a later date (Kolb, 2000 and Strong, 2001). Both parties gain from this swap arrangement. There are many analogies where two parties can gain through swapping an asset for a fixed time period and then swapping back. For example, if a professor from the University of California, Davis, plans to visit the University of Melbourne in Australia for a year, he or she might find a Melbourne professor who wants to spend a sabbatical in Davis. Most universities keep a listing of sabbatical homes for visiting professors, and faculty members often are willing to "swap" homes and cars with visitors. Both parties agree to swap homes and cars for a year, and maybe some cash changes hands. If rental rates in Davis are significantly higher than in Melbourne, then the Australian professor may agree to pay the Californian an agreed amount of cash as a supplement. In any event, both gain from this arrangement because they avoid the high transactions costs associated with finding or leasing rental property (such as search costs and realtor fees). On the Internet, there is also a very active international home exchange available to vacationers. If a New Yorker wishes to spend the summer in Italy, chances are that he or she can swap residences with an Italian through such home exchanges.

Essentially, a financial swap is an agreement by one party to make payments to the other for an agreed period of time and vice versa. Swaps can be used to either hedge or speculate, and they are instruments that are commonly used in the foreign currency and bond markets. **Over-the-counter swaps** have been used for many years by firms exposed to commodity, interest rate, or currency risk. More recently, exchange-traded standardized swaps have been introduced.

The most basic interest rate swap involves an exchange of a series of fixed interest payments for a series of floating (i.e., variable) interest payments. This is called a fixed-for-floating interest rate swap. Such an exchange is beneficial to both parties as long as each has a relative cost advantage in a specific credit market. The relative cost advantage in one market is used to obtain an equivalent advantage in the other market through the swap. For instance, firm A might be in a position where it cannot obtain an attractive long-term fixed interest rate, so it will have no choice but to borrow at a short-term rate and then "swap" interest payments with firm B, which can borrow at a more attractive long-term rate. In this case, a series of payments calculated by applying a fixed rate of interest to the principal amount is exchanged for a stream of payments similarly calculated but using a floating rate of interest.

A currency swap involves the simultaneous purchase and sale of a currency for two different dates against the sale and purchase of another currency. This is equivalent to borrowing one currency and lending another for a given time period.

In 2001, both the CBOT and the LIFFE introduced futures and options contracts based on interest rate swaps. The advantage of an exchange-traded swap is that it is standardized and therefore easier to buy or sell compared to the over-the-counter swaps.

The CBOT offers both 5- and 10-year interest rate swap futures and associated futures options contracts. These contracts are based on the underlying International Swaps and Derivatives Association's benchmark rate for 5- and 10-year U.S. dollar interest rate swaps. The contract is designed to offer a hedging tool for interest rate exposure tied to long-dated LIBOR.

In 1991, the CBOT introduced interest rate swap futures, but that contract failed. The 1991 contracts were based on 3- and 5-year swaps, whereas the contracts introduced in 2001 are based on a 10-year maturity swap. They are a less expensive alternative to the over-the-counter market and eliminate the counterparty risk of over-the-counter trading. Swap futures can be used to hedge interest rate risk and to create speculative opportunities for spread trading between swaps and other financial contracts.

EQUITY INSTRUMENTS

Futures contracts on stock market indices have been traded since 1982. As shown in Table 4.3, there are numerous futures (and options) contracts derived from stock indexes. Exchanges around the world have rapidly listed new indexes in the past

TABLE 4.3 Equity Index Futures Quotations

	OPEN	HIGH	LOW	SETTLE	CHG	LIFETIME HIGH	LOW	OPEN INT

Index Futures

DJ Industrial Average (CBOT)-$10 times average

	OPEN	HIGH	LOW	SETTLE	CHG	LIFETIME HIGH	LOW	OPEN INT
June	10274	10318	10226	10293	28	10951	9080	33,292
Sept	10260	10315	10235	10297	28	10705	9670	992

Est vol 15,000; vol Wed 23,663; open int 34,492, +451.
Idx prl: Hi 10318.83; Lo 10230.68; Close 10289.21, +45.53.

S&P 500 Index (CME)-$250 times index

June	109300	110080	108950	109910	460	170550	95030	473,671
Sept	109200	110180	109150	110060	450	165670	95530	58,333

Est vol 59,692; vol Wed 80,080; open int 538,072, -176.
Idx prl: Hi 1099.29; Lo 1089.17; Close 1098.23, +7.16.

Mini S&P 500 (CME)-$50 times index

June	109350	110075	108925	109900	450	118000	104575	231,886

Vol Wed 433,421; open int 232,090, +9,732.

S&P Midcap 400 (CME)-$500 times index

June	545.50	546.50	541.00	542.50	-2.50	555.90	417.85	16,643

Est vol 984; vol Wed 1,355; open int 16,645, +6.
Idx prl: Hi 545.72; Lo 540.91; Close 542.17, -2.36.

Nikkei 225 Stock Average (CME)-$5 times index

June	11700.	11780.	11680.	11775.	175	13400.	9245.	16,692

Est vol 1,455; vol Wed 1,426; open int 16,764, -172.
Idx prl: Hi 11747.35; Lo 11579.12; Close 11738.69, +95.72.

Nasdaq 100 (CME)-$100 times index

June	131600	133000	129700	132350	300	173650	112600	64,485

Est vol 19,680; vol Wed 28,576; open int 64,569, +3,578.
Idx prl: Hi 1319.52; Lo 1296.11; Close 1315.85, +4.80.

Mini Nasdaq 100 (CME)-$20 times index

June	1316.5	1331.0	1297.0	1323.5	3.0	1714.0	1144.5	161,165

Vol Wed 313,639; open int 161,186, +27,739.

GSCI (CME)-$250 times nearby index

June	205.50	205.70	201.30	204.00	-1.60	210.60	187.00	19,769

Est vol 165; vol Wed 529; open int 20,515, -193.
Idx prl: Hi 205.88; Lo 201.46; Close 203.92, -2.20.

Russell 2000 (CME)-$500 times index

June	513.50	514.00	505.75	506.65	-7.60	528.95	394.95	29,481

Est vol 2,306; vol Wed 2,763; open int 29,481, -40.
Idx prl: Hi 513.54; Lo 506.02; Close 507.40, -6.14.

Russell 1000 (NYFE)-$500 times index

June	579.75	584.00	578.50	584.00	3.00	622.00	555.00	49,383

Est vol 250; vol Wed 207; open int 49,393, -42.
Idx prl: Hi 582.68; Lo 577.97; Close 582.17, +2.81.

NYSE Composite Index (NYFE)-500 times index

June	579.25	582.50	579.00	581.40	1.15	611.50	550.00	2,768
Sept	...	...	...	582.40	1.15	607.00	561.40	410

Est vol 1,500; vol Wed 1,201; open int 3,378, -90.
Idx prl: Hi 582.44; Lo 578.98; Close 581.68, +2.14.

U.S. Dollar Index (FINEX)-$1,000 times index

June	114.29	114.65	114.01	114.34	.04	121.23	113.65	9,188
Sept	114.81	115.07	114.60	114.86	.04	121.00	114.18	2,925

Est vol 1,100; vol Wed 773; open int 12,126, -30.
Idx prl: Hi 114.47; Lo 113.84; Close 114.13, +.01.

Share Price Index (SFE)-A$25 times index

June	3381.0	3402.0	3369.0	3388.0	8.0	3516.0	2945.0	154,128
Sept	3388.0	3391.0	3388.0	3402.0	8.0	3511.0	3305.0	1,620
Dec	3407.0	3407.0	3407.0	3414.0	8.0	3497.0	3319.0	1,066
Mr03	3430.0	3430.0	3430.0	3431.0	8.0	3440.0	3335.0	658

Est vol 12,309; vol Wed 17,885; open int 157,666, +2,650.
Index: Hi 3403.5; Lo 3376.1; Close 3395.2, +19.1.

CAC-40 Stock Index (MATIF)-Euro 10.00 x index

May	4454.0	4473.0	4417.0	4444.0	-11.0	4627.0	4211.5	436,973
June	4423.0	4452.0	4410.0	4433.0	-10.5	4980.0	4200.0	102,506
Sept	4468.5	4496.0	4452.5	4467.5	-11.0	4645.5	4269.0	29,439

Est vol 43,580; vol Wed 46,293; open int 584,785, +3,536.

Xetra DAX (EUREX)-Euro 25 per DAX index point

June	5072.0	5120.0	5050.0	5068.5	-21.5	5520.0	4036.5	238,637
Sept	5117.0	5160.0	5100.0	5114.0	-21.5	5565.0	4806.5	5,862
Dec	5162.0	5162.0	5158.5	5165.0	-22.0	5552.5	4898.0	2,338

Vol Thu 54,961; open int 246,837, -7,945.
Index: Hi 5101.12; Lo 5032.08; Close 5047.45, -24.94.

FT-SE 100 Index (LIFFE)-£10 per index point

June	5274.5	5295.0	5250.5	5260.0	-19.0	5312.5	5089.5	316,357
Sept	5290.5	5307.5	5270.5	5276.0	-19.0	5321.0	5110.0	17,238
Dec	5329.0	5329.5	5329.0	5320.5	-18.5	5369.5	5151.0	9,498
Mr03	5349.5	5349.5	5341.0	5337.0	-17.5	5387.5	5192.0	3,089

Est vol 29,414; vol Wed 40,937; open int 346,182, -1,182.

DJ Euro STOXX 50 Index (EUREX)-Euro 10.00 x index

June	3563.0	3592.0	3520.0	3549.0	-47.0	3880.0	3010.0	899,527
Sept	3585.0	3604.0	3539.0	3561.0	-48.0	3871.0	3379.0	36,879
Dec	3626.0	3638.0	3572.0	3595.0	-47.0	3832.0	3412.0	14,196

Vol Thu 178,982; open int 950,602, +4,003.
Index: Hi 3606.48; Lo 3566.97; Close 3579.03, -16.70.

Source: Reprinted with permission from the *Wall Street Journal*, May 17, 2002

few years to try to accommodate investors and hedgers with complicated portfolios made up of domestic and international equities. Stock index futures and options are popular with speculators, and they also provide an important instrument for hedging portfolio risk.

The most actively traded equity index futures contracts are shown in Table 4.3, reproduced from the *Wall Street Journal*. These include the Standard and Poor's 500 (S&P 500) index on the CME, the electronic Mini S&P 500 Index, the Dow Jones Industrial Average on the CBOT, the CAC-40 Stock Index on the MATIF in France, the FT-SE 100 on the LIFFE in London, and the DJ Euro STOXX 50 on the EUREX. All these indices are designed to measure the performance of specific portfolios of stocks on various stock markets.

These indices are weighted averages of stocks and are designed to reflect movements in either the overall market (e.g., the S&P 500) or a particular segment of the market (e.g., the S&P Midcap 400). They serve as a proxy for a specific portfolio. The futures contract on the S&P 500 stock index was the first one traded (from

1982), and it is one of the largest volume contracts. The S&P 500 is a value-weighted average of 500 stocks, the majority of which are listed on the New York Stock Exchange. In the index, each stock is weighted by the market value of its outstanding shares, which means that the weights change over time.

Stock index futures are obviously settled by cash rather than by physical delivery because you cannot deliver a theoretical construct such as an index. This means that when a futures contract expires, the futures stock index equals the underlying spot market index. In Table 4.3, we find that the June futures price for the S&P 500 Index settled at 1099.10 (the *Wall Street Journal* does not report the decimal point). To calculate the total dollar value of this contract, we multiply this index by $250 because each index point is worth $250. Thus, the June contract was worth $274,775. The Mini S&P 500 Index is based on the same index but is 20% of the size of the S&P 500 contract. It is worth $50 times the S&P Index.

The Nasdaq 100 futures is also traded on the CME, and this index is based on 100 of the largest domestic, nonfinancial, common stocks listed on the Nasdaq Stock Market. There is a corresponding Mini Nasdaq 100 contract that is one-fifth the size of the Nasdaq 100. The S&P and the Nasdaq 100 futures (and options) contracts trade on the CME during "regular" trading hours (8:30 A.M. to 3:15 P.M. Central Standard Time) and electronically overnight on the GLOBEX (trading hours 3:45 P.M. to 8:15 A.M. the next day). The Mini S&P and Mini Nasdaq 100 virtually trade 24 hours a day (from 5:30 P.M. Sunday to 3:15 P.M. Friday).

The Dow Jones Industrial Average (DJIA, sometimes referred to as "the Dow") is another popular index with traders, and futures and options based on this index trade on the CBOT. The DJIA futures and options also trade electronically on the EUREX platform, where it can be traded 20 hours a day.

From Table 4.3, it is evident that European stock indexes also play an important role in financial futures and options trading. For instance, the Dow Jones Euro STOXX 50 Index is a large-volume contract traded on the EUREX. This index is comprised of 50 blue-chip stocks in the single Euro region of the European Union. Alternatively, the FT-SE Eurotop 100 Index, traded on the LIFFE, covers Europe's top 100 companies. The economic integration of Europe and the single currency (i.e., the Euro) has made cross-border trade more efficient in Europe and has helped develop financial markets in Europe.

The role of the stock index futures in the financial community became controversial soon after the first contract was launched on the CME. Many stock market investors and politicians did not fully understand how price movements in the futures market related to the underlying stock market. For example, some investors and politicians blamed the stock market crash in October 1987 on excessive trading in the stock index futures market and allegations that the futures market was manipulated. These critics singled out portfolio insurance, a hedging technique that involves the sale of stock index futures to protect a stock portfolio from a declining market. Stock index arbitrage trading, which involves the simultaneous buying and selling of stock and stock index futures, was also thought to be a factor in the stock market plunge.

President Reagan asked Nicholas Brady (former U.S. Treasury Secretary) to determine why the stock market collapsed during October 1987. Studies by The Brady Commission and others found no evidence to support the theory that futures-related trading constituted a major part of the October 1987 plunge in the New York Stock Exchange (Malkiel, 1988).

Stock index futures are of interest to the general public because so many small investors own stocks (i.e., equities). Investors are constantly trying to forecast the direction of the stock market, and some mistakenly look to the overnight trading in stock futures as a signal of where the New York or Nasdaq market is headed. Suppose the stock index futures market rallies during overnight and early morning trading. Does this mean that the New York stock market will necessarily open higher at 8:30 A.M.? The answer is no. Overnight futures trading establishes the market's valuation based on investor expectations on what might happen tomorrow, news that comes into the market overnight, and foreign stock market activity. This set of information could change once the New York stock market opens for the day. Overnight futures trading does not necessarily point to the next day's direction in the stock market. However, it is not unusual to hear "financial experts" on early morning television reporting that overnight stock index futures trading indicates which direction Wall Street is headed for the day. This type of financial advice is clearly wrong.

Spread Trading

Rather than taking an outright long or short futures position, many speculators in futures markets take a less risky approach through **spread trading**. Spread trading is popular with both **technical** and **fundamental** traders. The simplest spread involves the simultaneous purchase of one futures contract and the sale of another. This could involve trading two identical futures contracts but with different delivery months, known as a calendar spread. Calendar spreads are particularly common for nonstorables, such as lean hogs. For example, a trader might sell July lean hogs and buy February lean hogs. When the spread widens or narrows, the speculator can profit by buying the cheaper contract and selling the more expensive contract. Traders also spread the same contract but on different exchanges (e.g., silver in New York vs. silver in Japan). Alternatively, spread trading could involve trading two different futures contracts that are related in a way such that their relative prices have somewhat predictable patterns over time.

The objective with spread trading is to profit from an expected change in the relative prices of the two futures contracts. Rather than trying to predict absolute price changes, the spread trader is trying to predict relative price changes. There are an unlimited number of spread opportunities. In the commodity markets, examples of spread trading include cocoa/coffee spreads, wheat/corn spreads, and gold/silver spreads. In the financial markets, currency spreads are common.

Three types of spreads that are common in the financial markets are the MOB, NOB, and TED spreads. The MOB involves trading municipal bonds versus T-bonds, the NOB spread involves trading T-notes versus T-bonds, and the TED spread involves trading U.S. T-bills versus Eurodollars. The NOB spread is a spread between *maturities* (i.e., medium- vs. long-term interest rates). Alternatively, the MOB and TED spreads are spreads between *quality* levels. Municipal bonds are more risky than T-bonds, and Eurodollars are more risky than T-bills.

T-Bill Minus Eurodollar Rate

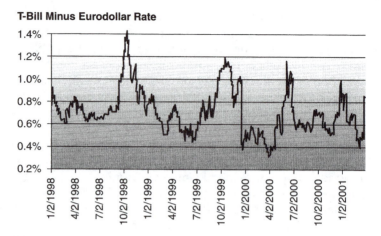

FIGURE 4.6
TED spread.

Consider the TED spread. The TED spread is the rate at which a Eurodollar futures contract is trading minus the rate at which a U.S. T-bill futures contract is trading. Assume that the rate of a nearby U.S. T-bill futures contract is 97.72 (implied discount rate of 2.28%) and that the Eurodollar future is trading at 97.02 (implied Eurodollar deposit rate of 2.98%). In this case, the TED spread would be 97.72 − 97.02 = 0.70. A speculator who trades this spread is evaluating the relative quality of the U.S. Treasury versus bank rates in Europe. One factor that can influence the spread is international politics. Investors tend to shift funds into and out of U.S. treasuries as the international political and economic climate changes. Assume in this example that the speculator expects the TED spread to widen from 0.70 to 1.0. In this case, she would buy T-bill futures and sell Eurodollar futures.

The actual TED spread from 1998 to 2001 is shown in Figure 4.6. The yield difference between T-bills and Eurodollars is always positive. The nearby futures contracts were used to generate Figure 4.6. The TED spread over this period averaged 0.7%, with a maximum spread of 1.3% and a minimum of 0.3%. This graph shows considerable variability in the spread over time.

SUMMARY

Most financial traders check the interest rate and currency markets first thing each morning, as do most commodity traders. This basic fact of a trader's life indicates that financials (i.e., currencies, interest rates, and stock indexes) are pervasive in our globalized economy.

This chapter has outlined price formation in the underlying spot markets for currencies, interest rates, and stock indexes. Additionally, it has traced the linkage between these spot markets and trading in financial futures and options. The workings of financial futures were explained for the major markets. Financial futures share many similar features with commodity futures, such as the cost-of-carry price spread relationship that ties together intertemporal prices.

Economic integration is increasing around the world, largely because of the efforts of the World Trade Organization and the examples set by those countries that have embraced globalization. Above-average economic growth has been achieved by countries that have opened their doors to more capital flows and more trade in merchandise and services. As a result of this globalization, financial futures and options markets will continue to expand and continue to offer new and innovative products for hedgers and speculators. Electronic exchanges are playing a vital role in the worldwide growth in financial futures and options trading.

DISCUSSION QUESTIONS

1. Explain why foreign exchange rates are important to a U.S.-based firm that exports final processed goods to Canada and imports raw materials from Mexico. How would changes in the Canadian and Mexican exchange rates affect the firm's sales and profits?
2. Which macroeconomic factors affect the exchange rate? Provide an example with an analysis of a recent currency move.
3. What have been the main economic impacts of the creation of the Euro single-currency zone? Describe the impacts within western Europe and for the rest of the world. Why didn't Britain initially replace the pound sterling with the Euro?
4. Explain the macroeconomic information that is embedded in the shape of the yield curve. If the yield curve steepens during a recession, is this good or bad news?
5. The 1988 Brady Commission called for higher margins on financial futures markets to limit wild price swings. Brady suggested that futures margins should be raised to the 50% of gross value required by the stock market. Discuss the most likely reasons why this recommendation was never implemented.
6. Should financial futures be regulated by the U.S. Securities and Exchange Commission instead of the Commodity Futures Trading Commission? What are the pros and cons of such a regulatory change?

SELECTED WEB SITES

The faculty of commerce at the University of British Columbia maintains a Web site dedicated to information on foreign currencies (*http://pacific.commerce. ubc.ca/xr/*). This site provides current and historic daily exchange rates and commentary on exchange rate fundamentals.

There are many excellent Web sites with daily price information on financial futures, such as *http://www.ino.com*, *http://money.msn.com*, and *http://www.bloomberg.com*; for charts and quotes, go to *http://tfc-charts.w2d.com*.

The Federal Reserve Bank of New York maintains a Web site with current financial statistics that cover global economic trends, exchange rates, and financial market analysis. Go to *http://www.ny.frb.org*.

The International Monetary Fund (*http://www.imf.org*) provides reports on economies around the world, and this Web site is helpful for currency-related economic information.

SELECTED REFERENCES

Copeland, L. S. (2000). *Exchange rates and international finance.* Harlow: Financial Times Prentice Hall.

della Paolera, G., & Taylor, A. M. (2001). *Straining at the anchor: The Argentine Currency Board and the search for macroeconomic stability, 1880–1935.* Chicago: University of Chicago Press.

Dornbusch, R. (1987). Exchange rate economics: 1986. *Economic Journal 97*(385), 1–18.

Friberg, R. (1999). *Exchange rates and the firm: Strategies to manage exposure and the impact of EMU.* New York: St. Martin's.

Harvey, J. T. (2001). Exchange rate theory and the fundamentals. *Journal of Post Keynesian Economics 24*(1), 3–15.

Isard, P. (1995). *Exchange rate economics.* Cambridge: Cambridge University Press.

Kolb, R. W. (2000). *Futures, options, and swaps.* Malden, MA: Blackwell.

Malkiel, B. G. (1988). The Brady Commission Report: A critique. *Journal of Portfolio Management 14*(4), 9–13.

Strong, R. A. (2001). *Derivatives: An introduction.* Cincinnati: South-Western.

Taylor, M. P. (1995). The economics of exchange rates. *Journal of Economic Literature 33*(1), 13–47.

CHAPTER 5

Fundamental Analysis

In this chapter and the next, two general categories of forecasting futures and options prices are introduced to the reader. This chapter discusses fundamental analysis, and Chapter 6 introduces technical analysis. A fundamental analyst looks forward in time, gathering information concerning future supply and demand conditions and determining what this information implies for market conditions and forthcoming prices. Alternatively, a technical analyst looks backward in time for information. He or she generates price forecasts based on historical market prices and historical volume and open interest data.

Fundamental analysis is more difficult than technical analysis because there is considerably more information to evaluate and the models used are much more complex. The use of fundamental tools requires a combination of extensive market knowledge and some training in economics and statistics. The old-fashioned fundamental traders[1] did not use formal economic models with multiple equations; instead, their models were "in their head." However, modern-day fundamental price forecasts are generated mostly using analytical tools. The same analytical tools can be applied to a number of different markets, but application requires detailed knowledge of a specific market. For example, a skilled econometrician can build and estimate a model of the world wheat market using the same analytical tools she would use to develop a model of the world coffee market or to model exchange rate movements. However, it would take a long time (e.g., weeks or months) to build these models, and it would be time consuming to keep the models updated.

Alternatively, technical trading rules can be effortlessly generated by a personal computer using relatively inexpensive software. Technical trading rules can be easily and quickly applied to a number of different markets. For example, with little or no background understanding of the wheat market, a technician could

---

[1] For examples of some of the more traditional fundamental approaches, see the collection of studies edited by Jiler (1975). Although dated, these studies illustrate a relevant approach to fundamental analysis as practiced by professional traders.

BOX 5.1

Sir Issac Newton was a fundamentalist.

Sir Issac Newton (1642–1727) was one of the greatest scientists in the history of the world. He was primarily a physicist and mathematician, but he became interested in economics in his 50s. As a result of his great mind and his fascination with economics, he was appointed Master of the British Royal Mint in 1699, a position he retained until his death.

When Newton took over the mint, the British government was facing a perceived money problem because of the rising price of gold relative to silver. At the time, "money" consisted of coins. The shilling was a silver coin and the guinea a gold coin. The price of one guinea had risen from 22 to 30 shillings over a relatively short time period, and the government of England was concerned with the speculative run-up in the price of gold relative to silver. Silver coins were being melted down and/or exported to buy up foreign gold, and a shortage of silver coins resulted.

Newton evaluated the problem by comparing the purchasing power of gold in terms of silver across Europe. He reckoned that in England, gold was overvalued relative to silver, and he argued that the laws of supply and demand (i.e., the fundamentals) would eventually solve the problem. Based on Newton's forecast, the government put a ceiling on the price of the guinea at 21 shillings and prohibited trading at a higher price. Eventually, the price of gold fell relative to the price of silver, and Newton's forecast was indeed correct.

For more background on this topic, see Bernstein (2000).

---

choose a forecasting approach from the family of technical procedures and generate wheat price forecasts in a matter of hours. The same approach could then be applied to the coffee market (or any other market) in a matter of minutes. Updating technical forecasts is also much easier than updating fundamental forecasts. Neither formal training in economics and statistics nor detailed market knowledge is required to become a technical trader.

These two alternative approaches to price forecasting—technical and fundamental analyses—are also used outside the futures and options markets, for example, in the equity (or stock) markets. Some investors in the stock market subscribe to forecasts generated by technical analysts, while others follow fundamental analysts. Strictly speaking, technical analysis of equities has nothing to do with stock valuation and instead focuses on historical price patterns in an attempt to determine the current price trend. Alternatively, fundamental analysis of the stock market focuses on price-to-earnings ratios, balance sheets, and industry profitability.

In the equity, futures, and options markets, the fundamentalist pays attention to both the "demand" and the "supply" side of the market and believes that the dynamics of the market are ultimately driven by the fundamentals. A fundamentalist tries to determine the intrinsic value of a product, which is a long-run approach to price analysis. Fundamentalist traders use different methods ranging from calculating simple ratios of economic variables (e.g., the ratio of the price of hogs to the price of corn indicates profitability of hog production and predicts the forthcoming supply of hogs) to building and estimating complex econometric supply and demand models.

EFFICIENCY OF FUTURES MARKETS

There is considerable controversy surrounding the profitability of technical versus fundamental analysis. The technicians argue that the fundamental approach is far too complex to be of any benefit to the small trader. Alternatively, the fundamentalists point out that technical trading is of no value because it is impossible to consistently predict forthcoming prices from historical prices. Which is the most dependable approach?

At the center of the debate is the issue of whether the futures and options markets are **efficient**. A very broad definition of an efficient market is one in which stock, futures, and options contract prices fully reflect available information at any point in time (Fama 1970). Alternatively, if information is costly, an efficient market is one that reflects information up to the point where the marginal benefits from trading (futures or options contracts) based on this information do not exceed the marginal costs of collecting the information (Fama 1991).

Markets can be tested for efficiency, and Fama has classified efficient market tests into three groups: the weak, semistrong, and strong forms.[2] The information set for weak-form tests is confined to historical market prices, semistrong-form tests measure the market's adjustment to historical prices plus all other relevant public information, and strong-form tests measure its adjustment to "inside" information not available to the public. For each form of the test, if markets are efficient, the test's information set cannot be used by traders to make above-average earnings. However, any test of market efficiency is necessarily a joint test of efficiency and a model of asset pricing, which means that market efficiency per se may not be strictly testable (Fama 1991). Furthermore, Figlewski (1978) has questioned the efficiency assumption in its most general form. He develops a model of a speculative market in which the redistribution of wealth among traders with different information is studied, and he theoretically demonstrates that in neither the short nor the long run is full efficiency (in Fama's strong-form sense) likely in a financial market if the participants are risk averse. As discussed in this chapter, the futures and options market is at least semistrong efficient.

Speculators who subscribe to either fundamental or technical analysis buy and sell futures and options contracts with the expectation of making a profit. They

---

[2] Fama's concept of efficient markets is different than the traditional welfare concept of efficiency in economic theory.

are not trading for their health. However, if the market is efficient, then predicting price changes is difficult if not impossible for these speculators, regardless of whether they are fundamentalists or technicians. The (semistrong) efficient market hypothesis states that today's market prices fully reflect all publicly available information. This implies that if a small speculator spends hours each morning studying the market "news" before trading, then he is wasting his time and money. If the market is efficient, then the news is reflected in the market price by the time the small speculator reads about it in the *Wall Street Journal* or on the Internet.

In statistical jargon, if the market is efficient, then prices approximately follow a **random walk**. This implies that day-to-day price changes are random so that you cannot predict the future from the past. The random walk theory states that

$$P_t = P_{t-1} + e_t, \tag{5.1}$$

where P_t is the current price, P_{t-1} is the price lagged one day, and e_t is an error term. Assume that P_t is today's closing price on the futures market and P_{t-1} is yesterday's closing price. According to this theory, the expected value of $e_t = 0$. In other words, if we rearrange equation 5.1, we find that

$$E(P_t - P_{t-1}) = e_t = 0. \tag{5.2}$$

So, Equation 5.2 indicates that day-to-day price changes average to zero, which is another way of saying that price changes are random. This means that the price change tomorrow (i.e., $P_{t+1} - P_t$) is independent of today's price change (i.e., $P_t - P_{t-1}$). According to this model, whether today's price change was positive or negative has no bearing on the sign of tomorrow's price change.

In an efficient market, competition among traders leads to a situation where, at any point in time, futures (and options) prices reflect both the effects of current information and events that are expected to occur in the future. In statistics, this is characterized as a "fair game," and in an efficient market the current price will be an accurate estimate of the commodity or asset's true intrinsic value. This means that it would be difficult to come up with a better price forecast to "beat" the market. If a trader did come up with a system to beat the market, then, in theory, other traders would soon exploit that profit opportunity, and the inefficiency would quickly disappear.

Prices quickly adjust to new information as it becomes available in an efficient market. Price changes from day to day are random because news events come into the market in a random fashion. Today the news might suggest that the market is going higher (i.e., **bullish** news), and tomorrow the news might be negative and suggest that the market price is going lower (i.e., **bearish** news). This random nature of news is illustrated with an example from the copper futures market shown in Box 5.2.

The random walk theory asserts that price movements will not follow any patterns or trends, which means that technical analysis is worthless because past price movements cannot be used to predict future price movements. The more participants and the faster the dissemination of information, the more efficient a mar-

---

BOX 5.2

Market news is random.

The arrival of important news into futures and options markets is difficult to predict. This point is illustrated with the following five news stories in the *Wall Street Journal* over a two-week period in 1995. The initial story on October 16 refers to an attempt by a Japanese trading house to corner copper stocks on the London Metal Exchange by putting a "squeeze" on the copper market, thus raising prices. Two days later, on October 18, there was a sharp drop in the price of copper. On October 20, prices reversed course and rose again, only to fall based on the news on October 25. The news was bullish on the following November 3, and as a result copper prices strongly rallied.

The titles of the *Wall Street Journal* news stories and the dates were as follows:

"Squeeze Rumors Rattle Copper Market" (October 16)
"Copper Prices Sink on Variety of Bearish Factors" (October 18)
"Copper Prices Reverse Course to Post Strong Gains" (October 20)
"Copper Scarcity Is Under Debate at London Metal Exchange" (October 25)
"Copper Prices Rally Again Amid Panic Buying" (November 3)

---

ket should be, and the less likely it will be for technical analysts to profit from their predictions of price movements.

The debate over the efficient market hypothesis has resulted in many empirical economic studies, and there is considerable evidence to suggest that most futures markets are approximately efficient but not fully efficient. For example, in an early study, Brinegar (1970) statistically tested the degree to which wheat, corn, and rye futures prices departed from behavior expected in a random series of prices. He found that prices reacted to exogenous "shocks" in a gradual fashion and consequently concluded that the behavior of the markets studied was less than "ideal."

Elam (1978) developed a semistrong test of efficiency and considered the question of whether profits can be earned by fundamentally trading the hog futures market. An econometric model of the U.S. hog market was estimated and used to generate price forecasts. His basic trading rule was to sell one hog futures contract if the futures contract price is x% above the price level forecast, and buy one contract if the futures contract price is x% below. This rule yielded profits over the period studied and led Elam to conclude that the hog futures market is not efficient. Leuthold and Hartmann (1979) also concluded that the live-hog futures market does not reflect all publicly available information and is inefficient.

Tomek and Gray (1970) and later Kofi (1973) were the first to test the forecasting ability of the futures market within the context of market efficiency. They argued that inventories of storable commodities provide a linkage between the springtime prices of the postharvest futures and the subsequent harvest-time prices, which helps

---

BOX 5.3

Can the futures market forecast freezing temperatures in Florida?

In the United States, the production of oranges for processing is concentrated in the state of Florida, which produces virtually all the frozen concentrated orange juice (FCOJ) in the country. Futures and options for FCOJ are traded on the New York Board of Trade.

The orange crop in Florida is susceptible to freezing temperatures from January through March in any given year. Because of the geographic concentration of production, FCOJ prices react sharply to the winter temperatures in Florida.

In a provocative research paper, Roll (1984) found that price movements in the orange juice futures market could predict freezing temperatures in Florida better than the U.S. National Weather Service could. In other words, the futures market was found to be efficient in terms of incorporating available weather information. In the winter, the best predictor of freezing temperatures in Florida is the price of FCOJ. If FCOJ futures prices were up sharply on a winter day, this could be a strong signal of a forthcoming freeze.

---

make the futures price a self-fulfilling forecast. Using the ordinary-least-squares technique, they estimated the coefficients of the following linear regression equation:

$$P_h = \alpha + \beta\, P_{fh} + e_h,\qquad\qquad (5.3)$$

where P_h = cash price at harvest time, P_{fh} = planting time futures quotation for the harvest time contract, and e_h = error term. A "perfect forecast" was one for which α and β were estimated to be zero and one, respectively.

Both studies found that the forward pricing function of futures markets was more reliable for continuous than for discontinuous inventory markets. For potatoes, coffee, wheat, corn, soybeans, and cocoa, Kofi's results from 1953–69 data clearly show that the farther away from the contract expiration date, the worse the futures market performs as a predictor of spot prices. Leuthold (1972) estimated Equation 5.3 for corn and cattle and similarly found the futures market to be an efficient predictor of spot prices for only near maturity dates. His results for cattle show that up until the 15th week prior to delivery, the cash price was a more accurate indicator of realized cash prices than was the futures price. This phenomena was also confirmed for Maine potatoes by Gray (1972) and for live beef cattle, corn, and Maine potatoes by Stein (1981). The estimated coefficients of the equivalent of Equation 5.3 led Stein to conclude that the futures price, earlier than four months to delivery, is a biased and useless forecast of the closing price.

Using a semistrong-form test, Rausser and Carter (1983) examined the efficiency of the soybean complex. In some cases, the models outperformed the futures market for both long- and short-range forecasts. However, they stressed that unless the forecast information from the models is sufficient to provide profitable trades, then superior forecasting performance in a statistical sense has no economic significance.

Kenyon, Jones, and McGuirk (1993) examined the forward pricing performance of soybeans and corn and how this may have changed over time. For the 1952–72 time period, they found both soybeans and corn futures to be unbiased forecasts of forthcoming spot prices. However, for the 1974–91 time period, they found both soybeans and corn futures to be biased estimates of forthcoming spot prices. Kenyon et al. reasoned that this decline in forecasting ability was due to the reduced role of the government in the marketplace and greater production uncertainty.[3]

Tomek (1997) stresses that futures prices can provide poor price forecasts but still be efficient as long as their forecasts are better than any alternative, such as an econometric model. If the futures market is efficient, then it should be able to out-forecast an econometric model.

Fama and French (1987) tested for evidence of whether commodity futures prices provided forecast information superior to the information contained in spot prices. They found that futures markets for seasonal commodities contain superior forecast power relative to spot prices. However, this was not the case for nonseasonal commodities.

What all this economic research means is that, in reality, markets are neither perfectly efficient nor completely inefficient. All markets are efficient to a certain extent, some more so than others. The reason that futures and options markets are not perfectly efficient is that these markets reflect imperfect information and reflect influences other than fundamental information. In the futures and options markets, every dollar has a vote regarding the forthcoming price, and traders with imperfect information regularly "cast a vote," as do technicians with complete disregard for fundamental information. To "beat" the market, a trader must somehow use existing information in a way other than the market does or interpret existing information more accurately than the market. Another successful strategy could be based on anticipating changes in noninformational aspects of the market.

FUNDAMENTAL APPROACH TO PRICE ANALYSIS

The fundamental factors of supply and demand are taken very seriously by fundamental futures and options traders because supply and demand actually works in commodity and financial markets. These markets are thought to be closer to being perfectly competitive than many other markets in the economy because there is less domestic and foreign government intervention. There are some exceptions

---

[3] Brenner and Kroner (1995) argue that a test for price bias with Equation 5.3 is inappropriate for commodity markets due the fact that spot and futures prices may not be cointegrated, because the cost of carry has a stochastic trend.

to this statement in the case of agricultural commodities, such as wheat, corn, cotton, rice, and soybeans, where government intervention remains prevalent, especially in the United States and in the European Union.

Economic theory says that prices in a competitive market are determined by the interaction of supply and demand. The operations of futures and options markets do, by design, come very close to fulfilling the following requirements of perfect competition:

a. There are a large number of traders so that no one trader has (too) much influence on market prices.
b. Product homogeneity is closely approached by the contract specifications.
c. Free entry and exit is closely approximated through relatively small contract sizes and trading on margin.
d. Full information is available to everyone (in fact, futures and options markets generate a vast amount of price information that would not otherwise exist).
e. Independence and impersonality of trading are dictated by the organization and regulation of the futures and options markets.

Fundamental traders believe that in a market so close to the competitive model described in economic theory, the key to price analysis is to interpret information concerning factors affecting supply or demand. Furthermore, the traders want to forcast the effects that this information will have on long-term price trends. Fundamentalists are not as concerned about *when* prices will move significantly as they are with the probability of *whether* prices will move in a given direction and the possible extent of such a move. If the direction of price movements can be predicted correctly, speculators can make profits, and hedgers can better identify the strategy most appropriate to them. Fundamentalists believe that prices are random in the short term (e.g., day-to-day price changes). Therefore, traders relying on fundamental analysis try to monitor and correctly evaluate new *long-term* information concerning general economic factors and specific market supply and demand variables.

A fundamentalist's analysis involves determining the answers to a number of questions, such as the following:

a. Is the price level higher or lower than the long-term average? What is the current price trend?
b. What is the seasonal pattern (if any) of prices?
c. What is the current government policy, and how will this affect supply and demand?
d. Are demand prospects relatively strong or weak?
e. How sensitive are prices to news events?
f. For commodities, how do production and stock levels compare to long-term averages?
g. For commodities, is the production of competitive products larger or smaller than the average level?
h. For financials, what are the trends in general economic conditions, including inflation, unemployment, exchange rates, and retail sales?

In order to answer these (and other related) questions, fundamentalists use a variety of both quantitative and qualitative techniques. A brief introduction to examples of techniques used by analysts in commodity and financial markets is presented in the following sections.

COMMODITIES

Futures and options markets for commodities respond to a wide array of supply and demand factors. Like financials, commodity markets have become truly globalized markets in that arbitrage is practiced around the world. As a result, prices of products on futures and options exchanges traded in the United States are influenced by worldwide conditions and vice versa. The only downside to the growing level of international economic integration is that it complicates fundamental analyses of markets because supply and demand factors from around the globe now influence futures and options prices.

BOX 5.4

Trading places.

In the classic comedy movie *Trading Places*, two wealthy brothers who are commodity traders have nothing better to do than argue with each other over whether environment plays a bigger role than heredity in developing a person's character. They bet that anyone could run their company, so they fire their president and replace him with a homeless man. The ex-president, played by Dan Akroyd, is discredited and winds up on skid row. Eddie Murphy plays the homeless person who takes over as president of the brokerage firm.

Once Akroyd and Murphy discover the switch played on them, they team up to teach the two wealthy brothers a lesson. Akroyd and Murphy arrange to have advance access to the U.S. Department of Agriculture's crop report on orange juice. Then they corner the frozen orange juice futures market with the advance information on the government reports and financially break the two wealthy brothers.

Carter and Galopin (1993) ran an economics experiment based partly on this movie. They examined the value of the informational content of quarterly government reports that estimate forthcoming supplies of hogs and pigs. They assumed that a hypothetical futures trader obtains the government reports one day in advance of their release. A futures market trading rule is established that uses early access to the reports together with *a priori* expectations of the reports' contents. They found that the market information in the government reports is of little or no value to a futures trader in advance of the release date because this information is already incorporated in the futures price. In other words, the market is efficient.

Commodity futures and options prices are affected by changes in the expectations of market participants concerning a wide variety of supply and demand factors. As discussed previously, efficient market studies have shown that commodity futures prices react quickly to new fundamental information factors. For commodities, important supply and demand factors include the weather, input costs, and government policy.

Weather Patterns

Weather may be the single most important influence on the short-run **supply** of agricultural commodities, and it is virtually impossible to accurately predict the weather more than a few weeks out. The primary effect of weather conditions takes place during the growing season, affecting crop yields and harvest quality. Weather variables include degree days, temperature, rainfall, and so on.

For the heating oil and natural gas futures and options markets, the weather is perhaps the single most important influence on the **demand** side of the market. In the summer months, hot weather increases the demand for electricity, which in turn increases the derived demand for natural gas. If instead mild temperatures are experienced during the summer, there is weak demand for natural gas. As an illustration, on August 10, 2001, the *Wall Street Journal* reported, "Natural-Gas Prices

---

BOX 5.5

Inputs often substitute for one another.

In many of the richer livestock-producing countries, feed grains are important inputs into the livestock production process. American agriculture is a large exporter of feed grains, especially to Asia and Europe.

Some analysts blamed the 1997 Asian financial crisis for a decline in U.S. corn shipments to South Korea. However, it is not obvious that the decline in corn shipments during this period can be attributed to the financial crisis. It is true that South Korea's livestock feed consumption did decline in 1998 with reduced livestock numbers. In fact, feed grain usage in Korea (and in some other key Asian nations) is on a declining trend, partly because of the impact of increased meat imports. But we cannot look at corn in isolation. Feed wheat represents as much as 20% of South Korea's compound feed in some years. Korea's imports of corn did fall by about 1.6 million metric tons from 1996 to 1998. However, the Koreans imported feed wheat instead of corn; in fact, feed wheat imports increased by 1.4 million metric tons from 1996 to 1998. It is possible that the Koreans imported feed wheat instead of U.S. corn because of Korean consumer concern over genetically modified corn grown in the United States. At the time, about 25% of U.S. corn was genetically modified, but there was no genetically modified wheat commercially grown anywhere in the world.

Sink, with Heat Wave in the Northeast Dismissed as a Factor." This story was reporting that the New York Mercantile Exchange natural gas prices plunged with the news that a cooling trend was overtaking the short-lived summer heat wave in the northeastern United States.

During the same summer, crude oil and natural gas futures prices were influenced by a tropical storm in the Gulf of Mexico. Tropical storm Barry threatened offshore oil and gas rigs and land-based refineries, handling, and storage facilities. Petroleum prices rose before the storm hit on the expectation of damage and lost production. However, the storm passed without disrupting petroleum supplies in a significant way. The winter season is also a high-usage season for natural gas, and winter weather plays a major factor in the New York Mercantile Exchange's heating oil market.

The following quote from the *Wall Street Journal* (August 1, 2001) is fairly typical of news surrounding the agricultural market's sensitivity to the weather during the growing season:

> Soybean prices at the Chicago Board of Trade tumbled on U.S. weather reports. Soybean prices recently were on a bull run on private weather forecasts showing extremely hot and dry conditions moving into the Midwest. Market watchers were concerned that record temperatures and a lack of rain would cause heat stress, which would lead to a shorter crop. But forecasts showing a reduced heat threat and scattered showers dried out the bullish sentiment and pushed November soybean futures down.

Every year, the soybean futures market is very sensitive to weather reports in late July and early to mid-August. This is typically the "podding" stage for the soybean plant and therefore the most critical time for yield potential for soybeans.

Despite the well-known relationship between weather and commodity supply, weather data have been of little help to analysts trying to forecast prices. This is evidenced by Roll's (1984) study, in which only 3% of frozen concentrated orange juice price movements could be explained using data from weather reports.

Even the prices of livestock products are affected by the weather. For instance, in the summer of 2001, unusually hot weather in the midwestern United States led to reduced hog marketings as farmers tried to keep their pigs cool. As a result, hog futures prices rose sharply in late July and early August.

Foreign weather conditions are extremely important for U.S. commodity markets as well. For example, cold weather in Brazil in July and August can demolish the coffee crop in the world's largest coffee-producing nation. During the Southern Hemipshere's winter, the coffee market is usually somewhat volatile and prone to a sharp price rally on any hint of a damaging frost in Brazil.

Commodity traders also watch the weather conditions in China very closely, as China is the world's largest producer of raw agricultural products. For instance, China is the largest producer of wheat in the world and the second-largest producer of corn after the United States. The degree of China's integration with world commodity markets is growing, and China is notorious for its erratic international trade in certain commodities, such as wheat, corn, oilseeds, tobacco, and cotton.

For example, if China has a bumper cotton crop, it will undoubtedly be a large cotton exporter in that particular year, and international cotton prices will be depressed. However, if the weather is poor and the cotton crop suffers, then China can quickly turn and become a very large importer of cotton because China is the world's largest cotton consumer. The North China Plain is a major cotton-growing area that depends on mother nature for rainfall and good growing conditions. Assessing the size of China's cotton harvest is always difficult, and for this reason small shifts in China's weather patterns impact the cotton futures market swiftly.

BOX 5.6

It's a state secret.

One of the most important variables in the world food equation is the size of China's grain reserves, and it is a state secret. China's State Statistical Bureau publishes an annual statistical yearbook on its agriculture that is about two inches thick and filled with hundreds of tables of obscure data. However, for economic security reasons, this yearbook has no information on domestic grain stocks; this number remains a state secret in China. This presents a big problem for international commodity market analysts because China is the world's largest producer and consumer of grain and may hold as much as one-half of the world's grain reserves of wheat, rice, and corn combined.

In an attempt to fill this huge gap in knowledge, the U.S. Department of Agriculture (USDA) and the UN Food and Agriculture Organization (FAO) have periodically attempted to estimate the size of China's grain stocks. However, there is tremendous uncertainty in these estimates, as some of the grain stocks are stored privately on farms in rudimentary small-scale facilities and some in large state-run storage facilities that are off limits to foreigners.

In 2001, both the FAO and the USDA suddenly revised their previous estimates of China's domestic stocks of wheat, rice, and corn. The abrupt fall in China's production in 2000 did not lead to large imports, as expected, and partly for this reason, the FAO and USDA decided that China must have been sitting on large stockpiles of grain.

With a stroke of a pen, the USDA increased its estimate of grain stocks from 66.1 to 230.1 million metric tons, more than a tripling of the figure. That is nothing, however, as a few months earlier the FAO had revised its cereal grain stock estimate for China from 28.1 to 364 million metric tons, nearly 13 times more than its previous estimate. The FAO's revisions for China were so large that it meant more than a doubling of its estimate of the amount of world cereal grain reserves to 640 million metric tons at the end of crop year 2001.

See U.S. Department of Agriculture (2001) and UN Food and Agriculture Organization (2001).

Input Costs

Inputs are factors of production. Therefore, input costs affect commodity supply. The demand for an input will depend on the producer's return from employing more of the input, or the marginal revenue product (MRP) of the input. It is profitable to employ more of the input only if the additional revenue that is generated exceeds the cost. So, as long as the MRP of an input exceeds the cost of an extra unit of the input, it is profitable for the producer to purchase and use more of the input. Alfred Marshall, the famous economist who demonstrated the theoretical power of understanding demand and supply curves, developed four main factors that determine the price elasticity of input demand. Marshall demonstrated that the (absolute value of the) elasticity of demand for an input varies directly with the following:

a. The (absolute value of) elasticity of demand for the product the input produces
b. The share of the input in the cost of production
c. The elasticity of supply of other factors
d. The elasticity of substitution between the factor in question and the other factors

Many commodity markets are linked with one another in that the output of one market becomes an input for other markets. For example, corn, soybean meal, and feeder cattle are all inputs into the production of live (fattened) cattle. Therefore, the futures prices of these inputs directly affect the supply response of live cattle producers, in turn affecting the market price of live cattle.

Government Policy

Some governments in rich countries have become a major factor in determining agricultural commodity prices. This is especially true in the United States, Japan, and the European Union. Agricultural policies in these areas protect their domestic farmers from global competition. Overall, these policies lead to overproduction, which tends to depress world commodity prices and makes these prices more volatile. This protection stabilizes domestic prices, and as a consequence the residual "free market" world prices become more unstable.

The U.S. government provides large annual payments to some of its farmers in various ways. It sets support prices for field crops, such as wheat, rice, corn, cotton, and soybeans. The U.S. government ties payments to individual producers based on historical plantings and yields. Individual farmers can obtain government payments totaling up to $210,000 per year, and some receive multiples of this limit through partnerships and other business arrangements. The U.S. Environmental Working Group (in Washington, DC) examined government payment records and found that high-income farms enjoy a disproportionate share of government payments. They found that 10% of the farms in the United States received more than 60% of the government subsidies (*http://www.ewg.org*). Both U.S. and European grain subsidies adversely affect the competitive position of farmers in low-cost agricultural producing nations, such as Argentina, Brazil, Australia, and Canada.

According to the Paris-based Organization for Economic Cooperation and Development (OECD), for every metric ton of wheat produced in Australia in 1999, about $10 (in U.S. dollars) was received from the government. In contrast, in the United States and the European Union, the subsidies per metric ton were $50 and $60, respectively. The world wheat price in 1999 was only about $100 per metric ton.

Reform of extravagant farm subsidies in rich countries is at the top of the agenda for the World Trade Organization, which suggests that the situation of excessive subsidies will not last forever. Indeed, these subsidies may end one day. However, in the meantime, government policy is instrumental in understanding price behavior in agricultural commodity markets.

The 1996 U.S. "farm bill" (called the "freedom to farm" act) actually involved a significant shift in U.S. farm policy. From 1996, farm payments from the government were no longer linked to plantings or market prices. This resulted in a rather dramatic shifting of acreage in the Midwest from wheat and other field crops toward soybeans. The 2002 U.S. farm bill (which set policy for six years) continued with the 1996 framework.

Under the 1996 legislation, government payments resulted in a situation where soybeans became more profitable per acre. The soybean loan rate was set at $5.26 per bushel, which was high relative to the corn loan rate of $1.89 per bushel. American soybean farmers took advantage of the marketing loan program, and in fiscal year 2000–1, for example, they collected loan deficiency payments (LDPs) on about 87% of the crop, at an average payment of 94¢ per bushel.

American farmers, responding to relatively high soybean loan rates, planted record soybean areas year after year under the 1996 farm bill. In the United States, planted soybean acreage in 2001 was 74.3 million acres, up from 57.8 million acres in 1990—almost a 30% expansion. In comparison, following the 1996 farm bill, U.S. wheat acreage declined from 75.1 million acres in 1996 to 62.5 million acres in 2000.

This rapid growth in U.S. soybean production softened oilseed prices worldwide and affected the prices of competing crops such as canola (traded on the Winnipeg Commodity Exchange in Canada), sunflower seed, and cottonseed. American farm legislation led not only to a dramatic expansion of soybean production but also to a situation where U.S. soybean acreage became less responsive to market prices. After the passage of the 1996 farm bill, soybean acreage expanded in years that had rising prices but did not contract in a symmetric fashion in years that had falling prices (Ash, 2001). Therefore, the 1996 change in U.S. farm legislation would render invalid any existing model of the world oilseed market.

The U.S. and the European Union governments also heavily interfere in the sugar market. According to the U.S. National Center for Policy Analysis (see *http://www.ncpa.org*), the subsidy per acre for U.S. sugar farmers is almost 30 times larger per acre than that for wheat farmers. The U.S. sugar program is so incredible that in 2000, because of a mounting domestic surplus, the U.S. government offered to give cash to farmers who would agree to destroy their crop.

Because of government regulation, only about 25% of the world's sugar production is subject to free-market prices. This means that a relatively small shift in

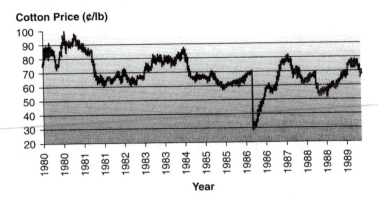

FIGURE 5.1
Cotton futures prices and the effects of policy shocks.
Source: Commodity Research Bureau

world production can represent a large shift in the supply of sugar on the "free" market. This is one of the reasons that world sugar prices are volatile. The U.S. government has isolated its domestic market by establishing support prices for both raw cane and refined beet sugar at levels well above world prices. The 1996 U.S. farm bill set the sugar loan rates at 18¢ and 22.9¢ per pound for raw cane and refined beet sugar, respectively. These support prices were continued under the 2002 farm bill. The U.S. government also imposes a steep import tariff on sugar to insulate the domestic market from world supply and demand conditions. As a result, the U.S. domestic price is often two to three times the world price. Given that the U.S. sugar market is segmented from the world market, the New York Board of Trade has two sugar contracts: Sugar No. 11 (world futures) and Sugar No. 14 (domestic futures). The price of world sugar is normally well below the price of U.S. domestic sugar, and there is little correlation between the two prices over time.

To drive home the point that government policy and changes in policy can have an important effect on commodity prices, refer to Figure 5.1, which displays the futures prices of the "nearby" cotton contract from 1980 to 1989. The figure shows the dramatic effect that the introduction of a new U.S. government marketing loan program had on cotton prices. During the summer of 1986, futures prices dropped immediately from approximately $0.70 to $0.30 per pound. Although cotton prices climbed back over $0.70 within a year, the short-term effects of the policy change were unmistakable and, to some futures and options traders, devastating.

Seasonal Price Patterns

Some commodity markets typically exhibit seasonal price patterns within a production period, known as **price seasonality**. For some commodities, seasonal patterns occur in a high percentage of years and are somewhat consistent. For instance, corn is an annual crop that is planted in the spring and harvested in the fall. In the Northern Hemisphere, corn is normally planted in April and May and

TABLE 5.1 Monthly Average Wheat Prices: Minneapolis Dark No. 1 Spring (13% Protein): 1990–91 Through 2000–1

CROP YEAR	JUNE	JULY	AUGUST	SEPTEMBER	OCTOBER	NOVEMBER	DECEMBER	JANUARY	FEBRUARY	MARCH	APRIL	MAY	AVERAGE
							$ PER BUSHEL						
1990–91	3.90	3.54	3.01	2.78	2.80	2.75	2.79	2.82	2.85	3.00	3.09	3.11	3.04
1991–92	3.03	2.93	3.11	3.19	3.68	3.76	4.12	4.36	4.56	4.35	4.28	4.44	3.82
1992–93	4.42	4.03	3.49	3.51	3.55	3.68	3.72	3.90	3.75	3.75	3.67	3.47	3.75
1993–94	3.49	4.08	3.84	4.23	4.54	4.68	4.82	4.77	4.56	4.23	4.50	4.44	4.35
1994–95	3.92	3.82	3.88	4.14	4.29	4.28	4.28	4.13	4.06	4.04	4.10	4.40	4.11
1995–96	4.70	5.40	4.98	5.22	5.45	5.56	5.70	5.54	5.75	5.72	6.34	7.31	5.64
1996–97	6.63	5.91	5.13	4.60	4.57	4.62	4.46	4.57	4.40	4.53	4.71	4.52	4.89
1997–98	4.31	4.08	4.34	4.33	4.32	4.30	4.18	4.03	4.05	4.19	4.19	4.06	4.20
1998–99	3.91	3.83	3.46	3.39	3.87	3.98	3.86	3.72	3.67	3.75	3.55	3.53	3.71
1999–00	3.65	3.46	3.29	3.32	3.23	3.42	3.38	3.19	3.37	3.44	3.50	3.50	3.40
2000–1	3.50	3.24	2.99	3.10	3.52	3.64	3.60	3.60	3.53	3.45	3.59	3.69	3.45
11-YEAR AVERAGE	4.13	4.03	3.77	3.80	3.98	4.06	4.08	4.06	4.05	4.04	4.14	4.22	4.03
SEASONAL INDEX	102.5	99.9	93.7	94.3	98.8	100.8	101.3	100.7	100.5	100.3	102.7	104.8	100.0

Source: Compiled from data in U.S. Department of Agriculture *Wheat Outlook*. Washington, DC: Economic Research Service

harvested in October and November. Once the harvest is completed, the market must ration the available supply until the following harvest, and the typical pattern is that prices rise after the fall harvest. This is fundamental price behavior because economic theory predicts that prices will rise after harvest in order to cover the full cost of storage until the following harvest one year later. A basic understanding of seasonal price cycles offers one of the simplest approaches to fundamental analysis in commodity markets.

As an illustration, the seasonal price pattern for U.S. wheat prices is shown in Table 5.1 and Figure 5.2 for the 1990–91 through 2000–1 crop years. Table 5.1 reports monthly wheat cash prices on a major U.S. market over an 11-year period. These data are monthly cash prices for Minneapolis Dark No. 1 Spring (13% Protein) wheat (Table 5.1).

The seasonal index is computed by expressing the average price for each month as a percentage of the overall average price for the entire 11-year period. We begin with the average price in June (the start of the crop year). From Table 5.1, the price in June averaged $4.13 per bushel from 1990–91 through 2000–1. At the same time, the overall average price (for all months) was $4.03 per bushel. So, the June index is (4.13/4.03) × 100 = 102.5. This suggests that the price in June is 2.5% above the yearly average in a normal year. The September index in Table 5.1 is 94.3, indicating that the September price is 5.7% below the yearly average price. Figure 5.2 is a plot of the seasonal index (i.e., the last row of Table 5.1).

We see from Figure 5.2 that, from 1990 to 2001, wheat prices were typically the lowest in the August–September period, just following the harvest. Wheat prices then increased seasonally from October through December before leveling off. Prices then rose again just prior to the next harvest, with a seasonal peak in May. Wheat prices tend to fall rather sharply from May through August.

Obviously, seasonal price indexes should not be relied on alone for price forecasts but instead should serve as a useful tool. Analysts should not assume that seasonality alone causes price changes within a year. Seasonal price moves may be

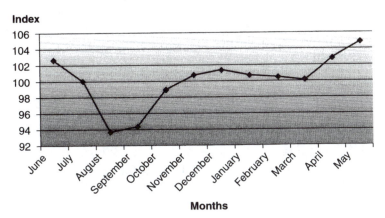

FIGURE 5.2
Seasonal index of wheat prices: 1990–91 to 2000–1.
Source: See Table 5.1

strong within a year, but if the trend is moving against the seasonal price pressure, the trend could certainly be stronger and outweigh the seasonal pressure.

There are a number of alternative approaches that can be used to calculate seasonal price patterns. The method used to calculate the wheat seasonal price pattern in Figure 5.2 is one of the simplest because the overall average price for the 11-year period was used in the denominator in order to calculate the index. Instead, if we had reason to believe there were long-term trends in the prices, we could have used a 12-month moving average in the denominator. With this alternative approach, the denominator would change every month.

FINANCIALS

All financial markets are influenced to some degree by a very long list of economic variables. For interest rate futures and options markets, macroeconomic variables and government macroeconomic policy are overriding fundamental factors. Stock index prices are subject to expectations concerning the general business climate and foreign currency markets reflect the relative strengths of national economies and gaps in global interest and inflation rates. Clearly, the number of factors that might have some impact on prices in financial markets is quite large, making fundamental analysis of financials a formidable task.

Fundamental traders in the financial markets keep abreast of business cycles, and the U.S. Conference Board, a private nonprofit organization, publishes a well-respected measure of these business cycles. The Conference Board indicators are key factors that influence financial markets, and the Conference Board groups 21 different economic variables into three categories: leading, concurrent, and lagging indicators (*http://www.conference-board.org*).

Leading indicators provide advance signals about the strength of the economy. They reflect expected changes in the business cycle and consequently provide an early warning system for identifying changes in financials. Concurrent and lagging indicators show the general direction of the economy and confirm or deny a trend or change in a trend implied by the leading indicators. Concurrent indicators show the degree of change that is taking place in the economy, while lagging indicators show the degree of change that has taken place.

There are 10 indicators that make up the Conference Board's "leading indicator" index:

1. Money supply
2. Vendor performance
3. Interest rate spread
4. Average weekly initial claims for unemployment insurance
5. Index of consumer expectations
6. Stock prices
7. Building permits
8. Average weekly manufacturing hours
9. Manufacturers' new orders for nondefense capital goods
10. Manufacturers' new orders for consumer goods and materials

There are four variables that make up the Conference Board's concurrent indicator:

1. Personal income less transfer payments
2. Manufacturing and trade sales
3. Industrial production
4. Employees on nonagricultural payrolls

And there are seven components in the Conference Board's index of lagging indicators:

1. Change in consumer price index for services
2. Change in labor costs per unit of output
3. Ratio of manufacturing and trade inventories to sales
4. Ratio of consumer installment credit to income
5. Commercial and industrial loans outstanding
6. Average duration of unemployment
7. Average prime rate charged by banks

The composite leading, concurrent, and lagging indexes signal peaks and troughs in the business cycle. Because they are averages, they are smoother than the individual variables that make up each index. Historically, the leading indicators have provided a reasonable measure of major turning points in economic variables, such as income and employment. The Conference Board also publishes global business cycle indicators and forecasts of economic performance in a number of different nations.

Purchasing Power Parity and Exchange Rate Forecasts

An exchange rate is the price of one currency in terms of another. In international markets, relative currency values are critical determinants of trade flows and the profitability of multinational firms. The role of exchange rates in the economy is becoming more and more important because of increased globalization. For example, a swing in the value of the U.S. dollar in terms of foreign currencies affects profits (and the competitiveness) for a large percentage of U.S. companies because of their multinational interests. Many U.S. companies earn sales revenues denominated in a foreign currency and/or they purchase inputs denominated in a foreign currency. When the revenues and costs are converted to U.S. dollars for the company's quarterly report, fluctuations in the exchange rate dramatically affect the U.S. dollar value. This is why multinationals typically hedge their exposure to currency risk in either the forward or the futures market. For example, exporters of wine from Australia typically receive payment from foreign buyers in either U.S. dollars or British pounds. The exporters convert the U.S. dollars or British pounds back into Australian dollars, and this means they are exposed to considerable exchange rate risk. To reduce this risk, the wine exporters typically hedge their exchange rate exposure because they are in the business of selling wine and not speculating on foreign currencies.

At the same time, speculators are attracted to the trading of currency futures, and they try to predict exchange rate changes. Just like the price of any asset, demand and supply establishes values in the spot, forward, futures, and options markets for currencies. However, some countries "fix" their exchange rate, and thus the price is not market determined. This is especially true of developing countries, such as China.

In the short run, such factors as interest rate differentials, economic growth rates, international capital flows, and trade balances are economic variables that affect market-determined exchange rates. However, in the short run, the markets do not always arrive at the same currency value that an accepted economic theory would predict as being the correct long-run value. Some traders use this discrepancy to predict the intrinsic value of a currency. That is, they appeal to the **purchasing power parity (PPP) theory** of exchange rate determination. They use this approach to adopt a long-run strategy of trading exchange rate futures. The reasoning is that a country's exchange rate cannot remain either "overvalued" or "undervalued" indefinitely, and eventually the exchange rate must return to its true equilibrium PPP rate.

Purchasing power parity is an economic theory that states that the exchange rate between two countries is in equilibrium when the "purchasing power" is the same in each of the two countries. This means that the exchange rate between two countries should equal the ratio of the two countries' price level for a fixed basket of goods and services. This is the country's "real" exchange rate. If we were interested in comparing the cost of living in the United States versus Europe, the real dollar/Euro exchange rate would provide an estimate of the cost of living in the United States relative to Europe. Alternatively, from an international trade perspective, the real exchange rate is a measure of how competitive Europe is in international markets relative to the United States. If the U.S. dollar has experienced real **appreciation** against the Euro, then Europe has become more competitive in world markets because the U.S. price level has risen relative to the European price level.

Suppose we are interested in the dollar/Euro exchange rate. Denote the dollar/Euro nominal exchange rate as $N_{\$/\epsilon}$. Then we can express the "real" dollar/Euro exchange rate $(R_{\$/\epsilon})$ as $R_{\$/\epsilon} = N_{\$/\epsilon} \times (P_E/P_{U.S.})$, where P_E is the overall price level in Europe and $P_{U.S.}$ is the overall price level in the United States. A rise in the real dollar/Euro exchange rate, $R_{\$/\epsilon}$, indicates a relative increase in European prices, and this is a real **depreciation** of the dollar. A depreciation of the dollar means that there is an increase in the dollar price of the Euro, and thus the dollar has become less valuable. At the same time, when the dollar depreciates, the Euro (measured in U.S. dollars) appreciates. Alternatively, a fall in the real dollar/Euro exchange rate, $R_{\$/\epsilon}$, indicates a relative increase in U.S. prices and a real "appreciation" of the dollar against the Euro. The dollar appreciates because if $R_{\$/\epsilon}$ falls, then the Euro is becoming cheaper in terms of U.S. dollars. The real exchange rate therefore provides information on the real costs of acquiring foreign goods when international prices are changing.

Comparing nominal exchange rates in the spot and futures market with PPP rates gives an indication of whether a currency is overvalued or undervalued. Another term for the PPP is the **law of one price**, which states that competition (i.e., arbitrage) will equalize the price of an identical good in two countries (adjusted for transportation costs and other transactions costs) when the prices are expressed in the same currency. When we express the exchange rate as dollars/foreign currency, an increase in the exchange rate is an appreciation of the foreign currency. So, if the real rate is greater than the nominal rate, then the foreign currency is thought to be overvalued. According to the PPP theory, we would expect an overvalued foreign currency to eventually fall in value.

Another way to describe the real exchange rate is the currency rate that equalizes the purchasing power of different currencies by eliminating the differences in price levels between countries. In its simplest form, the real rate is the ratio of the prices in national currencies of the same good in different countries. The concept of the real exchange rate can be illustrated by comparing the price of a single homogeneous good between countries, such as automobiles or hamburgers. However, this does not provide an accurate measure of the real rate because only one good is used for price comparisons instead of a complete basket of representative goods.

For example, if the price of a BMW 318i automobile in Europe is 35,000 Euros and in the United States it is $30,000, then the PPP between Europe and the United States is 35,000 Euros to $30,000, or 1.17 Euros to the dollar. This means that for every dollar spent in the United States, 1.17 Euros would have to be spent in Europe to obtain the identical goods.

The Economist magazine reports local currency prices of a McDonald's Big Mac for various countries of the world, and they call it the **Hamburger Standard**. The Hamburger Standard compares the price of a McDonald's hamburger in different countries, and the PPP theory predicts that a Big Mac should cost the same in all countries after converting the prices to a common currency.

Table 5.2 is an example of the Hamburger Standard from *The Economist*. The second column in the table reports the local currency price of a Big Mac in the United States and five other countries. A Big Mac purchased in Australia costs 2.59 Australian dollars, and in Japan the same Big Mac costs 294 yen. These local prices are converted to U.S. dollars using the actual exchange rate (column 5), and the results are reported in column 3 of the table. In U.S. dollars, the price of a Big Mac is

TABLE 5.2   The Hamburger Standard

	BIG MAC PRICES				
	IN LOCAL CURRENCY	IN U.S. DOLLARS	IMPLIED PPP OF THE DOLLAR[a]	ACTUAL $ EXCHANGE RATE	UNDER- (−)/ OVER- (+) VALUATION AGAINST THE DOLLAR
United States	$2.51	$2.51	—	—	—
Australia	A$2.59	$1.54	1.03	1.68	− 38%
Brazil	Real2.95	$1.65	1.18	1.79	− 34%
Canada	C$2.85	$1.94	1.14	1.47	− 23%
Euro	€ 2.56	$2.37	0.98	0.93	− 5%
Japan	¥ 294	$2.78	117	106	+ 11%

[a] The purchasing power parity (PPP) rate is the local price divided by the U.S. price (i.e., the local price divided by $2.51).
Source: *The Economist*, April 27, 2000

$2.51 in the United States, compared to $2.78 in Japan and only $1.54 in Australia. The fourth column in the table is the implied PPP rate, which is the local price divided by the U.S. price (i.e., the local price divided by $2.51). Comparing the implied PPP rate with the actual rate gives us an estimate of the extent to which each currency is under- or overvalued relative to the dollar. We see from the last column in the table that four of the currencies are undervalued relative to the dollar. The Australian dollar is the most undervalued at 38%. However, at the other end of the spectrum, the Japanese yen is 11% overvalued against the U.S. dollar.

Calculating a country's real exchange rate can be a complicated procedure given that price levels for a fixed basket of goods and services must be compared across international borders. The International Monetary Fund (in Washington, DC) publishes real exchange rate indices for the major industrialized countries (*http://www.imf.org*). In addition, the Organization for Economic Corporation and Development (OECD) in Paris also publishes PPP exchange rates for a large number of countries (*http://www.oecd.org*). Nominal and PPP exchange rates are provided in Figures 5.3 and 5.4, and these data were obtained from the OECD. Both

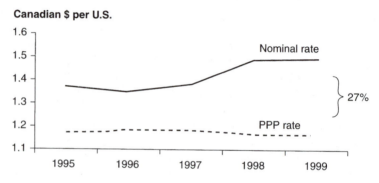

FIGURE 5.3
Canadian dollar: Nominal and PPP rate.
Source: OECD, Paris

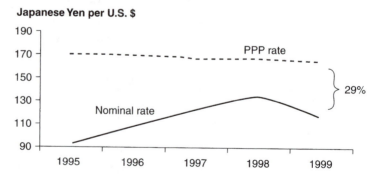

FIGURE 5.4
Japanese yen: Nominal and PPP rate.
Source: OECD, Paris

figures plot the annual PPP exchange rate and the nominal exchange rate from 1995 to 1999. According to these figures, the Canadian dollar was undervalued (in terms of the U.S. dollar) from 1995 to 1999, and in 1999 it was undervalued by an estimated 27%. During the same five-year period, the Japanese yen was overvalued relative to the U.S. dollar, and the extent of overvaluation stood at 29% in 1999.

EVALUATING THE FUNDAMENTAL DATA: FURTHER EXAMPLES

Elasticities

The price elasticities of demand and supply are both fundamental concepts that directly link price and quantity changes. Each is calculated as a percentage change in quantity (demanded or supplied) divided by the percentage change in the market price:

$$E = \frac{\%\Delta Q}{\%\Delta P}. \tag{5.4}$$

The price **elasticity of demand** measures the responsiveness of demand to a given change in price and is negative due to the "law of demand" (i.e., the inverse relationship between quantity demanded and price). The elasticity is independent of the units of measurement of price and quantity. It is related to the slope of the demand curve but is not identical to the slope. The (absolute) demand elasticity is greater than 1.0 for goods with elastic demand and less than 1.0 for inelastic goods. In the elastic range of the demand curve, any increase of price will result in a larger percentage decrease of quantity demanded, leading to a decrease in total revenue. So, for this portion of the demand curve, what is gained in raising the price is more than offset by the loss in quantity sold. On the other hand, for the inelastic range of the demand curve, a price hike will also lead to a decrease in quantity demanded, but the magnitude of the percentage change is smaller, meaning that the total revenue increases.

The economic significance of the price elasticity of demand is that it is indicative of what is likely to happen to the price of a commodity when the available quantity changes. If there is a supply shock (say, due to weather), then an analyst can infer the expected price change from knowledge of the price elasticity of demand. In addition, changes in industry revenue associated with price changes can be predicted.

The price **elasticity of supply** measures the responsiveness of supply to a given change in price and is positive. The **cross-price elasticity** of demand measures the responsiveness of demand for one good to a given change in the price of a second good. The cross-price elasticity is negative for complements and positive for substitutes.

In commodity markets often the elasticity of import demand or export supply is of more interest than domestic demand or supply elasticities because most countries are now very open to world markets and exports and imports move with relative freedom. The elasticity of demand for imports (also referred to as excess demand) is the percentage change in the quantity of imports demanded divided by

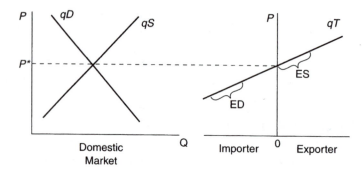

FIGURE 5.5
Elasticity of import demand (export supply).

the percentage change in the price of imports. Similarly, the elasticity of supply of exports (excess supply) is the percentage change in the quantity of exports supplied divided by the percentage change in the price of exports. With increasing globalization, these trade elasticities have become more and more important. For most commodities, the domestic elasticities can differ widely from trade elasticities.

The import demand and export supply functions are generally less steep and more price responsive than either domestic demand or supply functions. In fact, the price elasticity of both import demand (ED) and export supply (ES) is larger in absolute value than either domestic demand (D) or domestic supply (S). This is shown in Figure 5.5.

In Figure 5.5, the domestic demand (qD) and domestic supply (qS) are shown in the left-hand panel. Without international trade, the domestic market clears at price P^*. However, if we allow for international trade and the international price is different from P^*, there will be either excess demand (ED) or excess supply (ES) in the domestic market. If the world price lies above P^*, then ES is the horizontal difference between qS and qD, shown as the ES segment of qT in the right-hand panel of Figure 5.5. At this relatively high price, the home country becomes an exporter because quantity supplied exceeds quantity demanded. Alternatively, if the world price is below the domestic price before trade (i.e., P^*), then there is excess demand, shown as ED in Figure 5.5. The intuition is that as the price falls below P^*, the domestic producers move down the qS function and domestic consumers move down the qD function. For any given price level below P^*, $qD > qS$, which means that there is "excess demand" that must be satisfied by imports. The home country then becomes an importer, and the quantity of imports will be equal to the horizontal gap between qD and qS, which can be read off the ED portion of qT.

From Figure 5.5, we can see that for a given commodity, there will be excess supply at relatively high domestic prices and excess demand at relatively low domestic prices. Let the trade function (qT) be equal to the difference between the quantity of domestic demand (qD) and domestic supply (qS) at any given price, p:

So, $qT = qD - qS$, and $qT > 0$ for ED and $qT < 0$ for ES.   (5.5)

Using Δ to denote a change in a variable, we can rewrite Equation 5.5 as

$$(\Delta qT/\Delta p) = (\Delta qD/\Delta p) - (\Delta qS/\Delta p) \tag{5.6}$$

or by multiplying each component of the equation by p/qT as

$$\frac{\Delta qT}{\Delta p}\frac{p}{qT} = \frac{\Delta qD}{\Delta p}\frac{p}{qT}\frac{qD}{qD} - \frac{\Delta qS}{\Delta p}\frac{p}{qT}\frac{qS}{qS}. \tag{5.7}$$

In elasticity form, Equation 5.7 is

$$\varepsilon_T = \varepsilon_D\,(qD/qT) - \eta_S(qS/qT). \tag{5.8}$$

So, if we let $(qT/qD) = s$, then $(qS/qT) = (1-s)/s$. This means that Equation 5.8 can be expressed as

$$|\varepsilon_T| = (1/s)\,|\varepsilon_D| + (1-s)/s\,(|\eta_s|). \tag{5.9}$$

Equation 5.9 implies that $|\varepsilon_T| > |\varepsilon_D|$ since $|1/s| > 1.0$. In other words, the price elasticity of either the excess demand or excess supply is larger in absolute value than either the domestic demand or supply elasticity.

From Equation 5.9, we find that **import demand is more elastic**:

    a. the more elastic domestic demand (ε_D) is;
    b. the more elastic domestic supply (η_S) is; and,
    c. the smaller the market share of imports (s).

The economic intuition behind this result is that if the world price rises, then this implies a change in imports due to changes in both domestic demand and domestic supply. It is the induced change in domestic supply that results in the import demand being more elastic than the domestic demand.

An example will help illustrate why Equation 5.9 is useful. We can use Equation 5.9 to show that the absolute value of the price elasticity of domestic demand (ε_D) can be relatively low compared to the price elasticity of import demand (ε_T). Take beef as an example and suppose that 25% of domestic beef consumption is imported. For beef, let $(\varepsilon_D) = -1.0$ and $\eta_S = 1.5$. Thus, using Equation 5.9, we find that

$$|\varepsilon_T| = (1/.25)\,|-1.0| + [(1-.25)/.25]\,|1.5| = 8.5. \tag{5.10}$$

So, a 1% increase in the price of beef would induce a 1% decrease in domestic demand (with $\varepsilon_D = -1.0$) but an 8.5% change in the import demand for beef. The reason that the responsiveness of import demand exceeds the responsiveness of domestic demand is that the price increase also leads to a domestic supply response, which chokes off imports.

A more comprehensive example of the importance of trade elasticities is provided later in this chapter in the context of the Asian financial crisis that shocked world commodity and financial markets in the late 1990s.

Cycles

In commodity markets, **cycles** are defined by recurring patterns in production and prices that last more than one season (or production period). A complete cycle includes successive years of increases and decreases in either production or prices extending from one peak (or valley) to the next peak (or valley). For instance, the "hog cycle" is one of the most well-known cycles in agricultural commodity markets. In fact, cyclical fluctuations in prices and production have characterized the hog industry for a number of years (Shonkwiler and Spreen, 1986).

The hog cycle is thought to have developed because of a lag in the production period whereby current production is a function of past prices. Shonkwiler and Spreen found both a three- and a seven-year cycle in hogs. The three-year cycle was found to be due to biological factors in hog production and they argued that the time lag between farrowing and rebreeding retained sows is about eight to nine months. This means that it takes about one and a half years to expand production, which generates a three-year cycle.

Since corn is a major component of the cost of pork production in the United States, a crude indicator of hog profitability and of forthcoming cyclical changes in production and prices is the hog–corn ratio. This ratio is the price of hogs in dollars per hundred weight (cwt) divided by the price of corn in dollars per bushel. This ratio indicates how many bushels of corn that revenue from a hundred pounds of hogs will buy. A high ratio signals an increase in pork production, and a low ratio indicates a decrease in production. Producers decide to increase their supply of hogs when the hog–corn ratio is higher than the long-run average. Similarly, when the ratio is lower than the long-term average, producers often respond by reducing hog production. The hog–corn ratio depends on the price of the product (i.e., hogs) relative to the price of the input (i.e., corn). The ratio will increase when either the relative price of corn falls or the relative price of hogs increases. This means that an increase in the price of hogs could have the same effect on supply as a fall in the price of corn. However, a limitation of the hog–corn ratio as a profit indicator is that the ratio reflects only the price of one input (corn) and does not reflect price changes of other inputs. In addition, the ratio varies with the price of corn, which means that it takes a higher hog–corn ratio to represent a profitable situation when corn prices are low than when they are high. It may take a ratio of about 18:1 to be profitable when corn is $3.00 per bushel, but at $2.00 per bushel, a ratio around 20:1 may be needed to generate a similar profit level, assuming that nonfeed costs remain stable.

The hog–corn price ratio in the United States is shown in Figure 5.6 for the 1991–2000 time period. During this period, the ratio averaged 18:1. The maximum ratio during this period was 30:1, and the minimum was 7:1. The minimum ratio was experienced in late 1998 and early 1999, when there was record pork production.

As shown in Figure 5.7, high hog–corn price ratios have historically led to increases in production that bring hog prices down. On the other hand, low ratios indicate low profitability, so producers reduce hog farrowings (production), which eventually leads to tighter supplies and higher prices. Although ratios such as this are not always reliable, they are useful if combined with other fundamental techniques.

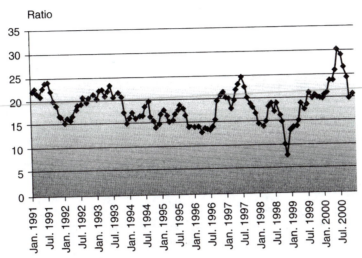

FIGURE 5.6
Hog–corn price ratio in the United States, 1991–2000.
Source: CRB Commodity Yearbook, 2001

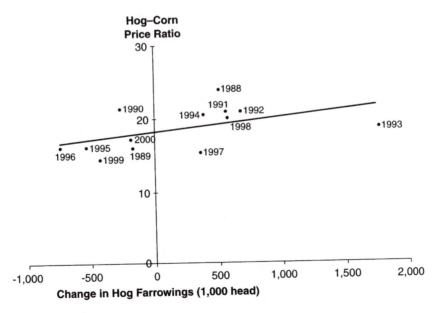

FIGURE 5.7
The hog–corn price ratio and production.
Source: CRB Commodity Yearbook, 2001

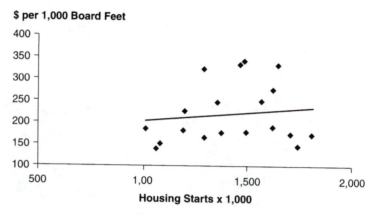

$ per 1,000 Board Feet

FIGURE 5.8
Lumber price as a function of housing starts, 1980–2000.
Source: CME and Bureau of the Census

Correlation

Correlation measures the degree of association (although not necessarily cause and effect) between two or more variables. Spreadsheets and regression packages available for use on personal computers have made this technique very easy to use, even with large data sets. For example, Figure 5.8 provides the results from a simple regression of annual U.S. lumber prices (LP) on the number of houses constructed or U.S. national housing starts (H): $LP = \alpha + \beta H + \varepsilon$. The line through the data points in Figure 5.8 represents the estimated linear relationship between lumber prices and housing starts. Once the regression line has been estimated, plotting the expected housing starts and comparing that point to the regression line gives a general indication of forthcoming lumber prices. In addition, if the point reflecting the current lumber price and housing starts is off the regression line, it is expected that market prices will gradually adjust so as to move toward the line.

A Case Study of the Asian Financial Crisis and Impacts on U.S. Commodity Exports

The purpose of this case study is to illustrate the important role that demand and supply elasticities play in determining a new market equilibrium (i.e., a new price and quantity equilibrium) following a major economic shock. There is no better example of a surprise economic shock than the 1997 Asian financial crisis, which caught the world's attention.

    After the Asian financial crisis hit in July 1997, stock markets and currencies in the region fell between 30% and 50%, and banks collapsed in the Philippines, Malaysia, and Indonesia. Trading losses to U.S. commodity exporters, including processed and consumer-ready food exporters, were expected

---

BOX 5.7

Globalization.
You can now buy a Big Mac in more than 100 countries in the world. This is but one illustration of the growing integration of the world economy, popularly known as "globalization." Since World War II, the World Trade Organization has been crucial in encouraging economies to open borders to international trade and investment. Greater interdependence among economies has raised standards of living around the world. In spite of the economic payoff from globalization, it is also politically divisive, as some critics believe it threatens the environment, threatens jobs, and destroys national cultures.

However, by some measures the degree of global economic integration today is not that high compared to the late 19th century, more than 100 years ago. Prior to World War I, there was a similar period of globalization, and the importance of international trade, measured as a share of income, was comparable to the situation today. In the late 1800s, the barriers to foreign trade were relatively low, and foreign investment was very high. World trade grew rapidly with the invention of the steamship and railroad, which lowered the costs of transportation. Some economists believe that global financial markets were as well integrated in the late 1800s as they are today.

See O'Rourke and Williamson (1999).

---

to be substantial.[4] The value of U.S. agricultural exports to those countries in East Asia most affected by the crisis were expected to decline by up to 40% in fiscal 1998 and 1999 (see Gajewski and Langley, 1998).

For this case study, we are interested in understanding what happened to the volume of U.S. food exports and food prices as a result of the crisis compared to what would have happened without the crisis. The case study illustrates how the volume and price impacts of a shock depend critically on demand and supply elasticities.

The actual commodity price effects resulting from the crisis were much less than some analysts were predicting. A futures trader in the United States may have sold beef or soybean futures when news of the crisis first hit in anticipation of a sharp drop in import demand in East Asia. While this may have been a reasonable trading strategy, this case study shows that the profitability of such a futures trade

---

[4] Our discussion of commodity markets in this case study does not include bulk commodities, such as cotton, wheat, or corn, because China is a large trader in these commodities and the financial crisis did not hit China directly. In addition, China's international trade in these bulk commodities is highly erratic because of swings in government policy; often, China's trading decisions are politically motivated and are not necessarily driven by underlying economic fundamentals.

depends critically on the elasticity of demand and supply for these commodities in the region hit by the crisis.

This case study suggests that there is a simple explanation as to why the price effect of the Asian economic flu was not as great as some expected. The reason lies with the elasticity of the U.S. supply curve facing that region. The Asian economies that were hit hardest by the crisis (Indonesia, Malaysia, South Korea, Thailand, and the Philippines) constitute less than 10% of the U.S. exports of high-valued and consumer-ready products, such as soybean products, meat, meat products, fruits, and vegetables. As a result, the elasticity of the U.S. supply curve facing the region is relatively high for these commodities. This is explained here with the aid of a graph and reference back to Equation 5.9.

Prior to the crisis, emerging Asia was experiencing strong growth in the 1990s and was becoming increasingly important in the global economy. Outside Asia, there was increased competition among exporting nations vying to capture the growing markets in Thailand, South Korea, Indonesia, and Malaysia. A significant factor contributing to the growth of the Asian nations was investment from both domestic and foreign sources that fueled a credit boom in these countries (Goldstein, 1998). However, bank lending standards were lax, and business loans were often based on political rather than financial considerations. Eventually, non-performing loans and corporate indebtedness began to pile up. By 1996, exports and growth started to slow, and in time the returns to foreign capital started to decline. Foreign investment quickly reversed course and started to flow out of the region in search of higher returns elsewhere. Some economists believe that this is what precipitated the Asian financial crisis.

Available U.S. trade statistics are shown in Figure 5.9. During the height of the crisis, from 1997 to 1998, annual U.S. exports of processed and consumer-ready food exports to East Asia declined from about $12.5 billion to $11 billion, a 12% drop. However, the subsequent recovery was sharp, as shown in Figure 5.9. The fact that the value of trade for U.S. exports did not fall as projected by the U.S. Department of Agriculture does not necessarily mean the government projections were wrong because it can always be argued that the export figures would have been higher without the crisis. However, there is reason to believe that the gov-

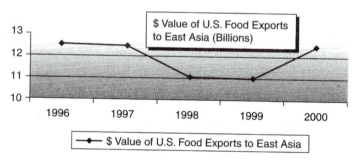

FIGURE 5.9
U.S. food commodity exports to East Asia during the Asian financial crisis.
Source: U.S. Department of Agriculture, Foreign Agricultural Service

FIGURE 5.10
Impact of demand shock in crisis region.

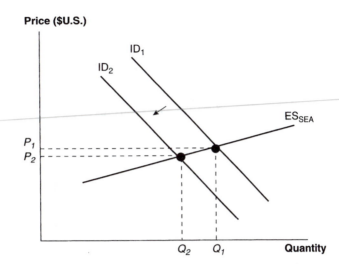

ernment economists were implicitly using the wrong supply and demand elasticities when they forecast a huge impact due to the financial crisis.

The Asian crisis led to a shift of the East Asian import demand schedule (the crisis region imported less quantity at a given price) because of the relative appreciation of the U.S. dollar and the decline of income growth in the importing region.

Figure 5.10 shows that if U.S. agriculture has a small customer whose demand has changed, this demand shock is relatively easy to accommodate without a large impact on the price. The same would not necessarily be true for a demand shock within a region that was a large customer.

In general, we know that in the case of a small customer, the U.S. export supply schedule, ES_{SEA}, is relatively flat (or "price elastic," meaning that the quantity exported is highly responsive to small price changes). The reason is that U.S. exporters quickly reduce shipments to the affected region (to match demand) and spread this residual supply among large customers outside East Asia. With the demand curve (ID) shifting leftward along the elastic supply curve, the market impact will fall mostly on quantity traded rather than price. In Figure 5.9, the U.S. export price falls a relatively small amount from P_1 to P_2, and the volume of trade declines significantly from Q_1 to Q_2.

SOURCES OF INFORMATION

Commodities

The Economic Research Service, U.S. Department of Agriculture, regularly publishes reports on specific commodity markets, such as wheat, soybeans, cattle, cotton, and coffee.

http://www.ers.usda.gov

The U.S. Department of Agriculture's Foreign Agricultural Service gathers intelligence on foreign markets. It has market analysts stationed abroad who write attaché reports with detailed supply and demand information on conditions within foreign countries. For example, if you are looking for current crop conditions for wheat in Australia or coffee in Brazil, this is a good place to start. It is also a good source for the latest information on international trade in commodities.
http://www.fas.usda.gov

The U.S. Department of Agriculture's National Agricultural Statistics Service (NASS) conducts extensive surveys of farmers and publishes reports with forecasts of supplies of food and fiber products. NASS produces the famous hogs and pigs report each quarter, which forecasts the U.S. pig crop.
http://www.usda.gov/nass

The U.S. Department of Agriculture's World Agricultural Outlook Board (WAOB) provides economic forecasts on the outlook for U.S. and world agriculture. The WAOB uses remote sensing and weather to help generate its forecasts.
http://www.usda.gov/agency/oce/waob/waob.htm

Cornell University's Mann Library has a comprehensive on-line collection of data and publications from the U.S. Department of Agriculture's economics and statistics system.
http://usda.mannlib.cornell.edu/usda/usda.html

The U.S. Department of Commerce's National Oceanic and Atmospheric Administration (NOAA) provides information on current weather conditions and weather forecasts. It is also an excellent source for historical weather information and weather links.
http://www.noaa.gov

The Food and Agriculture Organization (FAO) of the United Nations collects analyses information and data related to food, agriculture, forestry, and fisheries. The FAO has an excellent statistical database.
http://www.fao.org

Another good source for economic, business, and international trade information is STAT-USA, an Internet service provided by the U.S. Department of Commerce.
http://www.stat-usa.gov

Financials

For financial markets, the U.S. Department of the Treasury is an important source of information on Treasury securities.
http://www.ustreas.gov

The Federal Reserve system provides statistics and reports on monetary variables.
http://www.federalreserve.gov

The Federal Reserve Bank of New York is another good site with a searchable database and research reports.
http://www.newyorkfed.org

The University of British Columbia's Department of Commerce provides access to current and historic daily exchange rates and trend projections of the Canadian Dollar, the U.S. Dollar, and the Euro.

http://pacific.commerce.ubc.ca/xr

The Bureau of Economic Analysis (BEA) is an agency of the U.S. Department of Commerce. This agency generates important economic numbers, including national income and product accounts (NIPAs) and gross domestic product (GDP) estimates, for the nation. The BEA also generates regional, industry, and international statistics that present essential information on economic activity.

http://www.bea.doc.gov

In the private sector, Bloomberg is a news company with up-to-the minute and in-depth financial news and analysis, including information on interest rates and yield curves.

http://www.bloomberg.com

There are at least four other popular sites for financial investment information and trading techniques and tools.

http://www.morningstar.com
http://www.TheStreet.com
http://finance.yahoo.com
http://www.pimco.com

For information on European financial markets, visit the Bank of England's Web site.

http://www.bankofengland.co.uk

For information on Asian financial markets, visit the Asian Development Bank's Web site.

http://www.adb.org

Futures and Options Exchanges

All major futures and options exchanges issue statistical information on their products. The major exchanges are the following:

Chicago Board of Trade

http://www.cbot.com

Chicago Mercantile Exchange

http://www.cme.com

London International Financial Futures Exchange

http://www.liffe.com

For a comprehensive listing of exchanges around the world, visit the Web site of the Office for Futures and Options Research at the University of Illinois at Urbana, Champaign. This is a research center that promotes research on futures, options, and derivative markets.

http://www.ace.uiuc.edu/ofor

Newspapers and Magazines

The *New York Journal of Commerce* (*http://www.JOC.com*) is an excellent source for information concerning both demand and supply factors for commodities. *Investor's Business Daily* provides commodity and financial news, price quotes, and market analysis (*http://www.investors.com*). The *New York Times* (*http://www.nytimes.com*) and the *Wall Street Journal* (*http://www.wsj.com*) are helpful sources for commodity information but are especially useful in providing financial market data. Consensus is a weekly source (electronic and print form) of futures and financial reports, including market letters, special in-depth reports, and fundamental and technical buy/sell advice drawing from a broad cross section of public and private organizations (*http://www.consensus-inc.com*).

The *Economist* magazine provides well-researched articles on various topics related to commodity and financial markets (*http://www.economist.com*). *Futures* magazine reports on fundamental and technical developments, plus reports on managed futures funds. Articles in this magazine offer advice on trading techniques (*http://www.futuresmag.com*).

Brokerage Houses

A customer's representative in a full-service brokerage house is a good source for timely reports on important market changes. In addition, most large brokerage houses have a futures and options research unit that issues periodic reports. These reports usually provide a summary of market events and a price forecast based on fundamental (and/or technical) factors, reflecting the consensus of the firm's analysts, brokers, and traders.

SUMMARY

This chapter introduced fundamental analysis, one of two general categories of price analysis used by futures and options analysts and traders. The fundamental approach focuses on evaluating long-run supply and demand factors in an attempt to forecast the direction of price movements. A fundamental analyst looks forward in time, gathering information concerning future supply and demand conditions and determining what this information implies for market conditions and forthcoming prices. Factors that influence the supply of and demand for commodities and financials were outlined in this chapter, as were sources of information and simple fundamental techniques. Key points made include the following:

- A fundamentalist tries to estimate the intrinsic value of a product, which is a long-run approach to price analysis.
- There is a long-running debate between the fundamental versus technical camps. This debate is not confined to futures and options markets, however, as fundamental and technical approaches are also used in equity markets.
- Empirical research shows that futures and options markets are nearly efficient.

- If futures and options markets are efficient, then today's market prices fully reflect all publicly available information. This means that fundamental analysis is very difficult to use by speculators who have plans to earn consistent profits in futures and options markets.

DISCUSSION QUESTIONS

1. The Big Mac Index provides a rough guide to whether foreign currencies are at their correct level. It is based on the purchasing power parity (PPP) theory. This week, suppose the price of a Big Mac in Los Angeles is $2.25 and in Tokyo a 225 yen. If the actual exchange rate is 120 yen per dollar, to what extent is the Japanese yen over- or undervalued?
2. Suppose you heard the following two statements:

   "I do not believe in the random walk theory as an explanation of futures price behavior."

   "The futures market reacts to news quickly and soon discounts the information in the price. By the time the average trader hears the information, it is already reflected in the price."

   Are these two statements consistent with each other? Answer yes or no and explain your reasoning.
3. List the main factors that affect exchange rates and explain why the U.S. dollar has followed its recent pattern relative to the Euro and the yen. Explain what it means when there is a "strong dollar" and how domestic and foreign firms are affected by a strong dollar?
4. Why are firms willing to pay large fees to consultants for commodity and financial price forecasts if the futures and options markets are efficient?

SELECTED REFERENCES

Ash, M. (2001). *Soybeans: Background and issues for farm legislation* (Research Service OSC-0701-01). Washington, DC: U.S. Department of Agriculture, July.

Bernstein, P. (2000). *The Power of Gold*, New York, NY: John Wiley and Sons.

Brenner, R. J., & Kroner, K. F. (1995). Arbitrage, cointegration, and testing the unbiasedness hypothesis in financial markets. *Journal of Financial and Quantitative Analysis 30*(1), 23–42.

Brinegar, C. S. (1970). A statistical analysis of speculative price behavior. *Food Research Institute Studies, 9*(Suppl.), pp. 1–58.

Carter, C. A., & Galopin, C. A. (1993). Informational content of government hogs and pigs reports. *American Journal of Agricultural Economics, 3*(August), 711–718.

Elam, E. (1978). *A strong form test of the efficient market model applied to the U.S. hog futures market*. Doctoral dissertation, University of Illinois.

Fama, E. F. (1970). Efficient capital markets: A review of theory and empirical work. *Journal of Finance, 25*, 383–417.

———. (1991). Efficient capital markets: II. *Journal of Finance, 60*, 1575–1617.

Fama, E. F., & French, K. (1987). Commodity futures prices: Some evidence on fore-cast power, premiums, and the theory of storage. *Journal of Business 60*(1), 55–73.

Figlewski, S. C. (1978). Market efficiency in a market with heterogeneous information. *Journal of Political Economy, 86*(4), 581–597.

Gajewski, G., & Langley, S. (1998). Events in Asia lower prospects for U.S. farm and rural economy. *In Agricultural outlook*. Washington, DC: U.S. Department of Agriculture, Economic Research Service, February.

Goldstein, M. (1998). *The Asian financial crisis: Causes, cures, and systemic implications*. Washington, DC: Institute for International Economics.

Gray, R. W. (1972). The futures market for Maine potatoes: An appraisal. *Food Research Institute Studies, 11*(3). Reprinted in A. E. Peck (Ed.), *Selected writings on futures markets, II* (pp. 337–365). Chicago: Board of Trade, 1977.

Jiler, H. (Ed.). (1975). *Forecasting commodity prices: How the experts analyze the markets*. New York: Commodity Research Bureau.

Kenyon, D., Jones, E., & McGuirk, A. (1993). Forecasting performance of corn and soybean harvest futures contracts. *American Journal of Agricultural Economics, 75*(2), 399–407.

Kofi, T. (1973). A framework for comparing the efficiency of futures markets. *American Journal of Agricultural Markets, 55*, 584–594.

Leuthold, R. M. (1972). Random walk and price trends: The live cattle futures market. *Journal of Finance, 27*, 879–889.

Leuthold, R. M., & Hartmann, P. A. (1979). A semi-strong form evaluation of the efficiency of the hog futures market. *American Journal of Agricultural Economics, 61*(3), 482–489.

O'Rourke, K., & Williamson, J. (1999). *Globalization and history: The evolution of a nineteenth-century Atlantic economy*. Cambridge, MA: MIT Press.

Rausser, G. C., & Carter, C. (1983). Futures market efficiency in the soybean complex. *Review of Economics and Statistics, 65*(3), 469–478.

Roll, R. (1984). Orange juice and weather. *American Economic Review, 74*, 861–880.

Shonkwiler, S., & Spreen, T. (1986). Statistical significance and stability of the hog cycle. *Southern Journal of Agricultural Economics, 18*(2), 227–233.

Stein, J. L. (1981). Speculative price: Economic welfare and the idiot of chance. *Review of Economics and Statistics, 63*(2), 223–232.

Tomek, W. G. (1997). Commodity futures prices as forecasts. *Review of Agricultural Economics, 19*(1), 23–44.

Tomek, W. G., & Gray, R. W. (1970). Temporal relationships among prices on commodity futures markets: Their allocative and stabilizing roles. *American Journal of Agricultural Economics, 52*(3), 372–380.

UN Food and Agriculture Organization. (2001). *Food outlook*. Rome.

U.S. Department of Agriculture. (2001). *World agricultural supply and demand estimates* (WASDE-374). Washington, DC: Office of the Chief Economist.

U.S. Department of Agriculture. (2001). *Wheat outlook*. Washington, DC: Economic Research Service.

CHAPTER 6

Technical Analysis

Technical analysis is the study of historical market prices, usually conducted through examining price charts or computer-generated buy and sell signals. Technicians are also referred to as **chartists** and they attempt to predict forthcoming market price behavior from past prices, price variability, volume of trade, and open interest. According to chartists, examination of these historical variables will reveal implicit signals regarding the psychology of the market, which may signal the "strength" or "weakness" of a recent price move. While generating futures and options price forecasts, technicians ignore supply and demand facts and figures that are related to the underlying commodity or financial asset. In other words, they ignore economic fundamentals. Furthermore, they do not try to anticipate news events because such information is irrelevant to their trading system. For example, if technicians are studying price behavior in the natural gas futures market, they will not account for winter weather forecasts, even though a cold winter could shift the demand for natural gas and influence prices. They simply do not care about the relevance of such information to price behavior.

Technicians study the market itself rather than external supply and demand factors. With the development of inexpensive high-speed personal compucters and the fall in price of historical data banks (available on CD), quantitative analysis of historical market prices has grown in popularity.

Virtually all the futures and options charting techniques that are in use by futures and options chartists have been borrowed from stock market chartists. With only slight modifications to charting tools pioneered in the stock market, futures and options chartists are up and running forecasting prices, and some are even quick to begin selling trading advice. Charting does not require experience, knowledge, or understanding of the underlying commodity or financial asset. Rather, it requires blind faith that history will repeat itself in the way that price patterns are formed. This faith is not unlike the herd mentality that attracted "day traders" to the Nasdaq stock market prior to the tech stock crash in 2000.

Many futures and options traders who rely on charting do not actually run the historical numbers themselves. Rather, they subscribe to professional charting services, which usually includes all the hype that accompanies these services. The professional chartists make money selling their trading systems over the Internet, through videos and books, and through mail-order courses. Most of the technical advisory services that sell futures and options trading systems have catchy titles that entice naive speculators. If you visit yahoo.com on the Internet and search for "futures and options," you will find several Web sites pitching technical advice for steep fees. Their books and software titles are often misleading, as they suggest that the authors have the key to successful trading.

Chartists such as Jake Bernstein use late-night television infomercials to pitch technical trading secrets. He also writes books and sells videos. Similarly, Ken Roberts is a direct marketer who sells a trading system explaining how to become wealthy through trading futures and options. Jake and Ken are professional salesmen.

Technical trading authors such as Chande (2001), Kleinman (2001), and Luca (1997) write about "winning trading rules," "trading without fear," "trader's secrets," "robust trading systems," "techniques for bottom fishing," "sports psychology in trading," "Japanese candlesticks," "price filters," and "cycle analysis." There are hundreds of similar books available that describe winning ways to trade following the rules of technical analysis. You can find technical trading articles by these and other authors in *Futures magazine* (*http://www.futuresmag.com*). The magazine also runs classified advertising for technical trading methods. Another good source of technical information is a weekly electronic newspaper called Consensus (*http://www.consensus-inc.com*). Consensus provides technical buy and sell advice (with explanations and graphs) from a number of different technicians.

Chartists ignore economic fundamentals because they believe that supply and demand data are subject to too much individual interpretation and that the publicly available fundamental data are not current. With futures prices changing constantly, chartists believe that it is virtually impossible to keep up with all relevant "fundamental" supply and demand data and that long-term fundamental forecasts are too vulnerable to new information, hence the chartists focus on recent and current prices.

Technical analysts believe that the so-called problems with fundamental analysis can be avoided if instead you follow the "tracks in the sand" and let the market tell you when to buy and sell. They believe that by merely studying the direction and range of past price movements, information is revealed as to what other market participants are thinking. Chartists believe that trading based on fundamentals ignores the psychological mood of all other traders. They study a graph of price movements on their computer screen in hopes of finding a recognizable pattern that indicates that a predictable price movement is under way. In addition, they compute simple statistics that generate buy and sell signals from historical prices. In their books and courses, technicians stress trading discipline and claim to have made large profits over extended periods of time.

THE CHARTIST LOGIC

Charting is a subjective study of market price activity. A chartist attempts to anticipate the future direction of prices by appraising past and present trends and cycles. The traditional tools used in this analysis are a personal computer, access to a data bank, and a graph or chart showing the movement of prices over a specified period of time. Chartists reach their conclusions by diagnosing the chart formations or patterns. They believe that they know how the pattern will be further developed and played out in market prices. In other words, they believe that they know where the tracks in the sand are leading to.

One purpose of charting is to measure the relative strength of buying and selling pressures. According to a chartist, if it can be demonstrated that buying pressure at the prevailing price is more powerful than selling pressure, it is logical to assume that prices will rise. If the relative strengths of the market pressures are reversed, prices are expected to fall.

The actual forecasting process consists of identifying the various patterns established by prices as they trend up or down, cycle, or move sideways. These patterns are believed to disclose the relative strength of supply and demand forces. Each chart formation has its own significance that the chartist coordinates with various other technical considerations to determine where prices are going. Chartists use only three sets of historical data: price, volume, and open interest.

Technical analysis provides traders with empirical rather than theoretical guidance in generating price forecasts. Although chartists discuss buying and selling pressures, there is little or no economics in the process. In fact, it has sometimes been described as a method of evaluating "crowd psychology." Yet there are significant economic and statistical assumptions that are actually required to defend the logic of technical analysis. However, these assumptions are all implicit, and most chartists simply ignore them.

The technical approach to price forecasting assumes that "history repeats itself," which means that the future can be predicted from the past. In particular, charting implies that there is no "random walk" in day-to-day price changes. Recall from Chapter 5 that the random walk model says that day-to-day price changes average to zero. The important implication is that if price changes are random (and all the statistical evidence in academic publications suggests they are close to random), you cannot predict the future from the past. So, faith in technical trading methods implies a belief that prices do not follow a random walk. This, in turn, implies that the markets are inefficient[1] according to the usual economic definition. Chartists posit that random walk is nonsense, and to support this view, they point out that you need only look at any futures price chart to see how well the markets follow trends. Of course, statements like these are made *ex post*, after the trend has been completed. Just like the old adage says, technicians have 20:20 vision with hindsight.

There are numerous methods used by chartists, and they cannot all be described here. The reference section at the end of this chapter refers the interested reader to some books devoted to technical analysis. However, understanding the very basics of technical trading goes a long way to understanding this school of thought because even sophisticated-sounding technical methods are often just

---

[1] As explained in Chapter 5, an efficient market is one that accurately and rapidly reflects available supply and demand information (Fama, 1976).

slight variations of a basic technique. Technical proponents will go to great lengths to disguise what might be a small variation of a standard, simple technical approach. Technical methods fall into four general categories:

    a. Patterns on price charts
    b. Trend-following methods
    c. Character-of-market analysis
    d. Structural theories

Each of these four categories is discussed in the following sections.

PATTERNS ON PRICE CHARTS

The study of patterns on price charts mainly employs two types of basic charting tools: bar charts and point-and-figure charts. The bar chart is the simplest to construct and easiest to interpret. It is the most popular method of reporting price and volume data. When interpreting price charts, the three main objectives of technical analysts are the following:

    a. Identify the direction of current price trends
    b. Detect when the price trend is reversing
    c. Identify buy and sell signals

On a bar chart, each day (or week or month) is represented by a single vertical line on the graph that connects the high and low prices in order to indicate the price range for the trading period. To denote the period's closing price, a horizontal bar is placed across the vertical bar. Bar charts can easily be constructed with personal computers from data reported in newspapers or downloaded over the Internet. Microsoft Excel even has an option for charting high- and low-close bar charts. Figure 6.1 presents an example of a bar chart, which has time on the horizontal axis and price on the vertical axis.

Point-and-figure charts are used to show the direction of price changes while ignoring any time variable. Compared to bar charts, point-and-figure charts generate more clearly defined buy and sell signals. Such charts are constructed by filling in boxes with a combination of Xs (showing price increases) and Os (showing price decreases) in alternating columns, as illustrated in Figure 6.2. Price movements are depicted by either a rising column of Xs or a falling column of Os.

The point-and-figure box size is the unit price that a futures contract must move above the top of the current column of Xs (or below the bottom of the current column of Os) before another X (or O) is added to that column. The box size is arbitrary and determined by the technician.

Once the box sizes are determined, each trend reversal creates a new column. Contrary to bar charts, time is not plotted on the horizontal axis of point-and-figure charts. The final price square for each period is sometimes blackened.

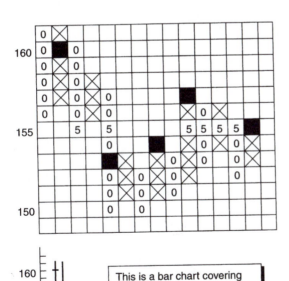

FIGURE 6.1
Vertical bar chart.

December Futures

	Day's high price
+	Close
	Day's low price

Cents per Pound

33.00

32.50

32.00

31.50

31.00

30.50

30.00

5 12 19 26

August

December Futures

(Note that Saturday and Sunday spaces are not included; the trading week is five days.)

FIGURE 6.2
Point-and-figure versus bar chart.

This is a bar chart covering the same price movements as the point-and-figure chart.

191

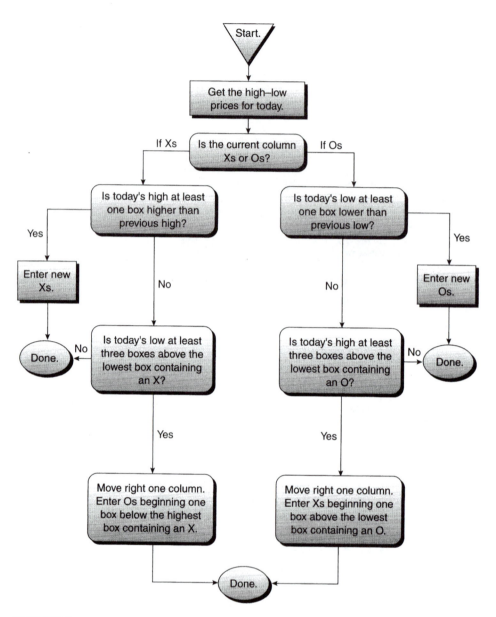

FIGURE 6.3
Flowchart for point-and-figure chart construction.

Figure 6.3 presents a flowchart that can be used to aid in the construction of a point-and-figure chart.

Interpreting bar chart formations requires some imagination on the part of the technician. To make the most of the information that price charts are believed to possess, an analyst must recognize patterns as they

BOX 6.1

What are hedge funds?

Hedge funds are private investment pools that employ sophisticated investment techniques in both asset (e.g., currencies and stocks) and derivative (e.g., futures, options, and swaps) markets. These managed funds pool investors' money and make extensive use of leverage. A leveraged fund purchases assets or derivatives with borrowed money or on margin. The term *hedge fund* is misleading because these funds do not necessarily hedge. Rather, the term refers to any type of private investment partnership. Unlike mutual funds, hedge funds are not required to register under the federal securities laws because they are not open to the public. This freedom from regulation gives hedge funds extensive latitude in their investment strategies. Some hedge funds operate from international tax havens such as Bermuda. Hedge funds accept only wealthy investors as partners and are relatively secretive because they are private funds.

However, the George Soros hedge fund made the world news in 1992, when it sold short the British pound, and made a reported profit of U.S.$1 billion. The Soros funds are the world's largest hedge fund group, and his Quantum hedge fund returned an average of 31% per year over the past 30 years. In 2001, the entire (global) hedge fund industry controlled an estimated U.S. $563 billion.

emerge so that trades can be made before the majority of the other technical traders recognize these same patterns. Clearly, this is not an exact science. Nevertheless, this chapter attempts to describe the basic logic used in interpreting charts. Because chartists are important players in the futures and options markets and hold significant open positions at any given time, it is useful to understand charting methods, even if little faith is placed in their forecasts. Chartists cannot be ignored because if all chartists believe that a market price will rise, the law of self-fulfilling expectations may ensure that the price actually does increase for a limited period of time. This could result in a small temporary bubble or market overshooting. Brunnermeier (2001) discusses technical trading and the impact on asset bubbles, while Zeira (1999) examines overshooting models.

BAR CHART PRICE PATTERNS

A key component of many bar chart price patterns is a cluster of bars called a **congestion area**. This represents a sideways movement of prices on a bar chart. Identifying these sideways clusters is usually the beginning point for a forecast in a break in prices, either up or down. Congestion areas are created during temporary periods of market stability around a certain price level. These **sideways**

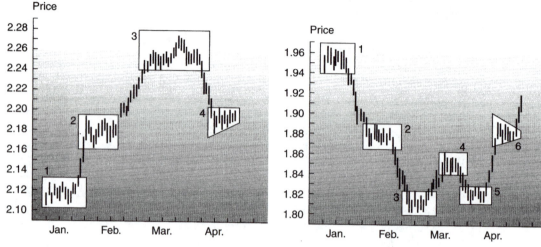

FIGURE 6.4
Congestion areas.

movements on a bar chart (Fig. 6.4) are sometimes considered to be indicators of market equilibrium because buy and sell pressures are relatively stable for a period. Chartists believe that the longer a congestion area lasts, the greater will be the impetus for any upcoming price move because significant buy or sell pressure may have accumulated.

Support and **resistance areas** are congestion areas in the middle of a trend. Chartists expect a congestion area to form whenever a trend reverses and returns to the same price range. This is expected whether the trend was originally up or down, as shown by boxes 2 and 4 in the left panel of Figure 6.4. It is also believed that congestion areas often form at psychological price levels, such as at even dollar amounts, half-dollar or quarter-dollar levels, and so on. This is usually attributed to the effects of large numbers of stop orders being placed at those price levels, temporarily stopping or reversing an established trend in prices.

Chartists always trade with an existing trend, never against it. This is because they believe that the key to successful technical trading is to follow a trend. The first rule of charting is that the "trend is your friend." Therefore, trend lines, such as the straight lines in Figure 6.5, receive a lot of attention from technical traders. Chartists believe that for some unknown reason, once a price trend gets started, the price fluctuations' limits during that trend tend to remain along a straight line. When prices break through that trend line, chartists take this as an indication of a coming price reversal. To someone who does not believe in charts, the reason for this reversal may simply be the self-fulfilling prophecy of technical trading. This criticism of charting is discussed at the end of this chapter.

A **double top** or **bottom** is formed when a trend reversal carries prices to the level of the previous congestion area, at which point the trend forces it back (Fig. 6.6). At the same reversal point, prices turn around, breaking the old trend line and beginning a trend in the opposite direction.

FIGURE 6.5
Trend lines.

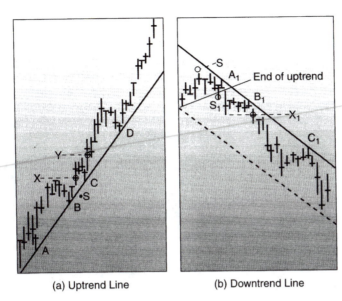

(a) Uptrend Line   (b) Downtrend Line

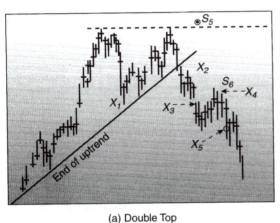

(a) Double Top

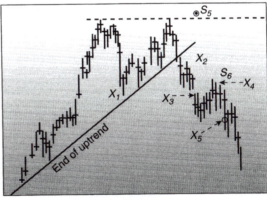

(b) Double Bottom

FIGURE 6.6
Double top and bottom.

Figure 6.7 shows two versions of a **head and shoulders formation**. These price patterns, similar in appearance to double tops and bottoms, also indicate the reversal of a trend. The **neckline** and return movement provide opportunities for placing buy or sell orders. At the top of Figure 6.7, as the neckline is completed and the right shoulder is being formed, a chartist believes that a clear indication of a coming downtrend is being signaled, meaning that short positions are recommended.

Triangles, flags, and pennants are specific types of congestion areas that interrupt an established trend when buying and selling pressures are temporarily balanced. A **pennant** is a triangle that (frequently) proves to be at the midpoint of the

FIGURE 6.7
Head and shoulders top
and bottom.

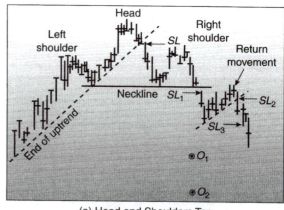

(a) Head and Shoulders Top

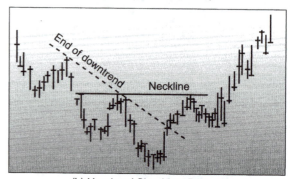

(b) Head and Shoulders Bottom

entire price move. As shown in Figure 6.8, ascending triangles are sometimes mistaken for double tops while forming. This pattern is similar to a descending triangle in that each successive price move is higher (lower), indicating that prices will eventually break out of the formation in the direction of their original move. Symmetrical triangles give no prior indication of the probable direction of their breakout from the formation. On the other hand, a flag's slope will be in the opposite direction from that of the main trend. Flags, as well as pennants and triangles, usually indicate that a major part of the price move is still to come. According to chartists' logic, these formations are all just temporary interruptions in an existing trend.

A **round top (or bottom)** is a formation produced by the gradual reversal of a price trend. They can resemble a congestion area but are distinguished by some gradual movement in the average price in the formation, whereas congestion areas usually have a stable average price.

A **gap** is a space on a bar chart between the high price of one day and the low price of the next day or vice versa. There are several ways in which gaps are formed, each given a special meaning by chartists. Figure 6.9 illustrates the most significant types of gaps. The **common gap** is usually formed in a market with very small trading volume. A **breakaway gap** forms at the beginning of a major price movement. It is usually accompanied by a sharp increase in the volume of trading

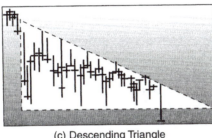
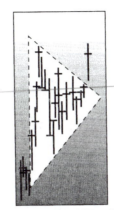

(a) Ascending Triangle   (b) Symmetrical Triangle

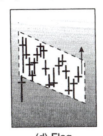

(c) Descending Triangle   (d) Flag

FIGURE 6.8
Triangles and flags.

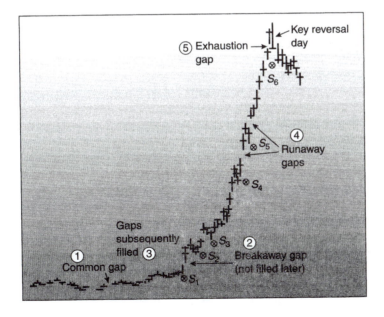

FIGURE 6.9
Gaps.

and a large price movement. It induces new traders into the market. **Runaway gaps** often prove to be approximately situated at the midpoint of a price move. **Exhaustion gaps** are soon followed by a key reversal day. During the formation of an exhaustion gap, prices continue to move with the established trend. Subsequently, support softens, liquidation begins, and the new trend reverses prices for the remainder of the trading session. This reversal is accompanied by very heavy trading volume. This series of events is interpreted by chartists as a strong sign that the original trend has turned.

POINT-AND-FIGURE CHART PRICE PATTERNS

Some chartists believe it is important to record price changes. As explained above, point-and-figure charts record price reversals with no reference to time; specifically, the size and direction of price moves are the focus of such charts. Although point-and-figure charts differ in their construction compared to bar charts, their interpretation is similar in that both provide a framework for identifying chart patterns that generate trading signals.

The simplest trading signals produced by a point-and-figure chart are buy and sell indicators. A buy signal is given when an X in the latest column has filled a box that is one box higher than the preceding column of Xs. A sell signal appears when the latest column is in Os that fill the box below the previous column of Os.

As with bar charts, point-and-figure charts produce many patterns that are interpreted as having special significance by technical analysts. Congestion areas, trend lines, resistance lines, support lines, and triangles can all be found on point-and-figure charts. These patterns are interpreted with the same meaning as identical patterns on bar charts, as discussed previously. Some patterns found only on point-and-figure charts include spread triple tops or bottoms and bullish and bearish catapults. Since fewer traders use point-and-figure charts compared to bar charts, detailed analysis of their patterns is not included here. Interested readers are referred to Luca (1997) and other similar books for extensive discussion of advanced point-and-figure signals.

TREND-FOLLOWING METHODS

The second category of technical analysis focuses on identifying price trends using **moving averages**.[2] A moving average (MA) is the average value of a contract's price over a given period of time, such as the past 10 days (i.e., a 10-day moving average). Moving averages are used to smooth noisy price data, such as daily set-

---

[2] A simple moving average is an updated average of a number of consecutive prices as they become available. At each time period t, the moving average is calculated as

$$MA_t = \frac{P_t + P_{t-1} + \ldots + P_{t-n+1}}{n} = \frac{\sum_{i=1}^{n} P_{t-i+1}}{n}, \quad n \leq t,$$

where n is the number of time periods used in the average. Each day, the oldest price is dropped out of this calculation and the more recent price added.

tlement (closing) prices. By charting the moving average of the settlement price, the technician can obtain a better idea of the underlying price trends. By plotting the moving average of closing prices over a specified time period, moving average chartists believe that they obtain a good picture of the true price trend by smoothing out the effects of short-term noisy price movements that can confound the interpretation of the chart.

When using moving average charts, the first thing chartists do is determine the number of days to be averaged. Any period may be chosen, but 5, 10, 20, or more days are typically used. The longer the period used, the longer the time lag between when a trend actually changes and when a chart signals that change. This could be considered a shortcoming if it generates a buy or sell signal too late. On the other hand, it could be considered a desirable characteristic if it causes a trader to hesitate before taking action in response to short-term temporary price moves that misrepresent the true trend situation.

There are a number of differerent ways to calculate moving averages, such as simple, weighted, smoothed, or exponential. Moving averages are typically charted against daily closing prices and perhaps with other moving averages to generate a buy or sell signal. Figures 6.10 and 6.11 illustrate these two examples. By plotting the moving average price against the daily closing price (Fig. 6.10) or against another moving average (Fig. 6.11), chartists believe that they can obtain an

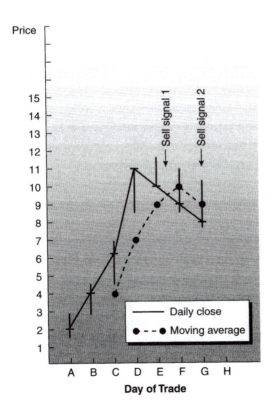

FIGURE 6.10
Vertical bar versus moving average.

FIGURE 6.11
Moving averages.

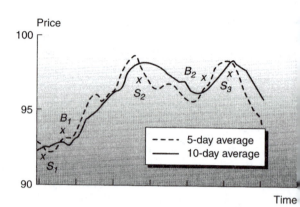

indication of when the trend is turning. Different types of buy and sell signals can be generated by combining prices with moving averages on the same chart.

Moving averages are used primarily as an indicator of long-term trends. Plotting a moving average of prices alone gives a general picture of historical market price movements. The moving average charts in Figures 6.10 and 6.11 combine the long-term trend information with bar or other moving average charts to detect short-term trading signals. With all types of moving average charts, a trading signal is given when lines on the chart cross. In Figure 6.10 a moving average and bar chart are used jointly to find two trading signals. The first signal is given when the bar chart line falls below the upward-trending moving average line. This indicates that long positions should be liquidated. The second sell signal is given when the moving average line turns down, indicating that the uptrend is reversing. This would tell chartists that a net short position should be initiated.

In Figure 6.11, 5- and 10-day moving averages are plotted. Notice that the 10-day moving average line is smoother than the 5-day line. This is to be expected because the longer the time period represented by the moving average, the smoother the moving average line will be. The lowercase x's in Figure 6.11 indicate when the 5- and 10-day moving average lines cross each other. As long as the 10-day moving average line is below the 5-day moving average line, the price trend is upward. Once the 5-day line crosses the 10-day line, this is taken as a signal that the trend has reversed itself. The buy signal (B_1) in Figure 6.11 is recorded when the 5-day moving average line crosses through the 10-day moving average line from below. At this point in time, the chartist goes long in the market and remains long until the next sell signal (S_2) is generated by the moving averages. Once the sell signal (S_2) is encountered, the trader reverses his or her position by going net short and so on.

CHARACTER-OF-MARKET ANALYSIS

Some technical analysts look beyond price information in making their assessments of price trends. They seek to identify characteristics of the markets that will give additional insights into what market participants are thinking. Character-of-market analysis, the third category of technical analysis, uses quantitative measures that are independent of price or uses price information more subtly in making price-trend forecasts. The principal factors considered are the size of a market (open interest), its level of market activity (volume of trade), its price variability (oscillators), and its composition (small- vs. large-scale traders).

Open interest refers to the total number of futures contracts outstanding at a particular point in time. It equals the number of long (or short) positions being held by traders in a market. When a trader settles a position by liquidating an outstanding contract, total open interest either declines or remains the same, depending on whether the trader on the other side of the market was also liquidating an outstanding position. When a contract reaches its maturity date, by definition, all individual traders' positions in that contract must be settled, and open interest declines to zero.

Chartists believe that changes in open interest, when viewed in conjunction with price changes, provides clues as to whether the market has been strengthened or weakened by recent trading activity. Changes in total open interest for all futures contract months are used in the analysis. When open interest goes up and prices are rising, the market is considered technically strong because of new buying. If prices decline during a rise in open interest, the market is technically weak because short hedging or short selling is taking place.

On the other hand, when open interest declines at the same time that prices are falling, a chartist considers the market technically strong because of long liquidation. The market is technically weak if prices are rising and open interest is falling, due to short covering. Therefore, when prices and open interest move in the same direction, it indicates that the existing price trend will continue. When prices and open interest are moving in opposite directions, it is considered a symptom of possible price weakness (trend reversal) ahead. It is important to remember, however, that there are seasonal patterns to open interest in many futures markets. These seasonal moves must be removed from the data before open interest calculations are made by the technicians.

Volume of trade refers to the total number of futures (or options) contracts traded during a specified period of time, such as a day. It is the total number of contracts bought or sold, and each individual transaction is composed of one buy and one sell.

Volume of trade is considered to be a major structural factor influencing a market and its prices. In addition, chartists believe that volume helps determine whether prices can be expected to continue moving in the same direction. They use total volume of trade on a given day for all delivery months combined and compare this figure with price movements. The technical rule of thumb that has developed is that prices will tend to move in the same direction as the change in the volume of trade.

Although volume of trade and open interest are related, changes in one variable cannot be used to predict the other, as explained in Chapter 1. For example, if there are only two trades during one day, volume is two, but open interest could have increased by two, decreased by two, or remained the same. If both trades established "new" positions, open interest would go up. If both trades liquidated existing positions, open interest would go down. In addition, open interest would not change if one-half the trades established new positions and one-half closed existing obligations. A "new" position is a trade that extends a trader's net long or net short position in a particular contract month. In other words, a new position does not liquidate a previously established position.

Oscillators are a family of technical indicators based on price changes rather than price levels. An example is a 10-day oscillator, which equals the current price minus the settlement price 10 days earlier. There are two basic principles behind the use of oscillators. First, users believe that a price rise or decline can become overextended if it gains too much velocity. A market rising (falling) too fast is called **overbought (oversold)**. Second, a price trend can simply disintegrate because of a loss of momentum, as everyone who wants to trade with the trend has already done so.

Both principles underlying the use of oscillators imply that there is some appropriate rate of change for prices in a market. If traders push prices at a rate that is too high, some factor, such as accumulated profits or losses for traders, will presumably cause those traders to react and correct the error. If this type of profit-taking behavior is prevalent in a market, using oscillators can benefit a trader by signaling the emotion level in that market. However, if prices are trending strongly in one direction because of an underlying change in the fundamentals, using oscillators can mislead a trader into thinking that the trend is reversing. Another shortcoming of this technical tool is that the subjective zones indicating an "overbought" or "oversold" market (shown in Fig. 6.12) change with time and market conditions. Figure 6.13 is an example of an oscillator in conjunction with a bar chart on the same graph. The oscillator is the solid line on the bottom of Figure 6.13. When the oscillator crosses above the horizontal solid line (shown at a price change of approximately 84), the maket is deemed to be "overbought," and when the oscillator falls below the solid horizontal line at approximately −84, the oscillator is signaling that the market is "oversold."

Other technical analysis systems based on characteristics of markets include evaluations of market composition and **contrary opinion**. To capitalize on this characteristic, some technical traders have developed trading rules based on market composition factors. Typically, buy and sell signals are derived from the studies of activities of large and small traders (distinguished by the size of their holdings). For example, if large traders hold short positions representing some arbitrary percentage of open interest, a sell signal is given. The logic is that large traders are assumed to be more successful than small traders; therefore, taking positions favored by a significant portion of the large traders in a market is more likely to be profitable than following the crowd of small traders. This approach obviously has a number of shortcomings, the most significant being the lack of timely data concerning traders' positions. The Commodity Futures Trading Commission (CFTC) publishes data on traders' positions (Box 6.2).

FIGURE 6.12
Oscillator.

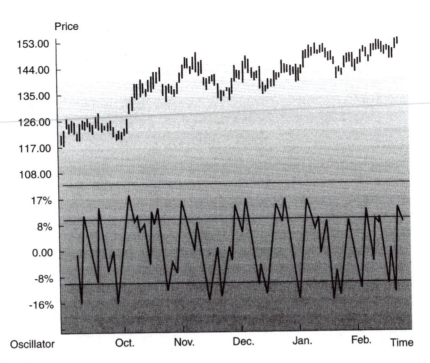

FIGURE 6.13
A sample oscillator and bar-chart.

BOX 6.2

Commitments of Traders *report.*

The Commodity Futures Trading Commission (CFTC) is the government regulatory agency that oversees futures and options trading. As part of their mandate, the CFTC publishes weekly reports of aggregate net open positions (i.e., long or short) of traders in the futures and options market. This is called the *Commitments of Traders* report.

For each commodity or asset, the CFTC first breaks open interest into "reportable" and "nonreportable" positions. Only the traders with a large position (above a CFTC-specified reporting level) must report whether they are commercial (i.e., a hedger) or noncommercial. For example, for heating oil the reporting level is 250 contracts, and for Eurodollars it is 1,000 contracts. The CFTC reports open positions as a percentage of open interest. See the CFTC's Web site for *Commitments of Traders* data at *http://www.cftc.gov.*

Contrary opinion is a strategy based on one concept: the herd mentality in the market is on the wrong side of the market. If the CFTC's *Commitments of Traders* report indicates that most speculators are long in the market, this approach would view this as a sign that the market is overbought and the price is about to fall.

Technicians favoring this approach use information from the CFTC concerning the open positions of large and small hedgers and speculators. When the market is overbought or oversold, contrarians see market prices as representing strong opinions supported by weak reasons. The weak reasons are that market information is well publicized and known for some time (meaning that the market has already responded). Using contrary opinion is highly subjective, even more so than some other technical analysis methods.

STRUCTURAL THEORIES

Structural theories, the fourth category of technical methods, involve intensive study of long-term historical prices with the goal of detecting recurring price patterns. These methods are different than charting because quantitative techniques are used more heavily in the structural analysis. Structural theories imply that

---

BOX 6.3

Triple witching hour.

Four times a year, futures and options traders brace themselves for a **triple witching hour**, when stock index futures and options and individual stock options expire simultaneously. Last-minute trading volume records have been set at the New York Stock Exchange on several of these Fridays.

The high trading volume concentrated into a very short period of time has significant effects on all markets involved. The volume is caused by arbitrage traders closing and "rolling over" positions into contracts that expire later. For particular stocks, the effects of these witching hours can be sizable price "bubbles" due to technical trading. In 1986, for example, the net changes in the Dow Jones Industrial Average on each of the four triple expiration Fridays was followed by a reverse move the following Monday:

	Friday	Monday
March	− 35.68	+ 14.37
June	+ 23.68	− 15.28
September	− 11.53	+ 30.80
December	+ 16.03	− 2.67

Futures and options exchanges and regulators have tried to reduce the triple witching hour effects by shifting the expiration of some stock index futures and options contracts to the opening of trading on quarterly expiration days instead of at the close of trading. Nevertheless, regulators and legislators are likely to continue scrutinizing the witching hour controversy in an effort to reduce technical trading effects on market efficiency.

prices follow a "blueprint" that creates patterns at irregular time intervals. The two general types of structural patterns are **seasonal** and **cyclical**. If these patterns are detected in a market, various quantitative methods are combined by technical analysts into a **trading** system. These systems are forecasting devices used to give buy and sell signals.

Studies on financial and commodity futures prices have found evidence of seasonality (e.g., Gay and Kim, 1987; Stevenson and Bear, 1970). As a result, numerous technical trading rules have been developed for measuring and predicting seasonality. These technical rules are partly based on a fundamental approach because the source of seasonality is either supply or demand driven. The distinction, however, is that technical traders view seasonal price patterns not as the result of interaction between supply and demand factors but as systematic patterns that happen to occur with regularity.

Cycles, on the other hand, are viewed by technical traders as price patterns that occur with less regularity and without regard for seasons. The logic behind the use of cycles is that past prices are believed to contain evidence of one or more cycles that will carry prices forward. Studies of cyclical price movements have shown these patterns to be more difficult to detect than seasonality (Herbst, McCormack, and West, 1987). Most futures traders believe cycles are too long term to be of use to make a profit. However, some technical traders have incorporated cyclical effects into forecasting models when long-term trends are relevant to the market and the trader's goals. Fang (2000), who discusses seasonality in the currency markets, finds evidence of seasonality in exchange rate volatility.

ELLIOTT WAVE THEORY

One of the most popular structural theories is based on the Elliott wave theory. Ralph Elliott was a stock market observer who wrote a book in 1946 with a modest title: *Nature's Law: The Secret of the Universe*. From that book and the work of supporters, the **Elliott wave theory** evolved. The theory is based on the belief that there is a rhythm in nature that spills over into all aspects of life, including the stock and futures markets. Elliott stressed that the rhythm is captured in the **Fibonacci summation series.** Fibonacci, an Italian mathematician who lived in the 13th century, created the series by summing the two previous numbers in the series to get the next number. The series begins 1, 1, 2, 3, 5, 8, 13, 21, 34, 55, 89, 144, and goes on to infinity.

Elliott used the Fibonacci series to describe the "ideal" market. According to his theory, Elliott believed that a major bull market consists of five waves followed by a major bear market of three waves. He believed that a five-wave bull market would consist of three "up" legs separated by two "down" legs. A three-wave bear market would consist of a downswing, a rally, and a final downswing. Elliott went on to say that within the major trends are intermediate trends and that within the intermediate trends (which also contain five and three waves) are minor trends (with five and three waves). As shown in Table 6.1, the sum of waves in each uptrend, downtrend, and complete cycle all correspond to the Fibonacci numbers.

TABLE 6.1 Principal Number of Elliott Waves			
	BULL MARKET	**BEAR MARKET**	**TOTAL CYCLE**
Number of major waves	5	3	8
Number of intermediate waves	21	13	34
Number of minor waves	89	55	144

The greatest shortcoming of the Elliott wave theory, like all cycle theories, is the difficulty in determining at what point in the complex wave system a market is currently in. There are hundreds of books available on the Elliott wave principle (e.g., see Prechter and Frost, 1995).

TRADING SYSTEMS

Technical trading systems have become increasingly popular among futures speculators, especially since personal computers and the Internet have become widely available. For a detailed description of specific technical systems, see Lukac, Brorsen, and Irwin (1988). It is worth noting that although these systems are used by many professional traders, they are probably not the best systems available. It is unlikely that developers of the most profitable systems would publish and sell them. Instead, they would presumably keep the system a secret and profit from trading the system themselves.

The most common type of technical trading system used by professionals is one that follows trends. They typically use five categories of technical analysis methods: price channels, moving averages, momentum oscillators, filter systems, and combination methods. All trading systems have trading rules that trigger buy and sell signals. The triggers are arbitrarily selected, usually based on some aspect of price variability in the market.

Channel systems look for a price breakout outside the range of past prices. The channel is defined by two trend lines drawn on a vertical bar chart. As shown in the box on the right side of Figure 6.5, one trend line is drawn along the top of the price pattern and the other along the bottom of the pattern. In computer-assisted versions of these systems, the line is expressed as a mathematical relationship. As soon as the current price breaks out of the channel formed by previous prices, a trade signal is given. In some systems, the signal is only to buy or sell. In others, the signal can be "neutral," meaning that no positions should be held. Different weights are given to prices in the channel by different systems, some favoring recent or distant prices. Virtually every combination of technical rules has been tried, and none has dominated sufficiently enough to be favored by a majority of system traders.

The **moving average** methods use recent prices to generate trading signals. Some systems simply use versions of the general approach to moving averages described earlier in this chapter, combining two averages or combining an average with some other technical indicator. A second type of moving average system uses

---

BOX 6.4

Famous investment bubbles.
What do tulips and Internet stocks have in common? Some would argue that the price of tulips and Internet stocks have both experienced price bubbles. The tulip price bubble swept through Holland in the 17th century as Dutch traders bought and sold tulips at incredible prices. Some tulip bulbs were reportedly traded for more than U.S.$10 million in today's value. The exorbitant tulip prices were not based on fundamentals, and the price spike lasted a relatively short time. The word *bourse* (which means "stock exchange") is derived from the tulip mania period. In the 17th century, tulips were traded at the offices of the Dutch noble family Van Bourse.

For a discussion of the most famous investment bubbles in history, see Garber (2000).

---

a band around the moving average line. This is similar to defining a channel around the moving average line with the width of the price band based on a percentage of the current futures price. When current prices cross the band, trade signals are given. A third type of moving average system uses moving averages of directional price changes. Increases and decreases in price are averaged separately to give trade signals.

Momentum oscillator systems determine relative overbought and oversold market conditions. As described earlier, most oscillators measure the relative strength in a market, and trading systems based on these indicators generate trading signals when some critical value is reached. Various oscillators are used in computer trading systems. Some are based on price differences over a particular length of time, and others are based on differences from an average over a period of time. Signals to buy, sell, or remain neutral are based on arbitrary levels of the oscillators used by the system.

Filter systems use trailing stops to give trading signals. One type of filter system follows price trends estimated with a linear model, using a trailing stop to reverse its signal. Another filter system also uses a trailing stop to generate a signal when the current price moves a certain percentage from a significant point in a trend. The key to these systems is to determine how far the stop should trail the trigger variable (i.e., the price).

Combination systems trade using two systems simultaneously. For example, one system uses both a moving average and a filter system to generate joint tests that must be met to generate buy or sell signals. A growing number of futures fund managers are using combination systems because of the built-in cross-checks that they provide for trading signals.

In summary, the increased variety and visibility of technical trading systems in futures and options markets has raised a number of questions. Does the tremendous growth in futures funds imply that these trading systems work? Why are technical trading systems so popular? Is one type of system better than the others?

The answers to these questions are still being debated, but trends in responses are beginning to take shape, as explained in the next section.

TO CHART OR NOT TO CHART

Supporters of technical analysis include a majority of futures brokers and managers of futures funds. In comparing fundamental and technical analysis, technical traders' arguments center on four reasons for using their method over the alternative:

1. It is impossible for any private trader to compete with large commercial firms in the rapid collection of accurate and costly market information. With technical analysis, a private trader can often determine whether the major commercial interests are trading long or short.
2. Fundamental analysis may succeed in predicting long-term price moves, but it is not too helpful in the short term. With the high level of financial leverage in futures trading, private futures traders cannot afford to be wrong in the short term.
3. Preoccupation with daily news events and rumors makes it very difficult to maintain the systematic and disciplined approach to trading decisions required for successful fundamental trading.
4. Technical analysis works. For decades, people have made money employing primarily technical methods. It is simple to use, and the same techniques can be applied to many different markets.

The first three points all focus on the need of a trader to quickly identify what other market participants are thinking and doing. This recognizes the fact that, for

---

BOX 6.5

Can a television talk show drive down cattle futures prices?

American cattlemen sued Oprah Winfrey for comments she made in 1996 on her daytime television talk show. Oprah reportedly said that her concern over Britain's mad-cow disease spreading to the United States "just stopped me cold from eating another burger!"

The mad-cow brain-destroying disease was not detected in the United States, but it did kill people in Britain. The lawsuit alleged that she had no right to make these comments because the United States was free of the disease. The cattlemen argued that cattle futures prices dropped drastically after the Winfrey television show aired.

The cattlemen had accused Winfrey and one of her guests of deliberately attacking the cattle industry and driving down futures prices through false statements. The cattlemen requested $16.5 million in damages. Eventually, the U.S. courts sided with Oprah and rejected the cattlemen's claims.

speculators, futures trading is a competition among traders in which market prices are the medium, not the objective. Ignoring commissions, futures trading is a zero sum game: profits must equal losses. To make a profit, a trader must out-forecast other traders, which leads to a preoccupation with access to market information and crowd psychology.

The fourth reason given above for using technical methods is the bottom line. Is technical analysis profitable? Several studies have tried to make an objective assessment of the performance of technical trading methods. For example, Irwin and Brorsen (1987) found that inflation rates affect returns to futures funds, implying that there are structural factors creating trends in prices that provide opportunities for systems trading profits. They also concluded that the amount of technical trading in a market does not affect returns to futures funds that trade based on the technicals. Neftci and Policano (1984) found that moving average systems seem to have some predictive power, while trend-following systems have mixed results.

Chartists assume that markets do not follow a random walk; rather, they assume that there are identifiable price trends. Indeed, it is argued by many economists that the survival of technical trading systems implies that futures markets are inefficient. Research results indicate that there are weak grounds for such an assumption. Several studies have shown that the markets are approximately efficient.

Critics argue that the short-term success of technical methods in general, and charting in particular, can be explained as self-fulfilling prophesies. The complaint goes as follows. A large proportion of futures traders use technical analysis as part of their decision-making process. As a result, if one of the well-known chart patterns begins to appear, many chartists will see it at the same time. Next, because each price pattern has a specific interpretation in the chartists' logic, everyone who sees the pattern taking shape will simultaneously make the same decision as to the appropriate market response. Finally, the weight of all the orders placed by those technical traders will help create the very momentum the chart supposedly predicted; therefore, prices will begin to move through the remainder of the price pattern, picking up more momentum as additional chartists see the pattern and react in the same way as other chartists had before them. Although the existence of this effect is difficult to measure, Lukac et al. (1988) found empirical evidence that it exists in computer-guided trading systems.

For a trader considering the use of technical analysis, many factors must be evaluated. The relatively short amount of time required for data collection and analysis is an advantage of technical methods. On the other hand, accuracy of forecasts is more relevant to traders' success. Therefore, the critical factor may be whether it is a profitable exercise compared to alternative forecasting methods.

In the long run, detailed economic models whose forecasts are sold commercially do no better than futures in predicting spot prices (Just & Rausser, 1981). However, traders' objectives are to forecast short-run futures prices. In this regard, technical methods can aid in order placement. However, there is no reason to expect that relying only on technical systems will produce abnormal profits on average. The performance of computer-guided technical trading systems has been generally poor. To improve profit performance, some additional (fundamental) information may be needed to help judge the recommendations produced by a technical system. Therefore, many successful chartists are probably not "true" chartists; they are probably doing some fundamental analysis whether they like to admit it or not.

COMMODITY POOLS AND PROGRAM TRADING

A commodity pool (or commodity fund) is a managed speculative futures fund similar to a mutual fund in either the stock or the bond market. It pools investors' money and then trades futures contracts using these funds. Any profits from the fund's trading are returned to the investors, net of management fees. An estimated $44 billion[3] has been invested in managed futures globally as of 2001. The pools are controversial participants in the futures market because, in aggregate, they control significant speculative funds.

Most pools use technical analysis exclusively (Brorsen and Irwin, 1987), and this has generated controversy over the price effects of futures pools. For example, too much technical trading can cause price swings unrelated to the fundamentals of the market, even if the technical traders correctly forecast price trends. The economics literature also suggests that technical analysis may adversely affect price volatility.

Irwin and Brorsen (1987) studied the role of public commodity pools in a portfolio of financial assets and found a beneficial diversification effect. Elton, Gruber, and Rentzler (1989) evaluated commodity funds' performance and found that less than half the funds they studied produced returns greater than Treasury bills. Additionally, the management fees and transactions costs of the funds were found to be high. Overall, they question the use of funds as an investment vehicle because they are a high-risk and low-return investment. Schneeweis, Savanayana, and McCarthy (1991) found that commodity pools may be rational investments as stand-alone investments, as additions to existing stock and bond portfolios, or as part of an optimal portfolio. Murphy (1986) found no compelling evidence that technical funds outperform a naive buy-and-hold strategy. Edwards and Ma (1988) found that a superior commodity fund could not be selected on the basis of historical performance. The research conducted on the value of funds to speculators has had mixed results, but nevertheless futures pools remain a popular investment option.

Economic research has concluded the following:

- Pools trade primarily in large markets
- Pools trade frequently
- Pools tend to trade when other market participants are trading (pools' trading volume is correlated with total market volume)

---

[3] This figure was reported by Managed Account Reports (*http://www.marhedge.com*). In addition, refer to the Managed Funds Association, a U.S.-based association of managed funds professionals, with more than 700 members that represent the managed futures and hedge fund industry throughout the world (*http://www.mfainfo.org*).

- Pools use similar trend-following methods when making trading decisions.
- Pool trading is a small percentage of futures and options total trading volume, but on some days it constitutes a large share of the total volume (up to 45%).

SUMMARY

This chapter has introduced technical analysis, the second method of price forecasting used by futures and option traders. Technical analysis focuses on a futures contract's price history, ignoring the fundamental factors of supply and demand. The chapter began by explaining the logic behind charting and describing the charting process, introduced quantitative approaches to technical analysis, and concluded with a summary of the debate over the value of technical analysis. Key points made in the chapter are the following:

- Technical analysis focuses on very short-term price forecasting, whereas fundamental analysis provides long-term price outlooks.
- Technical analysis is centered on trying to identify price trends and their turning points. It is intended to provide specific trade signals to enable the investor to trade with the trend.
- The most common charting methods use moving averages and/or high-low bar charts. Patterns in the temporal charts are believed to be significant and are used in price forecasting.
- Characteristics of a futures market are quantified by some technical analysts for use in price forecasting. Open interest and volume of trade, in particular, are watched closely by these analysts when attempting to determine whether existing trends will continue.
- The use of quantitative programs that run on personal computers is a popular approach to producing trading signals.
- Technical analysis can succeed only if there is no random walk in prices. Therefore, the survival of this forecasting approach implies (short-term) market inefficiency.
- Managed futures funds are popular investment vehicles for speculators, and the value controlled by managed futures funds exceeds $40 billion. Most of the managed pools use technical trading systems.

DISCUSSION QUESTIONS

1. Why do traditional technical analysts reject the use of any statistical supply or demand data when making price forecasts?
2. What criteria should be used in selecting the type of price chart to use in technical analysis?
3. Explain how to interpret a moving average chart for buy and sell signals.

4. Compare double top (bottom) and head and shoulders top (bottom) formations.
5. Define *open interest*. Explain why it is significant in technical analysis.
6. How can a market become overbought?
7. Why is using contrary opinion a risky approach to market analysis?
8. What is a price channel? How can it be used by a futures trader?
9. Explain the reasoning underlying the Elliott wave theory. What is the biggest shortcoming analysts face when trying to apply the Elliott wave theory in price forecasting?
10. Discuss the following statement: "The most convincing argument against the continued success of any technical trading rules (i.e., techniques) is that the process of exploiting the abnormal returns destroys the trading rule." As part of your answer, explain whether you believe this statement to be true or false.

SELECTED REFERENCES

Brorsen, B. W., & Irwin, S. H. (1987). Futures funds and price volatility. *Review of Futures Markets, 6,* 118–135.

Brunnermeier, M. K. (2001). *Asset pricing under asymmetric information: Bubbles, crashes, technical analysis, and herding.* New York: Oxford University Press.

Chande, T. S. (2001). *Beyond technical analysis: How to develop and implement a winning trading system.* New York: Wiley.

Edwards, F. R., & Ma, C. (1988). Commodity pool performance: Is the information contained in pool prospectuses useful? *Journal of Futures Markets, 8*(5), 589–616.

Elliott, R. N. (1946). *Nature's law: The secret of the universe.* New York: NY.

Elton, E. J., Gruber, M. J., & Rentzler, J. (1989). New public offerings, information, and investor rationality: The case of publicly offered commodity funds. *Journal of Business, 62*(1), 1–15.

Fama, E. F. (1976). *Foundations of finance.* New York: Basic Books.

Fang, Y. (2000). Seasonality in foreign exchange volatility. *Applied Economics, 32*(6), 697–703.

Garber, P. (2000). *Famous first bubbles: The fundamentals of early manias.* Cambridge, MA: MIT Press.

Gay, G., & Kim, T. (1987). An investigation into seasonality in the futures market. *Journal of Futures Markets, 7,* 169–181.

Herbst, A., McCormack, J., & West, E. (1987). Investigation of a lead-lag relationship between spot indices and their futures contracts. *Journal of Futures Markets, 7,* 373–381.

Irwin, S., & Brorsen, W. (1987). A note on the factors affecting technical trading system returns. *Journal of Futures Markets, 7,* 591–595.

Just, R., & Rausser, G. (1981). Commodity price forecasting with large-scale econometric models and the futures market. *American Journal of Agricultural Economics, 63,* 197–208.

Kleinman, G. (2001). *Commodity futures and options: A step-by-step guide to successful trading.* New York: Pearson Education.

Luca, C. (1997). *Technical analysis applications in the global currency markets.* Englewood Cliffs, NJ: Prentice Hall.

Lukac, L. P., Brorsen, B., & Irwin, S. (1988). Similarity of computer guided technical trading systems. *Journal of Futures Markets, 8,* 1–13.

Murphy, J. A. (1986). Futures fund performance: A test of the effectiveness of technical analysis. *Journal of Futures Markets, 6,* 175–186.

Neftci, S., & Policano, A. (1984). Can chartists outperform the market? Market efficiency tests for technical analysis. *Journal of Futures Markets, 4,* 465–478.

Prechter, R. R., Jr., & Frost, A. J. (1995). *Elliott wave principle: Key to market behavior.* Gainesville, GA: Charles J. Collins.

Schneeweis, T., Savanayana, U., & McCarthy, D. (1991). Alternative commodity trading vehicles: A performance analysis. *Journal of Futures Markets, 11*(4), 475–490.

Stevenson, R., & Bear, R. (1970). Commodity futures: "Trends or Random Walks"? *Journal of Finance, 25,* 65–81.

Zeira, J. (1999). Informational overshooting, booms, and crashes. *Journal of Monetary Economics, 43*(1), 237–257.

CHAPTER 7

Hedging

If military tension in the Middle East sends the price of oil higher, then this development will affect the profitability of airlines because the price of jet fuel rises with the price of crude oil. Likewise, if Japan devalues its exchange rate (the yen), the falling currency value will affect the profitability of German automobile manufacturers competing against Japanese firms in the world market. In both of these examples, the airline and the German automaker could partially mitigate the effect of lost profits through hedging.

Hedging is an all-encompassing term that, in the futures and options market literature, normally refers to simultaneously holding both cash and futures (or options) positions. There are many different types of hedgers, including airlines, exporters and importers, banks, manufacturers, mining companies, farmers, and so on. Because of the diversity of the underlying businesses that hedgers are engaged in, there are several different motives for hedging. In contrast, speculators' motives are very straightforward: buy low and sell high (or sell high and buy low). The traditional view is that hedgers are seeking to reduce price risk in the underlying cash market. Two other important and widely accepted explanations have hedgers either attempting to profit from expected movements in the futures–cash price spread (i.e., the basis) or endeavoring to use futures positions to diversify their portfolios made up of cash commodities and other assets.

Some of the most innovative research and writing on the subject of hedging has been carried out by Holbrook Working.[1] He was the first person to challenge the traditional and naive view that hedging is a method whereby producers and merchants can reduce or even eliminate the price risk associated with owning physical commodity stocks by taking an equal and opposite position in the futures market. Working (1962) correctly pointed out that hedging is practiced for a number of other legitimate business reasons, a major one being profit maximization by anticipating favorable basis changes. Following Working, the next major reformu-

---

[1] For a collection of Working's papers, see Peck (1977).

lation of the theory of hedging was presented separately by both Johnson (1960) and Stein (1961), who cast the motives for hedging within a portfolio framework.

The purpose of this chapter is to present the major theories and explanations for hedging based on the writings of Working, Stein, and Johnson. Empirical tests of the competing theories are also briefly reviewed. Additionally, this chapter discusses hedging in commodity and financial futures markets. The topic of hedging with options on futures is discussed in Chapter 9.

The concepts of hedging in financial futures and in commodity futures markets are very similar. Whether an oil refinery is balancing cash and futures positions in order to diversify a portfolio or a financial institution is balancing its assets and liabilities, the same economic principles apply. The primary determinant of the success of a hedge is how the basis changes during the hedging period.[2]

TRADITIONAL VIEW OF HEDGING

Hedgers are normally defined as those individuals or firms who produce, process, or utilize the underlying commodity, financial instrument, or asset that is being hedged. They manage the risk of adverse price changes by taking positions in the futures or options market. If they are long in the cash market, then they take a short position in the futures market and vice versa. Their main goal is to counterbalance price changes in the two markets against one another. This traditional view suggests that hedging is carried out to reduce price risk (Cootner, 1967).

BOX 7.1

Hedging jet fuel.
One of the first airlines in the world to hedge their jet fuel purchases was Quantas Airlines in Australia. They were hedged before the Persian Gulf War in 1990–91, and this turned out to be a huge cost saving maneuver because the war drove up jet fuel prices. Following the Gulf War price disruptions, several U.S. airlines started a similar hedging program. For example, Delta and Southwest Airlines started hedging programs in the mid-1990s.

For most airlines, jet fuel is one of the most significant expenses. Unhedged fuel is normally 15% to 20% of an airline's total operating costs, and the price of jet fuel is very volatile. For instance, Delta burns about three billion gallons of fuel per year. So, if the price of jet fuel jumps from 75¢ to $1 per gallon, which can easily happen, Delta's costs would be up by an extra $750 million for the year. Therefore, hedging plays an important role in their overall risk management strategy. There is no futures or options market for jet fuel, so most airlines cross-hedge by using heating oil futures and options.

---

[2] See Mahul (2002) for a discussion of hedging in futures and options with basis risk.

In the financial markets, the largest group of hedgers includes banks and financial portfolio managers and exporters and importers exposed to exchange rate risk. The largest group of hedgers in agricultural markets are merchants and processors who handle, process, and store the underlying physical commodity. In the metals and petroleum sector, producing and processing firms often utilize hedging programs. At any given time, it is too risky for mining companies, commodity merchants, and so on to hold large unhedged positions in the cash market because of potential losses due to price swings. Taking a position in the futures market opposite to the cash position allows the company to substantially reduce its exposure to this price risk.

Hedging Categories

In the 1960s, Holbrook Working categorized alternative motives for commercial hedging in commodity futures, and these motives continue to be valid today. The three broad categories are arbitrage hedging, operational hedging, and anticipatory hedging.

An **arbitrage hedge** is sometimes referred to as a **carrying charge hedge**. Since the futures and cash price converge in the delivery month, a commercial firm can "arbitrage" the two markets and earn a risk-free return from the predictable change in the basis. For instance, suppose that American Grain Inc. has access to warehouse space in Chicago. In early April, it may decide to buy wheat in the cash market for $3.50, put the wheat into storage, and simultaneously sell July wheat futures at a price of $4.00. Assuming full storage costs are less than $0.50 per bushel for three months, American Grain has successfully arbitraged the markets and locked in a riskless return (of $0.50 less storage costs) for storing the wheat. Of course, this type of arbitrage opportunity encourages firms to store commodities. Providing returns to those willing and able to carry products in storage is one of the many useful economic functions provided by futures markets.

Operational hedging facilitates commercial business practices by allowing firms to buy and sell contracts on the futures markets as temporary substitutes for subsequent cash market transactions. This use of futures markets provides firms with an avenue for being flexible in day-to-day operations and reducing price risk. Profiting from a change in the basis does not figure as prominently as an objective with this type of hedge. Suppose that in April a U.S. computer firm makes a large sale of hardware to a European importer and that the (forward) contract for the computers specifies delivery in August and payment in Euros on delivery. The U.S. company is exposed to the risk of an exchange rate change between April and August. However, the U.S. computer firm still has the flexibility to go ahead with the forward sale of the hardware because, as a temporary substitute for the sale of the Euros in the spot exchange rate market, the firm can sell Euro futures in order to reduce the exchange rate risk. Suppose that the computer hardware is worth 570,000 Euros, or approximately $500,000 if the Euro is currently trading at 0.88 in U.S. dollars. The forward contract specifies a price of 570,000 Euros, so if the Euro were to fall in value to 0.75, the computers would only fetch about $427,000 when converted back into U.S. dollars in August. This is the currency risk facing the computer firm.

BOX 7.2

Should farmers hedge or speculate?

Typically, futures brokers, textbooks, and journal articles praise hedging and suggest that all farmers should hedge. However, most farmers do not follow this advice. Despite the theoretical advantages of farmer hedging, a study by the Commodity Futures Trading Commission found that only about 7% of U.S. farmers use futures, and many of them were speculating rather than hedging. This is an interesting paradox.

Some of the reasons farmers give for not hedging include the following:

- Government programs provide a price floor
- Production risk
- Lack of knowledge of hedging process
- Margin calls make it too risky
- Availability of forward contracts as an alternative
- Production does not match size of futures contract

Actually, it is not totally surprising that so few farmers hedge and that many speculate instead. Production risk discourages hedging before harvest. After harvest, if a farmer expects prices to fall, he simply sells in the cash market (as long as the basis is not too wide). If, alternatively, he expects prices to rise, he might sell the physical and buy futures contracts or call options instead. He is speculating with futures or options rather than the physical inventory, which makes perfect sense. It is quite possible that speculation is a better use of futures and options by farmers.

Finally, U.S. government programs, such as loan deficiency payments, act like a put option with no premium. With lucrative government programs, there may be no need for farmers to hedge because the government programs have removed some of the downside risk associated with low market prices.

This example of the computer sale is an operational hedge because it facilitates the ability of the computer firm to make the forward sale to Europe, while at the same time limiting exposure to exchange rate risk. Of course, basis changes will affect the outcome of this hedge, as mentioned in Chapter 3 and as discussed in more detail in this chapter.

Anticipatory hedges involve the buying or selling of futures contracts by commercial firms in "anticipation" of forthcoming cash market transactions. Price expectations play an important role with this type of hedge. For example, Green Acres Inc. may have 1,000 acres planted to wheat and before harvest may sell wheat futures with the expectation that prices are on the decline. It is physically impossible for the manager of Green Acres to sell the actual wheat until it is harvested, and thus he is taking advantage of current prices by hedging in the futures market. In addition to price risk, this type of hedge also involves production risk— the size of the crop may fall short of expectations. A crop shortfall would result in

between the size of Green Acres' crop and the price of wheat, then the production risk may be manageable. The anticipatory hedge may still maximize expected return, even though it involves some risk. However, this yield-price correlation will depend on the commodity in question and the location of its production. For example, in an empirical study of soybean hedging, Miller and Kahl (1987) found negative correlation (− 0.3 to − 0.8) between yield and price for a sample of farms in Illinois. This means that as yield increases, the price of the commodity falls.

Examples of Hedging Basics

To illustrate the process of hedging, suppose that a grain merchant—American Grain Inc.—purchases 5,000 bushels of corn at $3.00 per bushel. This merchant is now long in the cash market, which means that the merchant possesses the actual physical commodity. In order to reduce the risk of a price decline and a reduction in the value of American Grain's physical stockpile of corn, American Grain takes an opposite position in the futures market. The company does this by going short a futures contract calling for delivery of 5,000 bushels of corn at some future point in time. This simultaneous purchase of the cash corn and sale of the futures contract will place the merchant in a hedged position. If the price of corn falls, American Grain will profit on its futures position and lose on its cash position, assuming that the cash and futures prices move in roughly a parallel fashion. On the other hand, if the price rises above $3.00, American Grain will lose on its futures position but gain on the cash position. Either way, profits (losses) in the cash market offset losses (profits) in the futures market. Therefore, American Grain has hedged its inventory of corn against a price decline.

In most cases, movements of cash and futures prices over time are not expected to be exactly parallel. The mathematical difference between the futures and

---

BOX 7.3

The Texas hedge.

Texans are often stereotyped as being risk takers. Some believe that individuals who are not afraid of risk built the state of Texas. A real Texan loves risk and is therefore not very interested in hedging. However, he may still use the futures (or options) market—but to speculate and not to hedge. For example, a Texas rancher might own 200 head of cattle that he plans to sell at a later date. At the same time, for example, he might purchase five live cattle futures contracts (or buy call options for five futures contracts). This transaction is referred to as a "Texas hedge." In reality, it is not a hedge but rather a large speculative move. It doubles the amount of risk the rancher is exposed to through ownership of the live cattle, and if cattle prices trend downward, his losses are double.

cash price, defined as the basis, will change over time. Examples of the numerous ways in which a basis may change with time are given in Chapter 3. Changes in the basis ensure that the merchant cannot eliminate price risk through hedging but only reduce it. Of course, if the merchant delivers on the futures contract, there is no basis risk. However, delivery on futures contracts is a relatively rare occurrence. Alternatively, if cash and futures prices were to move up and down in exact parallel fashion, then the basis would not change, and price risk could be totally eliminated. This is a "perfect" (or "textbook") hedge opportunity, but it is rarely present in commodity markets. Some examples of basis calculations are provided in Table 7.1.

An example of a changing basis is presented in the top panel of Table 7.2, where on December 1 American Grain Inc. simultaneously bought 5,000 bushels of physical corn for $3.00 per bushel and sold one May corn futures contract (calling for delivery of 5,000 bushels) at $3.25. Thus, the basis on December 1 is $0.25 per bushel, and once American Grain is fully hedged (i.e., the 5,000 bushels of physical corn inventory match the size of one futures contract), its only exposure to price

TABLE 7.1 Basis Calculations

TIME PERIOD	FUTURES CONTRACT	FUTURES PRICE ($)	CASH OR SPOT CONTRACT	CASH OR SPOT PRICE ($)	BASIS ($)
January	May corn	3.05	Duluth spot	2.85	0.20
January	May corn	3.05	Iowa local spot	2.55	0.50
March	July soybeans	6.95	Illinois local forward cash	6.50	0.45

TABLE 7.2 Hedging: Basis Examples

SHORT HEDGING CORN: AN ILLUSTRATION				
DATE	FUTURES PRICE ($)	BASIS ($ PER BUSHEL)	CASH PRICE ($)	HEDGER'S TRANSACTION
December 1	3.25	0.25	3.00	Sell one May corn futures contract
April 1	2.75	0.30	2.45	Buy one May corn futures contract
Gain (loss)	0.50		(0.55)	

LONG HEDGING CORN: AN ILLUSTRATION				
DATE	FUTURES PRICE ($)	BASIS ($ PER BUSHEL)	CASH PRICE ($)	HEDGER'S TRANSACTION
December 1	3.25	0.25	3.00	Buy one May corn futures contract
April 1	2.75	0.30	2.45	Sell one May corn futures contract
Gain (loss)	(0.50)		0.55	

risk is the risk of a basis change. Being a short hedger (i.e., simultaneously holding a long cash position and a short futures position), American Grain is concerned only with a widening of the basis because this will result in a loss of revenue. At the same time, American Grain will profit from the basis narrowing. A widening of the basis means that cash and futures prices move in such a fashion that the mathematical value of the basis increases. Conversely, a narrowing of the basis implies that the cash and futures price move in a way such that the mathematical value of the basis becomes smaller. For example, if in Table 7.2 the futures price remains unchanged at $3.25 and the cash price increases from $3.00 to $3.10, then the basis is narrowing because the difference between the futures and cash price has declined. If, instead, the cash remains at $3.00 and the futures price rises, then the basis is widening. Examples of the basis becoming either narrower or wider are shown in Table 7.3. The basis changes noted in the last column of Table 7.3 refer to a change from the previous time period. Each row in Table 7.3 represents a different time period.

On April 1, suppose that American Grain's hedge is lifted, while at the same time the physical corn is sold for $2.45 (refer to Table 7.2). American Grain lifts the hedge by buying a May corn futures contract, which is trading currently at $2.75. Its profit on the futures transaction will be $0.50 per bushel (ignoring brokerage fees and other transaction costs). This gain will approximately offset the loss of $0.55 on the physical corn. The merchant in this example reduced a potential opportunity loss of $0.55 per bushel to only $0.05 by exchanging price risk for basis risk via a short hedge. This example is referred to as a **short hedge** because the hedger has a short position in the futures market.

Alternatively, consider a **long hedge** in the corn market. Suppose that a cattle feeding company, Beef Barons Inc., has placed cattle on feed in early December and expects to feed them for about six months before shipping them off for slaughter. The marketing manager of Beef Barons has enough corn in storage for the first three months (December–February), but she will have to purchase an additional 5,000 bushels of corn in early March in order to finish feeding this particular herd of cattle. Obviously, a movement in corn prices between December and March will affect Beef Barons' profits. Fearing a rise in corn prices, the marketing manager buys one May futures contract at a price of $3.25 while the current cash price is $3.00. This example is a long hedge (because she is going long in the futures mar-

---

TABLE 7.3   Basis: Widening Versus Narrowing

TIME PERIOD	CASH ($)	FUTURES ($)	BASIS ($)	BASIS CHANGE
1	3.00	3.50	0.50	
2	3.00	3.25	0.25	Narrower
3	3.00	3.00	0.00	Narrower
4	3.00	2.90	− 0.10	Narrower
5	3.00	2.95	− 0.05	Wider
6	3.00	3.25	0.25	Wider
7	3.00	3.50	0.50	Wider

ket) and is shown in the bottom panel of Table 7.2. We know that corn prices fell between December 1 and April 1, as shown in the bottom half of Table 7.2. Cash prices fell by $0.55 per bushel to $2.45 and May futures by $0.50 to $2.75. Beef Barons lifts the hedge in April by selling one May futures contract and simultaneously purchasing 5,000 bushels of corn on the cash market. Ignoring brokerage fees, the outcome of this hedge is a loss of $0.50 per bushel on the futures transaction and an opportunity gain of $0.55 on the cash transaction. The net cost of the corn for Beef Barons is therefore $2.95 per bushel because they paid $2.45 on the cash market and lost an additional $0.50 on the futures position. Compared to the alternative of purchasing the corn in December (at $3.00) and paying storage, the hedging outcome is more cost effective. However, if Beef Barons had not hedged at all, they could have purchased the corn for $2.45 in March. This seems like the best alternative, but hindsight always gives a futures trader perfect vision. The important point is that Beef Barons did not wish to risk the possibility of higher corn prices, and hedging provided some insurance against such an unfavorable outcome. Barons ended up buying corn for $0.05 less than the cash price in December because the basis widened by $0.05, and this works in favor of the long hedge.

Long hedging in commodity markets is commonplace with grain merchants, cattle feedlots, processing firms, and so on. Consider another transaction where American Grain has made a forward cash sale of soybeans to Japan at an agreed price. If the merchant has made the forward sale and does not have an available inventory of soybeans on hand (i.e., is short the cash commodity), he may choose to hedge this sale by taking a long position in the futures market. The long futures position would provide interim price protection for American Grain in the event that soybean prices rise before the company has an opportunity to purchase the required physical inventory on the spot market. In this example, it is evident that the hedge serves as a temporary substitute for a subsequent transaction in the spot market and is thus a useful marketing tool. The initial decision by American Grain to hedge in this example is going to be dictated by the expected change in the basis. If American grain feels that the basis is going to narrow by a significant amount (i.e., the cash price gains on the futures), then it might attempt to buy the cash rather than going long in the futures market as a temporary substitute for buying the cash.

Choice of Market and Futures Month

So far, no mention has been made of the fact that for some commodities there is more than one exchange that trade futures contracts written for that commodity. For example, wheat contracts are traded on futures markets in Chicago, Kansas City, and Minneapolis. A hedger in wheat must first choose one of these exchanges and then choose the appropriate futures month. Hedgers may also have to decide how many contracts to buy or sell, as futures contract sizes do not always match the size of the cash position.

There are also many commodities for which no corresponding futures market exists: jet fuel, lettuce, peanuts, tomatoes, sunflowers, and California wine. A producer and/or commercial user of these nonfutures commodities might attempt to hedge in a related market where prices are highly correlated with the nonfutures cash commodity price. The higher the correlation between cash and futures prices, the greater the potential for risk reduction. This type of hedging is referred to as **cross-hedging** (i.e., placing a hedge in a related futures market [see Box 7.1]). Wilson (1984) investigated cross-hedging different classes of wheat in three different futures markets and found cross-hedging to be viable for wheat.

When choosing the exchange on which to hedge, several factors must be considered. These include the following:

- On which exchange is the underlying grade the closest to the grade of the product to be hedged? For example, soft wheat is not deliverable on a Minneapolis contract but is deliverable on a Chicago contract, and therefore a hedger of soft wheat should probably choose the Chicago market.
- Hedges are easier (and less costly) to place and lift on exchanges and contracts with relatively greater trading volume (i.e., liquid markets). In thinly traded markets, prices are more volatile, and the bid–ask spread is wider, compared to liquid markets.
- The location of the market may be important if delivery is a viable alternative. The location of the market will also affect the basis.
- The hedge should be in a futures delivery month far enough ahead to cover the entire duration of the hedge. The rule of thumb is to choose a contract that expires shortly after the date on which the hedge is lifted. This way, "rollovers" from one contract month to another are avoided (which keeps transactions costs at a minimum), and correlation between the futures contract price and the cash market price is likely to be as high as possible.[3]

Most futures markets trade contracts that do not expire until about 12 to 18 months into the future. In many practical hedging applications, this may not be far enough into the future. One method that is used to stretch a hedge beyond 12 to 18 months is to "roll over" short-term hedges into long-term hedges (see Box 7.4).

Consider the example of a soybean farmer who decides that current prices are at very high historical levels. He decides to sell his next three harvests at the present time and attempt to lock in the historically high price. He expects to harvest about 5,000 bushels per year. Because soybean futures trade for only 14 months into the future, the farmer immediately sells three futures contracts for delivery in 12 months' time. Next year, he sells his crop and buys back the three futures contracts. Simultaneously, he sells two futures contracts calling for delivery in 12 months' time and so on. The farmer is therefore "rolling" the hedge from one year to the next. Gardner (1989) empirically studied the effectiveness of long-term

---

[3] Since futures prices are the markets' estimate of cash prices expected to be prevailing at the time of contract maturity, one might expect the cash/futures price correlation to increase as the amount of time between futures maturity and cash market delivery is decreased. However, Samuelson (1965) predicted that futures prices will become more and more volatile as they approach maturity. Bessembinder, Coughenar, Seguin, and Smoller. (1996) found empirical support for Samuelson's law. This means that the volatility of the basis for a particular contract may tend to increase as the contract approaches maturity.

rollover hedging in soybean, corn, and cotton futures. He found that multiyear rollovers have some merit as a practical hedging strategy.

Arbitrage and Operational Hedges: Importance of Basis Changes

The basis (B) was defined in Chapter 3 as the mathematical difference between a futures price (FP) and a cash/spot price (CP): $B = FP - CP$. As discussed in that chapter, the basis may be calculated either as futures minus cash or as cash minus futures. The cash price often refers to the price for either immediate or forward delivery at any particular terminal[4] or local market, whereas the spot price is for immediate delivery. The cash price is sometimes referred to as the spot price, and these terms are often used interchangeably. There can be many different bases associated with one futures contract.

Once an arbitrage or operational hedge has been placed, the hedger becomes concerned primarily with basis changes rather than with changes in the absolute price level. For example, suppose that a grain merchant in rural Iowa, Central Grain Co., purchased 25,000 bushels of corn on the local spot market for $2.55 in January and then subsequently sold five May corn futures contracts on the Chicago Board of Trade at $3.05. Central Grain's basis was $0.50 when the hedge was placed (see Table 7.1), and until the hedge is lifted, the company is concerned more with a change in the Iowa basis than with a change in the absolute price level for corn.

One way of defining an arbitrage or operational hedge is an exchange of price risk for basis risk or, alternatively, as speculating on the basis. The reason the basis is of utmost importance is that the profitability of the hedge is determined largely by basis behavior. If a hedge is lifted at the same basis that prevailed when the hedge was initiated (a textbook hedge), then the hedger receives the cash price prevailing on the date the hedge was initiated. This rarely occurs, however, as the basis often changes daily.

If a hedger has one unit of inventory in storage, then (ignoring storage costs) the return from a short hedge from period 1 to period 2 is

$$\widetilde{R}_S = (\widetilde{p}_2 - p_1) - (\widetilde{f}_2 - f_1), \qquad (7.1)$$

where the tildes (~) denote a random variable and
$\widetilde{R}_{s,L}$ = hedger's revenue per unit, (S = short hedge, L = long hedge),
$\widetilde{p}_2$ = cash price in period 2,
$\widetilde{f}_2$ = futures price in period 2,
p_1 = cash price in period 1,
f_1 = futures price in period 1,
B_1 = basis in period 1 = $f_1 - p_1$, and
$\widetilde{B}_2$ = basis in period 2 = $\widetilde{f}_2 - \widetilde{p}_2$.

---

[4] The terminal market refers to the location or locations specified as delivery points in the futures contract.

The per-unit return on the hedge in Equation 7.1 is equal to the difference between the change in cash price and the change in the futures price. If there is no trend in prices, then the return is zero (ignoring storage costs).

Equation 7.1 can be rewritten as

$$\widetilde{R}_S = B_1 - \widetilde{B}_2. \tag{7.2}$$

This means that any change in the hedger's revenue (i.e., any return from hedging) depends on the change in the basis. If the basis is unchanged (i.e., a textbook hedge), then $\widetilde{B}_2 = B_1$, and the return from hedging is zero and revenue is unchanged. In this case, futures price changes exactly offset cash price changes. Alternatively, if $\widetilde{B}_2 < B_1$ (i.e., the basis narrows), then the short hedgers profit from the hedge. There is a loss of revenue on the short hedge if $B_1 < \widetilde{B}_2$.

Similarly, the return from a long hedge can be represented as

$$\widetilde{R}_L = (p_1 - \widetilde{p}_2) - (f_1 - \widetilde{f}_2) \tag{7.3}$$

or, rearranging terms, as

$$\widetilde{R}_L = \widetilde{B}_2 - B_1. \tag{7.4}$$

Thus, a narrowing of the basis occurs when $\widetilde{B}_2 < B_1$, and it detracts from the long hedge because Equation 7.4 becomes negative. If, on the other hand, $B_1 < \widetilde{B}_2$, then this outcome results in additional revenue for the hedger.

In addition, it is worth pointing out that the variance of $\widetilde{R}_s$ is equal to

$$\text{var}(\widetilde{R}_S) = \text{var}(\widetilde{p}_2) - 2\text{cov}(\widetilde{p}_2, \widetilde{f}_2) + \text{var}(\widetilde{f}_2). \tag{7.5}$$

From Equation 7.5, we find that the riskiness of the hedge depends on the sum of the variance of the cash price, the covariance between cash and futures prices, and the variance of the futures price.

For a perfect, textbook hedge, $\text{var}(\widetilde{p}_2) = \text{var}(\widetilde{f}_2) = \text{cov}(\widetilde{p}_2, \widetilde{f}_2)$, and the price risk is totally eliminated.

Table 7.4 shows the financial impact of a basis change on a hedger's revenue. As shown in the table, a short hedger gains financially from a narrowing basis and loses from a widening of the basis. The impact of a basis change on a long hedger is exactly the reverse of the impact on a short hedger.

For storable commodities, the size of the basis is determined largely by the supply and demand for inventories, and thus it changes over time (refer to Chapter 3 for more discussion on this point). However, basis trends or patterns within a crop-year are somewhat predictable by hedgers, at least more so than are absolute price patterns. This is due primarily to seasonal factors in the production of many agricultural commodities.[5]

---

[5] There is a significant amount of published empirical work that has investigated the changing components of the basis. For example, Tilley and Campbell (1988) ran regressions to explain the wheat basis at the Gulf of Mexico. They found that the basis varied with export movements and stock levels.

TABLE 7.4   Financial Impact of Basis Change on a Hedger's Revenue

	CHANGE IN BASIS OVER HEDGE PERIOD		
TYPE OF HEDGE	**UNCHANGED**	**NARROWS**[a]	**WIDENS**[b]
Short	No gain or loss	Gain	Lose
Long	No gain or loss	Lose	Gain

[a]A narrowing of the basis occurs when the cash price gains on the futures price and the mathematical value of the basis becomes smaller.

[b]A widening of the basis occurs when the cash price falls relative to the futures price and the mathematical value of the basis becomes larger.

It is the predictability of basis changes that often induces commodity merchants to hedge. If, for example, the basis is large and expected to decline, then the merchant will take a long cash position and a short futures position. Alternatively, if the basis is expected to widen, this will be an incentive for the merchant to be short in the cash market (say, by selling a forward cash contract) and long in the futures market. However, in practice this latter opportunity to sell a forward cash contract may not be as readily available as the opportunity to take a long cash position.

Holbrook Working was one of the first researchers to empirically study recurring basis patterns. His observations in the wheat market led him to posit that the cash price is positively correlated with the basis. With this correlation, seasonal trends in the cash price provide clues as to when hedging should be profitable. His theories have held in other storable markets as well, where it is often found that the basis is at its widest levels in the immediate postharvest period, with a gradual narrowing over the course of the year.

Theoretically, the basis for storable products is easier to predict than absolute price levels for two reasons. The first factor—an upper theoretical limit to the size of the basis—is equal to full carrying costs. The upper limit to the basis (at the delivery point) is equal to the sum of all carrying charges, such as interest, insurance, physical storage costs, and so on. If the futures price rose above the spot price by more than the full carrying charges, then grain merchants (for instance) would quickly arbitrage the two markets by simultaneously buying on the spot market and selling on the futures market. This would be essentially guaranteeing themselves a riskless return if the spot grain were purchased in storage in a terminal market (this is an example of an arbitrage hedge). The arbitrage mechanism would thus serve to reduce the basis down to the level equaling carrying charge costs. In theory, there is no lower limit to the size of the basis. The futures price may fall below the cash or spot price (called an inverted market) if there is a shortage of deliverable stocks (in or near the terminal markets). Since it is impossible to correct an inverted market by arbitrage, the amount of the inversion is theoretically limitless.

The second factor—a convergence of cash and futures—is by far the more important one, giving rise to recurring basis patterns. This relationship is shown

FIGURE 7.1
Theoretical basis trend
over time.

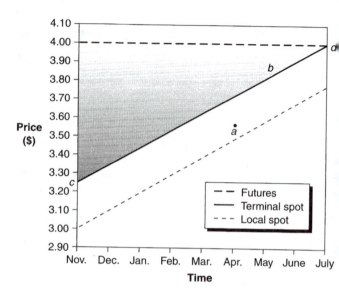

in Figure 7.1 for a hypothetical July wheat futures contract. Suppose that, on November 1, the July futures contract was trading at $4.00 per bushel. Ceteris paribus, this is the spot price expected to be prevailing in July. Furthermore, suppose that the spot price at the terminal delivery point (i.e., the location specified in the futures contract) was $3.25 in November. Also assume that the spot price at a local rural elevator was $3.00 on November 1. Under most conditions, the July basis can be expected to narrow between November and July. Once again, this occurs because the costs of storing wheat for delivery in July decline as time passes from November to July. In other words, it costs less to store wheat from March to July than it does from November to July. In Figure 7.1, this expected narrowing of the basis (shown by the shaded triangle) is based on the belief that the terminal spot price will gain on the July futures. The expected terminal market basis in the figure is the shaded area between the expected futures and the expected terminal market spot price. The extent of the narrowing in Figure 7.1 will be approximately equal to $0.75 because, in theory, the spot and the futures prices will converge. They rarely converge to zero, however, because in the delivery month the terminal market spot commodity will often sell at a slight premium to futures. This premium reflects the uncertainty of the exact delivery date and exact grade associated with purchasing a futures contract and taking delivery on it rather than buying the commodity outright on the spot market.

In Figure 7.1, the local or rural country basis is also shown to narrow by approximately the same extent as the terminal basis, but it will vary with *local* supply and demand conditions and changes in transport costs. The local basis will approach the cost of transportation from the local to the terminal delivery point, which is greater than zero. This phenomenon of the basis narrowing over time (within a crop-year) was particularly acute during the period of high interest rates in the early 1980s.

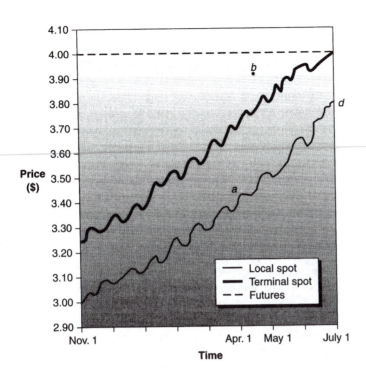

FIGURE 7.2
Theoretical basis behavior over time.

Thus, a grain merchant operating in the terminal market location in this example will be encouraged to take a short futures position if the basis is larger than that which returns zero economic profit. The basis that just returns zero profit is shown by the solid upward-sloping line, *cd*, in Figure 7.1. Profits are zero because the basis change covers carrying costs (as explained in Chapter 3, carrying cost refers to marginal cost). However, suppose that on April 1 the terminal spot price is at point *a* in Figure 7.1, which implies an abnormally wide basis. In the expectation of the basis returning to the solid trend line (*ed*), the merchant would attempt to buy cash wheat and sell July futures. Several of these opportunities to hedge and profit from a basis change may arise between November 1 and July 1. Figure 7.2 displays a normal basis pattern, which trends upward but not in a straight line. The basis pattern in Figure 7.2 would present several hedging opportunities for grain merchants.

Consider the alternative point *b* in Figure 7.2. Here the basis is smaller than expected for May 1, and it may be expected to widen over the short run. If, on May 1, the merchant had an opportunity to sell wheat in the forward cash market (for delivery before June 1), he would do so knowing that he could simultaneously go long in the July futures. In this case, he would be expecting to profit from a short-term widening of the basis.

The inability to arbitrage intertemporal markets periodically occurs between crop-years in a storable commodity. For example, if in June, July (old crop) corn futures closed at $2.14 per bushel and in December (new crop) closed at $1.78, then the futures market would be "inverted." This inversion of $0.36 per bushel could be a

FIGURE 7.3
Inverted market.

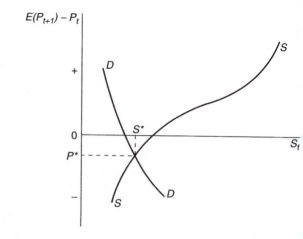

reflection of a low projected carryover of stocks from the old crop to the new crop-year. As Working has shown,[6] it is current stocks that determine intertemporal price relationships. Current stocks and intertemporal prices are simultaneously determined by the interaction of the demand for and supply of storage.

Figure 7.3 shows the demand and supply of storage, a model that was fully explained in Chapter 3. The demand for stocks (*DD* in Figure 7.3) relates the changes in price between the new crop period and the old crop period ($E[P_{t+1}] - P_t$) to the stocks held at the end of the old crop (S_t). The operator $E(\ )$ denotes that P_{t+1} is the expected spot price in period $t + 1$. Note again that the *DD* schedule has a negative slope. Also discussed in Chapter 3 was the net marginal cost of holding stocks, which is represented by the supply of storage (*SS*) in Figure 7.3. The supply of storage is the marginal cost of storage minus the marginal convenience yield.

Convenience yield refers to the benefit a firm receives from holding stocks. For example, it is important that a processing firm always maintain a certain minimum level of "pipeline" stocks. It would be costly to the firm if it periodically ran out of stocks. For low stock levels (i.e., the left-hand side of Fig. 7.3), the convenience yield is relatively high, and it outweighs the marginal physical costs of storage, such as interest, insurance, and so on. This is shown by the bottom portion of the *SS* curve, which lies below the horizontal line showing zero difference between the intertemporal prices. In this example, points below the horizontal line indicate that old crop futures are priced above new crop futures (i.e., an **inverted market**). For points above the line, a carrying charge price relationship exists. For example, if a more normal carryover were expected in the corn example represented in Figure 7.3, then a carrying charge market would probably exist where distant futures prices are priced higher than nearby futures prices.

In Figure 7.3, the demand for storage is positioned such that it reflects the fact that carryover stocks are relatively low (i.e., S^*). In commodity markets, this is most

----

[6] This explanation was more fully developed in Chapter 3, where the theory of storage was discussed.

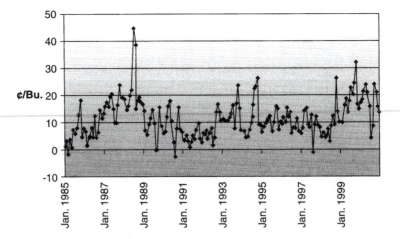

FIGURE 7.4
Monthly soybean basis.
Note: The basis is calculated as the monthly average nearby futures price minus the monthly central Illinois cash price. Nearby futures prices are for the nearest delivery month, but the next-to-delivery month is used one month before the delivery month expires.
Source: Commodity Research Bureau

often due to a crop failure in the current season (i.e., the "old crop" season). The position of DD gives rise to an inverted market. This equilibrium is shown by P^* and S^* in Figure 7.3. Note that stocks are carried out of the "old" crop and into the "new" crop, even though the expected return from storage is negative. This can be explained by convenience yield.

Some examples of actual basis patterns are shown in Figures 7.4 through 7.7. Figures 7.4 and 7.5 display monthly basis data for soybeans and coffee, respectively. This market price data was collected for a 15-year period (1985–2000). In both cases, the basis displays variability but much less than the cash price variability. For example, soybean cash prices ranged from a low of about $4.00 per bushel to a high of about $9.00 per bushel from 1985 to 2000. We can see in Figure 7.4 that during the same time period, the soybean basis ranged from + $0.45 to − $0.03 per bushel. Over the 15-year period, coffee cash prices ranged between $0.52 and $2.45 per pound, while the basis ranged from + 53¢ to − 3.71¢ per pound.

Using the underlying data from Figures 7.4 and 7.5, Figures 7.6 and 7.7 display the seasonal basis patterns for coffee and soybeans. The seasonal basis patterns are shown as the average monthly basis over the entire seven-year period. For the time period in question, the soybean basis in Figure 7.6 shows a fairly consistent pattern of rising from August through October, which means the basis is highest around harvest time, as theory would predict.

For coffee, the basis pattern in Figure 7.7 indicates that the basis tended to be at the lowest point from August through December and at the highest point from January through March. The coffee basis declined almost continuously throughout the calendar year.

FIGURE 7.5

Monthly coffee basis.
Note: The basis is calculated as the monthly average of the nearby futures price minus the monthly average New York cash price. Nearby futures prices are for the nearest delivery month, but the next-to-delivery month is used one month before, during the delivery month.
Source: Commodity Research Bureau

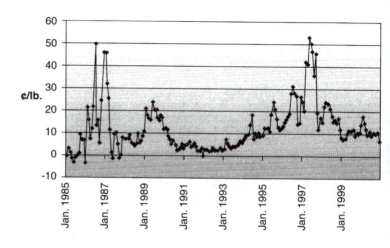

FIGURE 7.6

Seasonality of soy monthly bean basis, 1985–2000 data.
Source: See Figure 7.4

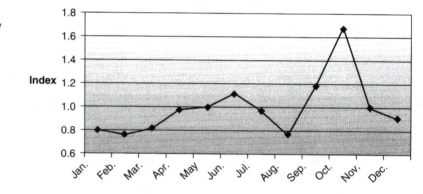

FIGURE 7.7

Seasonality of coffee basis, 1985–2000 monthly data.
Source: See Figure 7.5

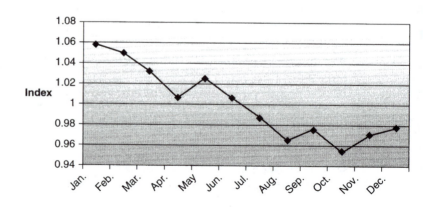

Anticipatory Hedge and Production Risk

As explained previously, anticipatory hedges may involve both price and production risk, and expected changes in the basis are not as relevant for this type of hedge.

The return from an anticipatory hedge from period 1 to period 2 is

$$\widetilde{R} = \widetilde{p}_2\widetilde{q}_2 - h(\widetilde{f}_2 - f_1), \tag{7.6}$$

where the tildes (~) denote a random variable and
$\widetilde{R}$= hedger's revenue,
$\widetilde{p}_2$= cash price in period 2,
h = quantity of futures sold ($-$) or bought ($+$),
f_1 = futures price in period 1,
$\widetilde{f}_2$ = futures price in period 2, and
$\widetilde{q}_2$ = hedger's production in period 2.

During period 1, the forthcoming cash price in period 2 ($\widetilde{p}_2$), the hedger's production ($\widetilde{q}_2$), and the futures price in period 2 ($\widetilde{f}_2$) are all unknown. Think of period 1 as the planting period (for, say, a soybean farmer) and period 2 as the harvest period. This can easily be generalized to commodities where there is no distinct "harvest." For example, an airline company might use anticipatory hedges for its fuel purchases, and in this case the "harvest" would be interpreted as the expected fuel consumption in the next time period. Airlines have to forecast the quantity of fuel they will be purchasing at the same time they are forecasting fuel prices.

The variance of the hedged position is

$$\text{var}(\widetilde{R}) = \text{var}(\widetilde{p}_2\widetilde{q}_2) - 2h(\widetilde{p}_2\widetilde{q}_2, \widetilde{f}_2) + h^2 \, \text{var}(\widetilde{f}_2). \tag{7.7}$$

This expression is much more complicated than Equation 7.5. In Equation 7.7, we find that the variance of the hedge depends on the correlation between prices and production (the first term in Equation 7.7), the correlation between revenue ($\widetilde{p}_2\widetilde{q}_2$) and the futures price, $\widetilde{f}_2$, (the second term), and the variability of the futures prices (the third term) and the quantity of futures sold or bought (h).

An anticipatory hedge is the type of hedge a farmer would enter into in the spring of the year if he were hedging his crop to be harvested later in the fall. Anticipatory hedges are also common for nonstorable commodities, such as live hogs or finished cattle, and the basis patterns are not as recurrent and predictable as in the case of storable commodities. Therefore, hedging to profit from basis changes is not really relevant in these markets. For example, a feedlot manager would not buy feeder cattle and sell fat cattle futures that mature after the feeding period (approximately six months) simply because of a wide basis. The feeder cattle cannot be placed in a warehouse and forgotten about. They must be fed daily and then sold for slaughter. During the feeding period, the hedge cannot easily be lifted until the cattle are "finished." For the fundamental reason that the storage activity cannot provide a linkage between the current supply of feeder cattle (or any other perishable product) and the demand 12 months hence, carrying charge markets and declining bases over time are not necessarily observed in nonstorable markets.

HEDGING WITH FINANCIAL FUTURES

The tremendous growth in financial futures trading volume indicates that these instruments have economic value to an increasing number of firms. Many firms have decided that the advantages of hedging outweigh the disadvantages of not hedging. Financial firms, commercial and mortgage bankers, pension fund managers, and insurance companies all face risks associated with fluctuations in interest rates that can be better managed through hedging. Mutual fund managers exposed to equity market risk can hedge their portfolios using stock index futures. In addition, exporters and importers can hedge foreign exchange transactions. However, there are still many firms and industries that do not share this view.

The general advantages and disadvantages of hedging with financials are similar to those for commodity futures hedging. Hedging enables firms to better manage price risk and provides additional flexibility in the timing of cash market transactions. This section explains how hedgers can use financial futures to achieve their business goals.

Hedging Exchange Rates: An Application

Volatile currency markets affect the profitability of firms that have either accounts receivable or payable in a foreign currency. Export or import companies take various strategies to cope with exchange rate uncertainty. Hedging exchange rates with futures is one such strategy, and it can be viewed as a firm's attempt to lock in an exchange rate over a period of time in order to insulate the firm against an adverse move in the exchange rate.

Consider the following example of a long hedge in Japanese yen. When foreign exchange expenditures (i.e., payables) are made after the U.S. dollar has fallen, the cost in U.S. dollars has risen. It now costs more dollars to buy yen. Consider the example of a U.S. firm in the Silicon Valley that, on November 1, orders computer components from Japan at a total expected cost of $100,000 at today's spot exchange rate of 130 yen per dollar (or $.0077/yen). Payment for the computer components is to be made in March in yen (13 million yen). Note that the size of this yen payment is slightly larger than the futures contract size of 12.5 million yen. The firm ordering the computer components is concerned that the yen will *rise* in value and therefore it goes *long* in the futures market for yen.

As shown in Table 7.5, a long hedge is placed by buying one June futures contract at a price of $.0082/yen. By March 1, the U.S. dollar has fallen, as was feared by the U.S. importer. The firm now lifts its hedge by selling one June yen futures contract at $.0103. The profit on the futures transaction is $26,250 (ignoring commission fees of approximately $100). The futures profit equals the futures price change (.0103 − .0082) × 12.5 million yen: the size of the futures contract. This profit partially off-

TABLE 7.5   Long Hedge with Japanese Yen: An Illustration

DATE	CASH PRICE	BASIS	FUTURES PRICE	HEDGER'S TRANSACTION
November 1	$.0077	$.0005	$.0082	Buy one June yen futures contract
March 1	$.0102	$.0001	$.0103	Sell one June yen futures contract
Gain (loss)	($32,500)		$26,250	

sets the opportunity loss of $32,500 that the computer firm experiences on its account payable in Japanese yen. The opportunity loss equals the change in the spot price (.0102 − .0077) × 13 million yen: the actual size of the payment made. The basis in this example narrowed from $.0005 to $.0001, which detracted from the long hedge. After completing the hedge, the importer's final cost of the computer components was $106,350 = 13 million yen × $.0102 − $26,250 (plus futures commission fees). While the final cost of the computer components was over $6,000 more than the $100,000 anticipated in November, it clearly would have been much higher without the hedge.

The impact of the weaker dollar on the computer firm's payables is shown in Figure 7.8, where the yen/dollar exchange rate is plotted on the left-hand vertical axis and the amount payable (in $U.S.) is on the right-hand vertical axis. Time is represented by the horizontal axis, moving from left to right. The current time period (say, November) is on the far left, and the far right represents a subsequent time period (say, March). The spot market exchange rate is shown as the solid line in Figure 7.8, declining from about 130 yen per dollar to about 98 yen per dollar over the time period represented. As the exchange rate moves from 130 to 98 (i.e., the dollar weakens), the amount payable (in $U.S.) rises, as shown by the dotted line in Figure 7.8. The move in the exchange rate raises the amount payable from about $100,000 to approximately $132,000. Conversely, if the solid exchange rate line in Figure 7.8 had a positive slope (i.e., representing a weaker yen), then the amount payable would be shown by a dashed line with a negative slope.

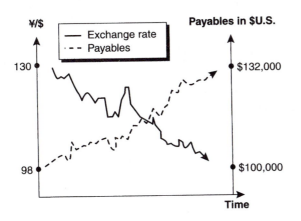

FIGURE 7.8
Impact of an exchange rate change on accounts payable.

FIGURE 7.9
Impact of an exchange
rate change on accounts
receivable.

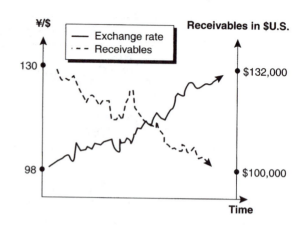

Figure 7.9 displays an alternative situation where a firm has $132,000 in receivables at the current spot yen/dollar exchange rate. This example would represent a firm that has sold some product or commodity to Japan and will eventually be paid in yen. In this case, if the yen falls in value (i.e., the dollar strengthens), the dollar value of the receivables declines. Figure 7.9 depicts a rise in the dollar from 98 yen to 130 yen, which translates into a fall in the amount of receivables from $132,000 to $100,000. A firm exposed to this type of risk would hedge by going short in the yen futures market.

Hedging Bonds: An Application

Consider an example of a pension fund manager who is motivated to preserve and expand the value of the portfolio under her management. Suppose the manager expects that the Federal Reserve will raise interest rates in the near term, a move that would erode the value of her portfolio because interest rates move in the opposite direction as bond prices. The portfolio manager therefore decides to try to reduce the effect of rising interest rates (i.e., bond yields) on the value of her portfolio by taking a short position in the futures market. A short bond futures position would yield a profit as interest rates rise.

Suppose it is September 1 and the fund manager is holding 10 $100,000 15-year, 6% Treasury bonds currently priced at 118-11, as shown in Table 7.6. A short hedge is placed by selling 10 December Treasury bond futures contracts at a price of 113-31. By November 1, suppose that interest rates have risen, as was expected by the fund manager, and she now lifts the hedge by buying back 10 December bond futures contracts at 111-15. As shown in Table 7.6, the profit on the futures transaction is $25,000 (before commission fees), which partially offsets the opportunity loss of $28,750 that the hedger experiences on her inventory of bonds.

In Table 7.6, notice that the December bond futures price falls from 113-31 to 111-15, or by 2-16, which amounts to $2,500 per contract. At the same time, each bond held in the portfolio falls by 2-28, or $2,875. The basis widened from minus 4-12 to minus 4-00 (i.e., became more positive), and this detracted somewhat from the hedge.

TABLE 7.6 Short Hedge with Treasury Bonds: An Illustration

DATE	CASH PRICE	BASIS	FUTURES PRICE	HEDGER'S TRANSACTION
September 1	118-11	– 4-12	113-31	Sell 10 December T-bond futures contracts
November 1	115-15	– 4-00	111-15	Buy 10 December T-bond futures contracts
Gain (loss)	($28,750)		$25,000	

HEDGING: A PORTFOLIO EXPLANATION

A portfolio explanation of hedging was first rigorously presented and developed by Johnson (1960), Stein (1961), and Telser (1958), who used the Markowitz foundations of portfolio management. With this approach, a hedger is viewed as being able to hold several different cash and futures assets in a portfolio and is assumed to maximize the expected value of his utility function by choosing among the alternative portfolios on the basis of their means and variances.[7]

The standard application of portfolio theory to futures markets assumes the following:

  a. A risk-averse hedger
  b. A fixed long cash position (e.g., some inventory in storage)
  c. A short futures position combined with a long cash position
  d. Each "portfolio" of cash and futures evaluated on the merits of its expected return and its variance
  e. A long cash position earning a higher (but riskier) return than a combined cash and futures (i.e., hedged) position
  f. Hedgers are not speculating on their price expectations

This model is displayed in Figure 7.10, where the expected return from a portfolio comprised of a hedged and an unhedged cash position is plotted on the vertical axis and the riskiness of the portfolio (measured by its variance) on the horizontal axis. The risk-return tradeoff associated with various combinations of hedged and unhedged portfolios is traced out by the curve *UH*. The shape of *UH* depends on the correlation between futures and cash prices. The higher the correlation, the more bowed out *UH* is. The expected return and variance associated with carrying the cash inventory unhedged is represented by point *U*. Point *H* represents the expected return

---

[7] For some individuals or firms, the size and exposure of the cash position determines the size and exposure of the futures position. For others, the opposite causal relationship holds or, more often, the cash and futures positions are simultaneously determined.

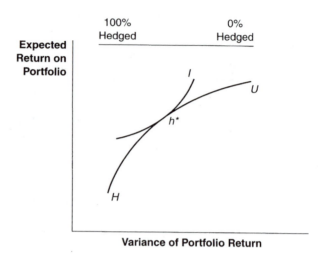

FIGURE 7.10
Portfolio solution to the
optimal hedge.

and variance associated with a full 100% hedge. In the case of this traditional, full hedge, the variance of returns is the basis risk. As drawn in this example, point *H* is the portfolio that offers the lowest level of variance. It is important to notice that the risk at point *H* is nonzero.

The **optimal hedge ratio** represents the most desirable combination of cash and futures positions and is chosen on the basis of shape of the indifference curves of the hedger. Indifference curves reflect a hedger's attitude toward risk and return. In Figure 7.10, an indifference curve, labeled *I*, is drawn as an upward-sloping convex curve, indicating that the hedger is risk averse to some degree. The hedger will have an entire set of indifference curves, but only one is drawn here. All portfolios that lie on curve *I* are equally desirable to the hedger. Risk aversion implies that a hedger requires a higher expected return from a more risky portfolio than from a less risky one. Indifference curves for a risk-seeking investor would be drawn as concave functions with a negative slope.

In order to maximize expected utility (i.e., attain the highest possible indifference curve), a hedger will choose point h^* in Figure 7.10. This point possesses minimum risk for a given level of expected return. It shows that the optimal hedge in this case is less than 100% the cash inventory level.

The portfolio approach to the understanding of hedging is appealing on several grounds. Most important, it is able to theoretically explain why an inventory position may not be fully hedged. Additionally, it explains why commodity merchants will hold a spot and futures position even if the expected return is negative, and it clearly differentiates between hedging and speculation. However, the practical usefulness of portfolio theory for hedgers has come into question by some researchers, as discussed in the next section.

Optimal Hedge Ratio

There are two standard formulas that have been developed for computing the optimal hedge ratio, that is, the optimal futures position relative to the cash position. The minimum risk hedge ratio is shown as point *H* in Figure 7.10. This ratio has been utilized by Ederington (1979) and others. Alternatively, there is the utility maximizing optimal ratio h^*, as shown in Figure 7.10. This has been developed by Heifner (1972), Johnson (1960), Telser (1958), and Ward and Fletcher (1971). If the expected profit from holding futures contracts is zero, then the utility-maximizing optimal hedge becomes equivalent to the risk-minimizing hedge ratio (Kahl, 1983). Empirical estimates of the optimal hedge ratios for commodities are often less than one (e.g., Rolfo, 1980) [See Appendix page 303].

Hedging can be viewed simply as the process of simultaneously choosing futures positions and underlying cash positions in order to construct a portfolio of assets. With this approach, a hedger is viewed as being able to hold several different cash and futures assets in a portfolio and is assumed to maximize the expected value of his utility function by choosing among the alternative portfolios on the basis of their means and variances. In a theoretical paper, McKinnon (1967) extended this concept and used a mean-variance objective function for the producer. In this framework, the objective function is $\Theta = EU(\Pi) - (\lambda/2)V(\Pi)$, where $EU(\Pi)$ is expected utility of profit (Π), $V(\Pi)$ is the variance of profit, and λ is the absolute risk aversion coefficient. McKinnon (1967) focused on the hedge decision (rather than the production decision) and calculated the optimal hedge ratio assuming minimum risk hedging.

Using an expected utility maximization framework but focusing on the production decision (rather than the hedge decision), Danthine (1978) incorporated the possibility of buying and selling futures contracts into the model of the competitive firm under price uncertainty. In the Danthine model, production is not risky, and it is assumed there is no basis risk. He demonstrated that planned production responds positively to the current futures contract price and that changes in the subjective distribution of futures or spot prices do not lead to changes in production decisions. The firm copes with price uncertainty by participating in the futures market, where a certain price is substituted for an uncertain one, while optimal production is unaltered. The futures price is the driving force affecting producer production decisions. With a futures market, production decisions are shown to be independent of both the producer's degree of risk aversion and price expectations, and they are separable from the producer's "portfolio problem" (i.e., just as under the Markowitz [1959] separation theorem). The optimal hedge in the Danthine-type model depends on the degree of risk aversion and the probability distribution of the forward price.

Anderson and Danthine (1983) showed that the "separation" result in Danthine (1978) does not hold when either output or the basis is random. For example, when basis risk is present, changes in the subjective distribution of the forthcoming spot price lead to changes in the production decision.

Anderson and Danthine (1983) modified the McKinnon (1967) model to allow for the simultaneous determination of hedging and production decisions. In a mean-variance framework and with price, yield, and basis risk, the Anderson–Danthine optimal hedge result is

$$\frac{h^*}{E(q)} = \frac{\rho(s,f)\sigma(s)}{\sigma(f)} + \frac{\rho(q,f)\sigma(q)/E(q)}{\sigma(f)/E(s)} + \frac{F - E(f)}{\lambda E(q)\sigma^2(f)}, \tag{7.8}$$

where h^* is the number of futures contracts ($h^* > 0$ indicates a short hedge); $s, f,$ and q are random variables representing the spot price at harvest, harvest time futures price, and quantity produced, respectively; ρ is the correlation coefficient; σ is the standard deviation; F is the planting time futures price; and E is the expectation operator. The first term on the right-hand side in Equation 7.8 represents the effect of basis risk on the optimal hedge. From the first term, the higher the correlation between the spot price and futures price at harvest, the larger the optimal hedge, ceteris paribus. The impact of yield risk is captured by the second term, where we find that the higher the correlation between harvest time futures price and production, the higher the optimal hedge. The numerator in the third term represents the extent to which futures prices are thought to be biased estimates of forthcoming spot prices. If there is no perceived bias, then this speculative component of the hedge ratio is zero.

Some firms prefer forward contracting to direct hedging with futures or options contracts. Forward contracts are a substitute for futures contracts, as both provide an opportunity to reduce price risk. However, from the firm's perspective, neither financial tool dominates the other, as there are pros and cons of using one versus the other. Perhaps the one key distinguishing feature is the absence of basis risk with forward contracting (Miller, 1986). Using the mean-variance framework, the first order conditions for forward contracting are

$$\frac{q^*}{E(q)} = 1 + \frac{\rho(q,f)\sigma(q)/E(q)}{\sigma(s)/E(s)} + \frac{G - E(s)}{\lambda E(q)\sigma^2(s)}, \tag{7.9}$$

where q^* is the quantity contracted and G is the cash forward contract price. Miller concluded that the absence of basis risk does not necessarily lead to higher levels of forward contracting relative to direct hedging with futures. This is true both theoretically and empirically.

Hartzmark (1988) has empirically tested the portfolio theory of hedging using Commodity Futures Trading Commission weekly data on cash and futures positions held by large commercial hedgers. He specifically tested for risk-minimizing behavior in wheat and oats by comparing cash and futures positions with risk-minimizing positions. Hartzmark found that the firms he studied adjusted their cash and futures positions in accordance with one another and that they did not adapt their expectations to changing market conditions. He therefore concluded that the firms acted as though they were risk minimizers. In a related paper, Peck and Nahmias (1989) came up with much different results. They analyzed quarterly cash and futures market positions for a number of U.S. flour mills aggregated together. They calculated the recommended hedging strategies from portfolio theory (optimal and minimum risk hedges) and compared it to actual behavior. Their results show little statistical relationship between either the optimal or the minimum risk ratios and actual hedge ratios. From this, Peck and Nahmias concluded that the portfolio model has little practical relevance. As pointed out by Hartzmark, Peck and Nahmias use more aggregate data than Hartzmark, and they analyze small long hedgers compared to Hartzmark's sample of large short hedgers.

BOX 7.4

Rollover hedging.

Most futures contracts expire in less than two years. Therefore, in an attempt to hedge against long-term risk, firms sometimes choose to enter into sequential short-term hedges: rollover hedging. Rollover hedging is therefore a financial transaction where a firm attempts to use futures markets to hedge price risk far into the future (e.g., 3 to 10 years). The firm buys/sells futures contracts that are actively trading and then "rolls over" these hedges in the most distant futures contracts as the old contracts mature. There is considerable controversy over this hedging procedure. Some argue that rollover hedging is not a sound financial strategy because it is too risky.

The question is: does sequential short-term hedging, or rollover hedging, serve as a beneficial mechanism for long-term hedging in commodity markets? Presently, there are several international companies that use rollover hedging.

The German-based firm Metallgesellschaft used this technique in the crude oil market but encountered huge financial losses of approximately $1 billion in the early 1990s. Why those losses accumulated is still a subject of debate. Economist and Nobel laureate Merton Miller argued in a court case that Metallgesellschaft's strategy was prudent hedging.

See Edwards and Canter (1995).

Castelino (2000) estimated minimum variance hedge ratios for wheat, corn, Treasury bills, and Eurodollars. He found a stronger linkage between cash and futures prices for wheat and corn compared to Treasury bills and Eurodollars. In other words, the basis risk was higher for interest rate futures contracts compared to grain futures. Castelino estimated the extent to which the optimal hedge ratio varies over time and found that the time dimension associated with the optimal hedge ratio was more important for financial futures than grain futures. Time-varying hedge ratios make sense in the business world because the factors that determine the optimal hedge ratio (see Equation 7.8) are not constant over time. For instance, the correlation coefficients and price and quantity expectations in Equation 7.8 are changing over time.

Hedging with Futures Versus Options

Hedging with options on futures will be described in Chapter 9. Sakong, Hayes, and Hallam (1993) compared hedging with options versus futures. They set up a standard hedging model with both price and production uncertainty and found that the introduction of production uncertainty alters the optimal futures and options position and almost always makes it optimal for the producing firm to purchase put options. This result is not surprising because event risk has long been one of the standard reasons for hedging with options rather than futures (Feiger & Jacquillat, 1979). Stoll and Whaley (1985) explain,

> Options not only provide insurance against price risk that is conditional on an event (receiving the bid, having a successful harvest, making the loan, making the stock offering) but also avoid any penalty if the event does not occur (the bid is rejected, the harvest is poor, the loan is not taken down, or the stock issue is not sold). It is in this sense that options provide protection against both price and quantity risk and are, therefore, a better hedging tool than futures contracts in some cases. (p. 229)

Lapan, Moschini, and Hanson (1991) compared hedging with options versus futures with nonstochastic production. First, they showed that if futures prices and options premiums are unbiased, options are a redundant hedging device. They went on to demonstrate that if prices are symmetrically distributed and if futures prices are biased, then options may be useful.

SUMMARY

This chapter has introduced the economics of hedging commodities and financials through the use of the futures market. The basic fundamentals and theoretical explanations of hedging have a wide application. A coffee importer in New York may use the futures market for the same hedging reasons and with the same objectives as a major bank in San Francisco. Commercial motives for hedging commodities are arbitrage hedging, operational hedging, and anticipatory hedging. Three different explanations of hedging activity were covered. These include hedgers' desires to reduce price risk, profit from basis movements, and diversify a portfolio.

This chapter has provided examples of hedging in both the commodity and financial futures markets. Hedging involves an exchange of price risk for basis risk and we examined the impact of basis movements over time on the hedger's revenue. A short (long) hedger benefits from a narrowing (widening) of the basis. Alternatively, a short (long) hedger loses from a widening (narrowing) of the basis. Research has found that the basis risk may be higher for financial futures compared to commodity futures. When the hedger faces both price risk and quantity risk, then hedging with options may be superior to hedging with futures contracts. Hedging with options is taken up in Chapter 9.

Hedging can also be viewed as constructing a portfolio of assets that includes futures (and/or options) contracts and short or long cash positions in commodities or financials. Standard portfolio theory can then be utilized to derive an optimal hedging strategy. This approach explains why optimal hedge ratios may be different than 1.0. If hedgers do not expect to profit from futures contracts (i.e., they are not price forecasters) then the utility maximizing optimal hedge is identical to the risk-minimizing hedge ratio. The optimal hedge ratio depends on the volatility of cash and futures prices and correlation between them.

DISCUSSION QUESTIONS

1. Explain some of the added risks associated with hedging on a futures market located in a foreign country.
2. Discuss factors giving rise to an inverted futures market for a storable versus a nonstorable commodity. What are the implications for a hedger?
3. Is convenience yield an important component of the basis for financial futures, or is it a concept that is applicable mostly to commodities?
4. Using Figure 7.10, discuss the conditions under which the utility-maximizing hedge ratio (h^*) would be equal to the risk minimizing hedge ratio (H).
5. Compare the Internal Revenue Service's definition of a hedger with that of the Commodity Futures Trading Commission.

SELECTED REFERENCES

Anderson, R. W., & Danthine, J. P. (1983). Time and pattern of hedging and the volatility of future prices. *Review of Economic Studies, 50*(2), 249–266.

Bessembinder, H., Coughenour, J. F., Seguin, P. J., & Smoller, M. M. (1996). Is there a term structure of futures volatilities? Reevaluating the Samuelson hypothesis. *Journal of Derivatives, 4*, 45–58.

Castelino, M. G. (2000). Hedge effectiveness: Basis risk and minimum-variance hedging. *Journal of Futures Markets, 20*, 89–103.

Cootner, P. H. (1967). Speculation and hedging. *Food Research Institute Studies, 7* (Suppl.), 65–106.

Danthine, J. P. (1978). Information, futures prices, and stabilizing speculation. *Journal of Economic Theory, 17*(1), 79–98.

Ederington, L. H. (1979). The hedging performance of the new futures markets. *Journal of Finance, 34*, 157–170.

Edwards, F. R., & Canter, M. S. (1995). The collapse of Metallgesellschaft: Unhedgeable risks, poor hedging strategy, or just bad luck? *Journal of Futures Markets, 15*(3), 211–264.

Feiger, G. M., & Jacquillat, B. (1979). Currency options bonds, puts and calls on spot exchange and the hedging of contingent foreign earnings. *Journal of Finance, 34*(5), 1129–1139.

Gardner, B. L. (1989). Rollover hedging and mission long-term futures markets. *American Journal of Agricultural Economics, 71*, 311–318.

Hartzmark, M. L. (1988). Is risk aversion a theoretical diversion? *Review of Futures Markets, 7*, 1–26.

Heifner, R. G. (1972). Optimal hedging levels and hedging effectiveness in cattle feeding. *Agricultural Economics Research, 24*, 25–36.

Johnson, L. (1960). The theory of hedging and speculation in commodity futures. *Review of Economic Studies, 27*, 139–151.

Kahl, K. H. (1983). Determination of the recommended hedging ratio. *American Journal of Agricultural Economics, 65*(3), 603–605.

Lapan, H. E., Moschini, G., & Hanson, S. D. (1991). Production, hedging, and speculative decisions with options and futures markets. *American Journal of Agricultural Economics, 73*(1), 66–74.

Mahul, O. (2002). Hedging in futures and options markets with basis risk. *Journal of Futures Markets, 22*(1), 59–72.

Markowitz, H. (1959). *Portfolio selection: Efficient diversification of investments.* New York: John Wiley & Sons.

McKinnon, R. I. (1967). Futures markets, buffer stocks, and income stability for primary producers. *Journal of Political Economy, 75*(6), 844–861.

Miller, S. (1986). Forward contracting versus hedging under price and yield uncertainty. *Southern Journal of Agricultural Economics, 18*(2), 139–146.

Miller, S. E., & Kahl, K. H. (1987). Forwarding pricing when yields are uncertain. *Review of Futures Markets, 6*, 21–39.

Peck, A. (Ed.). (1977). *Selected Writings of Holbrook Working.* Chicago: Chicago Board of Trade.

Peck, A. E., & Nahmias, A. M. (1989). Hedging your advice: Do portfolio models explain hedging? *Food Research Institute Studies, 21*(2), 193–204.

Rolfo, J. (1980). Optimal hedging under price and quantity uncertainty: The case of a cocoa producer. *Journal of Political Economy, 88*, 110–116.

Sakong, Y., Hayes, D., & Hallam, A. (1993). Hedging production risk with options. *American Journal of Agricultural Economics, 75*(2), 408–415.

Samuelson, P. A. (1965). Proof that properly anticipated prices fluctuate randomly. *Industrial Management Review, 6*, 41–49.

Stein, J. L. (1961). The simultaneous determination of spot and futures prices. *American Economic Review, 56*, 1012–1025.

Stoll, H. R., & Whaley, R. E. (1985). The new options market. In A. E. Peck (Ed.), *Futures markets: Their economic role.* Washington, DC: American Enterprise Institute for Public Policy Research.

Telser, L. G. (1958). Futures trading and the storage of cotton and wheat. *Journal of Political Economy, 57*, 233–255.

Tilley, D. S., & Campbell, S. K. (1988). Performance of the weekly Gulf–Kansas City hard-red winter wheat basis. *American Journal of Agricultural Economics, 70*, 929–935.

Ward, R. W., & Fletcher, L. B. (1971). From hedging to pure speculation: A micro model of optimal futures and cash positions. *American Journal of Agricultural Economics, 53*, 71–78.

Wilson, W. W. (1984). Hedging effectiveness of U.S. wheat futures markets. *Review of Research in Futures Markets, 3*, 64–79.

Working, H. (1962). New concepts concerning futures markets and prices. *American Economic Review, 52*, 432–459.

CHAPTER 8

Options Markets

Recall that an option on a futures contract is the *right* (i.e., the option) to either acquire or sell a futures contract. In financial markets, an **option** is the right to buy or sell a financial asset or security at a predetermined fixed price during a specified period of time. Private and institutional investors can buy or sell stock options for almost any major stock (i.e., security), for a number of foreign currencies, or for alternative debt instruments (i.e., interest rate options). If an investor believed that stock in Microsoft Corp. was a good buy, rather than buying the stock outright, she could purchase a call option, which would give her the right to buy the stock at a certain price (i.e., the **strike** price). The option would increase in value if there were an increase in the price of the underlying Microsoft stock.

Options on futures are traded on the same exchanges that trade the underlying futures contracts. The buyer of an option has the choice (or opportunity) to buy or sell a futures contract, and the seller provides the buyer with that opportunity. For example, the buyer of a "call" option purchases the right (by paying a "premium") to hold a long position in a futures contract. If the call option buyer chooses to exercise his option, then he would acquire the futures contract at the predetermined price (i.e., the "strike" price). Alternatively, the buyer of a "put" option purchases the right to a short futures position. The option has an expiry month that corresponds to the futures contract month of expiration, and the various strike prices are set by the exchange.

Options on futures contracts have many counterparts in our economy. For instance, some airline companies offer a plan whereby they are willing to fix the price of air travel for the next 10 years. For a 15% up-front payment, large volume clients may purchase an option to buy airline tickets at a fixed price that are redeemable for a certain number of miles. Those frequent travelers who expect travel costs to skyrocket can purchase these options as a form of insurance against higher airfares. But the option does not obligate the customer to eventually buy the tickets. If some new technology is developed that leads to a fall in the price of air travel, then the option buyer may choose not to use the "right" to buy tickets at the prearranged price. The traveler loses the 15% up-front payment if the "option" is not exercised. However, if airline ticket prices rise dramatically, the option buyer may exercise the option to buy the tickets or perhaps even sell the option to someone else for a profit.

BOX 8.1

Military aircraft options.
The C-17 is a relatively modern and huge cargo aircraft used extensively by the U.S. Air Force to deliver troops and cargo for both peacekeeping and humanitarian missions. The C-17 aircraft is manufactured by Boeing under contract with the Air Force. It is a versatile aircraft and can take off with a payload of about 170,000 pounds and land on short airfields if necessary. However, this plane is not cheap, with each costing approximately $240 million (constant 1998 dollars).

In an effort to save the U.S. taxpayers some money, the U.S. Air Force has constructed a type of options contract. Under this arrangement, Boeing can sell new C-17 planes to private air cargo companies (such as Federal Express), provided the Air Force can use the private fleet of C-17s in time of emergency. In return for the "option" to access the aircraft in time of need, the Air Force will provide the private buyers of the planes an initial fee plus annual payments. The Air Force reports that it will save several billions of dollars of taxpayers' money under this arrangement.

Options are a derivative security because their value depends on the underlying futures contract. Like futures contracts, options provide a form of price insurance for commercial hedgers. At the same time, they provide speculators with an opportunity to profit from price movements in the underlying commodity or financial asset.

This chapter covers the basic concepts of options written on futures contracts. It focuses on the important relationship between options prices (i.e., the premium) and the underlying futures prices and discusses factors that impact this relationship. The basics of the theory behind options on futures pricing are outlined in this chapter, and some examples are provided to illustrate the speculative use of options on futures. Hedging with options on futures is covered in the following chapter.

Options on futures contracts have rapidly emerged as an important risk management and trading tool (Kolb, 1997; Purcell and Koontz, 1999). As explained in Chapter 1, options written on futures contracts received formal government approval for trading on organized exchanges in the United States in early 1987. However, commodity options have a very long history that goes back two centuries. Options (or **privileges**[1]) were actively traded in the U.S. grain markets as far back as the 1860s, and they continued to be traded until the 1930s. The U.S. Congress then chose to ban commodity options trading in 1936 for two main reasons. The first was that option (or privilege) trading was unregulated at the time, and thus periodic trading abuses and defaults arose. Second, options were par-

---

[1] Privileges are very similar to modern-day options, the major difference being that privileges were normally of a shorter duration, such as overnight or for one week.

tially blamed for the excessive volatility and eventual collapse of commodity prices in the early 1930s. During the period in which they were banned in the United States, commodity options traded actively in London for such commodities as coffee, sugar, cocoa, copper, silver, and tin. During the ban on U.S. options trading, several firms specialized as intermediaries between their American customers and the London options markets.

WHAT IS AN OPTION ON FUTURES?

There are some important differences between futures and options contracts. First, for the buyer of an option, the risk involved in options trading is much different than the risk involved in futures trading. The holder of a futures contract has the obligation to either deliver or accept delivery of the underlying asset or financial instrument.[2] This obligation must either be "met" or "offset" by the owner of a futures contract. It is most often offset by the holder entering into an equal and opposite futures position rather than through delivery or cash settlement.

The owner of an option has the "right" but not an "obligation" to either buy or sell the underlying futures contract. For example, a buyer of a Treasury-bond (T-bond) futures contract must either accept delivery or sell an offsetting futures contract before contract expiration. On the other hand, a buyer of a T-bond "call" option can either exercise her right and obtain a long position in T-bond futures or sell her option at the prevailing market price (i.e., the premium). Alternatively, if the market has moved against her, she will choose not to exercise the option and simply let it expire worthless. The basic differences between futures and options contracts are outlined in Table 8.1.

TABLE 8.1   Basic Differences Between Futures Contracts and Options on Futures

ALTERNATIVE POSITIONS	TRADER'S RIGHTS	TRADER'S OBLIGATIONS	MARGIN REQUIRED
Futures contract buyer		Accept commodity or financial asset at contract price or cash settle	Yes
Futures contract seller		Deliver commodity or financial asset at contract price or cash settle	Yes
Put option buyer	Sell futures contract at strike price		No
Put option seller		Buy futures contract at strike price	Yes
Call option buyer	Buy futures contract at strike price		No
Call option seller		Sell futures contract at strike price	Yes

[2] Recall that there is cash settlement on some futures contracts. Options on futures contracts with cash settlement also have a cash settlement feature (see Garbade and Silber, 2000).

As shown in Table 8.1, an options contract gives the buyer of the option considerable flexibility and limited risk relative to the buyer of a futures contract. For the buyer of either a put or a call option, there are no margin calls because the premium is the maximum amount they can lose no matter what happens to the underlying futures price, and the premium is paid "up front" at the time the option is purchased. However, in order for the options buyer to earn a profit, the futures price must be above (for a call option) or below (for a put option) the option's strike price by more than the amount of the premium paid.

However, if the futures price is not above the strike (for a call option) or not below the strike (for a put option) by the amount of the premium, the buyer can still recover a portion of the premium through either exercising the option or selling it. The premium paid by the buyer is a type of "fixed" cost, and the buyer might decide to either exercise the option or sell it, even if a "profit" is not assured. In those cases where a portion of the "fixed" cost (i.e., the premium) can be recovered, the option buyer might well decide to cut his or her losses by either exercising the option or selling it.

Options that have been purchased can be subsequently sold before the month of expiry or simply allowed to expire. In contrast to the buyer's limited risk, the seller of an option must post margin calls because the seller's potential losses are high. The risk taken on by the options seller is very similar to the risk exposure experienced by the holder of a futures contract.

To reiterate, an option is a contractual agreement to either purchase or sell a futures contract at a preestablished price and within a specified time period. There are two types of options: puts and calls. A *call option* gives a buyer the right (but not the obligation) to purchase a futures contract at a specified "strike price" within a specified period of time (before the expiry date). A *put option* gives a buyer of the option the right (but not the obligation) to sell a futures contract at a specified price within a specified period of time. The seller (writer) of an option receives a *premium*, which is the amount paid by the buyer of the option in return for the right to control a futures contract. The premium is the price of the option; thus, it fluctuates with the supply and demand for the option itself. The holder can exercise his option on the futures contract at any time during the life of the option (Box 8.2). The seller of a put (call) option is obligated to buy (sell) the futures contract at the strike price if the buyer decides to exercise his option.

BOX 8.2

American versus European options.

Most calls and puts on futures contracts are classified as "American" options. This term characterizes the options contract specifications. Compared to European options, American options give the buyer more flexibility because an American option can be exercised or offset at any time prior to expiry. In contrast, European options can be offset or exercised only during the delivery month. These terms do not necessarily indicate where the options are traded because American options are traded on European exchanges and vice versa.

TABLE 8.2 Examples of Futures Options

CORN: CHICAGO BOARD OF TRADE, 5,000 BUSHELS (CENTS PER BUSHEL)

| | PREMIUMS | | | | | |
| | CALLS | | | PUTS | | |
STRIKE PRICE	DECEMBER	MARCH	MAY	DECEMBER	MARCH	MAY
250	16	23 ¼	29 ½	¼	2	3
260	7	17	22 ½	1	4 ½	6
270	1 ⅛	11 ½	16 ¾	5	8 ¾	9 ½
280	¼	7 ½	12 ¼	14	14 ½	15

GOLD: COMEX, 100 TROY OUNCES (DOLLARS PER TROY OUNCE)

| | PREMIUMS | | | | | |
| | CALLS | | | PUTS | | |
STRIKE PRICE	FEBRUARY	APRIL	JUNE	FEBRUARY	APRIL	JUNE
410	22.80	29.70	36.60	2.70	4.90	7.00
420	14.80	22.40	29.40	4.70	7.10	9.30
430	9.00	16.30	23.30	8.70	11.00	12.80
440	5.00	11.60	11.60	14.70	15.80	17.30

A few examples will help illustrate these basic concepts. Consider Table 8.2, where representative futures options prices are reported for options written on corn and gold futures contracts. The top panel of Table 8.2 reports corn option prices. On the day in question, the purchaser of a call option in corn would have four different "strike" prices to choose from, ranging from $2.50 to $2.80 per bushel. The exchange determines the range of strike prices available for trading. Normally, the strike prices are set so that they are spaced evenly around the price of the underlying futures prices, with fixed price intervals separating each strike price. For example, the corn strike prices are 10¢ apart. If the underlying futures price moves considerably, then new strike prices will typically be added to the list of strike prices by the exchange because options traders will be interested in trading options at these new strike prices.

Referring to Table 8.2, if the option buyer chooses $2.60 as the appropriate strike price, then she would pay 7¢ per bushel for the right to purchase one December corn futures contract at a strike price of $2.60 per bushel. The buyer may exercise this right any time before the month of December.[3] The total premium the buyer pays to the seller of the option is $350 ($0.07 per bushel × 5,000 bushels–the

---

[3] For most futures options, the expiration date is in the early portion of the contract month or late in the previous month. In contrast, most futures contracts expire near the end of the contract month.

size of the contract), and this is paid up front at the time the option is purchased. If the price of corn falls and the buyer chooses not to exercise the option, then the buyer's total loss is limited to $350 (plus brokerage fees). However, if the price of corn rises and the buyer exercises her option, then she will acquire a "long" futures position at the option strike price of $2.60. At the same time, the exchange clearinghouse will assign a "short" futures position to a trader who has previously sold an identical "call" option on the same underlying futures contract and with the same strike price. If the call option buyer has acquired a long futures position, then another trader must be assigned the corresponding short position—for every buyer in the futures market there must be a seller. The clearinghouse assigns the short futures position to one of the option writers (i.e., sellers). Recall that instead of exercising her option, the buyer could also reverse her position by selling an option with the same strike price and delivery month.

Suppose that after the buyer has purchased the call option, the price of December corn futures increases to $2.90 per bushel and she decides to exercise her option. On exercise, the exchange clearinghouse gives her a long position in December corn at $2.60 and at the same time assigns a call writer a corresponding short position in December corn at $2.60. The long and short futures positions are **marked to market** (up to $2.90) by the clearinghouse, and the original call writer[4] (who now is short December corn) is assessed a margin call. The original call buyer can immediately liquidate her futures position for a (gross) profit of $0.30 per bushel (= $2.90 − $2.60) or alternatively hold onto the long futures position. Similarly, the original writer of a December call can directly liquidate his futures position (for a loss of $0.30 per bushel) or instead hold onto the short futures position with the expectation that the upward price trend might reverse itself.

Turning to the gold example in Table 8.2, consider the buyer of a put option. If the purchaser chooses a strike price of $440 per ounce and a June expiry date, the premium to be paid in order to purchase the option from the seller is $17.30 per ounce, or $1,730 for one put option, as the contract is for 100 ounces. The holder of this option has the right to acquire a short position in June gold futures at a price of $440. If the price of gold falls before the month of June and this option is exercised, then the holder obtains a short futures position from the exchange clearinghouse. He must then liquidate his futures position in order to capture the full profit available to him at the time. Of course, if the premium increases in value, he could also sell a June gold put option, and his profit would equal the change in the value of the premium minus brokerage fees.

OPTION PAYOFFS

A call option buyer's possible profit and loss combinations are shown graphically in Figure 8.1. For comparison purposes, Figure 8.1 also depicts a payoff line for a holder of a long futures position. For ease of exposition, the current futures price is assumed

---

[4] An options *writer* and *seller* are terms that may be used interchangeably.

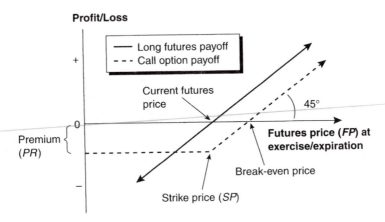

FIGURE 8.1
Long futures versus call options payoff.

to be equal to the strike price. The options **payoff line** is depicted as the kinked dotted line, and the futures payoff line is the straight 45-degree line with an arrow at each end of the line. Profits (losses) are shown on the vertical axis, and the underlying futures price at time of contract expiry (or at time of exercise) is shown on the horizontal line. When either an option or a futures contract is purchased, profits (losses) accruing to the holder depend largely on the extent to which the futures price moves in a favorable or unfavorable direction (assuming the option is not canceled by an offsetting trade in the options market). The expected profit from a long call position is

$$E(\pi_L{}^C) = \max[-PR, (FP - SP - PR)], \tag{8.1}$$

where E is the expectation operator, PR is the option premium, FP is the underlying futures price, and SP is the strike price.

On the left-hand side of Figure 8.1, the options payoff line lies below the horizontal axis by the amount of the premium. This premium is the maximum loss to the holder of the option and is given by the vertical distance between the horizontal axis (shown as 0) and the flat portion of the option payoff line. As the underlying futures price increases, we move to the right side of the graph, and the option payoff line becomes kinked at the strike price. Additionally, the call option payoff line crosses the horizontal axis at the futures **break-even price**. It is kinked at the strike price because once the futures price moves above the strike price, the option can be exercised for a monetary return. In other words, the option becomes **"in the money."** The option could be in the money, but the return could still be less than the premium paid. However, once the futures price rises high enough, the monetary return exceeds the premium. This is the point referred to as the break-even point. The break-even futures price can be solved by setting expected profits in equation 8.1 to zero, or

$$E(\pi_L{}^C) = (FP - SP - PR) = 0 \tag{8.2}$$

and therefore the break-even futures price equals

$$FP^{BC} = SP + PR. \tag{8.3}$$

In Figure 8.1, the futures payoff line is drawn for the holder of a long futures position. It is the 45-degree line crossing the horizontal axis at the current futures price, which is assumed to be equal to the strike price in order to simplify the example in the graph. Comparing the two payoff lines helps illustrate the risk/reward characteristics of options versus futures. The futures payoff line shows large potential profits if the futures price rises above the current level and large potential losses if the futures price falls. In contrast, the options payoff line shows large potential profits if the futures price rises above the current level but limited losses if the futures price falls. Losses to the holder of the call option are limited to $- PR$. When the futures price rises, the call option payoff line is parallel to but everywhere below the futures payoff line by the amount of the option premium. The maximum profit for a call option depends on the difference between the futures price and the strike price minus the premium, as shown in equation 8.1.

Now turn to Figure 8.2, which shows the payoff line for the holder of a put option. For comparison purposes, Figure 8.2 also has a payoff line for a short futures position, and it is assumed that the current futures price equals the strike price. The expected profit for the holder of a long put position is

$$E(\pi_L^P) = \max[- PR, (SP - FP - PR)], \tag{8.4}$$

where the variables are as defined previously. Equation 8.4, the payoff equation for the holder of a long put, is very similar to Equation 8.1, the payoff equation for the holder of a long call. In both cases, the maximum loss is the premium (i.e., $- PR$). The maximum profit for a call (put) depends on the difference between the futures (strike) price and the strike (futures) price minus the premium.

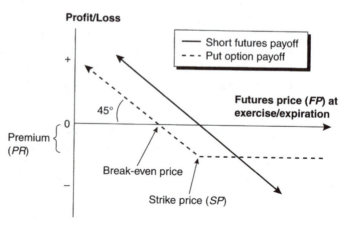

FIGURE 8.2
Short futures versus put options payoff.

BOX 8.3

Off-exchange options.

In 1984, the U.S. government permitted the trading of commodity options as long as trading was conducted on organized exchanges. In 2000, the Commodity Futures Trading Commission (CFTC) went one step further and lifted a long-standing government ban on the trading of off-exchange agricultural options. Trading in off-exchange commodity options was banned in 1936. The new rules were introduced following a change in U.S. farm policy that exposed farmers to greater price risk. The 1996 U.S. farm bill, known colloquially as the *Freedom to Farm Act*, placed more reliance on the free market to determine farm returns. The new farm legislation reduced the use of government programs that were designed to dampen fluctuating commodity prices. The *Freedom to Farm Act* separated government payments from production and prices and eliminated annual production controls for the major crops. As a result of their increased exposure to the market, farmers have a greater need for risk management instruments.

The off-exchange agricultural options are called "trade options." The CFTC intends to limit trade in these options to commercial producers or users of the commodity and to avoid off-exchange speculative trading in commodity options. The CFTC decided to allow off-exchange trading in order to increase the supply of option contracts available to farmers. Off-exchange options are nonstandardized, and this may allow farmers to hedge more precisely, as the off-exchange contracts can be tailored to individual situations.

Again, the flat portion of the options payoff line (on the right-hand side of Fig. 8.2) lies below the 0 horizontal line by the amount of the premium. If the futures price remains relatively high and is above the strike price, then $- PR$ is the loss incurred by the put option holder. Once the underlying futures price falls to the level of the strike price, the option moves in the money, and this is the point where the dashed option payoff line becomes kinked. For the put option, the break-even price is found by setting expected profits equal to zero:

$$E(\pi_L^P) = SP - FP - PR = 0, \tag{8.5}$$

and therefore the break-even futures price equals.

$$FP^{BP} = SP - PR. \tag{8.6}$$

Option payoff possibilities are perhaps best illustrated by some real-world examples. Turning to Figure 8.3, let us presume that a trader expects long-term interest rates to fall, and to capitalize on this expectation, she buys a March T-bond call option at a premium of 1-41 with a strike price equal to 100-00. The call option

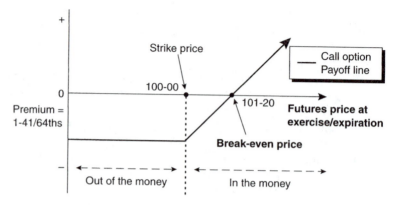

FIGURE 8.3
T-bond *call option* example.

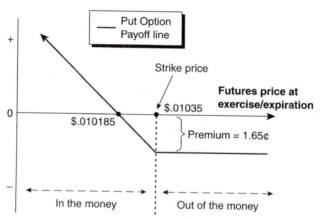

FIGURE 8.4
Yen *put option* example.

premium is 1-41/64ths, or $1,640 ($15.62 per 64th), and suppose the underlying March futures price is 99-18. In Figure 8.3, the payoff line is kinked at the strike price of 100-00, and the break-even futures price is 101-20 (= *SP* + *PR*). Note that the T-bond futures price is quoted in 32nds and the options prices in 64ths.

The call option depicted in Figure 8.3 is **"out of the money"** to the left of the strike price, where the payoff line is flat and where the *FP* < *SP*. The option is **"at the money"** where the *SP* = *FP*, and it is in the money to the right of the strike price, where the *FP* > *SP*. We can say that this option is out of the money because the underlying *FP* = 99-18, which is less than the strike price of 100-00.

As an alternative example, in Figure 8.4, the payoff chart is drawn for a trader who purchases a Japanese yen put option, with the expectation that the U.S. dollar is going to strengthen in value, thus decreasing the dollars-per-yen exchange rate. The trader therefore buys a March put option at 1.65¢ per 100 yen with a strike price equal to $.01035 per yen. The premium is thus equivalent to $2,062.50 (= $.000165 per yen × 12.5 million yen). Let us assume that the underlying March futures price is $.0103 per yen, which means that the option is currently in the money. The payoff line in Figure 8.4 is kinked at the strike price and crosses the horizontal axis at the break-even futures price of $.010185 (= $SP - PR$). Notice that yen futures are quoted in dollars per yen, while options prices are quoted in cents per 100 yen.

OPTION PRICING STRUCTURE

The buyer of an option is exposed to much less price risk than the seller (writer) of the option, so their risks are asymmetrical. The buyer's risk is limited to the premium paid at the time of purchase, whereas the seller's downside risk is proportional to the potential price movement of the underlying futures contract. This is unlike futures trading, where the buyer's and seller's risks are symmetrical.

Generally speaking, an option's premium consists of two components, **intrinsic value** and **time value**:

$$\text{Intrinsic Value} + \text{Time Value} = \text{Premium.} \qquad (8.7)$$

The intrinsic value refers to the amount by which an option is currently **in the money.** An option is in the money if there is some revenue that can be immediately realized by exercising the option. This revenue is derived from a gap between the option strike price and the futures contract price. Theoretically, a premium should never be less than the intrinsic value. For a call option, the intrinsic value (per unit) is the amount that the futures price is currently above the strike price. The option buyer can acquire the futures contract at the lower strike price (through exercising the option) and then immediately turn around and sell the futures contract at the higher futures prices. Alternatively, for a put option, the intrinsic value is equal to the amount by which the futures price is below the strike price. If an option is **out of the money,** it has no intrinsic value, and its premium consists solely of time value.

Essentially, "in the money" means the same thing as "intrinsic value." If an option has intrinsic value, then it is worth exercising. The relationship between the strike price and underlying futures price determines whether an option is in the money. This is shown in Table 8.3.

Time value represents the amount of money that buyers are willing to pay for an option with the expectation that the underlying futures price will change

TABLE 8.3 In and Out of the Money		
TERM	**CALL OPTION**	**PUT OPTION**
In the money (has intrinsic value)	Futures > strike	Futures < strike
At the money	Futures = strike	Futures = strike
Out of the money (no intrinsic value)	Futures < strike	Futures > strike

favorably to cause the option to increase in value. Of course, time value also reflects the return that sellers are willing to accept for writing an option. Therefore, time value is simply the market's assessment of the possibility that the option's intrinsic value may increase in the future.

Given the general definition outlined previously, it follows that time value (T) may be determined by subtracting intrinsic value (I) from the total market price of the option (i.e., its premium, PR). Thus, $T = PR - I$, which means that the time value is the amount by which an option's premium exceeds its intrinsic value. Options are sometimes referred to as a "decaying asset" because the time value decreases with time, becoming zero when the option expires.

For example, the possibility of a July soybean futures contract increasing by $1.00 per bushel in the six-month January–June period certainly exists because weather events alone could send soybean prices soaring during that period. However, the possibility of the same contract increasing $1.00 per bushel a few days prior to the expiry of the contract is very unlikely because there is little time for big surprises in the market just before expiry. A call option buyer might be willing to pay a $0.30-per-bushel premium in January for an out of the money option with a strike price $1.00 higher than the January price of the June futures contract since there is a seven-month period during which the option could move into the money. Likewise, the writer of that out of the money option might be willing to accept $0.30 per bushel as a premium. However, with a few days left until expiry, the buyer would not be willing to pay such a high premium, nor would the option writer demand it for an option so far out of the money. This concept of the decaying value of an option is shown in Figure 8.5. Basically, this figure illustrates the idea that, ceteris paribus, the more time an option has remaining until expiry, the larger is its premium.

The theoretical boundary prices for call and put options are shown in Table 8.4. For a call option, the maximum premium is the futures price because even if the strike price were zero, no rational buyer of an option would pay more than the futures price. At the same time, the minimum price is the current intrinsic value.

FIGURE 8.5
Decaying value of an option.

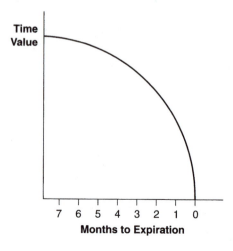

In Table 8.4, the operator Max [x, y] indicates the value is the maximum of either x or y. So, the minimum for a call option is either zero or the intrinsic value, whichever is greater.

Alternatively, for a put option, the maximum price is the strike price. It would be irrational to pay more than the strike price for a put option because this is the maximum intrinsic value even in the unlikely event that the futures price went to zero. Of course, the minimum premium for a put option is its current intrinsic value.

The information in Table 8.4 is shown graphically in Figures 8.6 and 8.7. Using crude oil futures options as an example, Figures 8.6 and 8.7 display the (theoretical) possible range of option premiums for a call and put option, respectively. Suppose that for both the call and the put option, the strike price is $19.50 per barrel. In both figures, the shaded areas give the range of possible option prices. The most likely prices are shown along the price paths A and B in both figures. In Figure 8.6, the maximum value of a call option is the futures price itself, so the left-hand side of the shaded area is a 45-degree line that rises with the futures price. Alternatively, the minimum price is the intrinsic value, which is either 0 or the futures price minus the strike price in the case of the call. This means that the bottom portion of the price border follows the 0 horizontal axis until the futures price hits the strike price (moving to the right). The bottom portion of the border becomes kinked at the point where the futures price equals the strike price, and then the border rises along the lower 45-degree line as long as the futures price continues to increase above the strike price.

The theoretical maximum price that a call buyer would pay for the crude oil option depicted in Figure 8.6 is an amount equal to the futures price. Suppose the

TABLE 8.4   Options Premium: Maximum and Minimum Price

	CALL	PUT
Maximum price	Futures price	Strike price
Minimum price	Max[0, (futures price − strike price)]	Max[0, (strike price − futures price)]

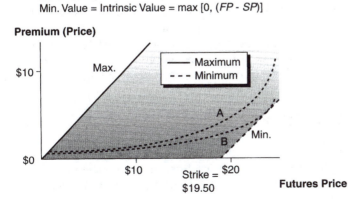

Max. Value = Futures Price
Min. Value = Intrinsic Value = max [0, (FP - SP)]

Premium (Price)

— Maximum
--- Minimum

$10 — Max.

A

B   Min.

$0

$10

Strike = $19.50 $20

Futures Price

FIGURE 8.6
Call option: Minimum and maximum prices.

Note: Either price path A or B: depends on volatility and time to expiry.

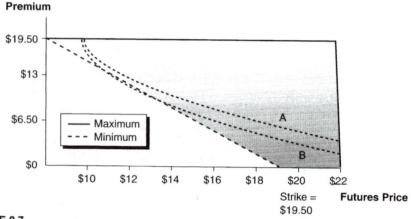

FIGURE 8.7
Put option: Minimum and maximum prices.
Note: Either price path A or B: depends on volatility and time to expiry.

futures price was $15 per barrel. In this case, the maximum revenue from exercising that option is $15 per barrel for the trader who buys a call option. So, even if the strike price were 0, the buyer would never pay more than $15 for the premium as long as the futures price was no greater than $15. If the futures price rose to $20, then the maximum price paid would rise to $20. In a competitive options market, the actual premiums paid would be much less than the theoretical maximum, and therefore the most likely premiums are shown along the curved lines A and B. If volatility decreases, then the price path might fall from line A to line B. In other words, premiums would fall, ceteris paribus. As time to expiry declines, the premium also falls (moving from line A to line B) because of the declining time value.

Figure 8.7 depicts the range of theoretical prices for a put option. Suppose the crude oil put also has a strike price of $19.50 per barrel. For a put, the maximum premium is equal to the strike price, so the top portion of the theoretical price border is a horizontal line at $19.50. No rational trader would pay more than $19.50 for the put option in this example because $19.50 is the maximum revenue that could be earned if the option is exercised, even if the futures price falls to zero. The minimum price is the intrinsic value, which is shown by the left-hand 45-degree line as the price border. If volatility increases, then the put option price would rise for a given futures price, and the price path would shift from the curved line B to that labeled A in Figure 8.7.

MARKET PRICING OF OPTIONS

To gain further understanding of option pricing, it is useful to look at some market-generated data on option premiums to help illustrate the concepts discussed so far in this chapter. Refer to Figure 8.8. Understanding the option premium data in

Cotton Options: 50,000 lb (¢/lb)

FIGURE 8.8
Market-determined options
premiums: A cotton example.

S.P.	Calls			Puts		
	Mar	May	July	Mar	May	July
54	4.05	4.25	6.6	1.58	1.95	2.6
55	3.15	4.65	6.0	2.1	2.4	3.0
56	2.95	4.2	5.5	2.2	2.95	3.4
57	2.4	3.65	5	2.95	3.35	
58	2.1	3.2	4.45	3.25	3.9	
59	1.7	2.8		3.65	4.45	

Underlying Futures: March 56.55, May 57.35, July 58.1

Figure 8.8 is facilitated by first computing the intrinsic value, if any, for each option. To review, call options will have intrinsic value only if the current futures price is above the strike price for that option, whereas put options will have intrinsic value only if the strike price is above the current futures price. The time value of each option may then be computed by subtracting the intrinsic value from the option premium. Those options that are in the money are circled in Figure 8.8.

In Figure 8.8, the 57¢ call option on the July cotton futures contract is trading at 5¢ per pound. This option has intrinsic value because the strike price of 57¢ is below the current July futures price of 58.1¢. The intrinsic value is therefore equal to 1.1¢ per pound (= 58.1¢ – 57¢). With a premium of 5¢ per pound and intrinsic value of 1.1¢ per pound, it follows from Equation 8.7 that the time value on that option must be 3.9¢ per pound. Alternatively, the March call option with the 57¢ strike price has no intrinsic value because the strike price of 57¢ exceeds the current March futures price of 56.55¢. The entire 2.4¢ premium for this option is therefore time value.

The May put option in Figure 8.8 with a 59¢ strike price has substantial intrinsic value since it gives the buyer the right to sell a futures contract at 59¢ that can be immediately purchased at the current futures market price of 57.35¢. With a premium of 4.45¢ and intrinsic value of 1.65¢ (= 59¢ – 57.35¢), the time value is 2.8¢ for this option. In contrast, the 54¢ strike on the March put option has no intrinsic value; rather, its entire 1.58¢ premium is time value.

Notice that for the March call in Figure 8.8, the premium for the 54¢ strike is 4.05¢ per pound. For the 59¢ strike, the premium is much lower—only 1.7¢ per pound. Actually, for the March call, the option premiums (in cents per pound) fall continuously from the 54¢ strike to the 59¢ strike (from 4.05¢ down to 1.7¢). Why do these premiums decline as we move from the lower to the higher strike prices? The answer is that the premiums fall largely because of the change in intrinsic value as the strike prices increase from 54¢ to 59¢. For call options, the intrinsic value declines with higher strike prices, and therefore the premiums decline.

Also observe that for the 58¢ calls, the premiums rise as we move along the row from March to July options. What explains this phenomenon of rising premiums as the expiry month becomes more distant? For the 58¢ strike price, the March premium is 2.1¢, and the July premium is more than double at 4.45¢. This increase in premiums for the same strike price but for more distant maturity months is due largely to the role of time value.

In Figure 8.8, the 59¢ July call and several of the July put options at higher strike prices have no premiums quoted. This is due to a lack of trading at these strike prices. The premiums asked by options sellers must be too high relative to the buyer's bid price, or we could alternatively say that the bid prices are too low. This indicates that options buyers and sellers, just like other markets, will "make a market" only when the bid–ask spread comes together.

OPTION TRADERS

An option's premium will respond to changes in a number of underlying factors. The most important factors include time to maturity, volatility of the underlying futures price, and the price of the underlying futures contract in relation to the strike price. At the most basic level, the relationship between the futures price and the option premium is shown in Table 8.5. A call option's premium is positively related to the price of the underlying futures contract. That is, if the futures price goes up, the call option's premium also goes up. If the futures price falls, then generally the call option's premium falls. Alternatively, a put option's premium is inversely related to the price of the underlying futures contract. The basic objective of the option trader is to sell the option for a higher premium than the original premium paid or alternatively to profit from exercising the option. This underscores the importance of understanding how changes in futures prices affect the call and put option premiums.

Put Option Buyer

As a speculator, a put option buyer expects that futures price will fall; but, as a hedger, the put option buyer wants to buy some protection from the consequences of the futures price falling below the strike price. The bearish expectation of falling prices is shown in the top right-hand panel of Table 8.6. As indicated earlier, a put option premium is composed of only time value if the futures price is equal to or above the strike price. A put option buyer can therefore realize a net gain only if the intrinsic value rises by more than the sum of any decline in time value plus the

TABLE 8.5 Relationship Between Futures Price and Options Premium		
	UNDERLYING FUTURES PRICES	
	DECLINES	**INCREASES**
Call option premium	Declines	Increases
Put option premium	Increases	Declines

TABLE 8.6   Option Traders' Positions and Their Price Expectations

	CALL OPTION	PUT OPTION
Buyer (holder)	Bullish	Bearish
Seller (writer)	Neutral to slightly bearish	Neutral to slightly bullish

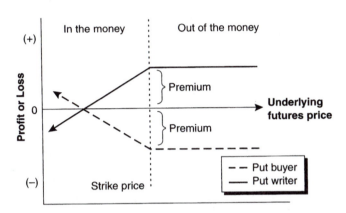

FIGURE 8.9
Risk/reward structure of a put option.

opportunity cost of the premium and brokerage charges. There is an absolute upper limit on the net gain that a put option buyer may realize. The worst outcome for a put option buyer is that the option has no intrinsic value near the end of trading and the option is allowed to expire with no remaining value. Therefore, a put option buyer knows at the time of purchase that the maximum possible loss is composed of the premium paid for the option plus brokerage fees. This relationship is depicted in Figure 8.9. When exercising a put option, a buyer profits by the amount the option is in the money less the premium paid and brokerage fees.

Put Option Seller

A put option seller is neutral to slightly bullish on prices (see Table 8.6). The seller receives the full premium immediately less brokerage charges. The total amount of a premium is the asset's "price," normally quoted in dollars per quantity unit, times the number of units specified in a futures contract. In addition, at the time a position is opened by a put option seller, the seller must deposit in a margin account the amount of the premium plus a sum of money similar to the margin that buyers and sellers of futures contracts must maintain. If the premium on a put option rises, option sellers must, in general, deposit additional margin money equal to this adverse change in the value of the option position. The clearinghouse sets these rules. If the premium declines after a put option seller opens a position, the seller will be allowed to withdraw from the margin account an amount generally equal to the decline in the premium.

A put option seller has the best possible outcome when an option is allowed to expire with no value to the option buyer. In this case, sellers keep the entire premium less brokerage costs. The maximum gain for a put option seller is limited to the net amount received in total premium at the time of sale. The worst possible outcome for a put option seller occurs when there has been a very large drop in the futures price and the option buyer closes the position either by selling the option in an offsetting transaction or by exercising the option. In the latter case, a put option seller must bear the full cost of acquiring a long futures position at the strike price and offsetting it at a lower price. The maximum loss for a put option seller is bounded by the total value of the associated futures contract (which requires the futures price going to zero). These relationships are shown in Figure 8.9. Of course, the total net gain or loss is also a function of interest earnings from holding the premium minus the margin deposit and brokerage fees during the period an option position is open.

Call Option Buyer

As a speculator, a call option buyer expects that the futures price will rise or alternatively, as a hedger, wishes to buy some protection from the consequences of the futures price rising above the strike price. As indicated earlier, the premium on a call is composed of time value only if the futures price is equal to or below the strike price. A call option buyer realizes a net gain if the intrinsic value rises by more than the sum of any decline in time value plus the opportunity cost of the premium and brokerage charges. There is no absolute upper limit on the net gain that a call option buyer may realize. The worst outcome for a call option buyer occurs if the option has no intrinsic value at the end of trading and is allowed to expire. Therefore, a call option buyer knows at the time of purchase that the limit to her possible loss is composed of the premium paid for the option plus brokerage fees. Figure 8.10 depicts the risk/reward structure for a call option.

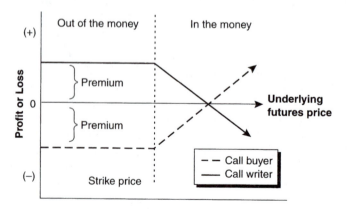

FIGURE 8.10
Risk/reward structure of a call option.

Call Option Seller

A call option seller knows when opening a position that she will be paid the full amount of the premium immediately less brokerage fees for the option sale. In addition, at the time a position is opened, a call option seller must make a deposit in a margin account. If the premium on a call option rises, option sellers must in general deposit additional margin equal to this adverse change in the value of the option position. If the premium declines after a call option seller opens a position, the seller will be allowed to withdraw from the margin account an amount generally equal to the decline in premium.

Just as described previously for puts, call option sellers have the best possible outcome when an option is allowed to expire with no value to buyers; sellers keep all the premium less brokerage costs. The maximum gain for a call option seller is limited to the net amount received in total premium at the time of initial sale. The worst possible outcome for a call option seller occurs when there has been a very large rise in the futures price and the option buyer makes an offsetting transaction or exercises the option. The maximum loss of a call option seller is unlimited theoretically. As long as futures prices rise, every dollar increase in total contract value represents a dollar lost to call option sellers. This relationship is depicted by the solid kinked arrow in Figure 8.10.

The previous discussion surrounding Figures 8.9 and 8.10 implicitly assumed that options were held until the date of expiry. This simplifies the presentation. It is also possible to either offset or exercise an **American option** before the date of expiry (Box 8.2). The results of this alternative trading strategy do not materially differ from those presented in Figures 8.9 and 8.10. For instance, if the intrinsic value increases to the point where it is profitable to exercise, the buyer of an option can choose to exercise the option at any time before expiry. Alternatively, he could sell the option for a higher premium than he initially paid. Traders usually take the second approach because selling an option enables both intrinsic and time value to be captured; exercising an option captures only its intrinsic value.

SPECULATION WITH OPTIONS ON FUTURES

There are *pros* and *cons* associated with speculative trading in options, as compared to futures. The pros include the following:

    a. The limited risk associated with buying an option
    b. The absence of margin calls when buying an option
    c. A greater number of investment opportunities and a higher degree of flexibility provided by options

As a result, options are an attractive investment alternative to most traders, and they provide risk/reward opportunities not available with futures. For example, options allow an investor to enter into a trade with an expected positive profit even if his price expectations are neither bullish nor bearish but "neutral" instead.

TABLE 8.7   Illustrative Sugar Options Prices

	PREMIUM	STRIKE PRICE
July call	$0.0194/lb	$0.095/lb
July put	$0.0028/lb	$0.095/lb

Note: Assume that the underlying July futures contract is trading at $0.1115 per pound.

Many investors also spread options and/or combine futures and options positions. All these advantages are not costless, however, since those who sell options must be paid for the risk they incur, and therefore they collect the option's premium. This is the downside of speculating with options rather than futures. There is nothing equivalent to the up-front premium when speculating with futures contracts.

Putting some numbers on payoff graphs helps one understand the impact of a futures price change on both the buyer and the seller of an option. For illustrative purposes, consider both a call and a put option on July sugar futures that have premiums (prices) prevailing during the month of March (see Table 8.7).

Using the prices in Table 8.7, the potential profits/losses of going long versus short in either a put or a call are graphed in Figure 8.11 against changes in the underlying sugar futures contract price. For simplicity, all brokerage fees are ignored in this example. The shape of the profit/loss lines for calls are mirror images of those for puts. Figure 8.11a displays the potential profit for the buyer (at the time of expiration) of a call option. This can be represented by

$$\pi_L^C = FP - SP - PR = \text{intrinsic value} - \text{premium paid} \qquad (8.8)$$

for $FP \geq SP - PR$, and

$$\pi_L^C = -PR, \text{otherwise,}$$

where FP is the futures price, SP is the strike price, and PR is the premium. Going long in the sugar call option will be profitable for a trader as long as the futures price is above the break-even amount of $0.1144 (= $0.095 + $0.0194) at the time the option expires. The potential profit is theoretically unlimited as futures prices could increase infinitely.

In Figure 8.11(c) the profit/loss opportunities for a short seller of a sugar call option are depicted. The maximum profit available to the seller is the premium, which is $0.0194. This represents a total of $2,172.80 because the sugar futures contract calls for delivery of 112,000 pounds. This profit potential begins to erode very quickly if futures prices rise above the strike price of $0.095, the point at which it becomes worthwhile for the buyer of the call option to exercise her right to obtain a long futures position. The expected profit for the holder of a short call position is given by

$$\pi_S^C = PR + SP - FP = \text{premium received} - \text{intrinsic value} \qquad (8.9)$$

for $FP \geq SP - PR$, and

$$\pi_S^C = PR, \text{otherwise.}$$

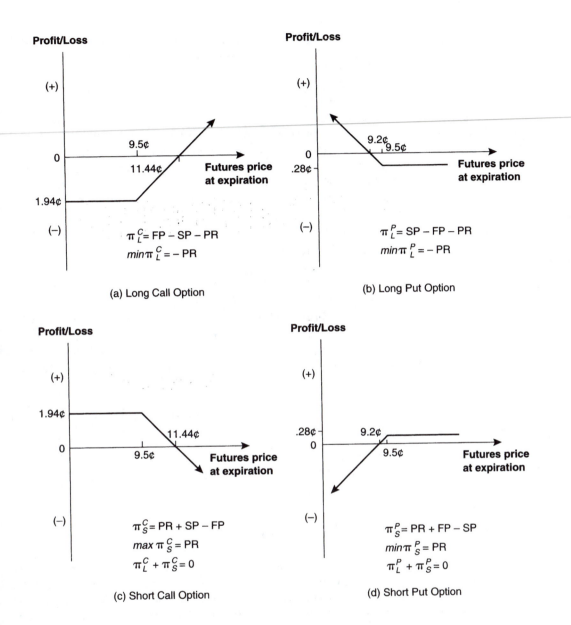

FIGURE 8.11
Options payoff at expiration: (a) long call option, (b) long put option, (c) short call option, (d) short put option.

This becomes a large negative number if at expiry $FP > (SP + PR)$ by a large margin. Recall that both PR and SP are constant after the option is sold, so the path of FP is all important.

Now consider the expected profits for a long and short put option. Figure 8.11(b) the payoff situation for a long put position. An investor would purchase a put if she expected futures prices to fall. In the example shown here, the premium paid is $0.0028 per pound, or $313.60 for an option on a 112,000-pound sugar contract. This premium is relatively low because the underlying July futures price is $0.1115 per pound at the time of the option purchase. The seller of the option is willing to accept a small premium because he believes that there is only a small probability that the price of sugar will fall from $0.1115 to $0.095 (or lower) between March and July. As long as the futures price remains above $0.095, it will not be worthwhile for the long position to be exercised, so an option holder would simply let the option expire. The put buyer recovers her premium and begins to reap a profit if the futures price is less than $0.0922 (= 9.5¢ − .28¢) when the option expires. The expected profit for the long put option position is given by the following equation:

$$\pi_L^P = SP - FP - PR = \text{intrinsic value} - \text{premium paid} \qquad (8.10)$$
$$\text{for } FP \leq SP - PR, \text{ and}$$
$$\pi_L^P = -PR, \text{ otherwise.}$$

This becomes a large positive number if $SP > (FP - PR)$ by a large amount.

Finally, Figure 8.11d shows the profit/loss opportunity for a short put option. In this case, the maximum profit is $313.60 (= $0.0028/lb × 112,000 lb). At the same time, the holder of the short put is exposed to a large potential loss if sugar futures prices fall below $0.092 per pound. The expected profit equation for the short call holder is

$$\pi_S^P = PR + FP - SP = \text{premium received} - \text{intrinsic value} \qquad (8.11)$$
$$\text{for } FP \leq SP - PR, \text{ and}$$
$$\pi_S^P = PR, \text{ otherwise,}$$
$$\text{which is positive if } FP > (SP - PR).$$

SPECULATIVE TRADING STRATEGIES

There are a large number of potential option strategies available to speculators.[5] Many of them are quite complex and offer varied risk/return opportunities. The more basic strategies are discussed here, concentrating on strategies based on price expectations, with some limited discussion of price volatility factors. These strategies focus on expectations concerning the underlying futures price at expiration rather than on more complex factors.

---

[5] Only the most basic trading strategies are covered in this chapter. The reader interested in more detail is referred to Jarrow and Turnbull (2000) for a more sophisticated treatment.

Basic Call Option Strategies

If a speculator has strong bullish price expectations, a straightforward strategy is to purchase a call option. The more bullish the expectation, the better it is to purchase an option that is far out of the money. This provides tremendous leverage in an up market, with relatively little downside risk because the premium paid is so low. Once a call option is purchased, the holder may choose (a) to exercise it and obtain a long futures position, (b) offset the position by selling the option, or (c) allow the option to expire.

If a speculator has strong price expectations that range from neutral to bearish, a reasonable strategy is to sell a call option. In the money call options provide maximum possible returns for the short trader who is very bearish. For a trader who has neutral to slightly bearish expectations, it is generally advised that she sell out of the money options with a relatively high strike price.

Basic Put Option Strategies

If a speculator is very bearish toward the market, a reasonable thing to do is to purchase a put option. The more bearish the expectation, the better it is to purchase an option far out of the money. This strategy gives a speculator maximum leverage.

Alternatively, a short put is the correct trade for a speculator who has strong neutral to bullish price expectations. If the trader's expectations are very bullish, maximum profit is obtained by selling a put with a strike price that is far in the money. Conversely, for a neutral to weakly bullish expectation, the best approach is to sell a put with a strike price that is far out of the money. A mildly bullish trader may sell a put that is at the money.

Basics of Spread Trading

The goal of spreading options, just as with futures spreads, is to profit from relative price movements of the two contracts. One of the simplest spreading strategies involves choosing two call options with the same expiry month but different strike prices and going long in one and simultaneously short in the other or alternatively going long and short in a put at the same time. These type of spreads are often referred to as **vertical spreads**.

Consider a vertical bull spread for the June gold call options reported in Table 8.8. The spread, illustrated in Figure 8.12, might involve buying the $380 strike at a premium of $17.30 per ounce ($1,730 in total for 100 ounces) and simultaneously selling the $410 strike at a premium of $4 per ounce (or $400 in total). The long call premium (PL) is higher than the short call premium (PS), and the difference (ML_{buc}) is the maximum loss that can be incurred from the spread; in this example, ML_{buc} is $13.30 per ounce (or $1,330 in total). The maximum profit (MP_{buc}) equals the difference between the strike prices, $SP_h - SP_l$, less the maximum loss, ML_{buc}. Thus, $MP_{buc} = SP_h - SP_l - ML_{buc} = \$16.70$. The break-even point for this spread is

TABLE 8.8   Gold Futures Options Premiums (100 Troy Ounces, $ per Troy Ounce)

UNDERLYING FUTURE PRICES; APRIL $386.60, JUNE $391.70, AUGUST $397.30

STRIKE PRICE	CALLS			PUTS		
	APRIL	JUNE	AUGUST	APRIL	JUNE	AUGUST
370	16.90	24.50	31.10	0.03	3.20	5.00
380	7.70	17.30	24.00	1.10	5.80	7.60
390	1.90	11.20	18.10	5.20	9.40	11.20
400	0.40	6.70	13.00	13.80	14.80	15.70
410	0.10	4.00	9.30	23.50	22.10	22.00
420	0.10	2.30	6.50	33.50	30.30	28.70

FIGURE 8.12
Vertical bull spread
payoff at expiration.

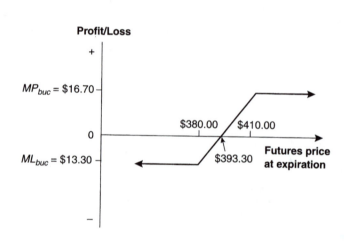

equal to $SP_l + ML_{buc}$, which is $380 + $13.30 = $393.30. By accepting a limit on the profit side, a spread trader gains a limit on the loss side of the spread.

A **bull vertical spread** involves buying an option with a relatively low strike price and selling an option with a relatively high strike price. Conversely, a **bear vertical spread** entails selling an option with a relatively low strike price and buying an option with a relatively high strike price. The payoff is exactly opposite that of the bull spread discussed in the previous paragraph. The maximum profit, MP_{bec}, is equal to the net premium received, which is $PL - PS$. In the example of June gold options discussed previously, this equals $13.30 per ounce. The maximum loss, ML_{bec}, is equal to the difference between the strike prices less the net premium received, which equals $16.70 per ounce. This payoff diagram is depicted in Figure 8.13. The break-even point is equal to $SP_l + MP_{bec}$, which is $393.30.

A vertical call bull spread is more common than a vertical put bull spread, although both spreads work much the same way. Both profits and losses are limited. For a bull put spread, the maximum loss, ML_{bup}, is equal to the difference in the strike prices less the net premium received. The maximum profit, MP_{bup}, is equal to the net premium received. The break-even point is equal to $SP_h - MP_{bup}$.

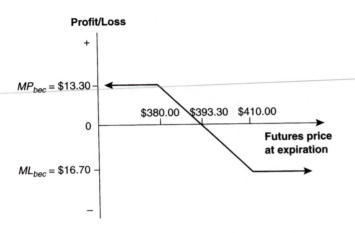

Profit/Loss

$MP_{bec} = \$13.30$

$\$380.00 \quad \$393.30 \quad \$410.00$

$ML_{bec} = \$16.70$

Futures price at expiration

FIGURE 8.13
Vertical bear spread payoff at expiration.

An opposite strategy involves trading a bear put spread, which means buying a put with a relatively high price and selling a low-priced put. The maximum loss is the net premium paid, and the maximum profit is equal to the difference in the strike prices less the maximum loss. The break-even price is equal to $SP_h - ML_{bep}$.

A Case Study: Spreading S&P 500 Index Options

An alternative trading strategy used by some speculators in options markets is spreading positions in two contracts with different delivery dates, called a **horizontal spread**. In a spread between options contracts expiring at two different times, two separate markets are involved, so two sets of supply and demand factors are relevant to the results. The key to such a trade, therefore, is to understand the economic relationship between the two markets.

An example of a horizontal option spread involves S&P 500 options contracts traded on the Chicago Mercantile Exchange. The goal of the trade is to take advantage of the different rates at which the time value of options decreases. Selling an at the money option that has at least a month before it expires and buying another option with the same strike price but with one additional month remaining in its life establishes the spread. The options can be either calls or puts, but either two puts or two calls must be used together to create this particular spread.

For example, suppose that it is late March and a speculator examines the May and June at the money calls. If the S&P 500 Index is around 1125 in the spot market, options with a strike price of 1125 would be approximately at the money. Suppose that the May 1125 call is currently trading at 27.20 points, or $6,800, at $25 per 0.1 index points. The speculator would sell the May call and, at the same time, purchase the June 1125 call. Assume that the June call is trading at 37.30 points (or $9,325) when it is purchased. The opening spread is therefore $37.30 - 27.20 = 10.10$ points, or $2,525.

A month later, suppose that the spot market for the S&P 500 index is unchanged at around 1125. The speculator sees that the May 1125 call option still has no intrinsic value and that its time value is decreasing more rapidly as its expiration date approaches. With a few days before the May option expires, the May 1125 call is trading at 5.00 points (or $1,250). The June 1125 call has no intrinsic value, either, but it still has a month before it expires, so its time value of 20.00 points ($5,000) exceeds that of the May call. As a result, the speculator closes the spread by making offsetting trades: a May 1125 call is purchased and a June 1125 call is sold. The closing spread is 20.00 − 5.00 = 15.00 points, or $3,750. The speculator has benefited by the change in the spread: 15 − 10.10 = 4.9 × $250 (the value of each point in the S&P 500 Index) equals a profit (before brokerage fees) of $1,225 per spread (one contract of each option). The cost to open this spread is the financing cost of the difference in premium paid for the June option ($9,325 per contract) and premium received from selling the May option ($6,800), or the cost of financing $2,525 per spread.

Option Straddles

Option straddles appear similar to option spreads but are traded for different reasons. Whereas spreads use either two calls or two puts (one long and one short), straddles combine one put and one call (both long or both short) for the same underlying futures contract. Unlike spreads, profits from straddles are earned from changes in absolute prices, not relative prices. As a result, straddles combine some aspects of basic option strategies and spread trading. This is illustrated in the following example.

An options speculator who expects the price of cattle to change but who is not confident about the direction of the change in absolute prices in the short run may choose to trade on using an option straddle. One strategy is to create a long straddle by simultaneously buying one put and one call, both at the money and with the same expiry date. Suppose that the underlying cattle futures contract is currently selling for $80 per hundredweight, and both options purchased would have an $80 strike price. As shown in the top half of Figure 8.14, the net effect of buying a call and a put is a maximum loss equal to the sum of the two premiums paid (assumed to be $4 per hundredweight for both the put and the call in this example). The maximum loss is incurred if the underlying futures price does not change during the period the straddle is held. However, if the price of cattle futures either rises or falls, one of the options will be in the money. If the price rises or falls by $8 per hundredweight (the total premiums paid), the profits on the option in the money will cover the premiums on both options. Additional price changes will produce profits net of premium costs.

As shown in Figure 8.14, the long straddle is a limited-risk strategy, while a short straddle is a very risky trade. A short straddle on the cattle market in the previous example generates outcomes that are opposite to those of a long straddle. The bottom half of Figure 8.14 indicates that a speculator would profit from this short straddle only if the underlying price of cattle does not change more than $4. In addition, $4 per hundredweight is the maximum profit available, while potential losses are virtually unlimited. In general, the limited risk of long straddles makes them more popular than short straddles, but traders planning to hold positions only a brief time may find short positions appealing in some markets.

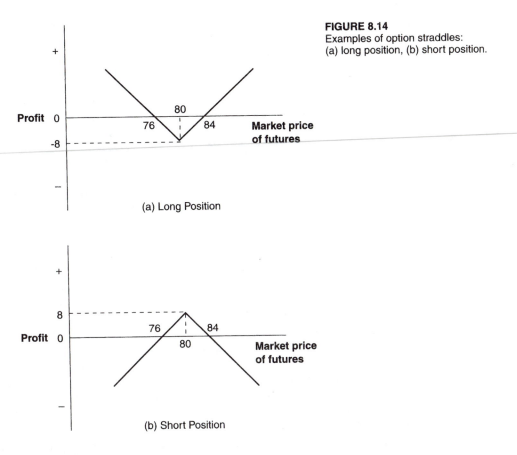

FIGURE 8.14
Examples of option straddles:
(a) long position, (b) short position.

(a) Long Position

(b) Short Position

OPTIONS PRICING IN GENERAL

The most accurate way to describe option pricing is to say that prices, usually known as "premiums," are determined by supply and demand for a particular option at a particular point in time. Supply and demand factors, and therefore option premiums, are influenced by the following:

    a. The relationship of the strike price to the underlying futures price
    b. The time remaining until the option expires
    c. The volatility of the price of the underlying futures contract
    d. Prevailing interest rates

    The market equilibrium for a call option is illustrated in Figure 8.15. Suppose that this option is out of the money. The demand curve intersects the vertical axis at the existing futures price, which is the maximum price that any trader would pay for a call option, as shown in Figure 8.6. The demand curve slopes down because there is a negative relation between the number of options contracts that traders are willing to purchase and the price (i.e., the premium). If the premium is relatively low, more options will be purchased, ceteris paribus.

FIGURE 8.15
Market equilibrium for a
call option.

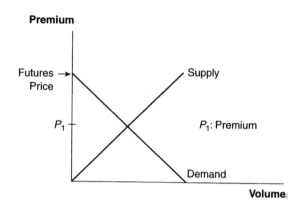

The supply curve is upward sloping, as the greater the premium, the larger the number of option contracts traders would be willing to write. The intersection of the supply and demand curves will determine the premium at any given point in time. The supply and demand functions will shift and/or rotate with changes in the four previously mentioned factors. For example, if the underlying futures price increases, the demand curve in Figure 8.15 will shift outward to the right, and the supply curve will rotate inward to the left, resulting in a new equilibrium with a higher premium.

The demand curve would shift (and not rotate) because the futures price establishes the point where the demand curve intersects the vertical axis. This means that if the futures price increases, then the demand curve's vertical intercept shifts upward, and the entire demand curve shifts out.

At the same time, when the futures price increases, the supply curve rotates to the left because the call option is moving closer to being in the money, and this concerns the writers (i.e., suppliers) of the call options. If the futures price rises sufficiently, the call option will move in the money, and the option will be exercised, which is a bad outcome for the option writer. Therefore, for a given volume of options, the writers require a higher premium if the futures price increases, ceteris paribus.

Think of the following example: If Mr. Castro buys a call option that gives him the right to buy an October sugar futures contract at $0.10 per pound and the current futures price for the same futures contract is $0.11 per pound, he should be willing to pay at least $0.01 per pound less transaction costs for that option. The option might be worth more than its $0.01 intrinsic value (meaning that it has some time value) based on Mr. Castro's expectations that the intrinsic value might become larger than $0.01 sometime before the option expires. In turn, no one would be willing to sell this option unless they were to receive its full intrinsic value because, otherwise, a buyer might immediately exercise the option or close it with an offsetting transaction. Additionally, option sellers would rationally attempt to obtain sufficient payment for time value to compensate them for the premium risk they have accepted. The required time value is based on their assessment of prospects that additional intrinsic value will be captured before the option expires, their risk preferences, and the cost of capital. In other words, time value represents the market's offer of return for the risk accepted by options sellers.

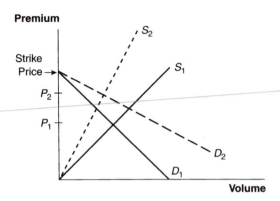

FIGURE 8.16
Market equilibrium for a put option.

In Figure 8.16, the market equilibrium is represented for a put option that is out of the money. The maximum premium is the strike price, and therefore the demand curve intersects the vertical axis at this price. Initially, the equilibrium premium is shown as P_1. Now suppose that the futures price declines. As a result, the demand curve rotates rightward, as options buyers are now willing to pay a higher premium for any given volume of options contracts. The reason the buyers are willing to pay more is that when the futures price declines, the put option is closer to being in the money. In other words, the expected payoff rises with a decline in the futures price (see Equation 8.4).

The dashed line (D_2) in Figure 8.16 shows the new demand curve. At the same time, the supply curve rotates to the left (to S_2), as writers of these put options now offer the same volume of put options at higher premiums. The intersection of the new demand and supply curves occurs at premium P_2, which is higher than P_1, because as the futures price falls, the options' premium rises. This graph illustrates the **delta** effect for put options, which is discussed in the next section.

Delta (δ)

A major preoccupation with option traders is determining how responsive the option premium is to changes in the price of the underlying futures contract. For example, if the November crude oil futures price increases from $17 to $18 per barrel, how much will the premium for an $18 November call option change?

The relationship between the price of an underlying futures contract and an option premium is measured by an option's **delta.** The delta, which lies between zero and one, is equal to the ratio of the price change of the option over the price change of the futures contract (i.e., $\delta = \Delta P / \Delta F$).

The delta value normally depends on the extent to which the option is either in the money or out of the money. Table 8.9 shows the general relationship between an option's delta and whether it is in the money.

Generally, options that are deep in the money have delta values that lie close to one, which means that there is almost a one-to-one relationship between a change in the underlying futures price and the option premium. For instance, if the S&P Index futures contract for June delivery is trading at 1300, an option to buy a

TABLE 8.9   Range of Option Deltas

	DELTA
In the money	0.5 to 1.0
At the money	0.5
Out of the money	0 to 0.5

June S&P Index contract for 1250 is worth at least 50 index points. This option is deep in the money and thus has a delta value near one. If the price of the June contract rises to 1310, then the premium will also increase by about 10 index points.

If an alternative call option on the same June futures contract had a strike price of 1350, then it would be deep out of the money (i.e., no intrinsic value), and its delta value would be near zero. In this case, a 10-point rise in the price of the contract would translate into only a small rise in the option premium, such as 1 index point. An at the money option on the June contract would have a strike price of 1300 index points, and its delta would be approximately 0.5.

Time Value: Theta (Θ)

Since time value reflects nothing more than the market's expectations concerning the prospects of an option having additional intrinsic value sometime before it expires, time value is affected by the amount of time remaining before expiry. A buyer would be willing to pay a higher premium, and a seller would insist on a higher premium, the longer the trading period remaining because this means that there is a greater probability that the option will take on increased intrinsic value. In practice, it appears that time value declines by very small increments per unit of time early in the trading period, while later in the trading period time value declines at an increasing rate as the last day of trading approaches. After trading has ended, an option has zero time value. This decline in an option's time value with the passage of time is frequently referred to as **time decay** of the premium (see Fig. 8.5). Therefore, $\Theta = \Delta P / \Delta T$.

Some option buyers will close their option position just before the rapid decline of time value begins and, in this way, recapture a large proportion of the original premium paid for an option, whether that option has intrinsic value at that time or not. However, if an option is far out of the money at the time the option position is closed, it will have very little premium to recapture even if the option has not yet reached the period of rapid time decay.

Options further in or out of the money have declining time value because the options have progressively lower probability of taking on additional intrinsic value. An option that is far out of the money will be of little interest to buyers. The seller of such an option expects that she will not sustain a loss on the option and is willing to sell at a low premium. Alternatively, an option that is far in the money will have relatively little time value because, to reach the in the money position, the price of the futures contract would have already experienced substantial price change. Hence, there is a reduced probability that the option will take on increased intrinsic value before trading ends.

Price Volatility: Lambda (λ)

An options buyer would be willing to pay a higher premium if the associated futures contract has recently experienced a high level of price volatility because high price volatility increases the probability that an option will have more intrinsic value sometime before its trading ends. In the same manner, option sellers would insist on receiving higher time values for options with higher price volatility because of the higher probability that intrinsic values will increase, causing them to lose money on the position.

For given levels of volatility, premiums would be higher as the price of the associated futures contract goes higher. This is true because a given level of volatility applied to a higher futures price means that potential gains and losses in holding an option position will be higher. In such a case, buyers like Mr. Castro are willing to pay higher prices, and sellers demand higher premiums for their increased risk.

An example of the relationship between volatility and time to expiration for silver futures is provided in Table 8.10. Looking down the columns, we see that as volatility increases, the call option premium increases. For example, with 40 days to expiration, as volatility rises from 15% to 35%, the premium rises from $0.157 to $0.367. The decaying time value is also clearly shown in Table 8.10 by looking across the rows. For a given volatility level, as the time to expiration is shortened from 40 to 10 days, the premium for the call option drops off.

Tables 8.11 and 8.12 provide examples of historical volatility of wheat futures prices and crude oil futures prices, respectively, over the 1995–2000 period. These were calculated as the standard deviation of percentage price changes of nearby futures. Volatility varies by both month and year.

From the perspective of a speculator, when volatility increases, the option's value rises, and when volatility decreases, the option's value falls. Therefore, rising volatility works to the benefit of those speculators who are "long" options and to the detriment of those investors who are "short" options.

TABLE 8.10 Time to Expiration Versus Volatility Change (Silver Futures = $7.00, Interest Rate = 7%)

	VALUE OF $7.00 CALL		
	TIME TO EXPIRATION		
VOLATILITY	40 DAYS	20 DAYS	10 DAYS
15%	15.7¢	11.1¢	7.9¢
25%	26.2¢	18.6¢	13.2¢
35%	36.7¢	26.0¢	18.4¢

Note: Calculated with the Black-Scholes model.

TABLE 8.11   Historical Monthly Volatility (%) of Wheat Futures Price

MONTH	1995	1996	1997	1998	1999	2000	AVERAGE
January	17.2	28.3	22.5	27.5	27.4	20.0	23.8
February	13.5	22.0	24.5	22.3	25.0	27.1	22.4
March	17.5	23.5	32.9	61.1	67.0	81.0	47.2
April	21.4	60.4	38.6	16.7	23.6	17.2	29.7
May	40.3	67.5	24.5	20.1	21.7	26.0	33.4
June	28.3	34.0	22.7	27.9	20.5	25.5	26.5
July	29.2	32.8	22.9	18.8	28.3	26.9	26.5
August	35.2	26.0	22.6	21.9	37.9	22.1	27.6
September	20.2	24.3	16.7	23.9	29.1	23.5	23.0
October	35.4	17.3	23.9	32.1	23.2	21.5	25.6
November	17.8	27.8	20.6	23.0	23.6	20.1	22.2
December	14.7	22.4	21.3	21.8	22.4	22.5	20.9
Average	24.2	32.2	24.5	26.4	29.1	27.8	

Note: Futures prices are measured by the annualized standard deviation of the natural log of the ratio between (t) and (t−1) daily settlement prices for the nearby futures contract 1995–2000.

TABLE 8.12   Historical Monthly Volatility (%) of Crude Oil Futures Price

MONTH	1995	1996	1997	1998	1999	2000	AVERAGE
January	16.0	21.0	27.9	23.7	22.6	23.8	22.5
February	92.6	26.7	22.9	22.5	24.5	24.9	21.8
March	10.3	13.1	21.1	43.9	26.9	45.4	26.8
April	17.0	21.6	16.5	23.6	21.6	39.2	23.2
May	18.0	29.6	21.6	19.6	21.5	31.2	23.6
June	14.9	25.5	18.6	24.0	26.4	30.0	23.3
July	16.7	20.8	20.4	24.7	22.6	31.0	22.7
August	11.3	21.0	17.0	33.7	18.0	27.0	21.3
September	20.3	31.1	11.4	36.5	16.3	50.4	27.7
October	17.0	31.7	21.7	39.1	34.3	56.2	33.3
November	15.6	33.0	15.8	39.2	31.2	122.9	42.9
December	46.7	151.8	10.5	56.9	28.8	40.1	72.5
Average	17.7	35.6	18.8	40.6	24.6	43.5	

Note: Futures prices are measured by the annualized standard deviation of the natural log of the ratio between (t) and (t−1) daily settlement prices for the nearby futures contract 1995–2000.

Most speculators who trade options on volatility expectations calculate what is referred to as the **implied volatility** of an option (Gallacher, 1999). That is, they calculate the volatility expectations that are currently built into an option's premium. Using an options pricing model or a simple spreadsheet program, they calculate implied volatility as a function of the premium, strike price, underlying futures price, term to expiration, and interest rates. Their trading is then based on whether they believe the implied volatility is too high or too low.

Whether the implied volatility is judged either too high or too low is often based on a comparison with historical volatility. For example, a trader may check historical prices and find a "normal" yearly price range for silver futures, using annual percentage changes as a yardstick. The addition and subtraction of the annual percentage change from the current futures price gives a range of expected prices for the year. As with the Black–Scholes formula, this assumes that returns are distributed normally and that commodity prices are distributed lognormally. For example, if the futures price is $8.00 per ounce and the speculator calculates the historical volatility to be 10%, then, using a normal probability distribution table, the implication is that she is 68% confident that silver futures prices will be in a range of $7.20 to $8.80 during the year.

Alternatively, the normal probability assumption can be used, for example, to calculate the probability that a long call option holder will lose his premium. This is the probability that, by expiration, the market will be trading at or below the strike price. Similarly, the chances of earning a profit can be calculated by determining the probability that the expiration price will be above the strike price by at least the amount of the premium. Suppose that July silver futures closed at $7.85 while the $8.00 call closed at $0.45, with an implied volatility of 10%. Assume that there are 120 days to expiration. What is the probability that the buyer of this call will make a profit? In other words, what is the probability that the futures price will reach $8.45 before expiration? The following formula can be employed:

$$N = \frac{\ln (F/C)}{v\sqrt{d/365}},$$ (8.12)

where
F = the "target" futures price level,
C = current futures price level,
v = futures price volatility, and
d = days until expiration.

The result gives $N = 1.276$, which corresponds to 0.898 on the cumulative normal probability distribution table. This means that there is an 89.8% chance the futures price will be at or below the break-even price of $8.45 before expiry. It also means there is a 100% − 89.8% = 10.2% probability that the market will be at or above the break-even price and the buyer of the call will earn a profit.

Interest Rates: Rho (ρ)

Higher interest rates are expected to discourage options buyers and encourage option sellers to add to their option positions. These incentives arise because buyers will pay a premium at the time an option position is opened, and if there is any price gain, it occurs only after the option has taken on increased intrinsic value. Therefore, a buyer must impute the time value of up-front money paid in the form of a premium as a cost of holding an option position. An option seller receives the premium when an option position is opened and holds those funds until the position is closed or is left to expire. This assumes that the seller can deposit a T-bill with the brokerage firm in order to satisfy margin requirement. An option seller may invest money received as premiums during the time a position is open and will derive somewhat greater benefits from this, as interest rates are higher. While theory and logic says that option premiums should decline with rising interest rates, other variables held constant, in practice premiums are rather insensitive to changes in interest rates. The relationship between interest rates and the options premium is $\rho = \Delta P / \Delta i$.

THE BLACK–SCHOLES MODEL

Figures 8.6 and 8.7 showed us the range of possible options prices (i.e., premiums). The options prices vary with the strike price, the underlying futures price, volatility, and other less important factors. The mathematical formula that captures this pricing relationship is known as the Black–Scholes model. Black and Scholes (1973) derived a stochastic partial differential equation explaining the price of an asset and then solved the equation to obtain the Black–Scholes formula for the price of the option on that asset. The 1997 Nobel Prize in Economics was awarded to Myron Scholes for the development of this options pricing model. Fischer Black passed away in 1995. He would undoubtedly have shared in the prize had he still been alive.

The mathematical economic model they developed was appropriate for the pricing of stock options (i.e., options on equities), and it therefore required modification to be directly applicable to the pricing of options on futures contracts or options on physical commodities. The principal difference is that stocks usually pay dividends while futures contracts do not. Black (1976) published a version of the Black and Scholes equation modified for commodity contracts.

The Black model of option pricing is really based on "European" options, which may be exercised only at the end of trading for the option, rather than "American" options, which may be exercised at any time prior to the end of trading. Since the Black model does not allow for the possibility of early exercise, it tends to slightly undervalue in the money options. Models (such as the one by Cox, Ross, and Rubinstein, 1979) have since been produced that are directly appropriate to American options, but these models are much more complex. However, these more complex models produce estimates of option premiums that are very similar to those produced by the Black model.

The equations used in the Black–Scholes model to estimate the value of commodity options are as follows:

Call:

$$e^{-rt} [x^* \, \text{NORM}(f_1) - s^* \, \text{NORM}(f_2)] \; \text{delta of call} = \text{NORM}(f_1) \qquad (8.13)$$

Put:

$$e^{-rt} [s^* \, \text{NORM}(-f_2) - x^* \, \text{NORM}(-f_1)] \; \text{delta of put} = -\text{NORM}(-f_1) \qquad (8.14)$$

where

$$f_1 = \frac{\log(x/s) \, + \, (vt/2)}{(vt)^{1/2}} \qquad (8.15)$$

and

$$f_2 = f_1 + v(vt)^{1/2} \qquad (8.16)$$

and NORM(f) is the cumulative normal distribution, evaluated at f.

The options parameters are as follows:

e = exponential term (2.7183)
t = days remaining in life of option
v = daily variance = volatility^2/365
r = daily rate of interest
x = price of futures contract
s = strike (exercise) price of option

The Black-Scholes model makes the following assumptions

1. The option can only be exercised on expiration (i.e., a European option)
2. The markets are efficient
3. No commissions are paid
4. Interest rates are constant and known
5. Returns are lognormally distributed (see equation 8.12)

Although the Black-Scholes model is complicated, it is very intuitive (see the put-call parity discussion below in the next section) and easy to calculate theoretical put and call option premiums generated by the model. The Internet has numerous user-friendly sites with an interactive Black-Scholes model and many hand financial calculators are sold with the model installed. In addition, there are Microsoft Excel add-ons for option pricing.

Go to a website such as *www.freeoptionpricing.com*, look up the model for futures contracts and type in the futures price, volatility, the interest rate, days to expiry, and the strike price. The web based model will give you back the theoretical call and put premiums, the delta value and so on.

In order to estimate an option premium with the Black–Scholes model, five variables are required. The variables (essentially the same as those discussed previously) are as follows:

a. Current price of the associated futures contract
b. Option strike price
c. Days to option maturity
d. Volatility of the associated futures contract price
e. The interest rate on a relatively safe investment

The factors influencing an option's premium are summarized in Table 8.13, and four of these factors are directly measurable. However, volatility is not directly observable and must be estimated. Tables 8.11 and 8.12 provide a simple example of one way to estimate volatility. Alternatively, if the Black–Scholes model is assumed to be accurate, the options premium can be inserted into the formula in order to solve for the *implied volatility*.

As explained previously, holding everything else constant, the change in the price of an option with respect to the underlying futures price is referred to as the

TABLE 8.13   Factors Affecting an Option's Price

FACTOR	MEASURE	COMMENTS
Change in option premium associated with a change in underlying futures price	Δ (delta)	Lies between 0 and 1 Approximately equal to 1 for deep in the money options, near 0 for deep out of the money options, and close to 0.5 for the at the money options
Rate of change in Δ	Γ (gamma)	Lies between 0 and ∞ Approximately 0 for deep in the money or deep out of the money options
Time	θ (theta)	Lies between 0 and the total value of the option; declines as option nears expiry
Volatility	Λ (lambda)	Lies between 0 and ∞; declines as option nears expiry
Interest rate	ρ (rho)	Lies between 0 and ∞; usually is near 0

option's delta (Δ), where $\Delta = \partial P / \partial F$. The price (premium) of the option, denoted by P and F, is the price of the underlying futures contract. The change of an option's price with respect to time is measured by theta (θ); thus, $\theta = \partial P / \partial t$, where t represents time. Gamma (Γ) measures the rate of change of an option's delta with respect to the price of the underlying futures price, so it is the second derivative of the option price with respect to the futures price $\Gamma = \partial^2 P / \partial F^2$. The rate of change of an option's price with respect to the volatility of the futures price is lambda (Λ). This means that, $\Lambda = \partial P / \partial \sigma$, where σ is the standard deviation of the futures price. Finally, the rho (ρ) of an option is the rate of change of an option's price with respect to the interest rate, $\rho = \partial P / \partial i$, where i is the interest rate.[6]

Research comparing market options prices with predicted prices from the Black model shows that the model is a very good approximation of what futures options markets actually discover in the way of premiums. Professional options traders (principally option sellers) either use a formal option pricing model, such as the Black model, or they (implicitly) have in their minds a good approximation of these formal models so that they can judge successfully when premiums available offer them a good profit opportunity. Of course, there are many reasons why the theoretical premium value may differ from the observed market value. These include the following:

a. Effects of trading liquidity
b. Different volatility expectations among traders
c. Differences between borrowing and lending rates
d. Distributional characteristic of the underlying futures prices that do not conform to theoretical expectations

---

[6] For more detail concerning these variables and their use, see Hull (2000).

TABLE 8.14   Sugar Options: 112,000 pounds (¢/lb)

STRIKE PRICE	CALLS			PUTS		
	JUNE	JULY	OCTOBER	JUNE	JULY	OCTOBER
7.5	1.05	1.15	1.09	0.03	0.13	0.50
8.0	0.60	0.77	0.82	0.08	0.25	0.72
8.5	0.27	0.49	0.60	0.25	0.47	0.99
9.0	0.09	0.30	0.44	0.57	0.78	1.33

PUT-CALL PARITY

Referring to Table 8.14, we see that the premium on a July sugar call option with a 7.5¢-per-pound strike price is 1.15¢ per pound. The July put option with the same strike price is 0.13¢ per pound. Given that the two options are linked to the same strike price and futures contract month, is there any expected relationship between the put and call option prices of 1.15¢ and 0.13¢ per pound, respectively? If nothing else was changed in Table 8.14, but the July put option premium was raised to 2¢ per pound instead of 1.15¢ per pound, would there be a riskless arbitrage opportunity? The answer to both questions is yes because of the **put-call parity** relationship. It is a fundamental pricing relationship that exists between the price of a put and call option, with an identical strike price and expiration date.

As discussed previously, with regard to the Black–Scholes formula, the same set of principal factors determines both put and call premiums. These factors are the strike price, the price of the underlying futures contract, the estimated price volatility, the time to expiry, and the interest rate. With these common factors, it is therefore intuitive that a predictable relationship exists between puts and calls— the put-call parity relationship.

To illustrate the put-call parity relationship, we assume that the option expiry date is the same as that of the futures contract. In other words, assume a European-style option. The put-call parity formula is then

$$\text{(Call Premium } - \text{ Put Premium)} = \text{(Futures Price } - \text{ Strike Price)}/[1 + r(t/360)], \qquad (8.17)$$

where r is the annualized risk-free interest rate and t is the number of days until expiry. This equation says that the difference between the call and put premiums is equal to the difference between the (present value of) the current underlying futures price and the options' strike price. Given a call premium, its strike price, time to maturity, and underlying futures price, we can use the put-call relationship to solve for the matching put option premium or vice versa.

If the put-call parity relationship does not hold, then there are riskless arbitrage opportunities for an options trader. This means that traders' arbitrage will force the put-call parity relationship to (approximately) hold. The hypothetical purchase of a put option and simultaneous sale of a call option, with the same strike price and expiration month, can be used to demonstrate this parity relationship. The simultaneous purchase of a put and sale of a call actually creates a synthetic short futures position. This means that the *synthetic* short futures position could be combined with a long futures position to create a riskless arbitrage portfolio.

We know that the value of an option at expiration is equal to its intrinsic value, so at expiration, the expected value of the long put is

$$E(EV_L^P) = \max [0, (SP - FP)] \tag{8.18}$$

and for the long call the expected value is

$$E(EV_L^C) = \max [0, (FP - SP)], \tag{8.19}$$

where $E(EV)$ is the expected value at the time of expiry.

If, at expiry, the $FP < SP$, then the put option is "in the money" and the buyer of the put earns $SP - FP$, while if $FP > SP$, then call option expires "in the money" and the writer of the call option earns a negative profit equal to $SP - FP$. Thus, on expiration, the payoff to a combined long position in a put option and a short position in a call option is $SP - FP$, meaning that $E(\pi_L^L) - E(\pi_S^C) = SP - FP$, which is the put-call parity formula, evaluated at $t = 0$. However, $SP - FP$ is also the expected payoff to a short position in the underlying futures contract, sold at a price SP. Thus, buying a put while selling a call with the same strike price and expiration date just replicates the return to a short futures position (i.e., it creates a synthetic short futures position).

We can illustrate the put-call parity formula with the sugar example in Table 8.14. Suppose that the underlying July futures price is 8.52¢ per pound, the riskless interest rate is 4%, and there are approximately 60 days remaining to expiry. Then, the put-call parity relationship for this example is

$$(1.15 - 0.13) \cong (8.52 - 7.50)/[1 + (0.04 \times 60/360)], \text{ or}$$
$$1.02 \cong 1.01.$$

This result verifies that the two July sugar options prices have the correct relationship. It also implies that the expected arbitrage profits would be approximately zero if a trader pursued a strategy of buying the underlying futures contract, selling the call option, and buying the put option.

This result is illustrated in Table 8.15 and Figure 8.17. In Table 8.15, the price of the futures contract at expiration is shown on the left-hand side of the table. The three middle columns in the table show the respective profits or losses accruing to each of the three positions: long futures, long put, and short call. In Table 8.15, the arbitrage strategy net profit is shown in the column on the right-hand side.

No matter where the futures price settles (either above, below, or at the strike price), the arbitrage strategy will generate a profit of $0. If the futures price settles at 9.5¢ per pound, then the profit from the long futures position is $1,097.60 (for one 112,000-pound sugar contract). There is a corresponding loss of $145.60 from the long put position and a loss of $952 for the short call position. These three fig-

TABLE 8.15 **Expected Profits and Losses from a Hypothetical Arbitrage in Sugar Options:** **112,000 pounds (¢/lb)**

PRICE OF FUTURES CONTRACT AT EXPIRATION (¢ / LB)	EXPECTED PROFIT FROM LONG FUTURES POSITION AT 8.52¢ / LB	EXPECTED PROFIT FROM LONG PUT POSITION AT 0.13¢ / LB AND STRIKE = 7.5¢ / LB	EXPECTED PROFIT FROM SHORT CALL POSITION AT 1.15¢ / LB AND STRIKE = 7.5¢ / LB	NET PROFIT
9.5	$1,097.60	– $145.60	– $952	$0.00
9.0	$537.60	– $145.60	– $392	$0.00
8.5	– $22.40	– $145.60	$168	$0.00
8.0	– $582.40	– $145.60	$728	$0.00
7.5	– $1,142.40	– $145.60	$1288	$0.00
7.0	– $1,702.40	$414.40	$1288	$0.00
6.5	– $2,262.40	$974.40	$1288	$0.00

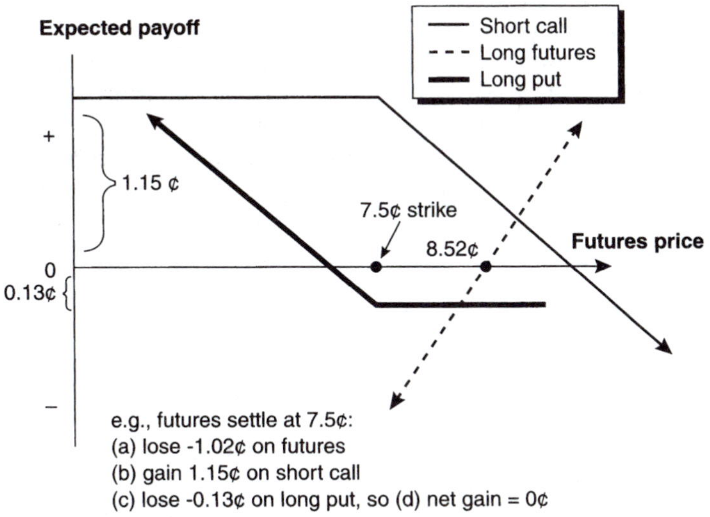

FIGURE 8.17
Expected payoff from a hypothetical arbitrage trade in sugar: 112,000 pounds (¢/lb).

ures sum to zero. As we move down the table, we see that for alternative futures prices at expiration, the result is exactly the same, with net profits equal to zero. This example ignores the time value of money, which appears in the put-call parity relationship but is not very empirically important in this formula.

Figure 8.17 shows the arbitrage strategy in graphical form. Combining a short call, long put, and long futures position will generate a net gain of zero, regardless of where the underlying futures price settles at expiry. For example, if the futures price happens to settle at the strike price (7.5¢ per pound), then the loss on the futures position is equal to 1.02¢ per pound (= 8.52 − 7.5), the loss on the long put is 0.13¢ per pound (i.e., the put premium), and the gain on the short call is 1.15¢ per pound (i.e., the call premium). So the net gain is zero.

Strictly speaking, the put-call parity relationship described here applies only to European-style options. The relationship does not exactly apply to American-style options because an option holder may exercise the option before expiration. However, in practice the empirical importance of this distinction is not very significant.

SUMMARY

This chapter has introduced the reader to call and put options on futures contracts, with examples drawn from the commodity and financial markets. The chapter builds on previous chapters that explained the fundamentals of futures markets. The focus here was on developing a basic understanding of how the market participants price both call and put options on futures. Buyer and seller motivations were discussed, and examples were provided of speculative strategies for trading options on futures.

Option payoff charts were utilized to explain the important relationship between futures prices and options prices. The fair market value of call and put options was discussed with an intuitive explanation of the factors underlying the famous Black–Scholes model of options pricing. The important factors include the strike price, the underlying futures price, days to expiry, and price volatility. Within the options market, there are also important relationships among put and call prices, and some of these price parity relationships were explained with examples.

DISCUSSION QUESTIONS

1. Compare and contrast the commitments taken on by a futures contract seller versus a buyer of a put option.
2. Compare and contrast the commitments taken on by a futures contract buyer versus a buyer of a call option.
3. A March cotton call option has a strike price of 60¢ per pound. The underlying futures price is 58.69¢ per pound, and the premium is 1.57¢. One cotton futures contract is 50,000 pounds.

   The intrinsic value is _____ (¢/lb) _____ ($ per contract).
   The time value is _____ (¢/lb) _____ ($ per contract).

4. A June T-bond put option with a strike price of 102-00 points has a premium of 5-30. The underlying futures price is 97-06. Recall that T-bond options are quoted in points and 64ths of 100%, while T-bond futures are quoted in points and 32nds of 100%.

   The intrinsic value is _____ (points and 64ths of 100%) _____ (per contract).
   The time value is _____ (points and 64ths of 100%) _____ (per contract).

5.

CORN OPTIONS (5,000 BU)
Option premiums are in cents per bushel

Strike ($/bu)	March Call	May Call	July Call	March Put	May Put	July Put
2.30	20	28	33	1	1	1
2.40	13	20	25	3	3	3
2.50	7	13	19	7	6	6
2.60	4	9	14	13	11	11
2.70	2	6	10	21	18	17
2.80	1	4	7	30	25	24

Underlying Corn Futures Prices

Delivery Month	Price ($/bu)
March	$2.50
May	$2.57
July	$2.61
Sept	$2.57
Dec	$2.53

Assuming zero transactions costs, does the put-call parity relationship hold exactly for the May put and call with a strike of $2.60? Answer yes or no and show your calculations. If the answer is no, indicate how far off the relationship is.

Given the corn options market information, draw the expected payoff chart for the following:

  a. Short July put with a $2.60 strike
  b. Long May call with a $2.40 strike

SELECTED REFERENCES

Black, F. (1976). The pricing of commodity contracts. *Journal of Financial Economics, 3* (no. 1/2), 167–179.

Black, F., & Scholes, M. (1973). The pricing of options and corporate liabilities. *Journal of Political Economy, 81,* 637–654.

Cox, J. C., Ross, S. A., & Rubinstein, M. (1979). Option pricing: A simplified approach. *Journal of Financial Economics, 7,* 229–263.

Gallacher, W. R. (1999). *The options edge: Winning the volatility game with options on futures.* New York: McGraw-Hill.

Garbade, K. D., & Silber, W. L. (2000). Cash settlement of futures contracts: An economic analysis. *Journal of Futures Markets, 20*(no 1), 19–40.

Hull, J. (2000). *Options, futures, and other derivatives.* Upper Saddle River, NJ: Prentice Hall.

Jarrow, R., & Turnbull, S. (2000). *Derivative securities* (2nd ed.). Cincinnati: South-Western.

Kolb, R. W. (1997). *Futures, options, and swaps.* Malden, MA: Blackwell.

Purcell, W. D., & Koontz, S. R. (1999). *Agricultural futures and options: Principles and strategies.* Upper Saddle River, NJ: Prentice Hall.

CHAPTER 9

Hedging with Options

Hedging with options provides commodity and financial instrument traders with many alternatives not available in a hedging program that utilizes only with futures contracts (Labuszewski and Nyhoff, 1988; Kolb, 1999). Although futures and options are similar in some ways, there are significant differences that make hedging strategies unique to each instrument. Table 9.1 sets out some of the fundamental differences between hedging with *options on futures* versus *futures* and we can see that a commercial firm enjoys substantially more versatility when it chooses to hedge with options rather than futures. Additionally, options come much closer to providing traditional price insurance than futures because either a **floor** or a **ceiling** price can be established with options. However, this does not imply that options are necessarily superior to futures as a hedging tool. In addition, it is important to note that futures and options are not mutually exclusive in the development of hedging strategies; in some cases, a complex strategy that uses both futures and options may be ideal.

TABLE 9.1 Pros and Cons of Hedging with Futures Versus Options

| | OPTIONS | |
FUTURES	BUYER	SELLER
Unlimited risk on long and short futures position	Limited risk with purchase of a put or call	Unlimited risk with the sale of a put or call
Margin calls with a long or short position	No margin calls with purchase of a put or call	Margin call with sale of a put or call
Establishes a "locked-in" price but may vary with basis risk	Establishes either a "floor" or "ceiling" price that may vary with basis risk	Establishes either a "floor" or "ceiling" price that may vary with basis risk
Limited number of hedging strategies	Multiple hedging strategies	Multiple hedging strategies
No premium is paid	Synthetic futures can be created	Synthetic futures can be created
	Premium is paid	Premium is received

In a general sense, hedging with options involves the management of risk through the use of derivative contracts in order to balance a portfolio. This strategy is therefore common in the commodity markets for inputs (such as corn) and outputs (such as oil) or in the financial markets for interest rates or exchange rates (such as Eurodollars or the Euro).

In this chapter, some very basic option hedging strategies are discussed. The strategies will then be compared to futures hedging methods in order to provide a base for evaluation. This evaluation will lead to an understanding of both the mechanics of hedging with options and the factors that affect whether options strategies provide a hedger with superior results.

BASIC OPTION HEDGING STRATEGIES

There are four basic option hedging strategies: two involve going either short or long *a put option,* and two involve being either short or long *a call option.* These four strategies are specified in Table 9.2. To illustrate the basic difference between option and futures hedges, consider the simplest case in which a commodity producer might be long in the cash market and at the same time desire protection against a steep price decline. A very simple hedge would involve buying a put option and thus establishing a price floor that protects the hedger from a steep price decline. However, if prices should suddenly rise, this producer does not have to forgo profit gains from the higher price. In contrast, with a short hedge in the futures market, profit opportunities from a higher price are forgone. For simplicity in the following examples, the basis is assumed to be constant and zero. In addition, the returns to option positions are based on the premium adjusted for the intrinsic value of the option at expiration. These simplifying assumptions do not alter the basic conclusions we can draw from the following examples.

Long Cash: Basic Option Hedges

As an example of a long put hedge, consider a commercial sugar trader who believes that sugar prices are going higher and thus purchased 112,000 pounds of sugar (the quantity in one futures contract) on the world market at a price of $0.11 per pound. Assume that it is now March and her intention is to sell the sugar in late September. However, the volatile sugar market is subject to weather and political

TABLE 9.2   Basic Hedging Strategies: Options Versus Futures

CASH MARKET POSITION	FUTURES HEDGES	OPTIONS HEDGE	
		PUTS	CALLS
Long	Short	Long	Short
Short	Long	Short	Long

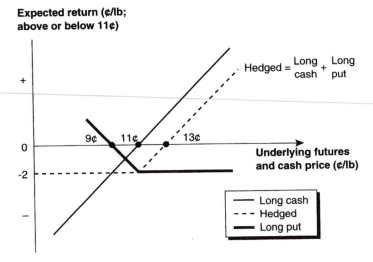

FIGURE 9.1
A long cash position and a long put hedge. The basis is assumed to be zero and constant.

shocks, and the trader is concerned about her exposure to a sudden price decline. In order to hedge her position, she may elect to buy an at the money put option on an October sugar futures contract for a premium of $0.02 per pound and a strike price of $0.11 per pound. In effect, she has a bullish position and has established a synthetic call.[1]

The trader's expected returns are shown in Figure 9.1. The figure shows that the long put reduces returns on the sugar inventory by 2¢ per pound (the amount of the premium paid) if futures prices go up. At a futures price of 11¢, the intrinsic value of the option is zero (since it is at the money), so the loss on the long put is 2¢ on the premium minus the intrinsic value, which is zero. As a result, the dashed line for potential outcomes for the hedged position is below the line for unhedged outcomes for all prices above 9¢ (the strike price minus the premium). Nevertheless, returns on a hedged position do increase with rising futures prices, unlike the outcomes from a short futures hedge. On the other hand, if prices decline, then the put has intrinsic value equal to the strike price minus the futures price, which keeps the hedged outcome line in Figure 9.1 flat below the strike price of 11¢ and the net return will be 9¢ no matter how far prices fall (ignoring basis risk).

Instead of being outright bullish, suppose that the trader was neutral to bullish. In this situation, she might still take a long cash position at $0.11. But, being of the belief that prices might not increase dramatically, she sells an in the money $0.10 call option at the same time and collects the premium, say, $0.025 per pound. She now has some cushion if prices fall below $0.11 because she will not lose

---

[1] This is a synthetic call because it is a combination of a long put and a long cash position and it replicates the behavior of a call option.

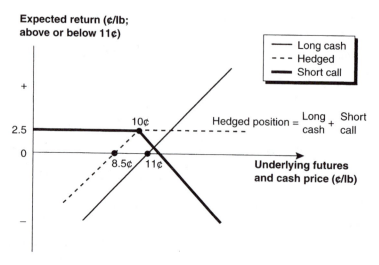

FIGURE 9.2
A long cash position and a short call hedge. The basis is assumed to be zero and constant.

money as long as prices remain above $0.085. As long as prices remain above $0.10, she is guaranteed an added return equaling the premium of $0.025, over and above the $0.11. Once the price rises above $0.11, the unlimited gains in the long cash position exactly offset the short call losses. This hedging strategy is depicted in Figure 9.2.

Short Cash: Basic Option Hedges

Alternatively, consider the purchase of a call option by a commercial trader who is bearish on sugar prices and has entered into a short position in the cash market. Suppose, for example, that at another point in time the same sugar trader from the previous example goes short in the cash market by making a forward sale (at a fixed price) to an importer without having the required inventory to meet the forward delivery commitment. In this case, the sugar trader profits if prices fall (because she can purchase the needed sugar at a price below that for which she has sold it) but is exposed to a loss if prices suddenly rise. She can hedge against an unexpected price rise by purchasing a call option on sugar. Suppose that the forward sale was for 112,000 pounds at a price of $0.14 per pound. As a hedge, the trader may elect to purchase an at the money July $0.14 call for $0.01. In essence, she has created a synthetic put and the trader's expected returns are graphed in Figure 9.3. By hedging, she has given up 1¢ per pound of potential return if prices decline, but at the same time has established a price ceiling if prices rise.

If instead of being outright bearish the trader is neutral to bearish and enters into a short cash position in a similar fashion as described previously, the hedge would involve selling a put option. Assume that the short cash position is at a strike price of $0.14 and an at the money $0.14 put is sold for a premium of $0.01. Thus, the sugar trader makes a profit on this hedge as long as prices remain below $0.15.

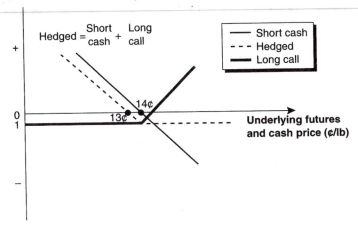

FIGURE 9.3
A short cash position and a long call hedge. The basis is assumed to be zero and constant.

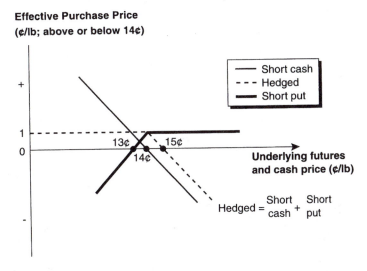

FIGURE 9.4
A short cash position and a short put hedge. The basis is assumed to be zero and constant.

This situation is depicted in Figure 9.4. The trader loses money only if prices rise above $0.15, whereas in the unhedged short cash position, losses are incurred as soon as prices rise above $0.14. As above, we are abstracting from basis risk.

In each of these basic option hedging strategies, an important question is whether to choose an option that is at, out of, or in the money. The answer really depends on how much protection the hedger wishes to purchase. The basic rule

LONG CASH

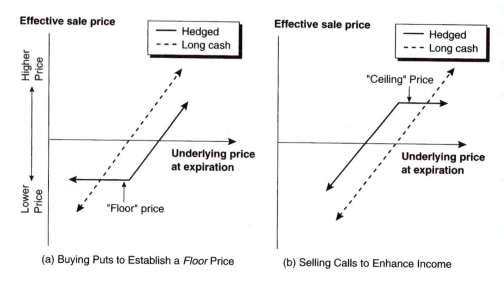

(a) Buying Puts to Establish a *Floor* Price   (b) Selling Calls to Enhance Income

SHORT CASH

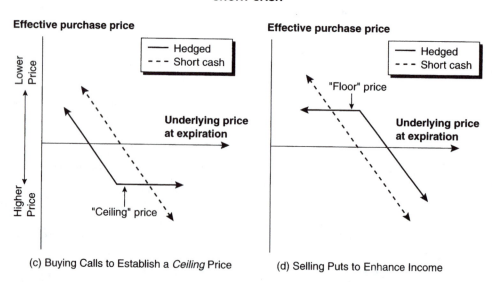

(c) Buying Calls to Establish a *Ceiling* Price   (d) Selling Puts to Enhance Income

FIGURE 9.5
Alternative option hedging strategies: (a) buying puts to establish a *floor* price, (b) selling calls to enhance income, (c) buying calls to establish a *ceiling* price, (d) selling puts to enhance income.

is that more protection costs more and less protection costs less. For example, in the situation depicted in Figure 9.1, the hedger is basically bullish. An out of the money put option will require much less premium, but its low delta means it will also provide less protection on the downside. A deep in the money option may offer protection at lower cost (because it has relatively less time value in its premium) but requires a much larger deposit initially; although the intrinsic value portion will be recaptured, paying the large premium may strain the hedger's cash flow while the option is held. This basic option hedging scenario is summarized in Figure 9.5a. Figure 9.5c is a general representation of the example shown in Figure 9.3. Figure 9.5b and d depict selling options as a possible hedging strategy.

Delta Hedging

As discussed in Chapter 8, an option's delta is a measure of the change in the option's premium relative to a change in the underlying futures price. An at the money foreign currency option, for example, which has a delta of 0.5, means that for every $0.01 change in the currency futures price, the option will change in value by $0.005. A long call delta implies that if currency futures' price rises by $0.01, the premium will also rise, but only by $0.005. Alternatively, for a long put option, a $0.01 rise in the currency price implies that the option's premium will fall by $0.005. Short put deltas are denoted by a positive number and short call deltas by a negative number. For deep in the money options, the delta is near 1.0, and for deep out of the money options, the delta is near zero. Of course, it is also important to remember that the delta value is not a constant and may fluctuate with underlying price changes and as the option approaches expiry. In other words, an option's delta moves with futures price changes and time to maturity. Toward expiry, the delta of an out of the money option approaches zero, and the delta of an in the money option approaches 1.0.

   Since the object of hedging is to offset a loss in the cash market with a gain in the options market, the delta is an important factor in a hedging program. A **neutral hedge ratio** is the reciprocal of a delta, and it is a measure of how many options contracts must be held in order to offset price changes in the underlying cash market (assuming either a constant basis or a favorable basis change). For example, a hedger who is long 40,000 pounds of beef in the cash market and wishes to offset the price risk must purchase or write two at the money 0.5 delta options to neutralize his cash position. If the delta is 0.25, four options are required. (This assumes the optimal hedge ratio for beef is 1.0.)

   However, optimal hedge ratios are not necessarily equal to 1.0. This means that the "neutral" ratio must be converted by the appropriate hedge ratio in order to derive a more effective option hedge. The **option hedge ratio (OHR)** is therefore

$$OHR = FHR \times NR, \text{ or } FHR \times \frac{1}{\Delta},$$

where *FHR* denotes the desired futures hedge ratio and *NR* the neutral ratio. For instance, in the previous beef example, suppose that $FHR = 0.8$ and $NR = 4$. This implies that 3.2, or approximately three options contracts would be required for the hedge.

   An option's delta is a function of the underlying commodity price and time; therefore, it changes over time. To account for changing deltas, an optimum hedge must be rebalanced over time. This leads to a dynamic hedging program.

> ## BOX 9.1
>
> ### How an airline uses call options to hedge.
>
> As mentioned in Chapter 7, all the nation's top airlines have turned to hedging in order to try and better manage wildly fluctuating fuel prices. A jump in fuel prices can quickly turn a profitable quarter into red numbers because fuel is the second most important expense for airlines after labor costs. By hedging, the airlines are able to manage some of the fuel costs, and some airline companies have reported that they saved hundreds of millions of dollars a year through hedging. United, Delta, Southwest, USAir, and Continental all have hedging programs.
>
> Some major U.S. airlines use call options to hedge. They buy heating oil call options as a type of cross-hedge because the price of heating oil and jet fuel is highly correlated. The airlines' goal is to protect themselves against sharp fuel price increases but still benefit from price declines. Of course, the downside is the option premium expenses that can also run into the hundreds of millions of dollars for a single airline.
>
> It is a long-term hedging program, and the airline tries to hedge in and around the long-term average price of fuel. This means that they purchase a lot of call options when fuel prices are low (e.g., in early 1999), and their hedge ratio varies over time. Some airlines were caught with low hedge ratios in the spring of 2002, when fuel prices jumped because of tension in the Middle East and Iraq's curtailment of oil exports.
>
> See McCartney and Trottman (2002).

COMPARISON OF ALTERNATIVE HEDGING STRATEGIES

Put options represent one method of establishing a forward price for a firm's inventory and/or output. Commodity producers can establish a forward price by either signing a forward pricing contract or hedging on either the futures or options market. The forward pricing alternative is the same as a futures or options hedge that has no basis risk.

An example here will illustrate how put options compare to cash marketing and forward pricing of oil. It is assumed that on June 1 a producer—First Oil Inc.—is considering the pricing of 5,000 barrels of crude oil that it plans to produce during the fall. If First Oil decides to wait until November 1 to price the oil, it has selected a cash marketing strategy.

Forward pricing locks First Oil in at a specific price. If prices go down and it has forward contracted at a higher price, the forward pricing decision would have been profitable. However, if cash prices increase significantly, First Oil would be unable to benefit from the price increases. Further, if First Oil's production falls short but has already been contracted at the lower price, it might have to buy oil on the spot market to meet the delivery requirements of the contract. This potential loss is unattractive from a risk management perspective because when the firm has short production volume, its net profit is likely to be either very small or negative. Paying a competitor for every contracted barrel not produced could lead to financial problems. To control this type of production risk, First Oil may limit the percentage of any future production that it forward contracts.

Put options are an attractive marketing alternative because they have the ability to partially overcome both of these limitations to forward contracting. First, a put option establishes a floor price but leaves open the possibility for a producer to benefit from upward price movements. In addition, if First Oil has a production shortfall, it may be able to sell its put option if prices decrease. The firm's maximum loss per unit would be the put option premium. The following two cases examine how a decrease or an increase in crude oil prices affects the outcomes of alternative marketing strategies.

Case 1: Crude Oil Decreases in Price

On June 1, First Oil Inc. is confronted with three marketing strategies: cash marketing in the fall, forward contracting, or purchasing a put option. Table 9.3 summarizes the prices and revenues under each alternative. The basis assumption is that futures and cash prices move perfectly together. Using the cash marketing alternative, First Oil does nothing to establish a price. If forward contracting, it signs a contract with a refinery for $17.50 per barrel for delivery on November 1. If it selects the put option alternative, it could buy five put options on the November futures contract (1,000 barrels each) that is traded on the New York Mercantile Exchange. On June 1, the November futures contract is trading for $18.00 per barrel.

TABLE 9.3   Comparison of Cash Marketing, Forward Contracting, and Put Option Marketing Strategies[a]

	MARKETING STRATEGY		
	CASH MARKETING	FORWARD CONTRACTING	PUT OPTIONS
Cash crude oil price decreases from $17.50 on June 1 to $16.00 on November 1			
1. Cash price received on November 1	$16.00	$17.50	$16.00
2. Plus premium for put option sold on November 1	N/A[b]	N/A	+ $1.60
3. Minus premium for put option bought on June 1	N/A	N/A	− $0.70
4. Total revenue per barrel	$16.00	$17.50	$16.90
Cash crude oil price increases from $17.50 on June 1 to $19.00 on November 1			
1. Cash price received on November 1	$19.00	$17.50	$19.00
2. Plus premium for put option sold on November 1	N/A	N/A	+ $0.10
3. Minus premium for put option brought on June 1	N/A	N/A	− $0.70
4. Total revenue per barrel	$19.00	$17.50	$18.40

[a]Producer forward contracted with refinery for November 1 delivery for a price of $17.50 per barrel. The basis is 50¢ per barrel. The put option has an $18.00-per-barrel strike price.
[b]N/A = not applicable.

Assume that First Oil must pay 70¢ per barrel for an $18.00 November put option. This means it has paid 70¢ to have the right to sell the November crude oil futures contract at $18.00 per barrel. Now jump ahead to November 1. First Oil had a good production run and has sufficient oil to sell or deliver. Cash oil prices dropped to $16.00 per barrel, and the November futures contract now is trading at $16.50. There has been a drop of $1.50 per barrel in both the cash and the futures market. The success of each alternative strategy can now be evaluated.

In hindsight, the inferior strategy would be cash marketing. The firm would receive only $16.00 per barrel. The best strategy would be forward contracting with the refinery for a price of $17.50. The put option strategy would require First Oil to sell its oil to the refinery for $16.00. Offsetting the drop in the cash market, however, is the profit from the puts. Assume that First Oil was able to obtain a premium of $1.60 by selling its $18.00 November put option back to the market. How can we explain the price increase in the put option? Remember that the put option repre-

---

BOX 9.2

What are hedging losses?

The popular press sometimes refers to "hedging losses" as a cause of concern for stockholders of corporations that have a hedging program. For example, Australia has several world class mining companies that rely on export markets for sales of gold, zinc, and so on. A weak Australian dollar (AD) is good for these export-oriented mines because the metal exports are priced in the stronger U.S. dollars (USD). When export revenue in USD is converted back to AD, the amount of AD generated rises as the AD weakens. Australian mutual fund managers with offshore investments also hedge the AD for essentially the same reasoning as the mining companies.

The AD fell almost continuously from $0.79 (USD) in late 1996 to $0.50 (USD) in late 2001. During this time period, the Australian mines were benefiting from the weak AD, but at the same time they were nervous about a turnaround in the AD and kept expecting a reversal.

To protect themselves against a possible rising AD, several Australian mines hedged the exchange rate, using futures, options, and forward markets. This was an attempt to "lock in" the existing exchange rate. However, AD continued to fall in value relative to the USD. Consequently, the mines "lost" money in their futures and options market positions, and these losses offset corresponding "gains" in the spot market. The mines no longer continued to benefit as much from the falling AD because they hedged against its rise. The futures and options losses were reported to shareholders, stock prices fell, and the Australian newspapers were full of stories about "hedging losses." Of course, these were not losses at all because they were offset by gains in the spot market. "Hedging losses" is an oxymoron.

See Gluyas (2002).

sents the right to sell the November futures contract for $18.00. If the November crude oil futures contract is selling for $16.50 on November 1, the right to sell the contract at $18.00 has a higher intrinsic value. The profit from the put option transaction would equal the $1.60 premium received minus the 70¢ that First Oil paid for the put option. The net price received by First Oil with a put option, therefore, would be $16.90 (cash price plus options profit). This is an intermediate price outcome that lies between the prices received from cash marketing and forward contracting.

Case 2: Crude Oil Increases in Price

Assume that First Oil's marketing activities and prices in the various markets are the same on June 1 as in Case 1. However, instead of declining, in this case cash crude oil prices increase in the local cash market to $19.00 per barrel, and the November futures contract price increases to $19.50 on November 1, as shown in the bottom half of Table 9.3. With hindsight, the superior strategy in this case is cash marketing because the firm sells its oil at $19.00 to the local refinery. The former preferred strategy, forward contracting, would have fetched a price of only $17.50 and is now the most inferior strategy.

The put option strategy means that the firm would deliver its oil to the local refinery for $19.00, but offsetting this price is a loss on the put option transaction. With the November futures contract trading for $19.50 per barrel, the right to sell contracts at $18.00 would not be attractive. Assuming that some other trader would be willing to buy First Oil's put option for 10¢, the net price received by First Oil would equal $18.40. The loss in the options market is 60¢ (the 70¢ paid for the option minus the 10¢ selling price). Unlike forward contracting, the put option let First Oil benefit from the price rise. However, again the option strategy is the second best strategy.

Can a put option strategy ever be the most inferior marketing alternative? Yes, this would happen if crude oil prices changed very little during the hedging period, for example, suppose that oil prices stayed at $17.50 per barrel in the cash market and $18.00 for the November crude oil futures contract between June 1 and November 1. Both the cash marketing and the forward contracting strategies would result in prices of $17.50. The option strategy would result in First Oil receiving $17.50 per barrel in the cash market, but the put option would be sold for less than was originally paid because of its decreased time value. This loss would lower the price received by First Oil to a level below that from the two other marketing alternatives. In the final analysis, however, we will see that numerous factors such as basis risk can impact on the ranking of puts as a hedging strategy.

Additional Factors Affecting the Ranking of Puts as a Marketing Strategy

In the cases outlined previously, only the absolute level of prices in the futures and cash markets were allowed to vary. Among other factors to consider when selecting a hedging strategy are the basis, transaction costs, and "insurance" premiums. Basis is the futures price minus the local cash price. In the previous case studies, basis was assumed to be constant at 50¢ or "50¢ under" the futures contract. For example, during the initial decision period of June 1, the cash market price was $17.50, and the futures market price was $18.00.

In order to use commodity options effectively, a hedger must understand the futures basis for his marketing location. If a basis "widens," the local cash market has become weaker relative to a specific futures contract. For example, the basis widens if the local cash price falls and the futures price remains constant. A narrowing basis implies that the local cash price has become stronger relative to the futures contract. This would occur if the cash market price increases and the futures contract price does not change.

Since cash marketing and put options do not establish a cash price for a future delivery date, these marketing strategies suffer a decline in revenues when the basis widens, but they gain revenues when the basis narrows. A forward pricing contract does establish a future cash price so that the producer's cash price is not affected by a change in the local basis. But with forward contracting, a producer does not benefit from a "narrowing" of the local cash basis. It is also important to note that increasing or decreasing volatility can affect the deltas, so price protection offered by an option contract will change over time.

Selling a Call Option

In selling a call option, a hedger has sold to another trader the right to buy a futures contract at a specific price. The hedger would receive the option premium rather than paying a premium. However, "shorting" a call is more risky than buying a put. With this strategy, a hedger limits his gains from any upside price potential and leaves himself exposed to downward price movements. Yet this strategy is appropriate when expectations are for prices to be relatively stable or increase.

In selling calls, several basic points must be remembered. Because of the risk of this type of transaction, a hedger will be required to have a margin account and be subject to margin calls. The original margin equals the option premium plus the margin required on the futures contract. If the option premium increases, the producer will be required to deposit additional margin money.

To illustrate this hedging example, assume that in March there is a rancher with fed cattle that he expects will be ready to deliver in May. He is considering using an option strategy. In this example, the cash price for his local market is assumed to be $1.00 under the Chicago Mercantile Exchange's June futures contract, which means that the basis equals $1.00. He is confronted with the option prices per 100 pounds (hundredweight [cwt]) specified in Table 9.4.

The rancher first checks the put premiums. He notes that the time values of the puts are as follows: $1.80 for the $64.00 put, $2.60 for the $66.00 put, and $2.20 for the $68.00 put. Since he is planning to deliver the cattle at the end of May, he expects to lose most of the time value component of the premium. Remember, time premiums disappear rapidly once the option approaches expiration. The loss of the time value is an expense to the put owner. He feels that this price insurance is too expensive given his expectations concerning prices.

TABLE 9.4   Sample of Put and Call Option Premiums for Cattle (June Futures Contract Price: $66.50 per 100 Pounds)

| | | CALL | | | PUT | |
STRIKE PRICE	PREMIUM	INTRINSIC VALUE	TIME VALUE	PREMIUM	INTRINSIC VALUE	TIME VALUE
$64.00	$4.20	$2.50	$1.70	$1.80	$0	$1.80
66.00	3.15	0.50	2.65	2.60	0	2.60
68.00	2.25	0	2.25	3.70	1.50	2.20

Instead of buying a put, he decides to short (sell) a call. In selling a call, he will receive the premium but will be required to place the premium in a margin account, along with margin money for the underlying futures contract. If the option increases in value, he will have to place additional money in his margin account. However, if the option premium declines, he will be able to withdraw funds from his margin account. When he decides to liquidate his option position, he will have to buy the call option back, unless it is going to expire worthless.

The rancher must now decide which call option to sell. To assist in this decision, he completed a set of calculations given in Table 9.5. He has estimated that the futures contract could trade in a range of $58.00 to $73.50 per hundredweight. After subtracting the expected basis of $1.00 from the June futures contract, he established the cash price for his cattle for five price levels. The cash prices were projected to range from $57.00 to $72.50 cwt. The next step is to establish the profits and losses for each of the call options at the different futures contract prices. The revenues will equal the call premium received. The cost of a call option in each transaction equals the premium he must pay to buy back the option. His gross profit or loss on the call option transaction equals the revenue from selling the option minus the cost of buying the option back.

If the option strike price is greater than the futures market price, the call option will expire worthless. For example, if the futures contract price is $60.00, the $66.00 call option will expire worthless because it would be cheaper to buy the futures contract on the exchange than to exercise the call option at the specified strike price. In Table 9.5, the hedger entered a zero for any situation where the option would expire worthless.

For the remaining options, he calculated the intrinsic value of the call option at a specific futures contract price and added some expected time value. Even though he is planning to buy the call option back on the day prior to expiration, he expects the in the money options to have some time value. If the futures contract price is $70.00, the $66.00 call will have $4.00 of intrinsic value ($70.00 minus $66.00). The rancher assumed that there would be $.05 of time value when he bought the $66.00 call option back. Therefore, the option premium would equal $4.05 (the time value plus intrinsic value).

TABLE 9.5   Calculation of Total Revenue Received When Shorting Different Calls

DESCRIPTION	FUTURES MARKET PRICE WHEN CALL OPTION IS REPURCHASED				
	$58.00	**$63.00**	**$66.50**	**$70.00**	**$73.50**
Adjust for the basis[a]	$ 1.00	$ 1.00	$ 1.00	$ 1.00	$ 1.00
Local cash price	$57.00	$62.00	$65.50	$69.00	$72.50
	Analysis of selling $68.00 call				
Revenue from selling call	$ 2.25	$ 2.25	$ 2.25	$ 2.25	$ 2.25
Cost of buying call back	$ 0.00	$ 0.00	$ 0.00	$ 2.10	$ 5.55
Total revenue from strategy	$59.25	$64.25	$67.75	$69.15	$69.20
	Analysis of selling $66.00 call				
Revenue from selling call	$ 3.15	$ 3.15	$ 3.15	$ 3.15	$ 3.15
Cost of buying call back	$ 0.00	$ 0.00	$ 0.65	$ 4.05	$ 7.53
Total revenue from strategy	$60.15	$65.15	$68.00	$68.10	$68.12
	Analysis of selling $64.00 call				
Revenue from selling call	$ 4.20	$ 4.20	$ 4.20	$ 4.20	$ 4.20
Cost of buying call back	$ 0.00	$ 0.00	$ 2.60	$ 6.05	$ 9.53
Total revenue from strategy	$61.20	$66.20	$67.10	$67.15	$67.18

[a] Estimated and actual bases are assumed to be identical in this analysis.

His total revenue from the strategy would equal the projected cash price for the cattle sold plus the gross profit or loss in the call option transactions. This amount represents the total revenue he would have available to offset transaction costs, margin account expenses, and the cost of production. To simplify the example, the transaction costs, margin expenses, and production expenses were not included in the calculations, but this should not affect the ranking of strategies.

In examining Table 9.5, the hedger notices that no single call option is the best strategy in all price scenarios. The $68.00 call would be the best option when futures prices run up to $73.50 since his total revenue is $69.20. But this total revenue is less than the projected cash price of $72.50. If the futures contract price drops to $58.00, his best strategy would be the $64.00 call with a total revenue of $61.20, which is greater than an estimated cash price of $57.00. What gives rise to these specific rankings?

If prices increased, the $68.00 call allowed the rancher to benefit from the fact that the strike price was higher than the futures contract ($66.50) price when he sold the call (i.e., there was no intrinsic value at the time of the sale of the option). In addition, the producer was able to benefit from the $2.25 of time value contained in the $68.00 call option when he sold the call. Only after the intrinsic value of the option became greater than its time value did the rancher have to pay more for the option in May than he sold it for in March.

If prices declined, the $64.00 call allowed the rancher to benefit from the fact that the strike price was lower than the futures contract price when he sold the call. The option had $2.50 of intrinsic value and $1.70 of time value. As the futures price dropped, the level of intrinsic value also decreased. In this case, only after the futures price decline totally offset the total premium received by the rancher did his total revenue begin to fall below the original cash value per unit of his inventory, $65.50.

Selecting which call option to sell is therefore based on futures contract price expectations. Producers must establish a marketing plan based on a specific price expectation and have plans for situations when prices move against their position. As indicated in this discussion, the size of the time premium is an important factor in determining strategies. Large time premiums make selling calls attractive, while small time premiums increase the attractiveness of buying puts. A systematic scheme for ranking the basic options hedging strategies is presented in the next section.

RANKING ALTERNATIVE STRATEGIES

The two marketing alternatives not incorporating options are cash marketing and forward/futures contracting. With calls and puts, a hedger must select between using in the money, at the money, or out of the money options. Each of these options represents a distinct strategy based on a specific price expectation. Table 9.6 provides rankings of the eight strategies for five basic price scenarios: major price decline, moderate price decline, no change in price, moderate price increase, and major price increase. For each price scenario, a ranking is given to the eight different strategies, with the first being the best strategy and the eighth strategy being the worst.

An implicit assumption behind the table is that there is no uncertainty in the hedger's production and total production in the industry. If prices and the production level of the hedger are uncertain, the ranking of the marketing alternatives may be different from those present in Table 9.6. For example, if the hedger's output is below what is planned and a significant number of other producers experience this decline in production, the price of the commodity will rise. Such a situation makes the put option more attractive because it allows the hedger to benefit from upward price movements. In the same manner, a production increase could imply lower prices, and the downward price protection of the put becomes more important. Keep in mind that Table 9.6 deals only with changes in the price level, not changes in both price and production levels.

An important conclusion from Table 9.6 involves the competitiveness of puts as a strategy. In none of the price scenarios would buying a put be the best strategy, and the highest rank achieved by any put strategy was third. Why? Time value is a deteriorating asset; that is, as an option approaches expiration, its time value declines. The decline in time value is a cost to the buyer of a put option. If the expectation is for a major price decline, the best strategy is forward contracting. However, if time premiums are large on options, selling call options may provide a significant source of price protection. Table 9.6 clearly indicates that the

TABLE 9.6 Ranking of Alternative Marketing Strategies Under Five Basic Price Change Scenarios for a Hedger Long in the Cash Market

RANKING OF SPECIFIC STRATEGY	CHANGES IN FUTURES PRICE				
	MAJOR PRICE DECLINE	MODERATE PRICE DECLINE	NO CHANGE IN THE PRICE	MODERATE PRICE INCREASE	MAJOR PRICE INCREASE
First	Forward contracting	In the money call	At the money call	Out of the money call	Cash marketing
Second	In the money put	At-the-money call	Out-of-the-money call	Cash marketing	Out-of-the-money put
Third	At the money put	Out-of-the-money call	In-the-money call	At-the-money call	At-the-money put
Fourth	Out of the money put	Forward contracting	Cash marketing	In-the-money call	In-the-money put
Fifth	In the money call	Cash marketing	Forward contracting	Out-of-the-money put	Out-of-the-money call
Sixth	At the money call	In-the-money put	Out-of-the-money put	At-the-money put	At-the-money call
Seventh	Out of the money call	At the money put	In-the-money put	Forward contracting	In-the-money call
Eighth	Cash marketing	Out of the money put	At the money put	In the money put	Forward contracting

Note: The hedger is long in the cash market and therefore sells call options and buys put options in this example.

task of price risk management by producers requires careful consideration of price forecasts. But the most important contribution of options may be their ability to provide hedgers with a middle ground in marketing. One does not have to trade away all the potential of improved prices to avoid some of the price risk associated with commodity marketing. Of course, the same is true of using options to hedge underlying positions in financial markets (Nandi and Waggoner, 2000).

SUMMARY

This chapter has discussed the pros and cons of hedging with options versus futures and forward contracts. Hedging with options has both advantages and disadvantages. It involves basis risk in the same way that hedging with futures does. Options clearly expand the hedging opportunities available to commercial firms.

Four basic hedging strategies were analyzed in this chapter:

- Long cash and either long puts or short calls
- Short cash and either short puts or long calls

Alternative hedging strategies were compared through case studies, and it was demonstrated that price expectations play an important role in the choice of the appropriate options contract. The benefits of hedging with options versus futures or forward contracts also depends on price expectations.

DISCUSSION QUESTIONS

1. What two option hedging strategies can a producer currently holding an inventory use to protect against a reduction in that inventory's value?
2. Which of the two strategies discussed in Question 1 is the least risky? Explain your answer.
3. Under what circumstances should a hedger choose an out of the money option?
4. Is basis less important in hedging with options than with futures?
5. Describe what happens to an option's delta as the contract approaches its expiration date.
6. How is an option's delta used in hedging?
7. In general, what is the advantage of using options to hedge compared to futures contracts?
8. When commodity or asset prices are expected to be stable over the period a hedge is to be held, why are short option strategies generally favored over long option strategies?
9. If options used by a hedger expire worthless, is that hedger worse off than he would have been if he had not hedged? Explain you answer.
10. If a hedger exercises options purchased, is that hedger better off than he would have been if he had not hedged? Explain your answer.

SELECTED REFERENCES

Gluyas, R. (2002). Costello not alone in currency hedge loss. *The Weekend Australian*, March 9, p. 10.

Kolb, R. W. (1999). *Futures, options, and swaps* (3rd ed.). Malden, MA: Blackwell.

Labuszewski, J. W., & Nyhoff, J. E. (1988). *Trading options on futures: Markets, methods, strategies, and tactics*. New York: John Wiley & Sons.

McCartney, S., & Trottman, M. (2002). Quick jump in fuel prices may leave some airlines short-changed on hedges. *Wall Street Journal*, April 9, p. A2.

Nandi, S., & Waggoner, D. F. (2000). "Issues in hedging options positions" *Federal Reserve Bank of Atlanta Economic Review*, 85(1), 24–39.

APPENDIX

Optimal Hedge Ratio

Lets assume that the utility-maximizing optimal hedge ratio is equivalent to the minimum-risk optimal hedge ratio. We can then elaborate on the fundamentals of the minimum risk (optimal) hedge ratio by assuming the objective is to minimize the following equation, which gives us the variance of a simple cash/futures portfolio (without production risk).

$$\text{Minimize } (\sigma^2_h) = \sigma^2_c + h^2 \sigma^2_f - 2h \sigma_{cf}, \tag{1}$$

where σ^2_h is the portfolio variance, σ^2_c is variance of the cash price, h is the proportion of the cash inventory that is hedged (i.e., the hedge ratio), σ^2_f is the variance of the futures price, and σ_{cf} is the covariance between the cash and futures price. If we minimize equation (1), the first order conditions are

$$\partial(\sigma^2_h)/\partial h = 2h \sigma^2_f - 2\sigma_{cf} = 0, \tag{2}$$

solving for h* yields the optimal hedge ratio

$$h^* = \sigma_{cf}/\sigma^2_f, \tag{3}$$

which is equal to the slope coefficient of a regression of P_{ct} on P_{ft} (i.e. $P_{ct} = \alpha + \beta P_{ft} + \varepsilon_t$), and the R^2 from this regression equation is the percentage reduction in price variance that is obtained by choosing the optimal hedge.

Equation (3) can be written as

$$h^* = \rho(\sigma_c/\sigma_f), \tag{4}$$

where ρ is the correlation coefficient and recall that $\rho = (\sigma_{cf}/\sigma_c\sigma_f)$. If futures prices have the same (or higher) price volatitlity than cash prices, h* can be no greater than the correlation coefficient between them, which is ≤ 1.0 in absolute value. Normally h* is < 1.0. Suppose a hedger determines that for his cash market $\rho = 0.8$, $\sigma_c = 0.4$, and $\sigma_f = 0.6$. Using equation (4) this implies the optimal hedge ratio h* = 0.5.

GLOSSARY

Add-on rate   Interest rate that is added onto the principal amount. If you borrow $1 million at 5% for one year, the add-on interest is $50,000.

American option   Options that can be exercised on or any time before the expiration date.

Anticipatory hedge   An anticipatory hedge involves buying or selling contracts by commercial firms in anticipation of forthcoming cash market transactions.

Appreciation   When a currency appreciates, its value increases. If the U.S. dollar were to appreciate, for example, it would take more of another currency to purchase $1. Appreciation is the opposite of depreciation.

Arbitrage   Attempting to profit by exploiting price differences of identical or similar commodities or financial instruments on different markets or in different forms. Arbitrage opportunities (if they exist) provide riskless profit opportunities.

Arbitrage hedge   Sometimes referred to as a carrying charge hedge. An arbitrage hedge is motivated by the tendency for futures and cash prices to converge in the delivery month.

Arbitrageurs   A subclassification of speculators that try to profit by taking very short term positions in the market to take advantage of market anomalies. One who practices arbitrage.

Ask   The price that a seller is willing to accept for a futures or options contract.

At the money   In options, when the strike price equals the price of the underlying futures contract.

Bar chart   Bar charts are used by technicians to report price and volume data. Each day (or week or month) is represented by a single vertical line on the graph connecting the high and low prices to indicate the period's price range.

Basis   The principle measure for linking cash and futures prices. Calculated as futures price − cash price or cash − futures.

Basis point   A basis point is also referred to as a tick. It is one-hundredth of a percentage point and is used for quoting bond yields or interest rates.

Bear vertical spread   A bear vertical spread involves selling an option with a relatively low strike price and buying an option with a relatively high strike price.

Bearish   A trader who is bearish expects prices to fall.

Bid   The price that a buyer is willing to pay for a futures or options contract.

Black–Scholes   The Black–Scholes formula estimates theoretical options prices using factors such as price volatility, interest rates, strike prices, underlying futures prices, and time to expiry.

Board of governors   The board is elected from the futures and options membership and manages the day-to-day affairs of the futures and options exchange.

Breakaway gap   Breakaway gaps, on bar charts, signal the beginning of a price move. They occur when a futures price that's been moving sideways breaks out of the base with a gap.

Break-even price   For a call option the break-even price is equal to the strike price plus the premium. For a put option the break-even price is equal to the strike price minus the premium.

Broker   A person or firm that executes futures and options trades on the floor of the exchange on behalf of a public investor.

Bullish   A trader who is bullish expects prices to increase.

Bull vertical spread   Bull vertical spreads involve buying an option with a relatively low strike price and selling an option with a relatively high strike price.

Butterfly option spread   A strategy aimed at taking advantage of differences in time value erosion in options markets with relatively stable prices. This spread is created by buying one in the money call option, buying one out of the money option, and simultaneously selling two at the money options, all with the same expiration date.

Buyer   The buyer of a futures or options contract.

Buying pressure   Buying pressure occurs when more traders are trying to buy rather than sell futures or options contracts. The price will therefore tend to increase.

Call option   A call option gives the buyer of the option the right but not the obligation to buy the underlying futures contract at a specified price.

Call option buyer   As a speculator, a call option buyer expects futures prices to rise. As a hedger, protection from price increases is obtained by buying a call option.

Call option seller   A call option seller is neutral to bearish. The most a call option seller can earn as profit is the premium less brokerage fees. The loss is theoretically unlimited as futures prices can continuously rise.

Carrying charge market   Also known as contango. A typical intertemporal price pattern that occurs when the prices for futures contracts with later maturity dates are higher than prices for contracts with earlier maturity dates.

Carrying charge hedge   Sometimes referred to as an arbitrage hedge. An arbitrage hedge is motivated by the tendency for the futures and cash prices to converge in the delivery month.

Cash delivery   The seller delivers the actual product or asset to the buyer.

Cash prices   Also known as spot prices. Cash prices refer to the actual market for immediate delivery of the physical commodity or financial instrument underlying a futures or options contract.

Cash settlement   Futures contracts that do not permit delivery, rather the contracts are settled at the cash price.

Ceiling price   A ceiling price can be established with options hedging, which creates a maximum price that a buyer will have to pay.

Channel systems   The goal of a technician's channel system is to look for a price breakout outside the range of past prices. The channel is defined by two trend lines drawn on a vertical bar chart.

Chartist   Also referred to as a technician. This term refers to those traders who use technical analysis and predict forthcoming prices from past price behavior.

Clearinghouse   The clearinghouse financially guarantees all contracts on the exchange and manages the financial settlement of futures and options contracts.

Combination systems   Combination systems include trading two systems simultaneously.

Commodity fund   Also referred to as a commodity pool. A commodity fund is a managed speculative futures fund similar to a mutual fund in either the stock or bond market. It pools investors' money and then trades futures and options contracts.

Commodity Futures Trading Commission   Abbreviated as CFTC, it is the U.S. government agency that regulates and oversees the futures industry.

Commodity pool   Also referred to as a commodity fund. See definition above.

Common gap   A common gap is formed in a market with small trading volume.

Congestion area   The area on a bar chart that contains a cluster of bars is referred to as a congestion area.

Contango   Also known as a carrying charge market. See above definition.

Contrary opinion   A technical trading system based upon the concept that the crowd mentality is wrong and the market is either over-bought or over-sold.

Convenience yield   The convenience yield refers to the benefit (the convenience) of holding inventory.

Convertible currencies   Currencies that can be freely exchanged for another country's currency in the open market.

Cross-hedging   Occurs when there is no futures contract corresponding to the underlying financial instrument or commodity. The hedger then hedges in another related futures market whose price movements are similar to those of the commodity or financial instrument being hedged.

Cross price elasticity   Measures the responsiveness of demand for one good to a given change in the price of a second good.

Cycles   Recurring patterns in production and prices that lasts more than one season.

Cyclical   Something that happens periodically, i.e., on a regular basis.

Delivery month   Indicates the month during which the futures contract expires.

Delta   Delta measures the relationship between the price of an underlying futures contract and the option premium. The delta is equal to the ratio of the price change of the option (i.e., the premium) over the price change of the futures contract. The absolute value of the delta lies between zero and one.

Demand for storage   The demand for the provision of inventories to be carried forward through time.

Depreciation   When a currency depreciates, its value decreases. It is the opposite of appreciation.

Derivative   Contracts whose value depends on an underlying asset. Futures and options are both examples of derivatives.

Discount   A bond is sold at a discount when it is traded at a price that is less than its par or face value.

Discount rate   The interest rate used in discounting future cash flows.

Double bottom   A technical chart pattern that shows a drop in price, then a rise, then another drop to the same price level.

Double top   A technical chart pattern that shows a rise to a high price, then a drop, and then another rise to the same high price.

Efficient   A market is efficient when futures and options contract prices fully reflect all available information at any point in time.

Elasticity   The percent change in quantity (demanded or supplied) divided by a percentage change in the market price.

Elasticity of demand   Measures the responsiveness of demand to a given change in price. It is negative.

Elasticity of supply   Measures the responsiveness of supply to a given change in price. It is positive.

Elliott wave theory   A technicial trading theory based on the belief that there is a rhythm in nature that spills over into all aspects of life, including futures markets.

Eurodollars   Deposits of U.S. dollars in foreign banks or foreign branches of U.S. banks.

European option   An option that can only be exercised on the date of expiry.

Exchange rate   The rate at which one country's currency can be converted into the currency of another country.

Exchanges   Organized futures and options market.

Exercise price   Also known as the strike price. It is the preestablished price that the buyer of a call option can purchase a futures contract at (or the price the buyer of a put can sell at).

Exhaustion gaps   Exhaustion gaps, in bar charts, signal the end of a price move.

Expectations theory   A possible explanation for the shape of the yield curve. This theory states that the shape of the yield curve is a market forecast of the forthcoming spot interest rate.

Farmgate prices   Prices received by farmers at the point of production.

Fibonacci series   This series is created by summing the previous two numbers in the series to get the next number. The series is 1, 1, 2, 3, 5, 8, 13, etc.

Filter systems   A system used by technicians that indicates trade signals given by trailing stops.

Fiscal policy   The government's expenditures on goods and services and the way in which the government finances these expenditures (through borrowing or taxes).

Flexible exchange rates   Also known as floating exchange rates. Under flexible exchange rates, supply and demand determine the value of a currency.

Floor price   A minimum price that will be received. Created through options hedging.

Forward contract   A forward contract is a contract calling for the future delivery of a commodity or asset at a specified price and at a set time period.

Fundamental trader   Fundamentalists focus on evaluating supply and demand in an attempt to forecast the direction of price movements.

Futures contract   An obligation to buy or sell a specific quantity and quality of a commodity or financial instrument at a certain price, and at a specified future date.

FX   The abbreviation for foreign exchange.

Gap   A space on a bar chart between the high price of one day and the low price of the next day, or vice versa.

Globalization   A term that describes a growing trend towards internationally integrated markets and the free movement of goods, services, and factors of production.

Head and shoulders formation   Patterns resembling the head and shoulders outline of a person that are used by technicians to chart and forecast price trends.

Hedging   Participating in the futures or options markets to neutralize the effects of commodity or financial price risk. Individuals who hedge are referred to as hedgers.

Horizontal spread   Created by holding opposite positions in two futures contracts with different delivery dates.

Implied volatility   Volatility expectations currently built into an option's premium. It can be estimated with the Black-Scholes formula.

Index futures   Futures contracts based upon indices such as the S&P 500 stock market index. These contracts are cash settled.

Interest rate parity   The relationship between international interest rates and exchange rates.

Intertemporal   Intertemporal means across time. It is one of the dimensions to cash and futures price relationships.

In the money   An option is in the money if there is some revenue that can be realized by exercising the option. If an option is in the money then it must have intrinsic value.

Intrinsic value   The difference between an option's premium and its time value. A call option has intrinsic value when the current futures price is above the strike price. A put option has intrinsic value when the strike price is above the futures price.

Inverted markets   Occurs when futures contracts for the nearer months are trading at a price premium to the more distant months.

Law of demand   Property of demand curves. If the market price rises, consumers buy less of the good or commodity, holding everything else constant.

Law of one price   The law of one price says that there is one price for a commodity, or financial asset the cash price of the underlying asset, and all other prices are related to that price through storage transformation, and transport costs.

Liquidity preference theory   A possible explanation for the shape of the yield curve. This theory states that the shape of the yield curve is affected by a liquidity premium between long and short-term securities. It maintains that long-term interest rates exceed short-term interest rates because investors prefer shorter maturities.

Liquidity premium   An extra component of yield on a financial instrument. The forward rate minus the expected future short-term interest rate.

London Inter-Bank Offered Rate (LIBOR)   The 90-day deposit rate on U.S. dollars traded between banks in London. The LIBOR is the yield on Eurodollar futures.

Long   To have bought a futures or options contract.

Long call   A long call gives the buyer of the option the right, but not the obligation, to buy the underlying futures contract at a specified price (See call option buyer).

Long hedge   A long hedge is taken when the hedger currently holds a short cash position and seeks protection from falling prices by taking a long position in futures or options.

Long put   A long put gives the buyer of the put the right, but not the obligation, to sell the underlying futures contract at a specified price (See put option buyer).

Margin call   A futures or options trader will receive a margin call when the market has moved unfavorably against his position. The trader must then deposit additional funds to bring the balance back up to the original margin deposit.

Margin deposit   A good-faith deposit a trader must make when buying or selling futures or options. If futures prices move adversely, the trader must deposit more money to meet margin requirements.

Market   A place or situation that puts sellers and buyers in communication with each other and presents the opportunity for them to trade.

Market segmentation theory   An explanation for the shape of the yield curve. This theory states that there are separate markets for short-term, medium-term, and long-term securities and interest rates are determined by supply and demand conditions in each market.

Monetary policy   Refers to actions taken by the central government to influence the amount of money and credit in the economy.

Moving averages   A technical analysis term meaning the average price over a specified time period. Used to identify trends in prices by flattening out noisy price fluctuations.

Naked option   Also known as uncovered options. When a trader sells (i.e., writes) an option for underlying futures contracts, which the writer does not own at the time, he is selling a naked option.

Neckline   The neckline is a part of the head and shoulders formation used in technical trading. It is formed during the correction of a price advance that represents the head.

Net cost of storage   The net cost of storage is a function of three components: physical costs of storage, a risk aversion factor, and convenience yield. Net cost = physical cost of storage + risk aversion − convenience yield.

Neutral hedge ratio   The reciprocal of a delta. It is an estimate of how many option contracts must be held by a hedger in order to offset price changes in the underlying cash market.

Nonstorable   Commodities are considered nonstorable if they cannot be held on to and used in future time periods. They are perishable.

Open interest   The number of open futures contracts for which a trader remains obligated to the clearinghouse because no offsetting purchase or sale has been made yet. Open interest can either be the number of open longs or the number of open shorts.

Operational hedge   Operational hedges facilitate commercial business by allowing firms to buy and sell on the futures markets as temporary substitutes for subsequent cash market transactions.

Optimal hedge ratio   The ratio of the number of futures contracts purchased or sold to the size of the cash position being hedged. It represents the most desirable combination of cash and futures positions.

Option hedge ratio   Equal to the futures hedge ratio × neutral hedge ratio. It is also equal to the futures hedge ratio × 1/delta.

Option straddles   This position is taken by either going long (a long option straddle) or short (a short option straddle) in both a put and a call.

Options   An option gives the buyer the right, but not the obligation, to exercise the option and obtain a long or short position in a futures contract at a predetermined price. There are two types of options: calls and puts.

Oscillators   A family of technical indicators based on price changes rather than price levels.

Out of the money   If an option is out of the money there is no intrinsic value and the premium consists solely of time value. A put option is out of the money when the futures price is greater than the strike price. A call option is out of the money when the futures price is less than the strike price.

Overbought   A market that is rising too fast, according to technical rules.

Oversold   A market that is falling too fast, according to technical rules.

Over-the-counter swaps   Financial swaps that are bought and sold outside an exchange.

Par delivery   A par delivery point is a cash market where no deductions (premiums) are taken from (added to) the futures contract price upon settlement.

Par value   Also referred to as face value. A bond trades at par when the coupon rate is equal to the interest rate.

Payoff line   A line that graphically shows the profits/losses to futures and options contracts as the futures price changes.

Pennant   In technical analysis, a chart pattern that occurs when the trading range formed by successive highs and lows narrows over time.

Point-and-figure (P&F)   A chart used by technicians that plots price movements only, without measuring the passage of time.

Premium   In options markets, the price paid for the right to buy or sell a futures contract.

Price inelastic   If a commodity is price inelastic, its demand expands by less than 1% when its price falls by 1%.

Price of storage theory   This theory is used to explain the pattern of intertemporal price relationships among futures contracts for storable commodities. It predicts that intertemporal price relationships are determined by the net cost of carrying inventory.

Price seasonality   Occurs in markets that exhibit recurring seasonal price patterns.

Price volatility   A measure of price risk, usually estimated by the standard deviation of the price.

Privileges   Privileges are an older form of futures contracts. They are very similar to modern futures with the major difference being that privileges were normally of a shorter duration.

Purchasing power parity (PPP) theory   This theory is based on the concept that goods and services in different countries should cost the same when measured in a common currency. If goods do not cost the same then the country's currency is either under or overvalued.

Put option   A put option gives the buyer of the option the right, but not the obligation, to sell the underlying futures contract at a specified price.

Put option buyer   As a speculator, a put option buyer expects prices will fall. As a hedger, the put option buyer seeks protection against prices falling below the strike price. The maximum loss is the premium plus brokerage fees. There is no limit on the potential gain.

Put option seller   A put option seller is neutral to bullish on prices. The maximum profit is the premium less brokerage fees. The maximum loss is limited to the total value of the futures contract.

Put-call parity   The relationship between the price of a put and call option on the same futures contract with the same strike price. If this relationship does not hold, there are arbitrage opportunities.

Random walk The Random walk theory implies that day-to-day price changes are random and forthcoming prices cannot be predicted from past price behavior.

Real rate of interest The difference between the nominal rate of interest and the expected rate of inflation.

Repo rate Repo is short for repurchase and the repo rate is the rate of interest in a repo transaction. The interest rate difference between the futures and spot price is an implied repo rate.

Reserve requirements In the United States the Federal Reserve Bank requires that financial institutions hold a certain percentage of deposits in reserve.

Resistance area Congestion areas in the middle of a trend as indentified by technical traders. Resistance is the inverse of support.

Risk premium The risk premium is the financial reward that an investor earns for holding a risky asset rather than a risk-free one.

Rollover hedging Hedging over a long time horizon by using a series of futures contracts. The hedger takes either a long or short position, closes the position at expiry, then opens another position and again closes the position at expiry. The hedger repeats this until the desired time frame is covered.

Round bottom A formation produced by the gradual reversal of a price trend on technical charts.

Round top A formation produced by the gradual reversal of a price trend on technical charts.

Runaway gaps A runaway gap in a bar chart is approximately the midpoint of a price move.

Seasonal Variations in business or economic activity that recur with regularity.

Seasonal pattern Any systematic pattern in prices within a marketing year.

Selling pressure Selling pressure occurs when more traders are trying to sell rather than buy futures and options. This will tend to drive prices down.

Semi-strong efficient If a market is semi-strong efficient then prices reflect all publicly available information.

Short To sell a futures or options contract.

Short call To sell a call option (See call option seller).

Short hedge A short hedge is taken when one holds a long cash position and at the same time takes a short position in the futures market.

Short put To sell a put option (See put option seller).

Sideways movements Sideways movements on bar charts created during temporary periods of market stability around a certain price level.

Speculating Speculators participate in the futures and options markets with the sole intention of making a profit.

Spot prices Also known as cash prices. The spot price is the price for immediate delivery.

Spread trading   Spread trading involves taking simultaneous positions in two different contracts rather than taking an outright long or short futures position.

Storable   A commodity is storable if it can be stored for use in future time periods.

Strike price   Also known as the exercise price. This is the predetermined price that the underlying commodity or asset is bought or sold at when an option is exercised.

Strong form efficient   If a market is strong form efficient, then private information is fully reflected in prices.

Supply   The total amount of a good or service available for purchase.

Supply of storage   Refers to the supply of commodities as inventories.

Support area   Congestion area in the middle of a trend on a technician's chart. Support is typically found at a level where a bottom was formed during a previous price decline.

Swap   An agreement between two parties whereby each party agrees to initially exchange an asset and then re-exchange assets at a later date. Swaps can be used to either hedge or speculate and they are instruments that are commonly used in foreign currency and bond markets.

Synthetic call   Created by simultaneously holding a long cash position and purchasing a put option. It mimics a call option.

Synthetic put   Created by simultaneously holding a short cash position and purchasing a call option. It mimics a put option.

Technical trading   The use of historical prices to predict forthcoming price behavior.

Technicians   Also referred to as chartists. This term refers to those who use technical analysis.

Texas hedge   A Texas hedge is not actually a hedge but is instead a large speculative position.

Theory of normal backwardation   This theory explains how positive carry markets have price differences between contracts that are insufficient to cover full costs of storage. This theory says that hedgers must compensate speculators for assuming the price risk associated with holding futures contracts.

Theory of price storage   This theory developed by Holbrook Working says that intertemporal price relationships are determined by the net cost of carrying stocks.

Thin market   A thin market is one that is inactive or illiquid. In such a market the volume of trading is small, there are relatively few transactions per unit of time and price fluctuations are high relative to the volume of trade.

Time decay   This term refers to how the time value of an option decays as expiry approaches.

Time value   Time value reflects the market's expectations concerning the prospects of an option having intrinsic value before expiry. It is the premium minus the intrinsic value.

Tradable   Goods are tradable if they can be consumed away from the point of production.

Trading system   Trading systems are technical forecasting models used to generate buy and sell signals.

Uncovered option   Also known as a naked option. (See naked option).

Vertical spreads   An option strategy involving the simultaneous purchase and sale of options of the same commodity or asset and expiration date but with different strike prices.

Volume   The number of contracts traded over a given time interval.

Weak form efficient   If a market is weak form efficient, then past prices contain no information about forthcoming prices and price changes are random.

Writer   The writer of an option is the person selling the option.

Yield   The average rate of return or the interest rate.

Yield curve   The yield curve is the relationship between yield and term to maturity.

INDEX

Note: The letter "b" following a page number indicates boxed text, the letter "f" indicates figures, and the letter "t" indicates tables.